THE FEDERAL BUDGET
Politics, Policy, Process

THE FEDERAL BUDGET
Politics, Policy, Process

REVISED EDITION

by Allen Schick

with the assistance of
Felix LoStracco

BROOKINGS INSTITUTION PRESS
Washington, D.C.

Copyright © 2000
THE BROOKINGS INSTITUTION
1775 Massachusetts Avenue, N.W., Washington, D.C. 20036
www.brookings.edu

Library of Congress Cataloging-in-Publication data
Schick, Allen.
    The federal budget : politics, policy, and process / by Allen Schick
with the assistance of Felix LoStracco.—Rev. ed.
        p.   cm.
    Includes bibliographical references and index.
    ISBN 0-8157-7726-4 (cloth : alk. paper)—
    ISBN 0-8157-7725-6 (paper : alk. paper)
    1. Budget—United States. 2. Budget process—United States. I.
LoStracco, Felix. II. Title.
    HJ2051 .S3424 2000   99-050857
    352.4'8'0973—dc21   CIP

9 8 7 6 5 4 3 2 1

The paper used in this publication meets minimum requirements of the
American National Standard for Information Sciences—Permanence of Paper for
Printed Library Materials: ANSI Z39.48-1984.

Typeset in Adobe Garamond

Book design and composition by Linda C. Humphrey

Printed by R. R. Donnelley and Sons
Harrisonburg, Virginia

Foreword

When the first edition of this book was published in 1995, the federal government had just completed twenty-five consecutive years of budget deficits. To many observers, the budget predicament was hopeless. The nation's leaders and institutions seemed to lack the political will and fiscal tools to rein in spending and produce sufficient revenue to balance the books. The country's economic future was at risk—if the budget could not be balanced when the elderly were a small, stable portion of the population, how would the government meet its commitments early in the twenty-first century, when an aging society would greatly add to its financial burdens?

Barely five years later, the federal government is now accumulating record surpluses that, according to official projections, may enable it to pay off the public debt by the time the baby-boom generation floods the retirement ranks. Like any other projection, those that foresee a rosy future are likely to be wide of the mark. Projections are predicated on assumptions about future economic performance and political actions. Variances from the expected economic course affect future budget outcomes, as do decisions by Congress and the president. Therefore, the odds are that the next edition of this book will show a different budget outlook than the current one. Change is constant in budgeting.

Budgetary change is an amalgam of politics, policy, and process; all three contributed to the turnaround in the budget's fortunes. During the late twentieth century, divided political control of government tempered demands for higher spending and impeded efforts to cut taxes. Policy changes—in particular, tax increases enacted during the Bush and Clinton presidencies—boosted federal revenue. Budget rules and procedures were reengineered in the 1990s to strengthen fiscal discipline. Notwithstanding the unprecedented economic growth that America has recently experienced, without these political, policy, and procedural changes there would have been no surplus today .

Much of the debate during the 2000 election season revolves around future budget policies. The budget's political importance is partly a matter of size, for the federal government collects almost $2 trillion annually—equal to approximately one-fifth of the nation's gross domestic product. The budget is also important because it is one of the principal means by which the government establishes priorities and defines programs.

Another side of the budget is less well known but no less significant. Budgeting entails complex rules and procedures that influence government policies and financial outcomes. Some rules deal with substantive policy, others with the manner in which the budget is compiled in the executive branch and voted on in Congress. In this book Allen Schick, a visiting fellow in the Brookings Governmental Studies program, assisted by Felix LoStracco, describes how budgeting works at each stage of executive and legislative action—from preparation of the president's budget through the appropriation and expenditure of funds—and assesses the impact of budget rules on policy decisions. He explains how the budget was transformed from deficit to surplus and discusses various proposals to change the rules.

The author wishes to thank Robert Keith of the Congressional Research Service and Edward Davis of the Congressional Budget Office for assistance in explaining some of the recent innovations in budgetary practice. Valerie Norville edited the manuscript, Carlotta Ribar proofread the pages, and Mary Mortensen prepared the index.

The views expressed here are those of the author and should not be ascribed to any person or organization acknowledged above, or to the trustees, officers, and other staff members of the Brookings Institution.

MICHAEL H. ARMACOST
President

June 2000
Washington, D.C.

Contents

FIGURES

TABLES

EXHIBITS

THE FEDERAL BUDGET
Politics, Policy, Process

1

Conflict and Resolution
in Federal Budgeting

This book is about the politics and processes of federal budgeting and the policies that emerge from them. No discussion of budgeting can be complete unless it takes all three aspects into account. Many governmental activities combine process and politics, but budgeting differs because certain basic tasks must be completed each year. No matter how difficult the choices or how uncertain the outlook, the president must submit a budget and Congress must make appropriations. If the president or Congress decides that the time is not right to change tax policy or to act on a particular legislative proposal, either can defer action until an agreement is reached. But they cannot default on their responsibility to decide the budget. When they do, federal programs and agencies shut down for lack of funding, and the work of government comes to a halt. Yet even when shutdowns occur, most recently in 1995–96, there ultimately is an agreement between the president and Congress.

In budgeting, then, there is conflict and resolution. Politics and process have a dual role in igniting conflict and in prodding the protagonists to set aside their differences. How the conflict unfolds and how it is resolved varies from year to year, but one can distinguish two broad patterns in federal budgeting. In one, the procedures of budgeting predominate; in the other, political factors hold sway. Much of this book details the procedures by which budgetary decisions are made.

This world of budgeting is one of regularity and predictability, in which players know what is expected of them and behave accordingly, conflict is muted, budget decisions are made at the margins, and the status quo predominates.

There is, however, another world of budgeting that is not so strongly bound by procedure and is unpredictable and turbulent. It is a world where substantial policy changes occur, or at least big changes are sought—a world in which Democrats and Republicans, sometimes members within each party as well, war not only over incremental issues but over past decisions and commitments. It is a world clouded by threat of breakdown, and resolution often comes through summit negotiations between the president and Congress. Here, the combatants write the rules and script as they go along. But like the world of budgetary order and calm, it is also a world in which there ultimately is resolution.

CONFLICT

The federal budget is an enormously complex undertaking. It entails the active participation of the president, key advisers, and many members of Congress, the efforts of thousands of staff in the executive and legislative branches, and the attention of numerous interest groups. It consists of thousands of big and small decisions, complicated rules and procedures, and debate over the composition and amount of public revenue and spending. The process is often tense and contentious because so much is at stake and so many institutions and interests are affected when budget decisions are made. The government takes in and spends almost $2 trillion annually—an amount equal to approximately one-fifth of the nation's gross domestic product. The federal government is the largest source of income for millions of American households and the largest investor in physical and human capital. Managing the federal debt makes the federal government the largest participant in capital markets.

However, the budget is much more than a matter of dollars. It finances federal programs and agencies and is a vital means of establishing and pursuing national priorities. In a fundamental sense, the federal government is what it spends. Through the budget, the government assists millions of families in meeting basic expenses and provides a financial safety net for the sick, elderly, and other dependent persons. The budget invests in the country's future by paying for roads and other physical assets, as well as for education and other human improvements. It signals to allies and adversaries the role of the United States in the world, and it is a key instrument of steering economic policy and stabilizing household income.

With so much at stake, it is not surprising that budgeting is often a difficult, conflict-laden process. As big as the budget is, there is never enough money to satisfy all demands. To budget is to fight over money and the things that money buys. The conflict sprawls between the Democratic and Republican parties (and frequently within them as well) and between the legislative and executive branches. Budgeting creates strife between Congress's authorizing committees, which have jurisdiction over federal programs, and its appropriations committees, which control a large chunk of federal spending, and between the committees responsible for tax legislation and those responsible for spending decisions.

As the budget has grown and become more prominent in U.S. political and economic life, the scope for conflict has expanded. Thousands of budget makers and influencers work in Washington, many on the staffs of congressional committees and executive agencies. Many others representing national corporations, trade associations, states and localities, foreign governments, and other interests mobilize to protect or expand their share of the budget's largess. The news media closely cover budget fights and issues, reporting developments in both executive suites and legislative chambers. In some years the budget is the centerpiece of the president's agenda as well as the vehicle for enacting much of Congress's legislative output. In national politics, it is now the age of budgeting.

But as the budget has grown in size and scope, it has become less supple and more constraining. A new-millennium president who inherits a $2 trillion budget may have fewer genuine choices than did predecessors who worked with budgets that were less than $100 billion. A generation ago, in 1970, this writer collaborated on a Brookings Institution project, *Setting National Priorities*, that analyzed and explained the president's budget options and choices. The title and tone of that publication optimistically intimated that by means of the budget the government could set priorities and policies that would make significant differences in the well-being of the United States and its citizens. In those not-so-distant years, the budget was still regarded as a malleable, empowering process; it enhanced the capacity of the government to govern. Through sound decisions, the budget could bolster economic conditions, buy cost-effective defense, humanely and efficiently allocate costs and benefits, and create a more bountiful future. Nowadays the budget often appears to be a limiting process, imprisoned in old commitments that narrow the options available to the government. A twenty-first century president has fewer options for Social Security than President Franklin Roosevelt had when the program was established in 1935 and fewer options for health care than President Lyndon Johnson had when Medicare and Medicaid were enacted in 1965. In some years the bud-

get appears to crowd out genuine choice and forces tomorrow's opportunities to give way to yesterday's decisions.

How can this be? How can the budget be both bigger but weaker? How can it have more resources but less choice, more programs but fewer options? A full consideration of these questions would require an inquiry into the condition of American democracy in the early twenty-first century. Budgeting is not the only process that has suffered a loss in capacity—as measured by the volume of public laws, legislating by Congress has also come upon hard times. Both have been weakened by a long spell of divided government, attrition in public trust and confidence, an imbalance between what Americans want from government and what they are willing to give it in political and financial support, protracted conflict over the role of government, social ills that seem irremediable through federal action, and more. Budgeting cannot be confident and efficacious when government is not.

To argue that the federal government and the machinery of budgeting are weaker than they once were is not to conclude that initiative and change are impossible. Ronald Reagan in 1981 and Bill Clinton in 1993 demonstrated that presidential leadership and budgetary resources are potent forces for redirecting national policies, changing tax laws, and reallocating federal money. They showed that the budget can be an instrument for change, that it need not be locked into old policies and priorities, that the opportunity to govern can be enlarged, and that the machinery of government can be deployed in pursuit of new political objectives. Both presidents exploited the rules and procedures of budgeting to alter established policies, even though the easier course would have been to accept the status quo. Each invested an enormous amount of scarce political capital in his first budget, and each stirred up vast amounts of budgetary conflict. In the end, each trimmed his objectives to get what he could, leaving other matters for future budget battles.

In budgeting, change and conflict go hand in hand. Without the latter, there would not likely be much of the former. Because 1981 and 1993 were inaugural years in which a president from one party succeeded a president from the other party, it is not surprising that change was the order of the day. In recent times, however, there have been quite a few other conflict-laden years: 1995–96, when a new Republican majority in Congress sought to revamp national priorities; 1997, when Congress and the president warred over and finally agreed on a measure to liquidate the deficit; and 1998 and 1999, when the president and Congress clashed over appropriations bills.

RESOLUTION

Regarding intense conflict as inevitable would miss the many years—rarer in the 1990s than in previous decades—when budget issues were resolved quietly, with little fanfare, and with little effort to significantly alter the course of government policy. The absence and mitigation of conflict are as indigenous to budgeting as are the flare-up and enlargement of conflict. Three of the ten years during the 1990s (1991, 1992, and 1994) had calm budget seasons in which the president called for, and Congress considered, few policy changes.

Budgeting has two inherent features—one that broadens the scope of conflict and the other that narrows it. Conflict is expanded by friction over who should pay and who should benefit, over how the tax burden should be distributed, and over which programs should grow and which should shrink. Budgeting is an allocative process in which there never is

enough money to allocate. It is also a redistributive process in which some gain because others lose—some get back more from government than they pay in taxes and others get less. It is a process of choosing among the many claims on public resources, which even in good times do not suffice to cover all demands. It is a rationing process in which the budget is resolved by excluding some claimants from its bounty. It is a process in which, expressly or indirectly, the government decides on its role and sets priorities. All these broaden the potential for conflict, not only on the large stage of American politics—between Republicans and Democrats and between the president and Congress—but also on thousands of back stages, in the bowels of government agencies when initial budgets are drawn up, in interest groups and lobbying firms where plots are hatched to seize a larger share of the pie, and in state and local governments, which see the federal Treasury as a vast pool of money from which they are entitled to their just share.

But there is another feature of budgeting that pulls it in the opposite direction, which contains conflict and constrains ambition. This arises out of the characteristic mentioned in the opening paragraph, that budgets must be resolved. Containing conflict begins in the earliest stages of the process, when claimants ask for less than they want, and continues to the last stages, when combatants set aside remaining differences in order to reach agreement. Budgeting rarely is all-out war, for if it were, even the best efforts of the various disputants would not bring closure.

It is not only self-denial that enables budgeting to achieve resolution. The process itself brings order and routine to budgetary demands and decisions. Budgetary procedures regulate conflict by parceling out tasks and roles, establishing expectations and deadlines for action, and limiting the scope of issues that are considered. Conflict is dampened by the routines of budgeting, the repetitive tasks that are completed with little or no change year after year, and by the patterned behavior of participants. Budget makers normally display a willingness to compromise that is often lacking when other matters are in dispute. When this accommodating disposition is lacking, as it was in 1995–96, routines break down and the process collapses.

THE TWO WORLDS OF BUDGETING

It would be facile to conclude that there are two worlds of budgeting—the political world in which conflict is pervasive and policy change is substantial and ambitious, and the procedural world in which order prevails and is tempered and incremental.

In reality, politics is as much a part of the world of budget resolution as it is of budget dispute. Similarly, rules and procedures inhabit the world of budgetary conflict as well as the world of budgetary peace. Incrementalism, which is the premier strategy for containing conflict, is as much an aspect of the politics of budgeting as are the conflagrations that engulfed budgeting in the 1990s. And when there is vast conflict, the various parties must rely on the machinery of budgeting to reach agreement.

As box 1-1 details, there are indeed two worlds of budgeting—one of big ambitions and large conflict, the other of modest ambition and minor flare-ups. The first is the world of change, the other the world of status quo. In most years, there is a bit of each in federal budgeting; budgeting without incremental routines would be chaotic, and budgeting without change would be unacceptable.

▼

BOX 1-1
Conflict and Calm in Budgeting: 1993 versus 1994

In 1993 President Clinton proposed major tax and spending changes, and the Democrat-controlled Congress reluctantly went along. The following year both sides opted for a status quo budget, as health care reform dominated the agenda. The budget resolution contained reconciliation instructions in 1993 but not in 1994. Continuing resolutions were necessary in 1993 to keep the government running, but in 1994 all regular appropriations cleared by the start of the fiscal year.

1993	1994
President Clinton's budget	
Inaugural budget, released on April 8, proposed major tax increases, changes in discretionary spending, and $500 billion in deficit reduction over five years	Status quo budget sought only minor adjustments in discretionary spending; Clinton's proposal to restructure the health care system occupied most of the congressional session
Congressional budget resolution	
Contained reconciliation instructions and was adopted before the statutory deadline for the first time since 1976	Made only minor adjustments to the president's request; adopted by the House on May 5; Senate adopted it one week later
Reconciliation bill	**Health care reform**
Conference report passed the House, 218-216, on August 5; Senate passed it the following day 51-50 by Vice President Al Gore's tie-breaking vote; signed by Clinton August 10	No reconciliation bill; Senate Majority Leader George Mitchell (D-Maine) announced on September 26 that health care reform was dead for the year
Appropriations	
Only two of thirteen regular appropriations bills completed by the start of the fiscal year; last one cleared the Senate November 10	All regular appropriations bills cleared Congress by October 1, the start of the fiscal year

In the 1992 election, Clinton talked about jobs, college education, the ability to own a home, affordable health care, and retirement with economic security. But when attention shifted to deficit reduction, Clinton, against the advice of close political advisers, altered his agenda and offered a massive package of tax increases, some spending cuts, and stimulus investments. He proposed $700 billion in gross deficit reduction over five years, slashing defense spending, making some cuts in domestic spending, imposing tax increases on high-income taxpayers and corporations, and seeking $200 billion in new spending and targeted tax relief. In the end Clinton got most of what he asked for, but he was forced to alter his energy tax and abandon his stimulus program.

continued

▼

BOX 1-1
Continued

In 1994 Clinton's budget sought little more than to rearrange a small amount of discretionary spending. OMB Director Leon Panetta said, "The real purpose of this budget is to stay on track with what was done last year." Many in Congress shared similar sentiments. Senator Kent Conrad (D-N.Dak.) said, "The fact is [that] we had a significant package of deficit reduction last year. That tells me we ought to stay the course [this year]." A fuller explanation is that Clinton's 1993 plan barely survived, and he expended much of his political capital to get a modified version enacted. By 1994 he was weaker and did not want to engage in another round of budgetary conflict with members of his own party.

Furthermore, the budget receded to the periphery as attention centered on health care reform. Despite the pressures to release the health proposal at the beginning of his administration, Clinton waited until the reconciliation bill was enacted before unveiling the mammoth 1,342-page overhaul. The House and Senate were fixated on health care reform throughout the 1994 session, although neither chamber voted on the plan. As did the budget in 1993, Clinton's health care plan crowded out other initiatives; not a single piece of substantive legislation was enacted before the mid-term election, which cost Democrats control of Congress.

When Congress debated the reconciliation package in 1993, Republicans, opposed to the tax increases and defense cutbacks, united against it. Clinton had to shop among his own party to find enough votes for this major piece of legislation. While no Democrat wanted, as Senator Bob Kerrey (D-Nebr.) said, "to cast the vote that brings down [Clinton's] presidency," liberals wanted additional spending for social programs, and conservatives sought smaller tax increases and more spending cuts. It took the all-out personal lobbying efforts of Clinton, Vice President Al Gore, and other administration officials to secure a bare House majority; 41 Democrats and all Republicans voted against the package. In the Senate, Mitch McConnell (R-Ky.) argued that "the only promise Bill Clinton has fulfilled is his promise of change—he has changed all of the policies that got him elected while making the middle class pay more." Six Democrats sided with all of the Republicans voting against the measure, but Vice President Gore's tie-breaking vote secured its passage.

During the 1993 appropriations process, Congress delivered on the deficit-cutting promise, but conflict delayed the bills. Eleven of the thirteen regular appropriations were unfinished by the start of the fiscal year. Three continuing resolutions later and for the first time in twenty years, Congress held discretionary spending to roughly the same level as the previous year. At the same time, Democrats reallocated spending to fund most of Clinton's earlier-reduced investment programs.

The following year Congress cleared all of the annual appropriations bills before the start of the fiscal year—at the time, only the third such occurrence since 1948. There were numerous pressures to wrap up the bills quickly—most notably, the appropriations chairs' determination to finish on time and Clinton's desire for action on health care reform before the session ended.

2

The Evolution of Federal Budgeting
From Surplus to Deficit to Surplus

The process and politics of budgeting revolve around two main institutions of government power: the presidency and Congress. The evolution of federal budgeting has been a long contest between these two political branches for control of the purse. Their weapons have been the rules and procedures of budgeting; each has sought to impose its policies and priorities on the other by leveraging public resources to dictate how big the government should be and how the money should be spent. For more than two hundred years these institutions have vied for political power, sometimes cooperating and sometimes confronting one another. Sometimes Congress has held the advantage; other times the president has. Rarely have the two sides enjoyed budgetary parity. Instead, the dominance of one has corresponded with the weakness of the other. The struggle has led each branch to establish its own budget process, each with its own budget staff and operating rules.

The evolution has not only resulted in distinct budgetary roles for the president and Congress—it has also given the federal government two very different ways of spending public funds: one centered on annual appropriations, the other on mandatory legislation. While appropriations are the form of congressional control envisioned by the Constitution, during the second half of the twentieth century Congress and the president increasingly relied on authorizing legislation to entitle

Americans to payments from the Treasury. Appropriations and entitlements take different paths through Congress and are subject to different budget rules and constraints. However, they are merged in both the presidential and congressional budgets to show total federal spending.

The rise of entitlements has been associated with another important budgetary development—prolonged deficit spending. Chronic deficits have been a recent phenomenon fueled in large part by the requirement that the government pay for entitlements regardless of its financial condition. It took a long time for Congress and the president to adjust to the fiscal realities of the "entitlement state." It was not until near the close of the twentieth century that they managed to do so, producing balanced budgets after decades of uninterrupted deficits.

This chapter tells the story of federal budgeting from the three vantage points mentioned thus far: the contest between the president and Congress for budgetary power, the changing composition of federal spending, and the shift from surpluses to deficits and back to surpluses. The chronicle is broken into three periods, which are delineated by important milestones in federal budgeting. The first period was from 1789, the First Congress, until 1921. It was characterized by congressional dominance, small government, and frequent surpluses. The second period was initiated by the Budget and Accounting Act of 1921 and continued until the Congressional Budget Act of 1974. It was characterized by presidential dominance, the growth of government, the enactment of major entitlement legislation, and frequent deficits. The most recent period, from 1974 to present, is one in which deficits ballooned and then disappeared, federal spending and entitlements continued to rise, and the president and Congress repeatedly fought over budget policies. Inasmuch as the focus of this book is on current budget process, politics, and policies, the account for the first two periods is brief, while that of the current period is longer and more detailed. In discussing the contemporary period, the book is particularly concerned with why large deficits emerged in the 1980s, how they were liquidated by the end of the 1990s, and how budgeting adjusted to the permanence of the entitlement state and to protracted warfare between the president and Congress.

In budgeting, the final chapter is never written. The next fiscal year is no more than 12 months away, and with it comes changes in the budget's numbers and new twists and turns in the relationships of those involved with budgeting. From afar, the process may appear to repeat itself year after year, but for those locked in combat, each year brings fresh opportunities and issues. At this writing, the newly won budget surplus seems secure; official projections show rising surpluses through the first decade of the twenty-first century. The history of budgeting, however, does not consist of promises and projections but of outcomes and experiences. Moreover, actual budgetary results rarely conform to expectations. Budgeting is full of shocks and surprises, which will forge a budgetary future that will be politically and financially different from the outlook at the start of the millennium.

LEGISLATIVE DOMINANCE: 1789–1921

The Constitution grants Congress the power to levy taxes and provides that money may be spent only pursuant to appropriations made by law. It does not specify how these powers are to be exercised, nor does it provide for a federal budget or for the president to have a significant role in the nation's financial matters (other than that of signing or vetoing bills passed by Congress). In fact, the practice of budgeting was unknown when the Constitution was written. Modern budgeting emerged in Europe during the nineteenth century and was imported into the United States early in the twentieth century.

But if budgeting was unknown, the role of Congress in deciding revenues and spending was well established. Centuries of struggle in England between Parliament and the Crown over the power of the purse culminated in the principle that the government's authority to tax and spend must be conferred by legislation. It took centuries to implant this principle in England, but by the time the American colonies were waging war for their independence, its acceptance on this side of the Atlantic was a basic tenet of limited, democratic government.

Congress's power of the purse was designed to constrain executive authority. The Constitution bars the president and federal agencies from spending money unless they have prior authorization from Congress. But it was not just the totals that Congress constrained; it also ruled over individual items of expenditure by making detailed appropriations. Exhibit 2-1, drawn from the 1799 appropriation for the Treasury Department, shows a typical line-item appropriation. Each line is a separate limitation on the specific amount permitted for a particular purpose. In some years Congress gave spending agencies limited discretion to transfer funds among items; in others it insisted that the funds be spent exactly as appropriated.

In the early years of American government, the House Ways and Means and the Senate Finance Committees handled revenue and spending legislation, as well as other financial matters. Although the government was small, the practices devised during the formative years set precedents for congressional action

during the next two centuries. From the start the House took the initiative on both revenue (as stated in the Constitution) and spending bills; the Senate acted only after the House had completed its work. Appropriations were made one year at a time, in bills whose sole purpose was to supply money to federal agencies. Legislation was handled in separate measures; it was taken for granted that appropriation and legislation should not be combined in the same bill. Thus, the First Congress passed one law creating the War Department and another law appropriating money to it. Although subsequent Congresses made appropriations in a number of separate bills, the First Congress folded all appropriations into a single bill.

While the Constitution does not prescribe any particular budgetary outcome, it was accepted that each year's spending should not exceed that year's revenues. As figure 2-1 shows, the balanced budget norm was adhered to in two-thirds of the years from 1789 through 1916. Most of the exceptions were during wartime, when a surge in federal spending led to deficits. But the deficits were small and short-lived; when the war ended, budgetary balance was restored. Deficits were also occasioned by adverse economic conditions; these too tended to disappear when the economy recovered.

The balanced budget norm coexisted with the notion that government should be small and limited. It was also accepted that the size of government should not vary significantly from year to year and that the amounts spent during the previous year should, with only small adjustments, determine the amount appropriated for the next. In contrast to contemporary government, in which compiling the annual budget often centers on the quest for money to expand federal programs, during much of the nineteenth century the process normally in-

▶ **EXHIBIT 2-1**
Line-Item Appropriations: Eighteenth-Century Style

For compensation to the Treasurer, clerks, and persons employed in his office, five thousand eight hundred and fifty dollars.

For expenses of firewood, stationery, printing, rent, and all other contingencies in the treasurer's office, six hundred dollars. . . .

For the payment of rent for the several houses employed in the Treasury department (except the treasurer's office) two thousand seven hundred and thirty dollars and sixty-six cents.

For the expense of firewood and candles in the several offices of the Treasury department, (except the treasurer's office,) three thousand five hundred dollars.

For defraying the expense incident to the stating and printing the public accounts for the year one thousand seven hundred and ninety-nine, (including an increase of two hundred dollars in consequence of an extension of the revenue and expenditures,) one thousand two hundred dollars.

For defraying the expense incident to the removal of books and records of the Treasury department from Philadelphia to Trenton, during part of the summer of the year one thousand seven hundred and ninety-eight, including the extra expenses of the several officers, clerks and messengers in each office, four thousand four hundred dollars. . . .

For the wages of persons employed at the different branches of melting, refining, coining, carpenters, millwrights, and smiths' work, including the sum of eight hundred dollars per annum, allowed to an assistant coiner and die forger, who also oversees the execution of the iron work, seven thousand.

For the purchase of ironmongery, lead, wool, coals, stationery, office furniture, and for all other contingencies of the establishment of the mint, six thousand three hundred dollars.

Source: *United States Statutes at Large*, 5th Cong., 3d sess., March 2, 1799, chapter 25, p. 717.

(a) Line-item appropriations were common up to the twentieth century, but the degree of itemization varied from year to year. Some were even more detailed than the appropriation exhibited here.

(b) With line-item appropriations, a perennial issue facing Congress was the extent to which it should authorize spending agencies to transfer funds among the items. Inasmuch as each line is a legal limit on expenditure, these transfers could be made only with Congress's approval.

(c) As government grew, the individual items receded in importance, and Congress was impelled to lump them into broad categories. Nowadays most federal agencies have a single appropriation covering all their operating expenses.

FIGURE 2-1
Deficits and Surpluses, Fiscal Years 1789–1916

Millions of dollars

Source: *Historical Statistics of the United States: Colonial Times to 1970,* 93d Cong., 1st sess., H. Doc, 78, part 2, Y 335–38.

volved estimating the next year's cost of activities already under way. Increases were modest and were more a reflection of territorial expansion and population growth than the drive to enlarge government. Nevertheless, federal spending was significantly higher in 1900 ($521 million) than it had been in 1800 ($11 million).

In nominal terms, federal spending quadrupled during the War of 1812, doubled during the Mexican War, and increased twenty-fold during the Civil War (table 2-1). Spending receded after each war (except for Vietnam), but always remained well above prewar levels. Between wars, while its composition changed, total spending remained stable. For example, the federal government spent $358 million in fiscal 1867 (the first full fiscal year after the Civil War) and only $366 million in fiscal 1897 (the last full fiscal year before the Spanish-American War). The government typically accumulated debt during wartime, was bur-

TABLE 2-1

Impact of War on Federal Spending, Selected Fiscal Years, 1811–1974

Millions of dollars, unless otherwise specified

War	Prewar			Wartime peak			Postwar		
	Outlays	Fiscal year	Surplus or deficit	Outlays	Fiscal year	Surplus or deficit	Outlays	Fiscal year	Surplus or deficit
War of 1812	8	1811	6	35	1814	−24	22	1817	11
Mexican War	23	1845	7	57	1847	−31	45	1849	−14
Civil War	63	1860	−7	1,298	1865	−964	358	1867	133
Spanish-American War	366	1897	−18	605	1899	−89	521	1900	46
World War I	713	1916	48	18,493	1919	−13,363	6,358	1920	291
World War II	13,653	1941	−4,941	92,712	1945	−47,553	34,496	1947	4,018
Korean War	38,835	1949	580	76,101	1953	−6,493	68,444	1955	−2,993
Vietnam War	118,528	1964	−5,915	183,640	1969	3,242	269,359	1974	−6,135

Sources: *Historical Statistics of the United States: Colonial Times to 1970*, 93d Cong., 1st sess., H. Doc. 78, part 2, Y 335–38; and *Budget of the United States, Historical Tables, Fiscal Year 2000*, table 1.1, pp. 19–20.

dened by interest payments after the war ended, and gradually undertook new spending as debt was paid off and interest charges declined. In the last decades of the nineteenth century, paydown of the public debt was financed by revenues that sufficed to cover total peacetime expenditures. With federal budgets consistently at or near balance, the public debt receded from $2.8 billion in 1866 to $1.3 billion in 1900.

Financial stability was maintained despite the lack of a presidential budget system to coordinate revenues and expenditures. As long as the government was small and its financial needs modest, a national budget was not necessary for producing acceptable outcomes. Congress managed to coordinate federal revenues and spending decisions by acting on the various bills affecting federal finances. Two related developments, however, brought this comfortable situation—coordinated outcomes without coordinated control—to a close. One was increased fragmentation in Congress; the other was the growth of federal spending and the emergence of peacetime deficits.

The first step toward fragmenting congressional action occurred as a byproduct of the Civil War, which greatly added to the cost of government and to Congress's workload. To ease the burden on the House Ways and Means and Senate Finance Committees, the House in 1865 and the Senate in 1867 separated revenue and spending jurisdictions by establishing new appropriations committees. The second step, which began in the 1870s in the House and then spread to the Senate, was the legislative committees' seizure of control over half of the appropriations bills. These committees wanted spending jurisdiction because they were dissatisfied with the tight constraints imposed by the new appropriations committees. This fragmentation of spending power led, some scholars have argued, to higher federal expenditures.

Legislative fragmentation was mirrored by decentralization in the executive branch. The president had a limited role in overseeing federal finances. Many agencies submitted spending requests directly to congressional committees, without prior review by the president.

The various requests were compiled by the Treasury in an annual *Book of Estimates*, but little effort was made to coordinate spending by individual agencies or to ensure that they totaled to an acceptable amount and were in accord with national policy.

Fragmentation and the progressive rise in federal spending (which doubled in nominal terms between 1894 and 1915) led to persistent peacetime deficits. Spending exceeded revenues in eleven of the seventeen years from 1894 to 1910. To battle these deficits, the government introduced a national income tax and created an executive budget process. While the income tax amendment was ratified in 1913, the budget proposal (promoted by a national commission headed by former president William Howard Taft) provoked considerable controversy. World War I erupted before Congress created an executive budget process. As a consequence of the war, federal spending soared from $726 million in 1914 to $19 billion five years later. The public debt followed a similar trend in those five years, escalating from $1 billion to $26 billion. Shortly after the war, Congress conceded that it needed strong presidential leadership to control spending. It passed the Budget and Accounting Act of 1921, which established the presidential budget system that has operated for the past 80 years. Box 2-1 lists this and other landmarks in federal budgeting.

PRESIDENTIAL DOMINANCE: 1921–74

The 1921 act did not expressly alter the manner in which Congress made revenue and spending decisions, though the House and Senate amended their rules to return jurisdiction over all spending bills to the appropriations committees. The main change was to give the president a formal role in budgeting before Congress acted on the appropriations bills. The 1921 act required him to submit an annual budget to Congress and barred agencies from giving their requests directly to Congress.

The act also created the Bureau of the Budget (renamed the Office of Management and Budget in 1970) to help the president decide the amounts to be requested. His annual budget sets forth revenue and spending recommendations that influence Congress, although it is not bound to follow them. For each element in the budget, Congress may appropriate more or less than the president requests. Similarly, it may diverge from the president's preferences on revenue legislation.

The 1921 act does not require a balanced budget, but it was predicated on the strong expectation that presidential coordination would restrain federal spending. In effect, the Budget and Accounting Act made the president an agent of congressional budget control. Every step of the way, it was expected that Congress would consider the president's proposals before making its own decisions. Reformers assumed that Congress would thereby act in a more disciplined and coordinated manner than it had when agencies directly lobbied for additional money. With the White House holding agencies on a tight spending leash, Congress would appropriate less, thereby enabling the government to balance its books.

These expectations were borne out during the early years of presidential budgeting. The new process had immediate success in regulating federal finance. In the 1920s taxes were reduced, and both expenditures and the public debt declined. These outcomes may have been partly due to the conservative mood of postwar America, but the single-minded fiscal discipline imposed by the new system was also an important factor. Throughout the 1920s the president's eager budget controllers maintained a tight grip on agency spending, demanded efficiency, and insisted that agencies

▼

BOX 2-1
Milestones in Federal Budgeting, 1789–1990

1789   **Constitution**
Gives Congress the power to lay and collect taxes and to borrow money; requires appropriations by Congress before funds can be drawn from the Treasury

1802–67   **Congressional Committees**
House Ways and Means Committee established as standing committee in 1802; Senate Finance Committee established in 1816; House Appropriations Committee established in 1865; Senate Appropriations Committee established in 1867

1837, 1850   **House and Senate Rules**
House and Senate bar unauthorized appropriations

1870, 1905–06   **Antideficiency Act**
Requires apportionment of funds to prevent overexpenditure

1921   **Budget and Accounting Act**
Provides for an executive budget; establishes the Bureau of the Budget in the Treasury Department and the General Accounting Office

1939   **Reorganization Plan No. 1**
Transfers the Bureau of the Budget to the new Executive Office of the President and expands the bureau's role

1967   **President's Commission on Budget Concepts**
Adoption of the unified budget, including trust funds

1974   **Congressional Budget and Impoundment Control Act**
Establishes the congressional budget process, procedures for legislative review of impoundments, House and Senate Budget Committees, and the Congressional Budget Office

1980   **Omnibus Reconciliation Process**
Reconciliation used for the first time at the start of the congressional budget process

1985, 1987   **Gramm-Rudman-Hollings Acts**
Set deficit reduction targets and created sequestration procedures

1990   **Budget Enforcement Act**
Shifts from fixed to adjustable deficit targets; establishes caps on discretionary spending, pay-as-you-go rules for revenue and direct spending, and new budgeting rules for direct and guaranteed loans

1990   **Chief Financial Officers Act**
Provides for a chief financial officer in all major agencies to oversee financial management and integrate accounting and budgeting

FIGURE 2-2
Deficits and Surpluses, Fiscal Years 1917–74

Billions of dollars

Source: *Budget of the United States, Historical Tables, Fiscal Year 2000,* table 1.1, pp. 19–20.

make do with either less or no more than they had the previous year.

Then came the Depression and in its wake the New Deal—a vast, permanent expansion in the scope, scale, and cost of government. At the eve of the Depression in 1929, federal spending totaled approximately 3 percent of GDP; a decade later, at the eve of World War II, it was 10 percent. Although expenditures tripled during the 1930s, revenues failed to keep pace, and the government incurred substantial deficits throughout the decade (figure 2-2). However, World War II brought a massive inflow of revenue, as Congress converted the individual income tax into a mass tax, imposed very high rates (reaching to 91 percent of taxable in-

come), and established a new system for withholding taxes from paychecks. These and other provisions produced a surge in revenues, which were seven times higher in 1945 than they had been five years earlier.

Following the pattern set after previous wars, Congress lowered taxes in peacetime but retained most of the additional revenue raised during the war to finance a permanent expansion of government. Congress maintained the broad-based, high-rate individual income tax, as well as the withholding system. Big government was here to stay, thanks in part to the taxes that were made politically palatable by war. Federal outlays average 18 percent of GDP during the 1950s, double the 1930s level. The upsurge in revenue enabled the president and Congress to produce budgets that were at or near balance.

The new money transformed the president's budget role from spending controller to program planner. During the 1950s and 1960s it became customary for the president to prepare a legislative program in tandem with the annual budget. The president used the budget to propose spending initiatives, which shaped Congress's agenda and media coverage. There was no opprobrium and little political cost for the president to ask for more, provided that his proposals were paid for out of existing revenues and not by borrowing or new taxes. Congress followed suit by authorizing and appropriating more—sometimes resisting or trimming presidential initiatives, other times providing even more than the president requested.

This was the age of the "imperial presidency," a term coined by scholars to characterize the extent to which the president dominated national policy. The budget was one of his chief tools, enabling him to formulate programs, promote spending initiatives, and preside over a new burst of governmental expansion that culminated in the Great Society legislation enacted in 1964 and 1965.

With the rise in revenue and spending as a proportion of GDP, the president increasingly used the budget to fine-tune the economy—keeping it on a high-employment, low-inflation course—by adjusting the budget to stimulate or dampen aggregate demand. The notion that the budget should balance the economy superseded the balanced budget norm. Deficits were acceptable to spur the economy to operate at full potential and to reduce unemployment. As long as the economy was booming, small deficits were seen as a prudent means of promoting national well-being.

But the Vietnam War and the growth in entitlements brought this idyllic period in national politics to an end. The war challenged presidential leadership; the growth in entitlements called into question the adequacy of existing budgetary instruments. Because the war was unpopular, Congress was reluctant to pay for it with tax increases. It did enact a small surtax in 1968, more than a year after President Lyndon Johnson had requested it and at only about half the rate he wanted. While the surtax and continued economic growth generated a small surplus in fiscal 1969, it was the last surplus the government achieved for nearly three decades.

Widespread distaste for the Vietnam War tainted attitudes toward budget deficits. Rather than considering deficit spending an appropriate means of financing military operations, many Americans regarded it as evidence of fiscal irresponsibility and of the destabilization and policy distortions brought about by the war. To make matters worse, when the war ended, federal spending did not recede as it had after previous wars and the budget did not return to balance. In fact, there was no post–Vietnam War year in which federal spending fell below the fiscal 1966 level—there was no peace dividend.

The post-Vietnam budgetary situation differed from the pattern set in previous wars because the composition of federal spending had changed. Figure 2-3 compares the shares of federal spending accounted for by payments to individuals and other categories at 20-year intervals from 1940 to 2000. During this period there was a fundamental reversal in the ratio of mandatory to discretionary spending. Payments to individuals (mostly entitlements) were 18 percent of total spending in 1940. In 1960 the government spent almost three dollars on discretionary defense and domestic programs for every dollar of individual payments; today it spends approximately two

FIGURE 2-3
Composition of Federal Outlays, Fiscal Years 1940, 1960, 1980, 2000[a]

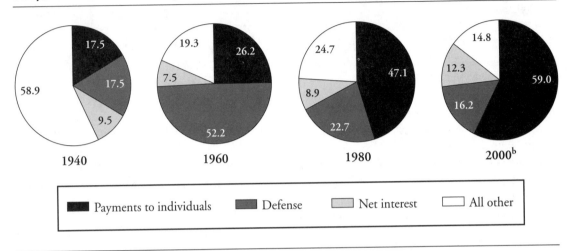

Source: *Budget of the United States, Historical Tables, Fiscal Year 2001*, table 6.1, pp. 103–09.

 a. Totals add to more than 100 percent because "undistributed offsetting receipts" are not included.

 b. Estimated.

mandatory dollars for every discretionary one. There was no peace dividend after Vietnam because the increase in mandatory payments exceeded the decrease in defense spending. Between 1969 and 1973 defense expenditures declined $6 billion, but payments to individuals soared almost $50 billion. Consequently, the budget was hobbled by large, persistent deficits (see figure 2-2).

The increased share of the budget determined by eligibility rules and payment formulas weakened the president's budget capacity. As table 2-2 indicates, federal payments to individuals have continued to escalate as a proportion of total outlays. In some years the president's budget has been more a means of estimating next year's cost of past commitments than of recommending the program and financial policies of government. Vietnam and Watergate, which undermined confidence in his leadership and soured relations with Congress, also weakened the president's budget power.

CONGRESS VERSUS THE PRESIDENT: 1974–2000

Things came to a head in the early 1970s, when President Richard Nixon warred with Congress over budget priorities and refused to spend billions of appropriated dollars. Spurred by concern that the budget was out of control and rejecting presidential leadership, Congress sought to bolster its role by creating a new legislative budget process.

Congress's quest for budgetary independence culminated in the Congressional Budget and Impoundment Control Act of 1974, which Nixon signed into law less than one month before Watergate drove him from office. This measure provides for Congress to adopt an annual budget resolution that sets revenue, spending, the surplus or deficit, and debt totals, and allocates spending among 20 functional categories.

In expanding Congress's budget responsibilities, the 1974 act did not alter the formal role of the president. As before, the president

TABLE 2-2
Federal Payments to Individuals by Selected Programs, by Decade, 1960–2000[a]

Program	1960	1970	1980	1990	2000[a]
Payments to individuals					
Total (billions of dollars)	24.2	64.8	278.5	584.1	1,055.7
Total constant (fiscal 1996)	109.0	232.9	510.3	683.8	980.1
Percent of total federal outlays	26.2	33.1	47.1	46.6	59.0
Percent of GDP	4.6	6.4	10.2	10.2	11.0
Outlays for selected programs (billions of dollars)					
Social Security (OASDI)	11.4	29.7	117.1	246.4	403.2
Medicare (HI)	0	4.8	23.8	65.9	132.4
Medicaid	0	2.7	14.0	41.1	116.1
Food stamps	0	0.6	9.1	15.9	19.7
Family support (AFDC/TANF)[b]	2.1	4.1	6.9	12.3	18.1
Civil service retirement	0.9	2.8	14.7	31.0	45.4
Veterans' assistance[c]	4.7	8.1	19.9	27.3	44.5
Military retirement	0.7	2.9	11.9	21.6	44.5
Supplemental Security Income (SSI)	0	0	5.7	11.5	32.9
Recipients (millions)					
Social Security (OASDI)	14.8	26.2	35.6	39.8	44.8
Medicare (HI)	0	20.4	25.1	30.5	39.3
Medicaid	0	14.5	21.6	25.3	33.4
Food stamps	0	4.3	21.1	20.0	18.1
Family support (AFDC/TANF)	3.0	8.5	10.8	11.7	7.3[d]

Sources: Payments to individuals: *Budget of the United States, Historical Tables, Fiscal Year 2001*, table 11.1, pp. 172–73; Outlays: *Budget of the United States, Historical Tables, Fiscal Year 2001*, table 11.3, pp. 182–204; Recipients for fiscal 1960–90: *Social Security Bulletin, Annual Statistical Supplement, 1998*, table 5.A4, p. 197, table 8.B1, p. 313, table 8.E1, p. 328, table 9.G1, p. 342, and table 9.H1, p. 344; for 2000: *Budget of the United States, Analytical Perspectives, Fiscal Year 2001*, table 14-3, p. 291; Health Care Financing Administration; Department of Health and Human Services.

    a. Estimated.

    b. AFDC was replaced with Temporary Assistance for Needy Families (TANF) in 1997.

    c. Includes service and nonservice connected compensation; grants to states; hospital and medical care; and education, insurance, and burial benefits.

    d. Actual figures from 1999.

submits a budget each year, and Congress has the option of accepting or rejecting his recommendations. But now Congress has its own budget blueprint, economic assumptions, program analyses, spending priorities, and its own ideas on whether revenues and spending should be changed.

To a degree that may have been unforeseen when the 1974 act was formulated, the new system institutionalized and expanded budgetary conflict. The president and Congress have their own budgets, and neither has a for-

mal say in what the other does. Congress has its own Congressional Budget Office (CBO) and no longer has to rely on the administration's economic projections and program estimates. Of course, the two branches have to resolve differences to make appropriations and legislate changes in revenue and entitlement laws. But first, they fight. Moreover, rather than fighting over the details, as was once common, they now fight over big policy matters—the size of government, defense versus domestic programs, how much total spending

TABLE 2-3
Era of Divided Government, 1969–2000

	White House	House	Senate
1969–76	Republican	Democrats	Democrats
1977–80	Democrat	Democrats	Republicans
1981–86	Republican	Democrats	Democrats
1987–92	Republican	Democrats	Democrats
1993–94	Democrat	Democrats	Democrats
1995–2000	Democrat	Republicans	Republicans

and revenues should rise from one year to the next, whether to cut the deficit by trimming expenditures or by boosting taxes, and so on.

If the new congressional budget process opened the door to conflict, a long spell of divided government and weak economic performance kept the door open for an extended period. Table 2-3 shows that in all but six of the years between 1969 and 2000, the White House was controlled by one party and at least one house of Congress was controlled by the other party. Not only was government divided, but Republicans and Democrats repeatedly clashed on budget policy—in particular, on the steps that should be taken to deal with chronic deficits.

The congressional budget process had the misfortune of being launched about the time the nation's economic performance deteriorated. The postwar economic boom, which brought large, steady gains in productivity, national income, and other measures of economic well-being, ended abruptly in 1973–74 with the first oil shock. Inflation, unemployment, and interest rates soared, productivity stagnated, and real disposable income dropped. New terms, such as stagflation and the misery index, entered economic language to describe the adverse conditions. A weak economy took its inextricable toll on the federal budget, and deficits, which had been relatively small before the establishment of the

congressional budget process, became much larger.

The 1974 Budget Act did not ordain that the budget be balanced, nor did it bar Congress from adopting budget resolutions with big deficits. But the new process was enacted on the expectation that deficits would be smaller because Congress had to expressly vote on them. This expectation was thwarted by economic distress: the deficit averaged $113 billion a year (3.6 percent of GDP) during the first decade of the new process (fiscal years 1976–85) compared with $16 billion (1.4 percent of GDP) during the previous decade (fiscal years 1966–75).

Divided government and chronic deficits locked both ends of Pennsylvania Avenue in prolonged budgetary conflict. The president had his budget; Congress had its budget resolution. Each branch acted unilaterally, but in some manner or another, there also had to be a meeting of the minds each year. Although there was budgetary conflict, there also was budgetary resolution.

During the 1980s budgetary conflict was resolved in ways that added to the deficit. Figure 2-4 shows a striking descent into deficits during the 1980s. Before fiscal 1982 the peak deficit was $79 billion (in fiscal 1981); in the dozen years after fiscal 1982, the smallest deficit was $150 billion (in fiscal 1987). One does not have to search far for the root causes

FIGURE 2-4
Deficits and Surpluses, Fiscal Years 1975–99[a]

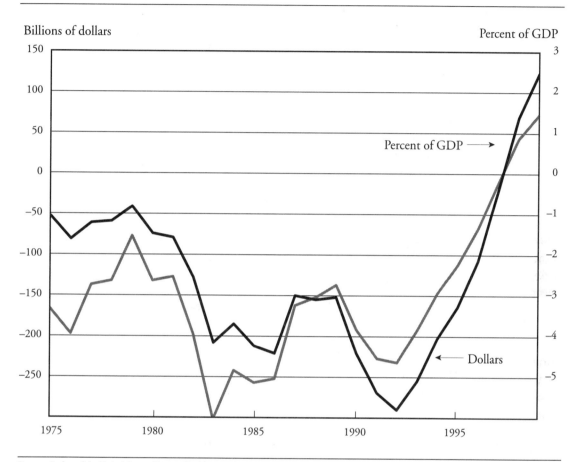

Source: *Budget of the United States, Historical Tables, Fiscal Year 2001*, table 1.1, pp. 19–20, and table 1.2, pp. 21–22.
  a. The transition quarter is evenly distributed between 1976 and 1977.

of the deficit explosion. It resulted from policy mistakes and political impasse during the Reagan presidency. Within months after he took office in 1981, Reagan got Congress to adopt a far-reaching economic program that slashed tax rates, boosted defense spending, but only modestly cut domestic programs. Individual income tax rates were cut by 25 percent, dozens of tax breaks were added to the revenue code, and future tax rates were automatically indexed to inflation. Official estimates made at the time projected a $749 billion revenue loss over the next five years. Through the appropriations process, Congress added more than $100 billion to annual defense spending, and although it made some material cuts in domestic spending, many cutbacks were subsequently reversed.

Reagan's budget program was vigorously promoted by "supply-siders" who argued that tax cuts would stimulate the economy and thereby generate higher revenues in the future.

Things did not work out this way. A recession in 1982 and budgetary stalemate between the president and Congress led to annual deficits of $200 billion—in the famous words of Reagan's budget director, David Stockman, "as far ahead as the eye can see." Congress responded to the deficit crisis by passing the Balanced Budget and Emergency Deficit Control Act of 1985, commonly referred to as Gramm-Rudman-Hollings (GRH), after the bill's principal sponsors. The act called for the progressive reduction in the deficit in each fiscal year from 1986 through 1990 and for a balanced budget in fiscal 1991. This objective was to be enforced by an automatic cancellation of budget resources if the projected deficit exceeded the target for a fiscal year by more than $10 billion. After the Supreme Court declared the original GRH law unconstitutional, Congress passed a revised version, which postponed the target year for a balanced budget to fiscal 1993.

Despite the threat of sequestration—withholding funds when deficit targets are exceeded—the actual deficit exceeded the GRH level in each fiscal year the law was in effect. Although it may have had a slight dampening effect on deficits, GRH was seriously defective. It did not require the actual deficit to be within the target, but only that the deficit projected at the start of each fiscal year be within that year's allowed level. Any increase in the deficit during the fiscal year, whether because of estimation errors, changes in economic conditions, or new policies, did not require congressional or presidential action to offset the increase. Reliance on projected rather than actual deficits led to manipulation of budget estimates, bookkeeping tricks instead of genuine savings, and much higher annual deficits than had been projected. In fact, the budget deficit was higher in GRH's last year (1990) than it had been in 1984, the year before the enactment of GRH.

Although GRH was a fiscal failure, it left an enduring imprint on budget practice. Figure 2-5 shows GRH and other legislation designed to control the deficit. In an age of divided government, it pioneered the notion that politicians should be restricted by budget rules when making revenue and spending decisions. Both the Budget and Accounting Act of 1921 and the Congressional Budget Act of 1974 authorized the president and Congress to take any budget action they deemed appropriate. In contrast, the premise of GRH was that politicians require prefixed rules barring them from making certain budget choices because they cannot be trusted to do the right thing on their own and they certainly cannot make the hard decisions needed to discipline federal revenue and spending.

Budget Enforcement Rules

Congress and the president were beset by an impending budget crisis in 1990. The GRH target allowed a deficit of only $64 billion for fiscal 1991, but budget projections made in July 1990 indicated a deficit in excess of $230 billion—far more than could be sequestered (withheld) without doing serious damage to national defense, social programs, and payments to needy households. Difficult negotiations produced an omnibus package of tax increases, some spending cuts, and new budget enforcement rules (box 2-2). The revenue and spending changes were estimated to slash $496 billion from deficits over the following five years. But because the nation plunged into recession in 1990, about the time the final touches were being put on the package deal, the deficit continued to rise, peaking at $290 billion in fiscal 1992 (see figure 2-5).

Despite this rise in the deficit, the new rules laid out in the Budget Enforcement Act of 1990 (BEA) do not require sequestration or any other response if the deficit exceeds tar-

FIGURE 2-5
Battling the Deficit: 1981–97ᵃ

Billions of dollars

1982:
Tax Equity and Fiscal Responsibility Act scaled back some of the tax cuts enacted in 1981 (see box 7-1)

1981:
Reagan's package enacted, including a $131 billion spending cut (fiscal 1982–84) and a $749 billion tax cut (fiscal 1982–86)

1984:
Deficit Reduction Act cut the deficit by $149 billion (fiscal 1985–87)

1985, 1987:
Gramm-Rudman-Hollings Acts; Set deficit targets to balance the budget and provided for sequesters if deficit projections exceed the targets

1990:
Reconciliation Act cut the deficit by $496 billion (fiscal 1991–95); the Budget Enforcement Act created discretionary spending caps and PAYGO rules for revenue and direct spending (see box 2-2)

1993:
Reconciliation Act extended PAYGO and spending caps through fiscal 1998; cut the deficit by $496 billion (fiscal 1994–98)

1995:
President Clinton vetoed a reconciliation bill that was the centerpiece of the new congressional Republican majority's agenda to balance the budget by fiscal 2002; sought to cut spending by $894 billion and lower taxes by $245 billion (fiscal 1996–2002) (see box 9-2)

1997:
Balanced Budget Act extended PAYGO and spending caps through fiscal 2002; cut spending by $263 billion and reduced the deficit by $127 billion (fiscal 1998–2002); companion measure cut taxes by $275 billion (fiscal 1998–2007)

Sources: *Congressional Quarterly Almanac*, 1981–97.
a. The years in bold within the graph are calendar years, while the years on the axis are fiscal years.

geted levels. One of the lessons Congress and the president derived from the failure of GRH was that it is futile to set fixed annual deficit limits that cannot be adjusted for changes in economic conditions or for reestimates of program expenditures. Fixed limits can be overtaken and rendered unworkable by unforeseen developments, such as the 1990–91 recession. By contrast, BEA gives the president the option to adjust the maximum deficit amount when he submits his budget to Congress, thereby greatly reducing the threat of a sequester. Political leaders came to understand that they must control the revenue raised and

the money spent in order to contain the deficit. In line with this reasoning, BEA established a new deficit control process that distinguishes between discretionary spending, controlled by annual appropriations, and direct spending, controlled by substantive legislation. The BEA rules were initially effective only for fiscal years 1991 through 1995, but they were subsequently extended through fiscal 1998 and then again through fiscal 2002. In view of the political attractiveness of these rules, they may be extended again.

The BEA rules are not complicated, but implementing them entails complex budget cal-

▼

BOX 2-2
Starting Down the Road to Liquidate the Deficit: The 1990 Budget Summit

The Gramm-Rudman-Hollings Act, which promised to balance the budget and calm budgetary strife between the Democratic-controlled Congress and the Republican White House, provoked renewed conflict between the warring branches in 1990. In January President George Bush insisted that he would veto any tax increase; in November he signed a big tax hike into law. When Congress convened, GRH threatened to sequester funds if statutory deficit targets were exceeded; by the end of the session a new set of rules replaced GRH. The year started with Congress and the president taking opposite positions on virtually every budgetary issue; it ended with them making budgetary peace through tense summit negotiations that produced the Omnibus Budget Reconciliation Act of 1990 (OBRA-

June 26
Bush announces that tax increases are necessary.

September 30
Agreement on budget summit package reached; first continuing resolution (CR) passed.

October 5
House rejects the budget resolution that would have codified the summit agreement; Congress passes second CR.

October 6
Bush vetoes the CR; partial federal government shutdown lasts three days.

October 26
The House, 228-200, and the Senate, 54-45, adopt the conference report on the budget reconciliation bill.

November 5
Bush signs the reconciliation bill.

90), the first and arguably most important step in turning massive deficits into surpluses.

Bush's fiscal 1991 budget relied on rosy economic assumptions to meet the GRH deficit target. But Democrats were reluctant to take the lead in proposing tax increases or additional spending cuts to realistically meet the target. As fiscal 1991 neared, revised projections estimated the deficit to be on a steep rise—$166 billion more than the figure released in Bush's budget six months earlier. With signs that the economy was slowing, Bush reluctantly agreed to negotiate with "no preconditions" concerning taxes and other budget issues. These talks initially failed to produce an agreement on how to avoid a GRH-triggered $100 billion cut in government programs. Unable to devise a tenable alternative, Bush admitted that "tax revenue increases" were necessary. This reversal handed Democrats two political victories—the president took the initiative on tax increases, and it split the Republican Party. Rank-and-file Republi-

continued

culations and procedures. BEA has three basic rules: adjustable deficit/surplus targets, discretionary spending caps, and pay-as-you-go (PAYGO) rules for revenues and direct spending. Although BEA was devised to deal with deficits, the rules also pertain to years in which the budget has a surplus. These rules and their implications are discussed in chapter four.

Budgeting during the Clinton Era
Bill Clinton campaigned for president in 1992 by emphasizing the need to rebuild the economy and remedy social problems. Nevertheless, shortly after taking office, Clinton put deficit reduction at the top of his agenda, giving it priority over health care reform, one of his main campaign promises. The package of

▼

BOX 2-2
Continued

cans openly criticized Bush, calling his proposal unacceptable. Bush replied that "getting this deficit down, continuing economic expansion and employment" were more important than campaign promises.

But an agreement still had to be reached on the mix of tax increases, spending cuts, and a new deficit target. Bush and Republican members of Congress advocated a cut in the capital gains tax; Democrats insisted on an accompanying increase in the income tax rate for high-income earners. Senate Minority Leader Robert Dole (R-Kans.) reminded the factions, "If we don't get a budget agreement, we're in real trouble. I mean everybody—Congress, the president. We just have to get it done." On the eve of the new fiscal year—the most important deadline in federal budgeting—negotiators announced that a deal had been struck.

When a budget resolution adopting the summit agreement was brought before the House, conservative Republicans and liberal Democrats who had been, as Rep. Tom DeLay (R-Tex.) quipped, locked out of the "fourth branch of government—the summit," joined to defeat it 179–254. To avoid a government shutdown, Congress passed a continuing resolution. An outraged Bush vetoed the measure to "put pressure on Congress." The president's veto tactics were effective—government offices closed and Congress was forced to act.

After passing a budget resolution, Congress cleared, and Bush signed, a reconciliation bill in three weeks—a task that usually consumes months. An examination of the roll call shows how far the bill had moved toward the Democratic position. In the House only 47 Republicans supported the package while 126 voted against it; 181 Democrats voted for it while 74 voted against. At the signing Bush called it "a compromise that merits enactment." The centerpiece of OBRA-90 were revenue and spending changes projected to reduce the deficit by an unprecedented $496 billion over five years. The reconciliation act also set five-year discretionary spending caps and established PAYGO rules but allowed the deficit to grow as long as Congress did not explicitly increase it. Yet this new process tightened the purse strings and set the budget on a path that led to a surplus eight years later.

The road to OBRA took a political toll. Bush suffered the most: in a single year he had abandoned his campaign promises of "no new taxes" and lower capital gains taxes, alienated the conservative wing in his party, and scarred relations with Democrats. In the end Bush paid the ultimate political price: two years after signing OBRA he was defeated for reelection.

tax increases and spending cuts that Clinton signed in August 1993 had short-term political costs but brought the president longer-term political gains. It enabled Clinton to wrest budget leadership from congressional Republicans and to preside over a truly extraordinary turnaround in the condition of the federal budget. In fact, Clinton had little to do with some of the main factors that transformed the budget from deficit to surplus, but one cannot fault him for taking credit for the budgetary improvement that occurred on his watch. After all, he would have been blamed if the nation's fiscal condition had deteriorated while he was in office.

Clinton's initial budget moves did not bring

immediate political gains because the deficit remained high from 1993 through 1995 (though it was lower than it had been) and because the president shifted political attention to his controversial universal health insurance plan. That plan preoccupied Washington from the time it was introduced in the fall of 1993 until its final death throes in the summer of 1994; its failure set the stage for the Republican capture of both the House and Senate in the 1994 midterm elections. Republicans controlled Congress for the first time in four decades and confronted Clinton by passing a budget measure that would have slashed taxes and benefit programs. When Clinton vetoed that bill, Republicans confronted him on annual appropriations, setting the stage for two partial shutdowns of the federal government that revitalized the Clinton presidency and profoundly affected recent budget history.

Historians will debate who was to blame for the shutdown—Clinton, who vetoed a measure that would have kept government offices open, or congressional Republicans, who wanted to force major budget changes on a recalcitrant president. But there can be no doubt that Republicans were blamed in the court of public opinion. Clinton's poll ratings soared and stayed high through subsequent budget battles, while Republicans lost House seats in both the 1996 and 1998 elections and Speaker Newt Gingrich (R-Ga.), the architect of the Republican takeover of the House and of their budget war with Clinton, resigned from Congress.

As Clinton's political fortunes soared and those of congressional Republicans foundered, there were annual budget battles between the president and Congress. The 1996 battle ended with Clinton stealing one of the Republicans' favorite campaign issues by leading the charge for welfare reform. In 1997 it ended by Clinton taking away the Republican claim that they were the only party that could balance the budget by negotiating an agreement that projected an end to deficits in 2002. In both 1996 and 1997 Clinton forced Congress to appropriate billions of dollars more for his priorities than Republican leaders wanted. Much the same occurred weeks before the midterm elections in 1998, when he got Republicans to agree to an omnibus appropriations bill that added billions for his programs. In this case, Republicans obtained more money for their priorities, but they were blamed for overspending on pork while Clinton got accolades for addressing the country's social needs. To top off his triumphs, the budget was balanced in 1998, four years earlier than had been projected in the 1997 budget deal, giving Clinton bragging rights on an extraordinary feat.

Clinton scored yet another achievement in 1999 when he ignored the discretionary spending caps and forced congressional Republicans to appropriate approximately $30 billion more than the caps allowed. Clinton once again got credit for spending on national priorities, such as education, while Republicans were blamed for an assortment of budget tricks that they had to use to fit the spending under the caps. What enabled Clinton to achieve victory was not only his political skills but a cooperative economy, which allowed him to spend more while maintaining a budget surplus. What also helped Clinton's cause was that he got away with vetoing a Republican-passed tax cut, despite receipts being at an all-time high relative to gross domestic product.

HOW THE BUDGET WAS BALANCED

Liquidating the deficit ranks as one of the supreme budgetary accomplishments in American history. In 1993 OMB projected that the fiscal 1998 deficit would be $339 billion; CBO estimated that it would reach $357

FIGURE 2-6
Projected versus Actual Deficits/Surpluses, Fiscal Years 1993–99[a]

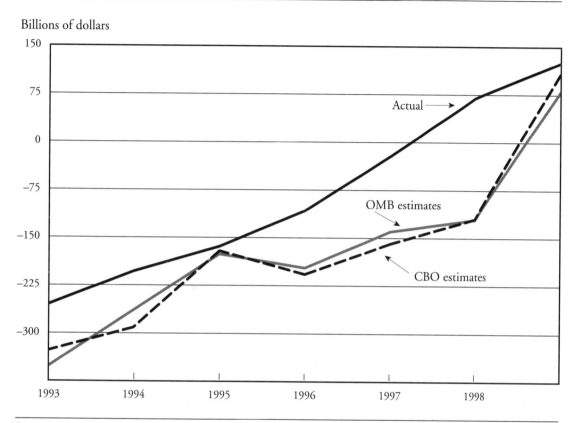

Billions of dollars

Sources: Congressional Budget Office, *The Economic and Budget Outlook,* January 1993–99; and *Budget of the United States, Historical Tables,* Fiscal Years 1992–2001.

a. These projections were made at the beginning of the previous calendar year for the fiscal year listed. For example, for fiscal 1996 CBO's projections were released in January 1995 and OMB's in February 1995.

billion. In fact, fiscal 1998 was not the only year for which budget experts were wide of the mark. Figure 2-6 shows that both OMB and CBO consistently overestimated the deficit for each year between 1993 and 1998. The estimates presented in this graph were issued at the time the president sent his annual budget to Congress, approximately nine months before the start of the fiscal year to which they pertained and 21 months before that fiscal year ended. Deficit overestimates were much higher in the five-year baselines.

In 1993 CBO projected that with the policies then in place, spending would exceed revenues by $1.5 trillion over the next five years. However, actual deficits totaled less than one-third of this amount.

In explaining how the deficit was liquidated, one must look at the performance of the economy, spending policies, and revenue trends. All three of these factors significantly contributed to deficit reduction. If any had been unfavorable, the government might still be running large deficits.

Economic Boom

Every budget is hostage to economic performance. Congress and the president cannot balance the budget when national output is declining and unemployment is soaring. Budget receipts are highly sensitive to changes in economic conditions, spending less so, but even a small shortfall in economic performance can have a big budgetary impact. CBO has estimated that if the annual real growth rate over the next decade were just one-tenth of a percentage point less than it has assumed, the fiscal 2010 budget surplus would be $40 billion below current projections.

When the deficit peaked in 1992, the United States was emerging from the recession that occurred at the start of the decade. When the budget was balanced in 1998, the economy was completing the seventh consecutive year of growth, during which 13 million jobs were added and inflation averaged less than 3 percent. The budget benefited from this economic success—revenues escalated as corporate profits and personal incomes rose, spending dropped as welfare rolls declined, the crisis in the banking sector was resolved, and inflation in the health care sector moderated.

But economic good times alone do not account for the budget's unexpected turnaround. Measured in terms of growth rates, the eight consecutive years of expansion during the 1980s (from the end of the Reagan-era recession in 1982 to the onset of the Bush-era recession in 1990) outperformed the boom of the 1990s, as table 2-4 shows. Real growth averaged 4.0 percent a year during the 1980s' expansion but only 3.6 percent during the 1990s' boom. The two expansions were structured differently, which may partly explain their different revenue impacts. The 1980s' growth began at a high rate and then tapered off; the 1990s' expansion began with low growth that accelerated as the expansion continued. More civilian jobs were created in the

1980s, but the unemployment rate was lower during the 1990s. A fair comparison of the two decades would have to take into account the fact that the boom of the 1980s followed a decade of "stagflation," while the 1990s' expansion followed a long period of growth that was briefly interrupted by the 1990–91 recession.

Spending Policies

Although the surplus would not have emerged without a cooperative economy, it also would not have occurred if budget policy in the 1990s had repeated the mistakes of the 1980s. Differences between the revenue and spending paths taken during the two decades led to very different budgetary outcomes.

The 1980s began with a steep boost in defense spending; the 1990s began with the collapse of the Soviet empire and the end of the Cold War. Defense spending, which started to level off during the second half of the 1980s, continued to decline through most of the 1990s.

As happened after previous wars, some defense savings were reallocated to domestic programs. Because the budget enforcement rules built a "firewall" between discretionary appropriations and other expenditures, most of the substitution occurred among discretionary accounts. Within the discretionary caps, the decline in defense spending made room for additional domestic spending. (In some years, separate caps on defense and domestic spending inhibited the shift in budget resources.)

Direct Spending

Spending growth in entitlements was constrained during the 1990s by the PAYGO rule requiring legislated increases in these programs to be offset by cuts in other direct spending or by revenue increases. It is highly probably that even in the absence of BEA rules, big deficits

TABLE 2-4
Comparison of Economic Performance from 1983–90 and 1992–99, by Selected Indicators

Economic indicator	1983–90	1992–99
Average real GDP growth rate[a]	4.0	3.6
Average annual civilian unemployment rate[b]	6.7	5.6
Total civilian jobs added (millions)	18.0	15.0
Cumulative percentage increase in real per capita disposable income[a]	20.5	14.5
Average annual consumer price index[b,c]	3.9	2.6
Average ten-year Treasury note rate[b]	9.5	6.3
Cumulative percentage increase in productivity[d]	12.5	13.9

Sources: *Economic Report of the President*, February 2000; Bureau of Economic Analysis; Bureau of Labor Statistics.
 a. Based on chained 1996 dollars.
 b. Calendar year average.
 c. For all urban consumers.
 d. Output per hour of all persons in business sector.

would have deterred the president and Congress from establishing new entitlements and impelled them to seek savings in old ones. In fact, few initiatives made it through Congress during the pre-BEA 1980s. But despite PAYGO, Clinton won some new entitlements, such as the children's health insurance program enacted in 1997.

The 1990s were a fiscally static period in entitlement policy. Leaving aside deposit insurance, mandatory spending was a higher proportion of GDP at the end of the decade than it had been at the start. The biggest increases were in means-tested entitlements; these were due both to new legislation (such as increases in the earned-income tax credit) and to built-in growth in old programs.

Tax Policies

If the economy and spending changes do not fully account for the surplus, the only other place to look is on the revenue side of the budget. There is ample evidence that a revenue

surge from 1993 through 1998 transformed the budget from deficit to surplus. Federal revenues were $63 billion higher in 1993 than in 1992, another $104 billion higher in 1994, $93 billion more in 1995, $101 billion more in 1996, $126 billion more in 1997, and $143 billion more in 1998. All told, the government took in $631 billion more in 1998 than it did in 1992. If projections materialize, revenues should double between 1995 and 2004.

Tax policy in the 1990s reversed many of the actions of the previous decade. During the 1980s the highest marginal tax rate (50 percent on earned income and 70 percent on unearned income—interest and dividends) was reduced to 28 percent (or 31 percent if a "bubble" in the rates is included). But in the 1990s the rate was boosted to 39.6 percent, and because of various phase-outs of exemptions and deductions, the highest marginal rate is actually above 40 percent. The first of these tax increases was enacted in 1990 when George Bush was president, the second in 1993 when Bill Clinton was in the White House. The first deprived Bush of reelection; the second contributed to the 1994 Republican takeover of Congress but ultimately aided Clinton's reelection. While politically risky, these tax increases pumped up federal revenues, which rose from 18.2 percent of GDP in 1990 to 20.5 percent in 1998. The 2.3 percentage point rise added $190 billion in federal revenue. If the 1989 tax structure were still in place, there would be no surplus to discuss.

The rate increases enacted in 1990 and 1993 targeted upper-income taxpayers. During the decade the income tax burden on low-income Americans was significantly reduced. Because of the widened gap between low and high earners, the government took in much more revenue than it would have if the tax increases had been spread evenly across income brackets. The government taxed the winners during the 1990s, redistributing income while boosting its revenue.

OVERVIEW OF THE ANNUAL BUDGET CYCLE

Two centuries of evolution have produced a complex budget process, with many players and stages, defined rules and roles, and layers of procedure. Each reform has deposited its distinctive requirements; some have faded away, and others have been incorporated into the ongoing activities of budgeting. The various requirements revolve around an annual cycle that begins with the formulation of the president's budget in the executive branch, involves four separate sets of congressional action, then moves to agencies, which implement their approved budgets, and concludes with the review and audit of expenditures. Table 2-5 lists the major actions taken during the fiscal year 2000 budget cycle. While the timetable is constructed on the assumption that each action is completed on schedule, it has become common for Congress and the

president to miss certain deadlines. Nevertheless, the basic steps are repeated year after year with little change, though particular procedures may vary with the style of the president, his relations with Congress, or in response to changes in economic or political conditions.

Table 2-5 indicates that the federal government has an annual budget process that sprawls over several years. This extended cycle means that at any given date, the federal government is typically juggling three fiscal years. The overlap of several fiscal years has made budgeting an arduous, year-round activity, which allows little time for pause and reflection and little opportunity for thinking strategically about the purposes and direction of federal programs.

In budgeting, the calendar is king, telling participants what they are supposed to do and when. Even when deadlines are missed, the calendar shapes actions and expectations, and it patterns the roles and behavior of those who make budgets and spend money. The most important date on the budget calendar is October 1, the day the new fiscal year begins. Agencies begin compiling their budgets with this date in mind, the president sends his budget to Congress mindful of the time required for legislative action, Congress organizes much of its work around this date, and agencies open and close their books on the basis of the October 1 starting point.

The President's Budget

Preparation of the president's budget generally begins in a decentralized manner, with each agency using its own procedures and guidelines for assembling its request. Formulation usually takes eight to ten months—longer in large agencies, shorter in very small ones. Because of the long lead times, agencies must make budget decisions with great uncertainty

TABLE 2-5
Timetable of the Fiscal 2000 Budget

Calendar[a]	Activities
1998	
March–June	Budget guidelines and preliminary policies are developed; agency budget offices issue call for estimates to operating units.
July–September	Agencies formulate detailed requests, which are submitted to OMB.
October–December	OMB reviews agencies' requests and issues passbacks; agencies appeal to OMB and/or the president; final decisions are made.
1999	
January	CBO releases *Economic and Budget Outlook* for fiscal 2000–09.
February	President submits his fiscal 2000 budget to Congress no later than the first Monday in February.
March 15	Congressional committees submit views and estimates on the budget to budget committees.
April 15	Congress adopts the fiscal 2000 budget resolution.
May 15	If budget resolution had not been adopted, appropriations could be considered in the House.
June–August	House and Senate act on regular appropriation bills for fiscal 2000; OMB and CBO release new revenue and expenditure projections for fiscal 2000.
September	Conference reports and enactment of regular appropriations.
October 1	Fiscal 2000 starts; continuing resolution is passed since regular appropriations have not been enacted.
October–November	CBO and OMB issue PAYGO reports for the past session of Congress.
October 1999–September 2000	Agencies spend resources and carry out activities as authorized by Congress; Congress may make supplemental appropriations for fiscal 2000.
2000	
February	New revenue and expenditure projections for fiscal 2000 are included in the fiscal 2001 budget.
September 30	Fiscal 2000 ends.
October–December	Agencies, Treasury, and OMB close the books on fiscal 2000.
2001	
January–December and beyond	Agencies prepare financial statements; postaudits and evaluations are conducted.
February	Actual revenue and expenditure data for fiscal 2000 are included in the fiscal 2002 budget.

a. The deadlines listed here represent a standard timetable. However, over the past twenty-five years certain targets have slipped more often than they have been met.

about the conditions that will prevail when the funds are actually spent.

Agency budget preparation is concentrated during the spring and summer of the calendar year preceding submission to Congress. OMB reviews agency requests in the fall, after which it recommends program and spending amounts. Agencies have a brief period to appeal for more than OMB recommended. Once all the issues have been resolved, the budget is printed and distributed to Congress and the interested public.

TABLE 2-6
Budget Functions of Congressional Committees

Budget	Authorizing	Appropriations	Revenue
Report budget resolution	Report authorizing and direct spending legislation	Report regular and supplemental appropriations bills	Report revenue legislation
Draft reconciliation instructions and compile reconciliation bill	Oversee executive agencies	Review proposed rescissions and deferrals	Report legislation on social security and certain other entitlements
Allocate new budget authority, outlays, and other aggregates to committees	Submit views and estimates to budget committees on matters in their jurisdiction	Submit views and estimates to budget committees	Submit views and estimates to budget committees
Monitor budget and advise Congress on budget impact of legislation	Recommend changes in laws pursuant to reconciliation instructions	Subdivide budget authority and outlays among their subcommittees	Recommend changes in laws pursuant to reconciliation instructions
	Include CBO cost estimates in reports on their legislation	Establish account structure for federal agencies and rules for reprogramming	
		Provide guidance to agencies on expenditure of funds	

The Congressional Budget Resolution

Congressional budget action involves the four sets of committees whose functions are set forth in table 2-6. A set of House and Senate committees has custody over one of the four types of budget actions—the annual budget resolution, revenue measures, authorizing legislation, and appropriations bills. The three legislative staff agencies listed in table 2-7—the Congressional Budget Office (CBO), the General Accounting Office (GAO), and the Congressional Research Service (CRS)—aid Congress in performing these tasks.

Each year the House and Senate budget committees prepare a resolution, covering the next five (or more) years, which specifies budget totals (total revenue, budget authority, outlays, surplus or deficit, and public debt) and allocates spending among twenty func-

tional categories, including national defense, agriculture, and health. Additionally, the budget resolution often contains reconciliation instructions directing specified House and Senate committees to report legislation that changes revenue or spending laws in accord with the policies set in the resolution. Legislation developed by committees pursuant to these instructions is packaged in an omnibus reconciliation bill that is considered by the House and Senate under special rules that expedite its passage.

The budget resolution is not a statute and does not have legal effect. Nor does it detail how federal funds are to be raised or spent. Rather, the resolution establishes the framework within which Congress considers revenue and spending measures. As a blueprint, the status of the budget resolution varies from year to year.

TABLE 2-7
Budget Functions of Congressional Support Agencies

Congressional Budget Office (CBO)	General Accounting Office (GAO)	Congressional Research Service (CRS)
Issues reports with ten-year projections on the budget and the economy	Issues accounting guidelines and reviews agency accounting systems	Analyzes legislative issues and proposals affecting agencies and programs
Estimates five- and ten-year cost of reported bills; prepares baseline budget projections and maintains database for scorekeeping	Audits operations of certain federal agencies; evaluates programs and recommends improvements	Assists committees and members by providing data and analyses relevant to their legislative responsibilities
Assists the budget, tax, appropriations, and other committees	Issues legal opinions concerning the use of funds	Compiles legislative histories of particular legislation and programs
Issues reports on options for changing federal revenue and spending policies	Reviews deferrals and rescissions to determine whether they have been properly reported and funds released as required	Issues reports on the status of legislation
Reviews the president's budget and other proposals	Investigates expenditures and agency operations as requested by congressional committees	Analyzes proposals to change federal budget practices
	Settles certain claims and debt collection issues or disputes	

In some years it strongly influences budgetary decisions; in others, it has very little impact.

Revenue Legislation
Although Congress takes some action affecting revenues just about every year, it has no regular schedule for doing so. In some years, it hardly does anything; in a few, it makes truly significant changes in tax laws.

Revenue legislation is in the jurisdiction of the House Ways and Means Committee and the Senate Finance Committee, two of the oldest and most powerful committees in Congress. The Ways and Means Committee usually acts first because the Constitution stipulates that revenue measures shall originate in the House. Although the Senate takes up these measures after the House, it often makes major changes, setting the stage for the conference committee.

Authorizations
Under House and Senate rules, before either chamber appropriates funds, the program or agency that is to receive the money must be authorized in law. That is, Congress must first pass a law setting up the program and specifying how it operates before it appropriates funds for that purpose. There are, however, many variations in this sequence, as discussed in chapter 8.

Most congressional committees are authorizing committees. They consider legislation establishing or changing federal programs and agencies, prescribing the terms and conditions under which these operate, and overseeing their performance. Some authorizing committees are active; others go through one or more sessions without reporting major legislation. There is no standard structure or style to authorizing legislation; each committee with jurisdiction over federal programs or agencies goes about the task in its own way.

Appropriations

Annual appropriations are provided in thirteen regular appropriations bills, each of which is in the jurisdiction of parallel House and Senate subcommittees. Shortly after the president submits his budget to Congress, the various appropriations subcommittees conduct hearings at which agency officials justify the amounts requested. Although the subcommittees are independent of one another, all are limited by the discretionary spending caps. To ensure that these caps are adhered to, the Congressional Budget Act requires the House and Senate appropriations committees to divide the total discretionary spending among their subcommittees. When the House or Senate considers an appropriations bill, the spending provided in the bill is compared with the amount allocated to the relevant subcommittee. In some circumstances the House or Senate may be barred from considering an appropriations bill that would cause the subcommittee allocation to be exceeded. This rarely occurs, however, because appropriations subcommittees usually take care to stay within their allocations. When they have exceeded the caps, they have done so by resorting to one or more of the bookkeeping tactics discussed in chapter 4.

Budget Implementation

Agencies cannot spend appropriations until OMB apportions the funds among periods or projects. Most federal agencies also have an allotment process that distributes available funds among their administrative units. With some exceptions, agencies are not permitted to obligate funds in excess of the appropriated or apportioned amounts.

Although agencies must spend funds according to the terms and conditions set by Congress, they sometimes reprogram funds by shifting them from one purpose to another in the same account. Deviations from authorized spending levels also occur when the president or other executive officials impound funds, either by delaying expenditures or by seeking to rescind the original appropriation. Special procedures, described in chapter 10, regulate impoundments.

Review and audit constitutes the final phase of the budget cycle. Because of the size of the federal government, financial management is decentralized, with each agency having responsibility for the propriety and efficiency of its expenditures and for maintaining complete, accurate financial records.

CONCLUSION

The history of budgeting shows periodic swings in relations between the president and Congress. At some points one branch of government dominates; at others the situation is reversed. The Constitution granted the power of the purse to Congress to constrain executive authority. Yet early in the twentieth century Congress enlisted the help of the president to restrict federal spending. When many felt that the president was overly dominating the process, changes in the rules of the game reestablished Congress's role. While there will never be a stable balance of power, each branch will continue to reposition itself to increase its leverage.

At one time the federal budget did little more than finance public works projects, national defense, and agency operations. Although never mandated, the norm was for the budget to be at or near balance. This was possible when government was small and had few costly obligations. Now the majority of federal spending is for payments to individuals. With these payments and interest charges mushrooming to absorb two-thirds of the budget, it seemed impossible to escape persistent peacetime deficits. There was continual conflict over what actions should be taken to put the nation's fiscal house back in order.

The additional layers of rules and laws added in the 1980s and 1990s to guide the politics, processes, and practices of budgeting center on one premise—politicians need to be restricted in the financial choices they make. But politicians have made some tough decisions on their own—for example, increasing taxes on upper income earners and capping discretionary spending—to help steer the budget to surplus. Within a surprisingly short period, the deficit was liquidated, but this turnaround did not end budgetary warfare. At this writing, multitrillion dollar surpluses have been forecast for the first decades of the new century. The only thing certain about these projections is that they will be wide of the mark. Perhaps the government will maintain a surplus for many years to come. If it does, the never-ending budget battle between the president and Congress will enter a new phase.

3

The Budget's Shifting Boundaries

An essential step in using or interpreting any budget is to understand what the numbers mean. In federal budgeting, not every dollar taken in is counted as a receipt, nor is every dollar paid out counted as an outlay. To say that the government collects or spends $2 trillion a year means that these are the official totals reported according to the budget rules currently in effect. But several types of numbers coexist in the federal budget. The next chapter explains the political arithmetic and rules of budgeting. This chapter explains the technical numbers, which are based on accounting rules as to how various transactions are counted and recorded, and maps out the boundaries of budgeting, describing which transactions are included or excluded from the budget.

RECEIPTS, BUDGETARY RESOURCES, AND OUTLAYS

The federal government has various accounting rules and conventions for computing receipts and expenditures. These practices affect the amounts recorded in the budget as well as the behavior of participants and the outcomes they produce. The key concepts are receipts, budget authority and other budgetary resources, and outlays.

Receipts

Most of the money the government receives is recorded as revenue; some is not. The basic rule is that money the government collects in the exercise of its sovereign power (such as the power to tax or to regulate) is counted as a budget receipt; money the government receives in the conduct of business-type operations is counted as an offsetting collection. Borrowed funds are not included in receipts, and repayment of debt principal is not counted as an outlay. The $2 trillion in annual revenues comes mostly from taxes, but customs duties, fines, and compulsory user charges also are included. Business-type revenue comes from the sale of assets, the income of government enterprises, and certain user charges. This income does not appear on the revenue side of the budget but is netted against outlays, usually of the agency or account that collects the money.

Budget Authority and Outlays

The federal government has an obligations-based budget system. The key points of decision and control pertain to the obligations authorized or incurred, not to the outlays disbursed during the year. When Congress appropriates money, it gives agencies *budget authority* to enter into obligations. Congress may also provide budget authority in direct spending measures that enable an agency to incur obligations. *Obligations* are incurred when an agency enters into a contract, executes a purchase order, or takes any action that commits the government to make payment. Some obligations, such as those ensuing from loan guarantees (discussed in chapter 4), are contingent on default or some other event. By law, contingent liabilities are excluded from budget authority, but an exception is made for guaranteed loans. In these cases the estimated sub-sidy cost of the loans is included in the computation of budget authority.

Money that first becomes available for obligation in a particular fiscal year is counted as *new budget authority* in that year's budget. Under this rule, when Congress makes an *advance appropriation*, the new budget authority is charged to the year in which the money first becomes available for obligation. For example, if Congress makes a $1 billion advance appropriation in an appropriations act for fiscal year 2000, the money is not counted as part of fiscal 2000 budget authority. This rule, discussed in chapter 4, has enabled Congress to appropriate more while staying within the discretionary spending caps.

Some programs, particularly those financed by trust funds, have *permanent budget authority* that becomes available each year without congressional action. By law, all money in the Social Security fund (and most other trust funds) is available for obligation, but only the amount obligated in a fiscal year is counted as new budget authority.

Executive and congressional budget documents sometimes refer to *budgetary resources*, a term that includes, in addition to new budget authority, all other money available for obligation in a fund or account. These resources may derive from transfers, user fees deposited in the account, unobligated balances carried over from previous year, or other sources.

Outlays occur when money is disbursed by check, electronic transfer, or cash. The budget surplus or deficit is calculated as the difference between cash receipts and outlays. (A small portion of outlays, associated with direct and guaranteed loans and certain other transactions, is not accounted for on a cash basis.) Although outlays generally receive more public attention than budget authority does, the latter is more important in managing the government's finances. Congress does not directly control total outlays or those of federal agencies; rather, it regulates outlays indirectly by providing budget authority. Each year's outlays derive principally from new budget authority, but a portion also derives from budget authority carried over from previous years. For example, the fiscal 2000 budget estimated that outlays would total $1.763 trillion. More than three-quarters of this amount ($1.445 trillion) was estimated to come from new budget authority, the remainder ($318 billion) from budget authority provided for previous fiscal years.

To clarify the relationship of budget authority and outlays, it may be useful to think of them as akin to deposits and withdrawals. When Congress provides budget authority, it deposits financial resources in an agency's account. When the agency incurs obligations, it encumbers these resources and they are no longer available for any other purpose. Finally, when the agency pays its obligations, it withdraws resources from the account.

The relation of budget authority and outlays varies among federal programs and depends on the rate at which budget resources are disbursed. In programs with high spendout rates, most new budget authority is outlaid during the year for which the funds are provided. Budget authority provided for salaries and other operating expenses typically has a high spendout rate; resources provided for construction or procurement have relatively low rates. For example, more than 95 percent of the new budget authority appropriated for military pay is spent during the year, but less than 5 percent of the new money allocated for shipbuilding is disbursed in the year for which it is provided. Spendout rates are used in enforcing the discretionary caps, which limit both new budget authority and outlays.

In estimating the amount of outlays to be derived from appropriations, CBO uses spendout rates (based on historical trends) to calculate the percentage of the new money that will be disbursed during the year. Because they are based on spendout rates, the outlays specified in the budget for the current or future fiscal years are (with only a few exceptions) merely estimates of the amounts to be disbursed.

In some programs, the numerical relationship between budget authority and outlays provides a useful clue to financial trends. When new budget authority is rising faster than outlays, more resources are being added than are being used; hence, future program activity is likely to expand. When new budget authority is flat or declining but outlays are increasing, however, future program activity is likely to decline because resources are being used faster than they are being replenished. (This pattern does not apply to trust funds.) Figure 3-1 charts trends in defense spending from 1976 through 1999. Note that at the start of this period, budget authority and outlays grew at approximately the same pace. However, during the Reagan defense buildup in the early 1980s, budget authority rose steeply, and the gap between it and outlays widened. The reverse occurred during the second half of the decade: defense budget authority leveled off, but outlays rose, narrowing the gap between them. During the 1990s defense budget authority and outlays were stable in nominal terms, and the gap between them was small.

SCOPE OF THE BUDGET

The president's budget for fiscal year 2001 estimated that the federal government would spend $1.835 trillion; it also estimated that the government would spend only $1.461 trillion—$374 billion less. Both estimates were accurate. The first was calculated on a unified basis; the second counted only on-

FIGURE 3-1
Defense Budget Authority and Outlays, Fiscal Years 1976–99[a]

Billions of dollars

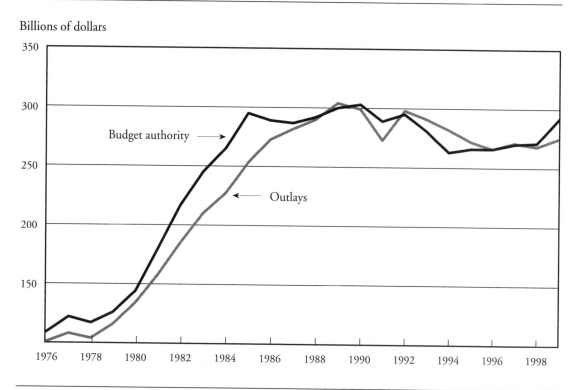

Source: *Budget of the United States, Historical Tables, Fiscal Year 2001,* table 3.1, pp. 42–49, and table 5.1, pp. 75–78.
    a. The transition quarter is evenly distributed between 1976 and 1977.

budget outlays. How much the budget takes in and spends depends on what is included and excluded. By some measures the totals are much higher than those reported in the unified budget.

In 1968 the government adopted the principle of a unified budget that accounts for all receipts and expenditures of federal entities. This principle, enunciated by the President's Commission on Budget Concepts, replaced an older method that excluded trust funds from the budget. The commission successfully argued that the unified budget has several advantages: it provides a fuller picture of financial transactions, it facilitates use of the budget

as an instrument of economic policy, and it enables the government to establish priorities among programs financed by different sources. The unified budget includes general funds and trust funds, current and capital expenditures, the transactions of government-owned enterprises, and loans issued or guaranteed by the government. But despite its broad scope, the budget does not provide a truly comprehensive account of federal revenues and expenditures. Certain funds and transactions, such as government-sponsored enterprises and the future costs of various federal insurance programs, are excluded. Yet some argue that the budget is too inclusive—that self-financing trust funds, such as Social Security and the Highway Trust Fund, should be walled off from the budget.

The scope of the budget is not merely a matter of how revenues and spending are classified. It affects the reported size of the budget surplus or deficit and involves conflict over the budgetary treatment of Social Security and other trust funds. Some have argued that budget accounting rules have discouraged the government from investing in capital improvements; others have argued that the rules fail to recognize the future costs of current budget commitments.

Funds in the Budget

The budget consists of four main types of funds: general, special, trust, and revolving. General funds are not earmarked by law for specific purposes; accordingly, there is no direct link between taxes paid and services provided. Almost all individual and corporate income taxes, and certain excise taxes and user charges, are deposited into the general fund. National defense, interest on the public debt, the operating expenses of most federal agencies, many grants to state and local governments, and some entitlements are paid for out of the general fund. It accounts for approximately two-thirds of federal revenues and outlays.

In contrast to the general fund, trust funds are designated by law for particular purposes. But inasmuch as Congress established these funds, it can abolish them, change the amounts paid in or out, and also change the purposes for which the fund's assets are used. For example, the revenue-sharing trust fund (financed by general revenues) was terminated during the 1980s. Some Highway Trust Fund money has been diverted to mass transit. In some years a portion of the federal gasoline tax has been paid to the general fund, while in other years all gasoline tax receipts have gone to the Highway Trust Fund. The federal government does not have a fiduciary obligation to manage trust funds for the benefit of those who pay into the fund or receive money from it. The only major exceptions are trust funds owned by Indian tribes, which the federal government manages on their behalf. In recognition of the unique status of Indian tribe trust funds, OMB removed them from the budget beginning with fiscal year 2000.

If the federal government can unilaterally dispose of trust funds, why does it establish them? What difference is there between money held in the general fund or in a trust fund? The answer to these questions lies more in the realm of politics than law. Politicians may prefer trust funds for several reasons: it may be easier to raise taxes when the money is earmarked for a particular purpose, trust funds may have an advantage in competing for scarce budget resources, and having a trust fund may offer some assurance that the money will be used for intended purposes. Trust funds are somewhat less than a contractual commitment but much more than an empty gesture. Although trust funds are sometimes raided, in almost all cases the money is used for the stated purpose.

Although trust funds are not inviolable, earmarking revenues to them does influence budget decisions. These funds generate strong expectations, bordering on entitlements in some cases, that the money will only be used for prescribed purposes. Moreover, when revenues are set aside in a trust fund, intended beneficiaries can more easily monitor government spending and thereby oppose diversion of the money to other uses. But a trust fund is only as secure as its beneficiaries are powerful. When beneficiaries are strong, the government may be unwilling to risk the political costs of raiding the trust fund. When they are weak, there may be little risk. With more than 45 million Americans receiving monthly payments from Social Security and more than 100 million workers expecting benefits in the future, Social Security is politically sensitive. It is off-budget, has its own budget enforcement rules, and is not subject to the reconciliation process. In contrast, the revenue-sharing trust fund lacked its own revenue source and made payments to state and local governments rather than to individuals or households. Its advocates were too weak to deter Congress from abolishing the fund when it wanted the money for other programs.

Trust funds have been a recurring source of budgetary controversy. One issue is whether these funds should be included in the budget; another is whether trust funds should be required to lend their balances to the federal government.

The unified budget combines all funds in a comprehensive set of accounts. However, Social Security's off-budget status excludes it from the computation of budget totals. Despite this, most official and media reports on the budget continue to include the Social Security trust funds, as well as other off-budget entities such as the Postal Service. Some critics argue that by including Social Security and other trust funds in the overall budget, the federal government uses the balances in trust funds to finance its general operations. The long-standing practice has been for the government to borrow all trust fund balances and to pay the prevailing rate of interest on Treasury bonds of comparable maturity. Trust funds have no choice in the matter; they must lend their balances to the government. At one time these balances were relatively small, but during the 1980s and 1990s, they spiraled from $200 billion to $1.6 trillion, largely because of the buildup in Social Security reserves. In fiscal 1999 the government paid ap-

proximately $120 billion in interest to various trust funds.

Some regard this as merely a bookkeeping arrangement that enables the trust funds to earn interest on retained balances. Others believe there should be an arm's-length relationship between the budget and the trust funds. They argue that the trust funds should be managed to achieve a higher rate of return than is earned on Treasuries and that combining trust and general funds masks the true condition of the federal budget. Resolution of this issue is likely to be linked to decisions on the future of Social Security. (This issue is briefly discussed later in this chapter in connection with measurement of budget surpluses and deficits and in the concluding chapter.)

Special funds share characteristics of both the general fund and trust funds. Most special funds, such as the Land and Water Conservation Fund and the National Wildlife Refuge Fund, are financed by user fees and other earmarked revenue. Although they are accounted for separately, special funds are grouped together with general funds under the label "federal funds." Diversion of money is more common in special funds than in trust funds.

The final category consists of revolving funds, most of which carry out businesslike activities, selling goods and services and using the income to finance their operations. Revolving funds are recorded in the budget on a net basis—income minus outlays. Thus if a revolving fund has $1 billion in income and $1.2 billion in outlays, the unified budget will report $200 million in outlays.

Government-Owned and Government-Sponsored Enterprises

The federal government owns and operates various businesses, including the U.S. Postal Service, the Government National Mortgage

Association, and the Pension Benefit Guaranty Corporation. All corporations owned in whole or in part by the government are included in the budget on a net basis—expenses are subtracted from income to show the net budgetary impact. For example, the Bonneville Power Administration, which produces and sells hydroelectric power in the Pacific Northwest, had $2.3 billion in expenses in fiscal 1998, all of which was offset by income.

The budget publishes special statements for most government-owned corporations, including a statement of income and expense, and a balance sheet. Because these statements are based on commercial accounting standards, they differ from the financial data provided for federal agencies, and they cannot be combined with regular budget schedules.

In contrast to government-owned corporations, enterprises established but not owned by the government are excluded from the budget because they are deemed to be private entities. The government does not have any equity in these government-sponsored enterprises (GSEs), most of which obtain financing from private sources. The biggest GSEs, such as the Federal National Mortgage Association (Fannie Mae) and the Federal Home Loan Mortgage Corporation (Freddie Mac), engage in credit activities that finance agriculture, home ownership, student loans, and other activities.

Although GSEs serve public objectives and benefit from governmental sponsorship—they borrow at highly favorable interest rates, and some enjoy special tax breaks—neither the president nor Congress reviews their finances. The aggregate liabilities of GSEs exceed $2 trillion, and the annual lending by these institutions exceeds $1 trillion (table 3-1). Although GSEs are self-financed, a few have a standby line of credit at the Treasury, and most have obligations that the government implicitly guarantees. Financial schedules of GSEs

TABLE 3-1
Investment Outlays, Direct and Guaranteed Loans, and Government-Sponsored Enterprises, Fiscal 1999[a]

Billions of dollars

Description	Amount
Investment outlays	240.2
Subtotal, physical assets	118.6
National defense	53.9
Grants to state and local governments	43.9
Nondefense	20.8
Subtotal, research and development	74.1
National defense	40.3
Nondefense	33.9
Subtotal, education and training	47.4
Grants to state and local governments	28.4
Direct federal	19.0
Direct loans	
Obligations	38.4
Disbursements	41.8
Outstanding	234.0
Primary loan guarantees	
Commitments	252.4
New guaranteed loans	224.7
Outstanding	975.8
Government-sponsored enterprises	
Assets	2,506.0
Liabilities	2,453.7
Direct loan obligations	3,209.8

Sources: *Budget of the United States, Analytical Perspectives, Fiscal Year 2001*, table 6-1, p. 146, table 8-9, p. 229, table 8-10, p. 236; *Budget of the United States, Appendix, Fiscal Year 2001*, pp. 1251–59.

a. Amounts may not add to subtotals due to rounding.

are published in the budget appendix but are not included in the totals.

Direct and Guaranteed Loans

The government participates in two types of loan transactions: it directly lends to borrowers, and it guarantees loans made by others. The Federal Credit Reform Act of 1990 changed the budgetary treatment of both

TABLE 3-2
Accounting for Direct and Guaranteed Loans

Description	Program account	Financing account	Liquidating account
Purpose of account	Receives appropriation for the subsidy cost of loans and associated administrative expenses	Handles all cash flows for loans and guarantees	Handles all loans made before fiscal 1992
Budget status	Subsidy cost included in budget authority and outlays	Means of financing; not included in receipts or outlays	Cash receipts and payments included in the budget
Cash flows	Transfers subsidy cost appropriations to financing account	Receives subsidy payment from program account Borrows unsubsidized part of loans from Treasury Collects repayments, fees, and interest from borrowers Disburses new loans, makes payments on defaulted loan guarantees, repays the Treasury with interest	Collects repayments, interest, and fees on old loans Pays defaults and interest subsidies on old loans

types of loans from a cash basis, in which disbursements were recorded as outlays, to a new system that shows the estimated subsidy cost of these loans as outlays.

The new system requires that funds be budgeted and appropriated to finance the estimated subsidy cost of loans. The subsidy cost is defined in the 1990 act as "the estimated long-term cost to the government of a direct loan or a loan guarantee, calculated on a net present value basis, excluding administrative costs." The net present value is calculated by discounting estimated future cash flows (disbursements by the government and repayments to it) of each loan program using a discount rate equal to the interest paid by the Treasury on borrowings of comparable maturity. In general, loans may be obligated or guaranteed only to the extent that Congress has appropriated funds to cover the subsidy cost.

Estimating this cost is a complex undertaking that is done annually for each credit account. The process differentiates between the subsidized portion of loans—the cost to the government—and the unsubsidized portion—the amount that will be repaid, recovered, or not defaulted. In the case of direct loans, the subsidy cost may be due either to default by borrowers or to below-market rates of interest. In the case of guaranteed loans, the subsidy cost may be due to default.

Budgeting for these loans entails three types of accounts: *program accounts* receive appropriations for the subsidy cost of loans and for associated administrative expenses, *financing accounts* handle all cash flows for direct and guaranteed loans, and *liquidating accounts* manage cash flows deriving from loans made before 1992. Table 3-2 explains the purpose and budgetary status of these accounts.

Although the rules of the 1990 act are complicated and involve assumptions about the volume and timing of defaults, recoveries, and payments, there also is a political dimension to the credit budgeting system. In shifting from a cash basis to subsidy cost, credit reform made direct loans less expensive to budget makers and guaranteed loans more expensive. In the past the entire amount paid out for direct loans was budgeted as an outlay. Now only the subsidized portion appears in the budget as an outlay. For guaranteed loans, the old system did not record outlays until a default occurred and the government made good on its obligation. Now estimated payments for default are budgeted as outlays. In fiscal 1998 the federal government disbursed $29 billion in direct loans and made $218 billion in new loan commitments. To cover the subsidy cost of these transactions, Congress appropriated $7 billion for direct loans and $2.6 billion for loan guarantees. These amounts are low because of the federal government's favorable experience with its loan portfolio. In 1998 the government wrote off less than 2 percent of its direct loans because of defaults and terminated only 1 percent of loan guarantees for default.

MEASURING THE BUDGET

The fact that some items are included and some excluded from the budget raises questions as to how revenue and spending totals are measured. The reported surplus or deficit is not the only correct measure, nor is it always the one that the media discuss. The surplus or deficit is commonly defined as the difference between the total the government takes in and the total it spends. But this is not the way transactions are measured in the federal budget. The official surplus or deficit is the difference between the receipts and outlays recorded in the budget. Consequently, the scope of the budget affects the official budget outcome. To

the extent that receipts and outlays are not budgeted on a cash basis, neither is the surplus or deficit. To the extent certain items are excluded from the budget, they also are excluded from its totals. The actual totals may vary by tens of billions of dollars, depending on what is included or excluded. The alternative measures shown in figure 3-2 are used for various budget purposes.

The Unified Budget

The unified budget is the broadest measure, though it does not include all payments for which the government may be liable. It includes the off-budget entities, trust funds, and both capital and operating accounts, but it does not include government-sponsored enterprises or (with the exception of loans) the future costs of current budget commitments. It does not cover contingent liabilities (except guaranteed loans), such as those the government incurs in insuring bank deposits and private pensions, nor does it recognize the future outlays that will result from the obligation to pay Social Security, Medicare, and other entitlements. The amounts involved in future claims on the federal Treasury are truly gargantuan. By some estimates, the government's exposure to various insurance schemes exceeds $5 trillion. We return to this issue in chapter 10 in discussing a balance sheet approach to federal finances.

On-Budget Totals

On-budget totals differ from the unified budget in their exclusion of Social Security and the Postal Service. The off-budget status of these entities is designed to protect them from spending constraints in the rest of the budget. By itself off-budget status makes little difference. However, Social Security's protected sta-

FIGURE 3-2
Alternative Measures of the Deficit and Surplus, Five-Fiscal-Year Intervals, 1980–2000

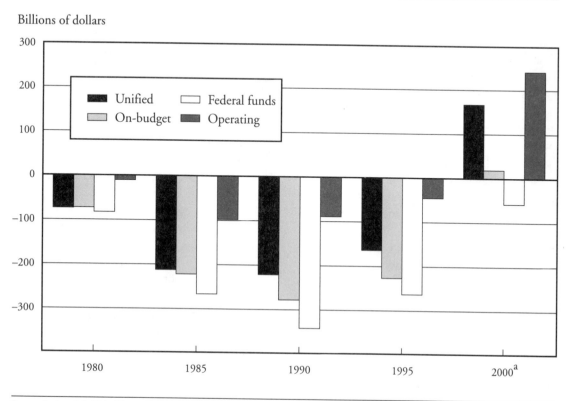

Billions of dollars

Source: *Budget of the United States, Historical Tables, Fiscal Year 2001,* table 1.1, p. 20, table 1.4, pp. 25–26, table 9.2, pp. 146–47.
  a. Estimated.

tus is reinforced by its exemption from recon-ciliation and sequestration, two of the govern-ment's tools for cutting expenditures. Because Social Security is so large, excluding it from budget totals would impair the government's ability to measure the fiscal impact of its bud-get decisions. In fact, Social Security is almost always included in governmental and media reports on the budget.

Since 1983, when Social Security was last overhauled, the on-budget totals have been less favorable than those reported on a unified basis. In fiscal 1992, for example, the on-bud-get deficit was $340 billion, $50 billion more than was shown in the unified budget. And in fiscal 1998 when the unified budget achieved a surplus, the on-budget accounts still had a $30 billion deficit. The difference between the two sets of numbers is due almost entirely to the buildup of surpluses in Social Security funds in preparation for the upsurge in the re-tired population early in the new century. Under current policy, when Social Security draws down its accumulated balances, the uni-fied budget will have a smaller surplus or a big-ger deficit than the on-budget totals. However, there is a strong probability that both Social Security and its budgetary status will be significantly altered by the time baby boomers begin entering the retirement stream.

The Federal Funds Budget

The federal funds budget excludes all trust funds. As noted earlier, it consists of the general fund and special funds. The federal funds deficit peaked at $386 billion in fiscal 1992, almost $100 billion higher than the unified budget deficit. It has since receded to $58 billion and will disappear early in the new century if budget projections materialize. The favorable outlook for federal funds is due principally to the surge in general revenue, fueled (as was explained in the previous chapter) by a steep rise in income tax collections. Most tax increases during the 1990s went into the general fund, not into trust funds, as had been the practice throughout the post–World War II period. Moreover, the general fund has improved with the end of the Cold War (and the consequent drop-off in defense spending) and with the introduction of discretionary spending caps.

The Capital and Operating Budgets

In contrast to the practice of state and local governments, the federal budget does not segregate capital and operating expenses. Both expenditures for current operations and for the acquisition of buildings, roads, and other fixed assets are budgeted as outlays. From time to time, proposals have been made to separate the two types of expenditures, but none have been adopted. However, the budget provides supplementary information on capital investments. Figure 3-2 uses a restrictive definition of such outlays: it includes spending on physical assets but excludes research and development as well as investment in human capital through education and training. See table 3-1 for a list of the

various types of investment outlays for fiscal 1999. The narrowest category, covering the acquisition of physical assets, amounted to $119 billion. Adding research and development increases this amount to $193 billion, and adding education and training raises it to $240 billion in investments.

Clearly, having a separate investment budget would paint the government's fiscal position in a more favorable light than the unified budget shows. But subtracting the gross amount invested in physical or human capital from the operating budget would misstate the government's financial condition. If a separate capital budget were introduced, the operating budget would have to be charged for depreciation and write-offs of capital assets. If these adjustments were made, the operating surplus or deficit would differ from that reported on a unified basis only to the extent that there was a net change in the government's stock of capital assets. If the government had a separate capital budget in fiscal 2000, the operating budget would have recorded an estimated $82 billion for depreciation.

The main reason for combining current and capital investment expenditures is to show the budget's aggregate impact on economic activity. Some have argued, however, that having a single budget hinders planning and financing of capital improvements, shortens the time horizon of budget makers, and leads politicians to cut investment spending when the budget is tight. But a number of difficult questions would arise if a capital budget were to be seriously considered. Should the capital budget be confined to investment in fixed assets or should it be expanded to include investment in human capital? Would a broad definition of investment weaken budget control by enabling politicians to shift spending from the operating budget to the capital budget? How should the federal government budget for roads and other facilities that it finances but that states or other governments own? Would the federal government be required to charge the operating budget for depreciation, for the loss of military weapons, and for other costs that are written off under generally accepted accounting rules?

Interest in a capital budget peaked when the federal government was running a large budget deficit. Some thought that segregating investment expenditure would enable the government to reduce the reported size of the deficit. Now that the government has a surplus, interest in a separate capital budget may wane. On the other hand, it may be that a surplus provides the most propitious opportunity to change the budget treatment of investment expenditure. Inasmuch as there is no deficit to hide, the government can base its decision on prudent accounting rules rather than on efforts to weaken budget control.

CONCLUSION

After two centuries of adaptation, the budget is still in a state of flux. Its boundaries are uncertain, and there are several alternative ways of measuring the government's financial flows and condition. How the surplus or deficit is measured depends on how the budget is defined. This problem cannot be resolved, however, by replacing one measure of the budget with another. The budget has multiple measures because it has multiple uses. Each measure tells a different story; none provides a snapshot of the budget from all appropriate vantage points. A budget constructed on the basis of cash flows provides essential information on the financing needs of government and is cast in a form that politicians can understand and deal with. But a cash flow bud-

get discloses little about the future financial claims on the government. For this purpose a balance sheet might be more useful, especially if it is refined to prudently evaluate the risks associated with insurance programs and other contingent liabilities. For other purposes a budget segregated by funds or between capital and operating expenditures might be more appropriate.

Although there are many ways to tell the budget's story, there can be only one basis for deciding the budget. Congress cannot review the budget one day and make allocations on the basis of cash flows, return the next day and independently decide how much should be invested in capital improvements, take a fresh look on another day and determine what should be done to each budgetary fund. More than a generation ago the government decided that the unified budget provides the most comprehensive basis for making and reporting budget decisions. However, the short-term Social Security surplus and the long-term Social Security deficit have called into question the adequacy of the unified budget. On the one hand, it has enabled the government to borrow the surplus for other uses; on the other hand, it has masked the approaching problem of paying for an aging population.

Congress has responded to these pressures by trying to wall off Social Security from the budget. In the future, it may also exclude other trust funds or establish a separate investment budget. But these possible developments will not put an end to debate on the proper boundaries of the budget. As long as there is a federal budget, questions will be raised as to whether particular transactions should be in or out. What is put in at one time might be taken out at another. This has been budgeting's history; it will also be its future.

4

The Political Rules and Arithmetic of Budgeting

E very budget is a compilation of numbers on the revenues, financial resources, obligations, outlays, borrowing, and deficit or surplus of the government. The federal budget has millions of these
numbers, computed and reported on the basis of rules and practices
that have accumulated over the years. The rules do not always conform
to the way businesses or other governments account for their finances.
Some are derived from laws, such as the Budget Enforcement Act of
1990 (BEA); many are not recognized in law or in accounting principles but nevertheless determine how financial transactions are recorded
in the budget. But different rules produce different numbers. An increase does not always mean more money is being raised or spent than
in the previous year, and a decrease does not necessarily mean that less
money is being raised or spent. Changes in revenue and spending are
also measured in terms of assumptions and projections that pertain to
federal budgeting.

This chapter explains the main rules laid out in, and the practices and
outcomes stemming from, BEA. It compares two types of spending, discretionary and direct, and describes the different processes for each.
Next, it focuses on the injection of politics into baseline projections, assumptions, and the complex world of scoring—measuring the budgetary impact of legislation and other actions that affect the budget.
Since the budget is hostage to the performance of the economy, the

TABLE 4-1

Total Discretionary Spending Caps, Fiscal Years 1991–2002

Billions of dollars

Year cap set	1991	1992	1993	1994[a]	1995[a]	1996	1997	1998[a]	1999	2000	2001[b]	2002[b]
1990												
Budget authority	491.7	503.4	511.5	510.8	517.7							
Outlays	514.4	524.9	534.0	534.8	540.8							
1993												
Budget authority					509.9	517.4	519.1	528.1	530.6			
Outlays					537.3	538.95	547.3	547.3	547.9			
1997												
Budget authority								526.9	533.0	537.2	542.0	551.1
Outlays								556.3	559.4	564.3	564.4	560.8

Sources: *Congressional Quarterly Almanac*, 1990, 1993, 1997.

a. For fiscal years 1994 and 1995 the caps were revised in 1993. For fiscal 1998, the caps were revised in 1997.

b. In his last budget sent to Congress in February 2000, President Clinton proposed to extend the discretionary spending caps for another ten years, beginning with a cap of $614.3 billion in budget authority and $626.4 billion in outlays in fiscal 2001 and ending with $757.7 billion in budget authority and $780.2 billion in outlays in fiscal 2010.

chapter concludes with an assessment of the role of economics in budgeting.

BUDGET ENFORCEMENT RULES

The BEA has three main rules—adjustable deficit targets, discretionary spending caps, and pay-as-you-go (PAYGO) rules for revenue and direct spending.

While the Gramm-Rudman-Hollings Act (discussed in chapter 2) fixed a target, the BEA permits the deficit or surplus to be adjusted each year in light of current economic and budget conditions. Yet removal of a maximum limit has not ushered in an "anything goes" permissiveness in federal budgeting. The focus of control has shifted to the spending and revenue decisions that affect budget aggregates. In effect, the federal government has two distinct budget processes, each with its own path and players. One involves discretionary spending, controlled by caps, the other, direct spending and revenues, governed by PAYGO rules.

The caps pertain to the one-third of federal spending annually appropriated. This discretionary spending includes virtually all defense expenditures, the operating costs of most federal agencies, and dozens of grant programs. Table 4-1 shows the spending caps in effect for fiscal years 1991 through 2002, which limit both the amounts appropriated by Congress and the outlays estimated to be disbursed pursuant to past and new appropriations. For some years (1994, 1995, and 1998) two sets of caps are shown—the original ones set for that year and the revised amounts when the caps were extended. Thus in 1997 when Congress extended the caps to 2002, it also changed the amounts permitted for the fiscal year immediately ahead.

Direct spending is not controlled by annual appropriations, but by the legislation that established eligibility criteria and payment formulas. It consists mostly of entitlement programs that are financed either by annual or permanent appropriations but also includes other budgetary resources provided by authorizing committees. When Congress appropriates for entitlements, such as Medicaid and food stamps, it must provide sufficient funds to cover the government's obligations. In other words, the appropriations committees do not have discretion to provide less money than the government is obligated to pay.

PAYGO rules mandate that new legislation increasing direct spending or reducing revenues must be fully offset so that the deficit is not increased or the surplus diminished. PAYGO does not require any offsetting action when the change in spending or revenue occurs pursuant to existing law. Thus spending rising because of inflation in health costs or revenues falling because of a weak economy would not trigger PAYGO. Nor does PAYGO bar Congress from passing revenue or spending legislation that adds to the deficit or cuts the surplus. Rather, it requires that any such change be offset by direct spending or revenue legislation, or by sequestering (withholding) certain funds. In practice, however, Congress generally has not approved direct spending increases nor revenue reductions unless the same measure also contained offsets.

After each session of Congress, the Office of Management and Budget (OMB) issues official estimates as to the impact on the surplus or deficit of measures enacted into law. Exhibit 4-1 displays excerpts from the December 1999 PAYGO scorecard. The Congressional Budget Office (CBO) also estimates budgetary impacts, and Congress relies on these while it is considering legislation. But once a measure has been enacted, OMB's estimate is authoritative in determining whether PAYGO has been breached. If OMB finds a net increase in the deficit or reduction in the surplus, budget resources would be sequestered from certain direct spending programs. Because most direct spending is exempt from sequestration, the brunt of any enforced cutbacks would fall on a few programs.

DISCRETIONARY AND DIRECT SPENDING

As the previous section shows, budgeting for discretionary spending is a very different exercise than budgeting for direct spending. In discretionary spending the basic task is to decide future spending levels; in mandatory spending it is to estimate the cost of past decisions. While the two processes converge at various points, such as the president's budget and the congressional budget resolution, they differ on a number of key institutional and financial dimensions. Although there are some exceptions to the distinctions drawn in table 4-2, the generalizations provide a useful comparison of two different budget conditions. The paragraphs below correspond to the entries in the table.

Budgetary Impact of Authorizing Legislation

An authorization of discretionary spending is only a license (required by House and Senate rules) to consider an appropriation. The amount authorized may be spent only to the extent that funds are appropriated. In contrast, an authorization of direct spending (such as entitlement legislation) either provides funds or effectively mandates the appropriation of budget resources. Spending control tends to be weaker when authorizing committees rather than appropriators dictate the amount to be spent because these committees often function as advocates for the programs under their jurisdiction. For example, the political role of the veterans' affairs committees is to look after the interests of veterans. Unlike the appropriations committees, they do not have to make spending decisions in light of other demands on the budget.

Role of the Appropriations Committees

The appropriations committees have effective jurisdiction over all discretionary spending;

▶ **EXHIBIT 4-1**

OMB and CBO Deficit Impact Estimates of Pay-As-You-Go Legislation

Act title	1998	1999	2000	2001	2002	2003	1998–2003
PAYGO balances: fiscal 1999 preview report			(in millions of dollars)				
OMB estimate	−153	11	16	14	10	9	−93
CBO estimate	−156	68	95	96	22	−68	57
Selected legislation enacted in 2d session–105th Congress							
IRS Restructuring and Reform Act							
OMB estimate	338	82	−33	543	1,018	1,234	3,182
CBO estimate	−168	−659	−519	241	806	1,157	858
VA-HUD Appropriations Act							
OMB estimate	(OMB does not believe this bill is subject to PAYGO)						
CBO estimate	0	4	23	57	78	98	260
Transportation Equity Act (TEA-21)							
OMB estimate	−421	−306	−93	−91	−275	−362	−1,548
CBO estimate	−440	−392	249	320	194	133	64
Omnibus Appropriation Act for fiscal 1999							
OMB estimate	0	250	−2,880	−1,506	−1,118	−2,394	−7,648
CBO estimate	0	−80	120	−1,051	836	200	25
Subtotal: legislation enacted in 2d session–105th Congress							
OMB estimate	−118	−883	−2,943	−847	−174	−1,101	−6,066
CBO estimate	−598	−1,499	492	241	2,737	2,494	3,867
Total: all legislation enacted through the 2d session–105th Congress							
OMB estimate	−271	−872	−2,927	−833	−164	−1,092	−6,159
CBO estimate	−754	−1,431	587	337	2,759	2,426	3,924

Source: *OMB Final Sequestration Report to the President and Congress for Fiscal Year 1999*, table 7, pp. 17–20.

(a) The Budget Enforcement Act of 1990 (BEA) requires OMB to submit a final sequestration report (usually in October or November) for each congressional session; one section of the report provides the status of PAYGO legislation (exhibited here). This report is determinative of whether a discretionary or PAYGO sequester is needed.

(b) In the session reported on here, Congress passed more than ninety measures that affected the budget. Only four are listed here, as well as the totals for all the measures.

(c) CBO and OMB often disagree on the budget implications of legislation. Once enacted, OMB's estimates determine the impact on the budget. The estimate made at the time of enactment is determinative; the BEA does not require that the budget impact be remeasured when additional data become available.

(d) Although the federal budget had a surplus when this report was issued, the BEA still requires that the impact be measured in terms of the deficit. A minus sign in the entries means that the legislation would reduce the deficit or add to the surplus.

TABLE 4-2
Comparison of Discretionary and Direct Spending

Feature	Discretionary spending	Direct spending
Budgetary impact of authorizing legislation	Authorizes consideration of appropriations measures	Provides budget resources
Role of the appropriations committees	Provide budget resources	Little or no control over budget resources
Frequency of action	Annual	Irregular, no fixed schedule
Budget enforcement rules	Spending caps	PAYGO rules
Enforcing budget decisions	Section 302(b) allocations	Reconciliation procedures
Basis of calculating budget impacts	Amount appropriated compared with current year's level and president's request for next year	Baseline projections and estimated effects of policy changes
Economic sensitivity	Low, indirect	Direct, often automatic
Political sensitivity	Variable: high for some programs, low for others	Often very high
Correspondence of budgeted and actual spending	Usually high	Sometimes low

the amounts available are specified in appropriations acts. However, these committees do not control mandatory spending. Some mandatory programs are funded by permanent appropriations and bypass the annual appropriations process. Many are funded by annual appropriations, but because the spending is mandated by law, the appropriations committees have little or no control over the amounts they provide.

Frequency of Congressional Action

With few exceptions discretionary appropriations are voted annually for the next (or current) fiscal year. Direct spending, however, is typically enacted in permanent law that continues in effect unless it is terminated or revised by subsequent legislation. The fact that many entitlements are financed by annual appropriations does not diminish the perma-

nence of the laws governing the amounts spent. Some entitlements, such as Medicare, have been subjected to frequent legislative action; others, such as Social Security, have gone years without new legislation.

Budget Enforcement Rules

Under BEA, discretionary spending has been controlled by caps, which (if they are adhered to) constrain the amount appropriated each year. Mandatory spending is not capped but operates under the PAYGO rule that new legislation cutting revenues or increasing direct spending must be offset.

Enforcing Budget Decisions

Congress expresses its budget policy, including the changes it seeks in existing revenue or spending laws, in an annual resolution. Because this resolution is not a statute, Congress must implement its policy in other measures. For discretionary spending, it does so in annual appropriations; for direct spending and taxes, it does so in new legislation. In both cases Congress needs a mechanism for ensuring that the actions taken are in accord with its budget policy. A procedure known as section 302 allocations links annual appropriations to the congressional budget resolution. By means of this procedure the House and Senate appropriations committees are given their share of the spending amounts in the budget resolution; each then allocates its spending among the thirteen appropriations subcommittees. In most cases total spending in each appropriations bill must be within the amounts allocated to the relevant subcommittee. In the case of direct spending and revenues, Congress relies on reconciliation procedures to implement its budget decisions; it does not apply reconciliation to discretionary spending. Although it can be a potent instrument, reconciliation is used only in those years when Congress wants to change budget outcomes; it is not applied in years when Congress accepts the outcomes that ensue from existing law.

Basis of Calculating Budget Impacts

Virtually all discretionary appropriations are for definite amounts. In making and reporting their decisions, the appropriations committees often compare the amounts recommended to the previous year's appropriation and to the amounts the president has requested. Thus, if an account had an appropriation of $100 million, and the president requested $120 million for the next year but the appropriations bill provided $110 million, this action would be counted as both a $10 million increase and a $10 million reduction. Direct spending legislation, however, is scored against baseline esti-

mates of the amount that would be spent if current law continues in effect without change. Moreover, inasmuch as most mandatory spending is open-ended—the law establishing entitlements usually does not specify or limit the amount to be spent—calculations of budgetary impact are based on assumed rather than actual spending levels.

Economic Sensitivity

All budgets are sensitive to changes in economic conditions, but the response may be weaker in discretionary programs than in mandatory ones. Discretionary spending is not automatically adjusted for economic changes. When prices rise, Congress may appropriate more funds, or it may require agencies to absorb the inflation with the same resources they had for the previous year. But in direct spending there often is an automatic adjustment. Rising prices trigger cost-of-living adjustments in Social Security and other transfer payments; rising unemployment boosts the number of people receiving unemployment benefits and certain other payments. In being more sensitive to the performance of the economy, direct spending may be less responsive to the will of politicians.

Political Sensitivity

Political considerations influence all budgets. Both discretionary and direct spending programs have constituents who benefit from federal dollars and actively guard their interests. But political interest in discretionary programs is highly variable. Some programs have powerful political constituencies that lobby for additional funds; others hardly attract any attention.

Direct spending is inherently sensitive because it affects the financial well-being of so many Americans. For the 45 million Americans receiving monthly Social Security checks and the 40 million enrolled in Medicare, the flow of money from Washington is a key determinant of their living standard. Cutting these and other entitlements has just about the same impact on household finances as cutting the pay of workers. It is just as visible, direct, and immediate, and as likely to provoke strong protest.

It is not only their size that augments the political prominence of mandatory programs. When Congress establishes an entitlement, it gives recipients a legal right to the money, and when it indexes these payments to price increases, it entitles beneficiaries to protection against inflation. These legal rights have political value; they strengthen claims on the budget. If Congress cuts payments, it not only takes money from recipients but also infringes on their perceived rights.

Correspondence of Budgeted and Actual Spending

The final distinction in table 4-2 pertains to the amounts spent. Discretionary spending usually conforms closely to appropriated levels, but mandatory spending often varies significantly from budgeted amounts. Variances may be due to estimation errors, unanticipated changes in economic conditions, or policy changes. When spending veers sharply off course, it is most likely because of changes in external conditions that were not considered when the budget estimates were made.

THE POLITICS OF BUDGETARY ARITHMETIC

The arithmetic of budgeting is political arithmetic—it influences budgetary policies and outcomes, and it is influenced in turn by the president, Congress, and others with a stake in budget decisions. Even when the numbers are compiled strictly in accord with technical rules and established practices, as is usually the case, they have political consequences. The numbers influence public perceptions about the budget, such as the size of the surplus or deficit. They may influence the behavior of politicians by making some types of transactions more or less expensive than others and may facilitate or impede the passage of legislation by increasing or reducing the estimated budgetary impact of a particular measure.

Although the rules for recording revenues and outlays have always been important, the appropriations caps and PAYGO rules have given them added prominence. How legislation is scored may determine whether a measure under consideration (or passed by Congress) is in compliance with current budget rules. Enforcing these rules is rarely straightforward, for much depends on assumptions about the behavior of firms and individuals affected by existing or new policies. For example, every budget specifies the amounts to be spent during the next year (or beyond) on Medicare, unemployment insurance, and other benefit programs. These figures are not firm; they are based on assumptions about future economic conditions, participation rates, and the payments those eligible will receive. In most cases these assumptions are wrong, sometimes by small amounts, but occasionally they are wide of the mark. Even when they are wrong, however, budget decisions are based on them as if they were certain.

Budgeting pertains to the future, and since the future is unknown, it can only be assumed. Small changes in the underlying assumptions can yield quite large differences in budget entries. Yet the budget says more about its numbers than about its assumptions. The assumptions are where political opportunism and manipulation thrive.

The budget staffs in the executive (OMB) and legislative (CBO) branches manage these rules and assumptions. Each staff has a strong interest in upholding the integrity of the budget process, but neither can avoid some entanglement in the politics of budgeting. As the president's largest staff agency, OMB has the lead role in preparing and defending his budget; it cannot openly take positions contrary to the policies the White House prefers. Both OMB's political operatives and career staff devise bookkeeping ploys that add up the president's budget to the numbers he wants. As a congressional agency beholden to both Democrats and Republicans, CBO vigilantly guards its independence, but as the scoring of legislation has gained prominence in enforcing budget rules, it has become part of the battle between the two parties and between the president and Congress. On many routine matters of budgetary arithmetic, CBO and OMB coordinate their work and produce the same numbers, but major disagreements occasionally explode into the open.

One such clash occurred over President Clinton's health care reforms, and it indicates how outcomes can be swayed by budgetary arithmetic. When Clinton sent his health proposal to Congress in 1994, he estimated that the reforms would reduce projected deficits by almost $60 billion over the next seven years. Reviewing the same proposal, however, CBO informed Congress that they would add $70 billion to the deficit. The wide discrepancy between the two estimates derived principally from differing assumptions about future health care costs.

Both OMB and CBO claimed that their estimates were free of political influence. Surely, however, it was no accident that OMB's numbers supported the president's position while CBO's challenged it. OMB's buoyant estimate helped Clinton reconcile his twin objectives of health reform and deficit reduction; CBO's

skeptical numbers gave doubting congressional committees more reasons for thwarting the president's initiative.

With so much riding on the numbers and underlying assumptions, it matters whose calculations have greater credence. By law, OMB officially measures the budgetary impact of legislation and determines whether congressional action complies with BEA rules. In practice, however, CBO often has the upper hand when its estimates diverge from OMB's. The reason is that Congress generally relies on CBO's judgment while it is considering legislation; OMB's score is authoritative only after a measure has been enacted.

Having two scorekeepers is not just a matter of getting a second opinion. This arrangement is rooted in the constitutional separation of powers. In most cases, Congress wants to maintain its independence on budgetary matters; this was its principal objective in establishing CBO. But it is in the president's interest to use estimates and assumptions prepared by OMB that are responsive to his legislative objectives. When Clinton became president, he expected that there would be no need for separate projections because Democrats controlled both branches. In his February 1993 budget speech to Congress, Clinton promised to rely on CBO economic estimates. "Let's at least argue about the same set of numbers," Clinton urged, "so the American people will think we're shooting straight with them." Within a few months, however, the administration was insisting on its own budget and economic assumptions when they differed from those CBO issued.

There are two situations under which one branch may base its budgetary action on the other's numbers. One is when congressional leaders and the president rely on summit negotiations to resolve a budgetary impasse; the other is when Congress finds it advantageous to use OMB data rather than its own. When they go to the summit, the two sides cannot make much headway unless they agree on what the numbers mean. They must have the same starting points, assumptions, and scoring rules. If they do not, any agreement would quickly evaporate.

In arithmetic disputes between the two branches, CBO often takes the more cautious position, estimating somewhat lower economic growth and higher outlays. Consequently, Congress sometimes finds itself at a disadvantage using CBO numbers. On occasion, therefore, Congress has directed CBO to use OMB assumptions in scoring legislation. This practice, known as "directed scoring," is discussed later in the chapter.

Arithmetic, like much else in budgeting, is an amalgam of procedures and politics. To conclude that the numbers are manipulated to serve political interests would ignore the extent to which numerical entries in the budget are determined by technical rules. But to assume that the numbers are churned out by a politics-free process would miss the extent to which budget makers bend the numbers to their liking. The balance between technical and political factors varies with different facets of budgeting. When the numbers represent actual transactions, such as the amount appropriated, technical rules predominate. When they represent assumptions about future conditions, such as the rate of inflation, there is greater scope for political influence. Because the budget is increasingly driven by assumptions, political arithmetic has become more important than it was a generation ago.

BASELINE PROJECTIONS

To enforce its budget rules during consideration of revenue or spending legislation, Congress must measure the budgetary impact of its actions. This task is relatively easy for programs funded in annual appropriations; Congress compares the amounts provided to the previous year's appropriation or to the president's request. But the task can be difficult when Congress acts on revenue or entitlement legislation. In these cases it must take account of factors that influence the amount taken in or spent, including the performance of the economy, price changes, participation rates, and the behavior of those affected by federal policy. The revenue yield of tax legislation depends primarily on future economic conditions and on the responses of taxpayers to changes in tax laws. The cost of entitlement legislation depends on economic variables, demographic trends, and the extent to which those who are eligible avail themselves of the benefits. Each program has its own factors that drive budgetary responses to legislative changes. Medicaid depends, among other things, on the actions of states in enrolling beneficiaries and setting benefits, the food stamps program on income trends, Medicare on the age structure of the population, and the child health insurance program relies on the speed with which states and families take advantage of this recent federal initiative. A complex program such as Medicare is sensitive to dozens of variables; each has to be analyzed in estimating future program expenditures.

In budget making, the future is assumed. Assumptions are used to estimate spending and revenue under existing laws and to establish changes in these laws. When Congress legislates, the estimated budgetary impact of its actions depends on assumptions about (1) the amounts that would be raised or spent without new legislation and (2) the amounts by which the legislation would change projected future revenue or spending. In contemporary budgeting, the first set of numbers is known as the baseline; the second set is the score. Both sets

TABLE 4-3
Hypothetical Baseline Projection and Policy Changes, Fiscal Years 2000–04

Millions of dollars

	2000	2001	2002	2003	2004
Previous year's baseline	100.00	107.12	114.74	122.91	131.66
Assumptions					
4 percent inflation	+4.00	+4.28	+4.59	+4.92	+5.27
3 percent workload increase	+3.12	+3.34	+3.58	+3.83	+4.11
Baseline projection	107.12	114.74	122.91	131.66	141.04
Policy changes					
Cap inflation increases at 2 percent	−2.00	−4.20	−6.63	−9.30	−12.23
Slow workload increase to 2 percent	−1.08	−2.30	−3.67	−5.20	−6.92
Projected spending	104.04	108.24	112.61	117.16	121.89
Total policy changes (score)	−3.08	−6.50	−10.30	−14.50	−19.15

of numbers appear in table 4-3, which provides a hypothetical illustration of baseline projections and legislative scoring.

Both OMB and CBO prepare baseline projections for budget aggregates (total revenue, total budget authority, and so on), particular categories of the budget (for example, national defense, income support), and for particular programs or accounts. The projections once covered the next five years; they recently have been expanded to ten years. They assume that current policy will continue in effect and that spending levels will be fully adjusted for inflation. In the case of mandatory programs, the baseline is adjusted for estimated changes in workload, such as increases in the number of people receiving Social Security checks or Medicare services. It also accounts for discretionary workload changes, such as an increase in the number of applications processed.

Once a baseline has been constructed, any variance from it due to legislation is measured as a policy change. In other words, legislation is scored and its budgetary impact is measured in terms of changes from the baseline. In the hypothetical case (table 4-3), baseline spend-

ing is projected to increase from $100 million in the current year to $141 million five years later. The $41 million increase, like all other baseline projections, is an assumed number; it will materialize only if the assumptions underlying the baseline—4 percent annual inflation and 3 percent annual workload increases—also materialize.

In this hypothetical case, legislated policy changes result in new projections below the baseline—$104 million in the first year compared with the $107 million baseline, growing to $122 million in the fifth year compared with the $141 million baseline. Although these new projections show nominal spending increases, they are scored as cuts—a reduction of $3 million in the first year, rising to a $19 million reduction in the fifth year. The usual practice is to compute the score as the cumulative budgetary changes over the full period covered by the baseline. In this case, the score would be a $54 million spending reduction. If the baseline were extended to ten years, the score would be much higher because estimated policy changes would be computed for twice as many years.

This feature of baselines can distort public perceptions of budgetary legislation. In 1999 Congress passed and Clinton vetoed a tax cut that was estimated to reduce federal revenues by $792 billion over a ten-year period. This seems to be an enormous reduction, but if the measure had been scored for only five years, the estimated revenue loss would have been less than one-quarter of that amount. In fact, the proposed tax cut would have amounted to less than 3 percent of the revenue expected to be collected over the ten years.

The hypothetical example reveals another interesting feature of baselines. Legislation often results in spending that is higher than the current level but below the baseline. This pattern enables politicians to portray their actions as both a spending cut and a spending increase. They can use the baseline to make the case that spending has been reduced and they can point to current spending levels to show that programs have been protected. Making the case both ways is no small political feat; it enables cross-pressured politicians to satisfy the conflicting demands that they cut the size of government and increase the size of programs.

The 1993 deficit reduction package President Clinton pushed through Congress illustrates how sizable savings can be enacted while program cutbacks are minimized. According to CBO estimates made when the package was enacted, Medicare was to be cut by $56 billion over five years. On its face, this cutback violated Clinton's pledge to Congress on February 17, 1993, when he launched his deficit reduction drive. "Let me be clear. There also will be no new cuts in Medicare. . . . Let me repeat this because I know it matters to a lot of you on both sides of the aisle. This plan does not make a recommendation for new cuts in Medicare benefits for any beneficiary."

How did the president and Congress manage to pare so much without cutting benefits?

The Medicare program shows that the task is not as difficult as one might think. About $50 billion came from reductions in baseline payments to providers, some of which would not be counted as cuts if more stringent criteria had been used. For example, fees for surgical services were increased by 8.6 percent, far above general inflation and even above inflation in the health sector. Nevertheless, this increase was scored as a multibillion dollar cut because the baseline assumed a 12.2 percent inflation adjustment. Payments to hospitals were reduced by 7.4 percent, a smaller reduction than was provided by the law it replaced. Nevertheless, CBO scored this as savings because the new spending level was below the baseline. Several billion dollars more were saved by extending the existing requirement that Medicare Part B premiums cover 25 percent of program costs. The reported spending cuts produced by these and other maneuvers enabled Congress to enact a smattering of Medicare enhancements in the deficit reduction measure.

Like other features of budgeting, the baseline was developed for technical reasons—to give Congress a neutral starting point not tainted by the president's budget recommendations—but it also serves political ends. The baseline strongly influences public perceptions about the budget, gives budget makers incentives to structure tax and spending legislation in certain ways rather than others, and protects some programs against inflation. In discretionary spending it strengthens arguments that appropriations should be increased to compensate agencies for inflation; in entitlements it transforms decisions facing the president and Congress from how much should be spent to how much should be cut.

Because the baseline hinges on assumptions, it provides ample scope for politicians to save programs by assuming savings will occur. They can meet savings targets by making some

FIGURE 4-1
Alternative Projections of Medicare Spending, 1996–2002

Billions of dollars

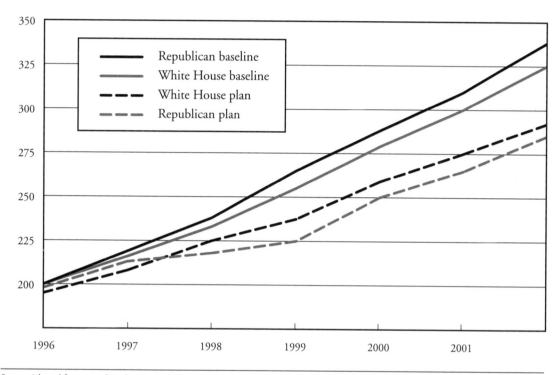

Source: Adapted from a graph in the *New York Times,* December 11, 1995, p. A1, based on Congressional Budget Office and White House estimates.

provisions temporary and taking credit for additional savings each time the provisions are extended. They can manipulate the score by enacting legislation that is effective at different periods covered by the baseline.

Inasmuch as Congress and the president sometimes rely on different baseline assumptions, policy differences between them are distorted. This problem occurred in 1995, enabling Clinton to gain a political victory that scarred congressional Republicans through the remainder of his presidency. In 1995 OMB and CBO drew seven-year baselines that showed Medicare spending rising steeply over the period (figure 4-1). OMB assumed less

health care inflation than CBO, and it therefore projected smaller spending increases in Medicare. Over the seven years, OMB estimated that Medicare spending would total $1.624 trillion; CBO's baseline totaled $1.692 trillion, $68 billion higher. Given the uncertainties in estimating future health care costs, the difference was quite small—only 4 percent of total spending. But this gap made an enormous difference in how the proposed Medicare cutbacks appeared. Because Congress used the CBO baseline, Republicans showed much deeper cuts than Clinton proposed. In fact, congressional Republicans reported $146 billion more in cuts than Clinton recommended, yet 47 percent of the difference was due to different baselines, not to policy differences. If Republicans had used Clinton's baseline, the size of their cut in 2002 would have been approximately $40 billion rather than $55 billion. If Clinton had used the Republican baseline, his cut in that year would have been about $50 billion instead of $35 billion. In terms of spending, the two plans differed by approximately $10 billion in 2002.

The moral of this story is that politicians have to be careful in choosing the baselines they use. In a dispute between the president and Congress, the side using the more cautious assumptions (for example, lower economic growth, higher inflation) exposes itself to blame for reducing spending, raising taxes, or doing other unwelcome things to the budget.

THE POLITICS OF SCORING

Scoring is not a static exercise in which budget experts wait until legislation has been proposed or enacted before measuring budgetary impact. As scoring has become more important, it has moved from the end of the process to the beginning. Legislation is framed so as to affect the score, and scorekeepers estimate the cost of alternatives before they are introduced. As legislative ideas are bounced around, there is a lot of behind-the-scenes interaction between budget scorers and politicians. Increasingly, lobbyists and consultants get into the act, trying to persuade budget specialists to score matters their way.

The subterranean world of scoring has rules and precedents, some of which have been published (exhibit 4-2), but there also are ad hoc accommodations in special cases. The "fingerprints rule" (rule 3 in the exhibit) is applied by OMB and CBO to classify spending as discretionary or direct. This rule specifies that legislated changes are scored to the committee reporting the measure—if an appropriations committee reports the bill, the ensuing spending is discretionary; if any other committee produces the bill, the spending is direct. The purpose of this rule is to deter evasion of budget controls, but it can produce some strange scoring outcomes. In 1999, for example, a legislative committee proposed that an automatic continuing resolution take effect whenever the fiscal year starts without enactment of all regular appropriations. Although the measure would pertain only to appropriations, CBO scored it as a $500 billion increase in direct spending because it was reported by an authorizing committee; the CBO score helped kill the proposal.

From time to time, Congress suspends the fingerprints rule when it enacts budget deals. One such case occurred in the 1998 omnibus appropriations act (see box 5-4), which packed eight appropriations acts and numerous authorizing laws in a single measure that was worked out in summit negotiations with the White House. A strict application of the fingerprints rule would have required that the legislative provisions be scored as discretionary spending, but Congress directed CBO to score them as direct spending.

Scorekeeping rules are sometimes changed to accommodate political interests. In the 1980s, when scoring rules were first formalized, revenue from the sale of assets was not scored; the additional revenue was disregarded in measuring budget impact. This rule recognizes that the government's financial condition is not changed by the sale of an asset, as it is merely exchanging one type of asset (such as real estate or a promissory note) for another type (cash). In the 1990s, however, the rules were changed to score savings but not losses from asset sales.

When an interest group lobbies Congress for a tax cut or spending increase, it no longer

▶ **EXHIBIT 4-2**
Scorekeeping Guidelines

3. Direct Spending Programs: Substantive changes to or restrictions on entitlement law or other mandatory spending law in appropriations laws will be scored against the Appropriations Committee section 302(b) allocations in the House and the Senate. For the purpose of CBA scoring, direct spending savings that are included in both an appropriation bill and a reconciliation bill will be scored to the reconciliation bill and not to the appropriation bill. . . .

6. Reappropriations: Reappropriations of expiring balances of budget authority will be scored as new budget authority in the fiscal year in which the balances become newly available.

7. Advance Appropriations: Advance appropriations of budget authority will be scored as new budget authority in the fiscal year in which the funds become newly available for obligation, not when the appropriations are enacted.

8. Rescissions of Unobligated Balances: Rescissions of unobligated balances will be scored as reductions in current budget authority and outlays in the year the money is rescinded. . . .

9. Delay of Obligations: Appropriation acts specify a date when funds will become available for obligation. It is this date that determines the year for which new budget authority is scored. In the absence of such a date, the act is assumed to be effective upon enactment.

If the new appropriation provides that a portion of the budget authority shall not be available for obligation until a future fiscal year, that portion shall be treated as an advance appropriation of budget authority. . . .

15. Asset Sales: If the net financial cost to the government of an asset sale is zero or negative (a savings), the amount scored shall be the estimated change in receipts and mandatory outlays in each fiscal year on a cash basis. If the cost to the government is positive (a loss), the proceeds from the sale shall not be scored for the purposes of the CBA or GRH.

Source: *Balanced Budget Act of 1997*, conference report to accompany H.R. 2015, H. Rept. 217, 105th Cong., 1st sess., 1997, pp. 1007–12.

(a) The House and Senate Budget Committees, CBO, and OMB use these scorekeeping guidelines in measuring compliance with the amended Congressional Budget Act (CBA) and Gramm-Rudman-Hollings Act (GRH).

(b) The purpose of the guidelines is to ensure that scorekeepers measure the effects of legislation on the deficit or surplus consistent with established conventions and with the specific requirements in CBA and GRH regarding discretionary spending, direct spending, and receipts.

(c) All of the scorekeepers must agree before any of the rules are changed. New accounts or activities are classified only after consultation among the scorekeepers. Accounts and activities shall not be reclassified unless all of the scorekeepers agree.

suffices that the proposal be palatable to members of Congress; it is also necessary that the proposal get a favorable score. Quite a few former budget or appropriations committees' staff members now provide expert advice on how to structure legislative proposals to influence the score. This game is played by both parties and in both the legislative and executive branches. Some tactics apply only to direct or discretionary spending, others to both. Although there are many variations, the tactics fall into two categories—one is to make the money (a spending increase or a tax cut) disappear; the other is to change the timing of the transaction. The discussion below deals with spending, but similar tactics, discussed in chapter 7, are deployed in structuring revenue legislation.

Discretionary Appropriations

The spending caps have spurred Congress to rearrange appropriations in ways that enable it to spend more while professing to stay within the caps. The tighter the caps, the greater the incentive to evade them. The following paragraphs explain some of the tactics devised to lower the discretionary spending score. Congress and the president employed many of the tactics discussed here in 1999 (for fiscal 2000 appropriations) because the gap between the discretionary caps and spending pressures was extraordinarily wide in that year.

Emergency Spending

This simple and effective approach has become a significant loophole in the budget enforcement rules. When the president and Congress want to spend more than the caps allow, they have a strong incentive to designate the excess spending as an emergency because its budget authority and related outlays are outside the caps. No criteria or assessments are required to ensure that the additional spending is for true emergencies such as natural disaster relief. As detailed in boxes 5-4 and 4-1, $21 billion of emergency spending was crammed into the fiscal 1999 omnibus appropriations act to resolve a preelection impasse, and an additional $15 billion was provided in that year's supplemental appropriation. The ploy was used again in fiscal 2000 appropriations because the caps did not provide sufficient room for maintaining existing programs and fully funding priorities; Congress and the president designated $20 billion, including funds for the decennial census required by the Constitution, as emergency spending. Because emergency spending raises that year's appropriation level, the odds are that without an upward adjustment in the caps, this tactic will be repeated in subsequent years with even more emergency money.

Led by Clinton, Democrats came out ahead in the emergency spending contests in the 1990s; they got credit for fiscal prudence while securing more money for popular programs. At times, congressional Republicans have taken the position that emergency spending should be offset by cuts in other discretionary programs, but they have not consistently followed this policy. Often outmaneuvered, they reluctantly approved the increases, sometimes after getting billions more for defense.

Offsets

A second way of making money "disappear" is to offset some spending increases by rescinding previous appropriations or by increasing offsetting collections from user fees or other sources. This is one reason that the volume of rescissions Congress initiated rose during the 1990s (see chapter 10). In 1999, for example, some Republicans proposed to rescind billions of unspent welfare dollars previously appropriated to the states to offset above-cap appropriations sought by Congress. Although state protests thwarted this proposed rescission, this example illustrates how the offsets game operates.

Under BEA rules, appropriations offsets are supposed to come only from discretionary accounts; any other offsets are to be scored in the PAYGO budget. Nevertheless, Congress and the president sometimes raid PAYGO accounts to boost discretionary spending. For fiscal years 1992 through 1998, there were about one hundred instances in which reductions in mandatory spending were scored as offsets to increase discretionary spending. One such instance occurred in the 1997 balanced budget deal, which diverted $3 billion in income from the sale of radio frequencies to the discretionary part of the budget. Another instance occurred a year earlier, when $1 billion from mortgage insurance reforms was used as offsets. Clinton disregarded the firewall in his fiscal 2000 budget, which proposed appropriations that were many billions of dollars above the discretionary caps but would have been offset with increased tobacco taxes. Clinton's démarche put congressional Republicans in a difficult position—either vote for tax increases or against education. Republicans tried to wriggle out of this predicament by designating routine expenditures as emergencies.

Directed Scoring

Money can be made to disappear by instructing CBO scorers to use OMB assumptions rather than its own. It was noted earlier that CBO tends to use more cautious assumptions than OMB; when this occurs, Congress appears to be spending more than it would if OMB's estimates were used. At times, therefore, the budget committees direct CBO to score certain appropriations with OMB's as-

sumptions. A related tactic is for Congress to make unilateral scoring adjustments, such as a slower spendout rate or quicker revenue flow, that have the effect of reducing total budget authority and outlays. In some cases, Congress picks and chooses between OMB and CBO assumptions, taking from each those that score its appropriations as less costly.

The foregoing tactics are intended to make appropriations disappear; the ones that follow are designed to defer their appearance in the score until a later fiscal year.

Advance Appropriations

Scorekeeping rule 7 (see exhibit 4-2) provides that advance appropriations are scored as new budget authority in the fiscal year in which the funds become available. This rule enables Congress to make appropriations in one year but to have the money scored against the caps for a later year. This tactic is attractive in grant programs because the federal fiscal year does not coincide with that of state and local governments. The federal fiscal year runs from October through September, that of many states from July through June.

Congress resorted extensively to advance appropriations in fiscal 1999 and even more so the following year. In evading one year's caps, advance appropriations can make it more difficult to comply with the next year's limit. If, for example, Congress provides $10 billion in advance appropriations, the effect is to reduce the amount available within the next year's caps by an equivalent amount. Underlying advance appropriations is the hope that sooner or later Congress will raise the caps to accommodate more spending. If they are not adjusted, the volume of advance appropriations will almost certainly rise from one year to the next.

Clinton's fiscal 2001 budget contained yet another way of hiding the budgetary impact of

BOX 4-1
Evading the Spending Caps: Emergency Spending in 1999

A bill that started out in 1999 as an ordinary emergency supplemental appropriation for hurricane disaster relief ended up as a vehicle for blowing a $15 billion hole in the discretionary spending cap. Evading the caps is not a particularly difficult task because BEA does not define "emergency"; an emergency is whatever the president and Congress deem it to be. There are political land mines, however; the White House and Capitol Hill have to share in the joys of emergency spending, legislative voices calling for the additional spending to be offset by cuts in other areas have to be silenced, and Congress has to minimize legislative riders that might provoke a presidential veto.

When the 1999 legislative session opened, the two branches had a recent precedent to guide them through the budget maze. Just months earlier, Congress ended the 1998 session by negotiating an omnibus appropriations act with the president that included $21 billion in emergency supplemental spending (see box 5-4). Enacted in October 1998, a mere three weeks into the new fiscal year, that measure started with President Clinton asking for $9 billion in emergency spending, Republicans then added their own list of priority items at a cost of $5 billion, and congressional Democrats anted up another $6 billion.

But that spending frenzy did not sate political appetites. In politics, emergency spending begets more emergency spending. The pressure to spend escalated: Clinton was seeking another $3 billion in emergency funds, revenues were surging into the Treasury, the budget surplus was growing, farmers were clamoring for additional aid, hurricanes ravaged Central American countries, and the United States promised to bankroll Israeli-Arab peace agreements.

Congressional Republicans, tarnished by their avid participation in the previous year's spending spree, opened legislative consideration of the supplemental by demanding that the additional spending be offset by cuts in other programs. Senate Appropriations Committee Chair Ted Stevens (R-Alaska) argued that "only defense funds [should be] rescinded to offset defense spending and only nondefense amounts to balance the nondefense spending." Clinton maintained, however, that the additional spending was "urgent, unanticipated, and essential"; hence, it should "be funded quickly, fully, and without requiring offsets that could force unanticipated reductions in important programs." He also urged Congress "not to add extraneous authorizations to the bill, particularly narrow, objectionable riders that would serve only to generate controversy, unnecessarily delaying the urgent needed assistance contained in this bill."

The House and Senate disregarded Clinton's demands, but the two chambers passed very different bills. The House bill cost about half as much as the Senate's and targeted different items for rescissions. The House applied the emergency designation to some spending while the Senate proposed across-the-board cuts in the omnibus appropriations enacted in the previous session. Clinton criticized both bills and threatened a veto if the offsets were retained.

Before House-Senate differences could be worked out in conference, the United States began military operations in the Balkans, leading the president to request another $6 billion in emer-

continued

▼

BOX 4-1
Continued

gency spending. With the supplemental at a level that ruled out legitimate offsets, the House Appropriations Committee entered into a bidding war to boost defense spending. Adding money for dozens of projects the Pentagon had not requested, the committee reported a $13 billion emergency supplemental. Speaker Dennis Hastert (R-Ill.) defended the committee's action, claiming that the armed forces had been "hollowed out" by six years of Clinton-imposed budget cuts. For his part, the president again asked Congress to "resist the temptation to add unrelated expenditures." Despite this urging, more than half of the House Democrats joined with Republicans to pass the bill by a lopsided margin.

The Senate did not bother to take up the military supplemental. Instead it opted to get what it wanted in the conference. The first thing that the House-Senate conference did was to package the military supplemental into the hurricane relief bill, in effect giving Clinton the message that the price for getting the latter would be to accept the former.

In conference, Democratic and Republican senators vied for the most costly add-ons to the bill. Senator Pete Domenici (R-N. Mex.) wanted a $500 million loan program for oil and gas companies. Not to be outdone, Senator Robert Byrd (D-W.Va.) demanded $1 billion in guaranteed loans for steel companies. In a burst of Sunbelt cooperation, Senators Bob Graham (D-Fla.) and Kay Bailey Hutchinson (R-Texas) insisted on a provision allowing states unrestricted use of $246 billion in tobacco settlement money. And in a display of corn and wheat state harmony, Democratic senators Tom Harkin (Iowa) and Byron Dorgan (N. Dak.) lobbied for $5 billion in emergency aid for farmers. In addition to these spending items, a slew of legislative riders dealing with (among other things) fishing rights in Alaska, dumping waste on federal lands, and the endangered silvery minnow and Alabama sturgeon were proposed in conference.

Not surprisingly, some in Congress who were not fortunate enough to have a front seat at the conference were upset by what had happened. Representative James Leach (R-Iowa) pleaded that "emergency supplementals should never be a vehicle for passage of measures that under ordinary conditions would be viewed with utmost skepticism." But Senator Pat Roberts (R-Kans.) explained why the riders were placed in the supplemental; it "was the only vehicle we had at the time."

For the first time, an appropriations conference was televised, giving the public an unusual glimpse of the give-and-take by which compromises are forged and legislation is passed. Representative Randy Cunningham (R-Calif.) said, "Most of us who watched . . . were appalled. It made the term 'good government' an oxymoron." Many of the controversial riders and some of the additional spending were dropped in conference, but the final tally was $15 billion. Senator Stevens used the fig leaf of "emergency" to assure his colleagues that "this additional money will remain safely in the U.S. Treasury and will only be used if the President determines emergencies exist that require the expenditure of these funds." Clinton thanked Congress for the supplemental and for ensuring that the government "will continue to be there for [American families] throughout their time of need."

advance appropriations. He proposed that $14 billion of advance appropriations made the previous year be shifted back to fiscal 2000. Under this guise, the $14 billion was not charged to the fiscal 2000 caps when they were enacted, nor to the fiscal 2001 caps when the money was spent. The government got $14 billion more to spend, and both the president and Congress declared with a straight face that they were living within the caps.

Delayed Obligations

In this scheme, which was applied in fiscal 2000 appropriations to the National Institutes of Health and other agencies, a portion of the appropriation is withheld from obligation by law until the last days of the fiscal year. Although the new budget authority is scored in the year for which appropriations are made, the outlays are deferred to the next year. This approach has been used when the cap on outlays is tighter than that on budget authority.

Delayed Payment

A related practice is to declare in an appropriations act that some payments are to be delayed until the next fiscal year. The effect is to reduce the estimated spendout rate and the amount of outlays scored against the appropriation. In 2000, some government workers and military personnel had their payday, which fell on the last Saturday in September, delayed until the next fiscal year. By delaying the payment for one day, over $4 billion in spending was shifted to fiscal 2001.

Effectiveness of the Caps

In constant dollars, discretionary domestic spending fared better under the caps in the 1990s than it did in the previous decade when

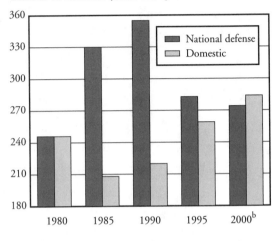

FIGURE 4-2
Discretionary Defense and Domestic Outlays, Five-Fiscal-Year Intervals, 1980–2000[a]

Billions of constant (fiscal 1996) dollars

Source: *Budget of the United States, Historical Tables, Fiscal Year 2001*, table 8.2, p. 118.
a. International discretionary spending is omitted. It has remained fairly constant during the period covered here, accounting for only 4.9 percent of total discretionary outlays in 1980 and an estimated 3.6 percent in 2000.
b. Estimated.

there were no caps. These programs declined 14 percent in the 1980s but increased 21 percent during the next decade. As figure 4-2 indicates, real discretionary domestic spending was significantly higher at the start of the millennium than it was when Ronald Reagan launched his campaign to roll back social programs. But despite the dollar increases in this part of the budget, it has not recovered as a share of GDP; discretionary domestic spending was 4.7 percent of GDP in 1981 but only 3.1 percent nineteen years later.

Most of the increases for domestic programs came at the expense of the other major component of discretionary spending—national defense. Adjusted for inflation, defense outlays were $106 billion less in 1999 than

TABLE 4-4
Defense Force Structure, Five-Fiscal-Year Intervals, 1980–2000

Defense force	1980	1985	1990	1995	2000[a]
Active Army divisions	16	17	18	12	10
Active Marine divisions	3	3	3	3	3
Total Naval ships	477	542	546	373	314
Active Air Force tactical wings	26	25	24	13	13
Active duty personnel (in thousands)[b]	3,053	3,335	3,216	2,432	2,149

Source: Congressional Research Service, *Defense Budget for Fiscal 2000: Data Summary*, February 16, 1999, table 9, and Office of the Under Secretary of Defense (Comptroller), *National Defense Budget Estimates for Fiscal 2000*, March 1999, table 7-5.
   a. Estimated.
   b. Includes military and civilian personnel.

they had been a decade earlier. Steep cutbacks in defense forces mirrored this drop. During the 1990s the Army lost eight of its eighteen active divisions, the Air Force disbanded almost half of its active tactical air wings, the Navy deactivated more than 40 percent of the fleet, and the Pentagon shed one-third (nearly one million) of its civilian and active duty military personnel (table 4-4). Regardless of the caps, if the Cold War were still raging, there probably would have been no surplus in 1998 or in subsequent years.

Through most of the 1990s the president and Congress managed to live with the discretionary spending caps, but political nature being what it is, the constraint could not withstand the good times of a revenue surge and expanding economy. Clinton prodded Congress to vote for marginal increases in discretionary appropriations while claiming a commitment to controlling the budget and reducing the size of government. Although the amounts were large in dollar terms—discretionary outlays rose from $549 billion in 1997 to approximately $618 billion three years later—the amounts were too small to derail the march to a balanced budget. A year after the deficit was liquidated, Clinton and the Congress resorted to a slew of mechanisms to spend $49 billion more than the caps allowed

(table 4-5). The following year in his fiscal 2001 budget, Clinton designated this amount as "spending funded by alternative mechanisms" and proposed to shift $14 billion in advance appropriations and certain other funds back to fiscal 2000.

The caps have not worked perfectly, as the heightened reliance on loopholes shows, but politicians have a strong incentive to continue them because the caps foster an appearance of fiscal discipline. At this writing, Clinton proposed to extend the caps for ten years. While final decisions have yet to be made, there is a high probability that the caps will be extended in the years ahead. The extent to which future caps are effective depends on the state of the budget. If the surplus declines or the budget tightens, the caps will play a prominent role in constraining federal spending. If the budget continues to be awash in revenue, it is inevitable that a portion of the bounty will be spent on expanding federal programs.

Direct Spending

Most of the tactics described below can be applied to both discretionary and direct spending. The following paragraphs elaborate how some methods have been used to influence the scoring of the latter.

TABLE 4-5
Spending Outside the Caps: Fiscal 2000 Appropriations[a]

Billions of dollars

Tactic	Budget authority	Outlays
Designated as emergency spending		
Defense Department operations and maintenance	7.2	5.4
Decennial census	4.5	3.8
Defense Department pay raise	1.8	1.8
Head Start	1.7	0.9
Other	8.5	2.6
Subtotal emergency spending	23.7	14.3
Offsets		
Federal Reserve balance transfer	3.8	3.8
Acceleration of spectrum auction receipts	2.6	2.6
Other	2.4	2.5
Subtotal offsets	8.7	8.8
Delayed obligations and delayed payments		
Pay delay	. . .	3.6
Defense progress payments	. . .	1.3
National Institutes of Health	. . .	0.9
Other	. . .	0.8
Subtotal delayed obligations and delayed payments	. . .	6.5
Fiscal 2001 advance appropriations		
Housing certificate fund	4.2	. . .
Special education	3.7	. . .
Training and employment services	2.5	. . .
School improvement programs	1.5	. . .
Administration for children and families	1.4	. . .
Other	1.1	. . .
Subtotal advance appropriations	14.4	. . .
Total	49.3	29.8

Source: Office of Management and Budget, *Final Sequestration Report*, January 25, 2000, table 2, pp. 4–6.
   a. Amounts may not add to subtotals due to rounding.

Backloaded Spending Increases

The easiest way to remove a spending increase from the score is to schedule it to take effect beyond the period covered by the baseline. This tactic facilitated major expansions in Medicaid enacted in the late 1980s and early 1990s. The expansions were phased in over more than a decade, with the result that they were never scored as spending increases. When enacted, the first year of expansion was beyond the baseline period; when that year finally was incorporated into the baseline, the expansion already was authorized by current law.

With the lengthening of baselines to ten years, it is harder to make new spending disappear. However, Congress can still reduce the score by scheduling a portion of the spending increase to take effect late in the baseline period.

Offsets

The fingerprints rule dictates that offsets to direct spending increases come from revenue or substantive legislation, not from measures in the jurisdiction of the appropriations committees. At times Congress exploits differences between Medicare and Medicaid to generate more spending in the latter by making small cuts in the former. Because it shares Medicaid responsibility with the states, the federal government pays less than 60 percent of the program's cost. However, it pays all of Medicare's expenses. This means that a $1 cut in Medicare makes room in the budget for almost $2 in Medicaid increases. The typical Medicare cuts involve reductions in payments to providers below baseline levels and an increase or extension in premiums; it rarely entails cuts in covered services.

Assessing the Impact of PAYGO

In addition to considering the scoring rules and the tactics used to lower the score, one must assess the budgetary and political contexts in which PAYGO has operated in order to evaluate its impact. Inasmuch as direct spending changes are calculated in reference to the baseline, Congress and the president can make room for spending cuts that do not impair program activity by using assumptions that raise the baseline. This game has been played repeatedly in Medicare, generating hundreds of billions of dollars in scored cuts without cutting any benefits. Although some of the claimed savings from publicized cutbacks have been illusory and had a small net effect on federal spending, they have been ap-

plied to offset the cost of benefits enhancements. At century's end, Clinton transformed the Medicare debate from a preoccupation with the retirement boom to a discussion of whether to add prescription drugs to the list of eligible benefits.

PAYGO has also significantly affected congressional behavior. Although it has not halted the enactment of new spending and revenue legislation, it has changed the types of measures Congress produces. Welfare, in the form of Aid to Families with Dependent Children (AFDC), was converted from an open-ended entitlement to a fixed block grant, and important changes were made in eligibility rules and program benefits to move recipients from welfare to work. When these reforms were enacted in 1996, official estimates projected a six-year savings of $54 billion. But because of the steep, largely unexpected decline in welfare rolls—6.5 million fewer recipients in 1998 than in 1993—welfare reform boosted spending (above what it might have been if the old program had been continued). Over the longer term, however, welfare spending will decline if the block grants and limits on eligibility remain. Another overhaul in 1996 was of agricultural price supports, but it is doubtful that the projected savings will be realized. Whenever the farm sector runs into trouble, Congress and the president pour in billions of dollars of emergency money.

PAYGO contributed to the liquidation of budget deficits by hampering enactment of new direct spending legislation and making it easier for the government to hold on to its revenue dividend (PAYGO's impact on revenue legislation is discussed in chapter 7). Congress now favors targeted tax cuts rather than across-the-board reductions because the former loses much less revenue than the latter. During the revenue surge in the 1990s, Clinton adroitly used PAYGO to thwart Republican demands for slashing tax rates, despite the emergence of a surplus and a steep rise in federal revenue as a share of the gross domestic product (GDP). However, without Clinton's strong opposition, PAYGO would not have sufficed to block the proposed across-the-board tax relief.

ECONOMIC ARITHMETIC

Assumptions about the future performance of the economy are among the main variables in constructing budget baselines. The relationship of the budget and the economy is reciprocal: budget policy influences economic performance, and economic conditions influence budget outcomes. The size of the budget surplus or deficit, the structure and amount of taxes, the pattern of expenditure, and the volume of debt financing affect economic growth, employment levels, price changes, interest rates, and other variables. In making budget decisions, the president and Congress must be mindful of the potential impacts on the economy. They must also take into account the impact of current and projected economic conditions. They must make assumptions about nominal and real growth, inflation and employment trends, and interest rates. The president's budget usually forecasts economic performance for the current and next five calendar years; Congress relies on CBO's projections, which typically vary slightly from the president's.

Because the budget, like the baseline, is predicated on assumptions, the extent to which revenue and spending expectations are achieved depends significantly on whether assumed economic conditions materialize. Variances between assumed and actual conditions may translate into significant discrepancies between expected and actual budget results. Table 4-6 shows the budget's high sensitivity to swings in economic conditions. Much of

the budget's adjustment to economic change is automatic; it occurs without presidential or congressional action and whether it is welcome or not. Outlays are sensitive to interest rates and inflation. Revenues are particularly sensitive to growth rates: a shortfall in economic performance invariably means lower-than-projected receipts. Even a minor shortfall can take a big bite out of federal revenues.

A temporary deviation from the expected economic course has lingering effects. According to OMB estimates (from which table 4-6 is drawn), if actual growth were one percentage point less than forecast in 2000 but achieved expected levels in each of the next five years, the fiscal 2005 surplus would be $38 billion less than the amount projected five years earlier. Approximately 60 percent of the shortfall would in revenues.

The most recent recession (as of this writing) occurred in 1990–91. By standard measures, it was brief and shallow, lasting barely a year and causing a decline of only 0.9 percent in real growth. Although the recession was a blip in a long-term growth trend, it contributed to the peak deficit of $290 billion in fiscal 1992. The recession left an imprint on the budget for the next three to five years, for though the deficit declined, it remained much higher than it would have been if economic growth had not been interrupted at the start of the decade.

The longer the economy veers off course, the greater the impact on the budget. If economic growth were one percentage point lower each year from 2000 through 2005, the surplus in the fifth year would be $146 billion below projections. The variance from budgeted levels widens each year the economy stagnates. One percentage point lower growth would subtract an estimated $9 billion from federal revenues in the first year and $126 billion in the sixth year; a one percentage point rise in interest rates would add $5 billion to

TABLE 4-6
Budget Sensitivity to Variances from Economic Projections, Fiscal Years 2000–05[a]

Billions of dollars

Assumption	2000	2001	2002	2003	2004	2005
Real growth: 1 percentage point less than projected in 2000; growth as projected in later years[b]						
Receipts	–9	–18	–22	–22	–23	–24
Outlays	2	7	8	9	11	14
Surplus decrease	–11	–25	–29	–32	–35	–38
Real growth: 1 percentage point less than projected each year, 2000–05						
Receipts	–9	–27	–50	–73	–99	–126
Outlays	0	1	3	7	12	19
Surplus decrease	–9	–28	–53	–80	–111	–146
Inflation: 1 percentage point more than projected each year, 2000–05						
Receipts	9	27	47	66	88	112
Outlays	1	6	12	20	28	36
Surplus increase	7	21	34	46	60	76
Interest rates: 1 percentage point more than projected each year, 2000–05						
Receipts	1	4	4	5	5	6
Outlays	5	12	15	17	17	17
Surplus decrease	–3	–9	–11	–12	–12	–11

Source: *Budget of the United States, Analytical Perspectives, Fiscal Year 2001*, table 1-6, p. 15.
a. Numbers may not add to totals due to rounding.
b. Assumes half a percentage point rise in the unemployment rate.

federal outlays in the first year and $17 billion in the sixth year.

Scoring the Economic Effects of Policy Changes

When CBO and OMB score legislation, they generally estimate the behavioral changes that would ensue from policy changes. For example, when Congress increased the earned income tax credit for the working poor, budget scorers estimated the costs that would result from giving more people an incentive to apply for this benefit. As a general rule, however, scorers do not consider possible changes in overall economic activity due to new legislation. For example, when the capital gains tax rate was lowered, the score did not include estimates of whether increased savings and investment might make the economy more productive and thereby boost federal revenues. But it did include an estimate of the capital gains that would be cashed in through the sale of stock and other assets.

The question of which economic impacts should be measured is often framed in terms of static versus dynamic scoring. Static scoring takes account of behavioral responses that can be reliably estimated; it does not measure changes in aggregate economic performance. Dynamic scoring includes macroeconomic effects such as changes in national output, employment levels, and investment. Differences between the two approaches can be significant: static scoring generally estimates that a lower capital gains rate will lose revenue; dynamic scoring concludes it will generate higher revenue.

Legislation is often promoted on the grounds that it will improve economic performance. If this is so, why is the feedback from the economy to the budget not included in the score? Why not incorporate dynamic models of economic impact? Those who oppose dynamic scoring offer two main justifications for excluding macroeconomic impacts: first, these effects are exceedingly difficult to measure; second, including them would open the door to opportunistic scoring that could damage the credibility of the budget. Taken to the extreme, dynamic scoring would generate perverse conclusions that the federal government raises more money when it taxes less, and spends less when it increases expenditures. These are the kinds of justifications that condemned the federal government to high deficits from the early 1980s to the late 1990s.

WHEN POLITICS MEETS ECONOMICS

The president and Congress are hostage to the performance of the economy. Because the future economy is uncertain when the budget is prepared, there are errors in revenue and spending projections. But because budget plans are based on assumed conditions, there may be an incentive to construct rosier economic scenarios than are warranted. This bias occurred in the early 1980s, when the Reagan administration projected that a booming economy would finance tax cuts and defense spending increases, and again later in the decade when the Gramm-Rudman-Hollings process threatened the automatic cancellation of budgetary resources if the projected deficit exceeded the targets set in law. Reagan won more tax cuts by pretending that the economic outlook was better than it was, and Congress and the president avoided sequestration by projecting a more favorable economic future than the facts indicated.

Even when there is no effort to manipulate economic forecasts for political advantage, it is extremely difficult to foretell when a recession will arrive, how deep or lasting it will be, and how long its impact on the budget will linger. In 40 years of budget watching, this writer can recall no instance in which a budget predicted a future recession or the worsening of an ongoing one.

The missteps of the 1980s had a chastening effect on politicians in the 1990s. During the long economic expansion that began in 1991 and continued into the next century, both the president and CBO repeatedly underestimated the rate of growth and resulting revenue. Part of the underestimate was due to the surprising strength of the economy, part to prudential budgeting. Regardless of the reason, the fact that the economy outperformed budget projections had much to do with the liquidation of the deficit.

The economy has the last word on the budget. There is a strong correlation between the rate of economic growth and the budget outcome. Fast, sustained growth is associated with small deficits or surpluses, slow growth with big, long-lasting deficits. The lesson of recent budget history is that cutting expenditures and raising taxes does not suffice to close the deficit when the economy is weak. The budget can grow out of a deficit only when the economy is sufficiently vigorous to produce incremental revenues that rise faster than the escalation in expenditures.

But this is not the only lesson. The evidence presented in chapter 2 clearly indicates that policy matters; budget decisions also influence the performance of the economy and therefore the size of the deficit or surplus. Stabilizing the budget requires realistic economic assumptions and realistic fiscal policies. Neither was present in the 1980s; both were in the 1990s. It is not inevitable that when politics and economics meet, the former corrupts the latter. It sometimes happens that good sense about the economy spurs politicians to do the right thing.

CONCLUSION

As budget enforcement has become more stringent and important, these rules have been elaborated, and what once was left to negotiation is now often codified. Some numbers are political and are compiled based on the preferences of those who make or implement budgets. Some numbers are economic or programmatic; they pertain to external factors that impinge on the budget. Many entries in the budget are composites of all three types.

When the budget states that a certain amount of outlays will be incurred in the food stamps program, the estimate is based on technical rules concerning the timing and recognition of transactions, political influences on projections of the number of food stamp recipients, and programmatic requirements concerning the benefits participants are entitled to receive.

In the private worlds of budgeting, where many of the numbers are compiled, technical considerations often prevail. But in the public arenas, political forces are on display, with politicians tweaking the budget at the margins to obtain more spending or tax cuts than a strict application of the technical rules would allow. Although only a few percentage points (or less) of the totals, the margins are the political battlegrounds in budgeting. They represent the incremental changes from one year to the next, differences between Democrats and Republicans, and elusive accommodations between the president and Congress. In budgetary battle each side is armed with numbers that make its case; the numbers disagree because the political combatants disagree. In the end, however, there can be budgetary peace only if presidential and congressional political arithmetic add up to the same numbers.

5

The President's Budget

The Constitution does not require the president to prepare a budget recommending the revenues and expenditures of the government. Nevertheless, the budget has become one of the president's recurring obligations as well as one of his most important policy tools to set legislative and program objectives while charting the nation's fiscal course. Early in each legislative session, normally the first Monday in February, the president submits an annual budget to Congress. The executive budget estimates spending, revenues, and other financial amounts for the next five or more fiscal years, contains policy and legislative recommendations consistent with those estimates, presents data on the actual and projected performance of the economy, and provides detailed information on the finances of federal agencies and programs.

As detailed in chapter 2, the Budget and Accounting Act of 1921 provides the legal basis for the presidential budget system. Before the law was enacted, the federal government did not have a comprehensive budget system. Agencies submitted financial schedules to the secretary of the treasury, who compiled them in an annual *Book of Estimates*. The president was not formally involved in the process, although some activity intervened to influence Congress's revenue and spending decisions. The 1921 act made the president responsible for the national budget by requiring him to prepare and submit revenue and spending estimates to Congress annually. The act established the Bureau of the Budget, now the Office of

Management and Budget (OMB), to assist him in formulating and implementing the executive budget. Although amended many times, this statute is still the principal legal source of the president's budget power. It prescribes some of the budget's form and content and also defines the responsibilities of the president and spending agencies in the process.

The president's budget is only a request to Congress; federal agencies can neither spend money nor initiate programs based on the president's recommendations. Congress is not required to adopt the recommendations, and it typically makes hundreds of changes in the course of appropriating funds and acting on legislation. Still, the president's proposals are often the starting point for congressional revenue and spending actions. The extent of presidential influence varies from year to year, however, and is dependent upon political and economic conditions.

PRESIDENTIAL ROLES AND STYLES

The formal role assigned to the president by the Budget and Accounting Act does not tell the full story of presidential involvement in the budget process. Each president brings to the office personal characteristics, along with political skills and weaknesses. Some are interested in financial matters and welcome the opportunity to make expenditure policy; others distance themselves from the budget and its myriad decisions and details. Some have robust program ambitions that can be realized only by shaping the budget to their liking; others have limited agendas that can be served with status quo budgets. Some seek to avoid friction in the annual budget and appropriations cycle; others see conflict as a necessary means of promoting their program objectives.

A comparison of Bill Clinton and other recent presidents reveals significant differences in their budgetary styles and roles (box 5-1). Clinton did not run for president to serve as the chief budget officer of the United States. During his first election campaign in 1992, he concentrated on domestic issues: jobs, the economy, education, and health care. But once elected, he made the budget his highest legislative priority for 1993. Later in his presidency, Clinton again gave top billing to budgetary matters. In 1995 he opposed efforts by a new Republican majority in Congress to make significant cutbacks in various domestic programs, and again in 1997 he negotiated an agreement with the Republicans that included modest spending increases and some tax cuts and allowed him to take credit for balancing the budget. Clinton's level of involvement—sending Congress change-oriented budgets and actively wielding his veto pen when Congress proposed bills that ran counter to his budgetary preferences—welled out of personal temperament and political calculation.

George Bush, Clinton's predecessor, was largely disengaged from the budget process. Bush left the task of formulating and negotiating major budget policies to Richard Darman, his wily OMB director. In fact, Bush alone among post–World War II presidents submitted budgets without a presidential message setting forth his major policies. Instead, Darman signed the policy statement printed in the budget. Bush was also on the sidelines when the economy went into a mild recession in 1990–91 and was maneuvered into signing a 1990 tax increase that was sharply at variance with his oft-stated "no new taxes" pledge (see box 5-1). But the president paid a political price for distancing himself from the budget. He was defeated for reelection in 1992 and never got political credit for taking the first strong steps to liquidate the budget deficit.

In budgeting, as in other areas of national policy and presidential activity, Clinton and

---

BOX 5-1
The Age of Negotiated Budgets

Reagan Presidency: Unofficial Negotiations That Led to Tax Increases and Spending Cuts in 1982:
"The Gang [White House aides and members of Congress] conducted its meetings at Blair House, at Jim Baker's home, at the residence of Vice President Bush, and at other unusual locations to conceal the meetings from the press, and also from others in the administration and Congress. By the time the package was finally presented to President [Ronald Reagan], it was treated virtually as a *fait accompli*—something to which 'the process' had committed us. The President, along with cabinet members and senior advisors not in the Gang, was briefed on the TEFRA [Tax Equity and Fiscal Responsibility Act of 1982] proposal and participated in decision meetings with congressional leaders; but the legislative package was rolling ahead with such momentum—in the news media and among both parties in Congress—that it would have been virtually impossible to stop or even modify it."

Bush Presidency: Formal Negotiations That Produced the Reconciliation Act in 1990:
"President [George Bush] met for 1 hour and 40 minutes this afternoon with congressional budget negotiators to consider a federal budget that would reduce the deficit substantially on a multiyear basis, allow the economy to continue to grow, strengthen the budget process, and avoid the adverse economic and programmatic effects of a stalemate that otherwise might ensue. The President and the negotiators agreed that it was important to reach an agreement as soon as possible. The President discussed the reasons for these summit meetings. . . . The President concluded his opening remarks by saying, 'The American people are tired of seeing the budget process seem to fail year after year. They would welcome our doing the job right and our fixing the process at the same time.'

The congressional leadership gave opening remarks concerning their interest in achieving a suc-

continued

Bush were very different chief executives. The budget bore Clinton's imprint: he actively participated in making budget policy, was well informed on matters in dispute, and was familiar with salient details of federal programs (box 5-2). He made decisions concerning the size and direction of government, the composition of tax legislation, and the shape of policy initiatives. He invested time in mastering the details of the budget, meeting with department heads to discuss their budgets and to resolve issues that remained after OMB completed its review.

Clinton was not the first president who

shaped the budget to his will. Ronald Reagan put his stamp on the budget in 1981 (his first year in office) when he won enactment of major revenue and spending changes. Like Clinton, Reagan had to fight to get his budget through Congress. But in policy preferences, the two presidents moved in opposite directions. Reagan lowered taxes, Clinton raised them; Reagan boosted defense spending and slashed social programs, Clinton trimmed defense while adding to social expenditures. Yet these ideologically different presidents took similar approaches to the budget. Both under-

▼

BOX 5-1
Continued

cessful agreement, and all indicated a shared responsibility by both branches of the Government to reach agreement."

Clinton Presidency: Breakdown in Negotiations That Shut Down Part of the Government in 1995–96:

"President [Bill Clinton] has been working since the very good meeting on Saturday with a cross-section of Democratic members of the House and the Senate to see if we can't frame some of these budget issues in a way that will break this impasse and move the balanced budget discussions forward. We've had good conversations. There are some different approaches within the Democratic caucus, but the President is working with all points of view within the Democratic caucus to see if we can't have a more unified approach. And we're encouraged by the discussions that we've been having.

He's been doing a lot of work on this personally. He had a long meeting on Saturday, as you know, with Democratic members. And we believe it's important and vital to move forward with the balanced budget discussions and achieve the result the American people want. . . .

He's got specific ideas that he will be willing to entertain. But this has got to be a negotiation in which both sides show flexibility. And certainly, there's no one who would dispute the notion that the President has been flexible, has been willing to address the concerns of the Republican majority in Congress, has been willing to adopt their timetable for consideration of a balanced budget. What we've failed to see thus far is any sign of flexibility on their part that would acknowledge the importance of the President's priorities."

Sources: Edwin Meese III, *With Reagan: The Inside Story* (Regnery Gateway, 1992), p. 145; Office of the Press Secretary, White House, "Statement by Press Secretary Fitzwater on the Federal Budget Negotiations," May 15, 1990; Office of the Press Secretary, White House, "Press Briefing by Press Secretary Mike McCurry," December 18, 1995.

stood that political success depends on changing budget policies, acted to reshape budget policy almost immediately after taking office, and got Congress to pass most of what they wanted. Both invested much time and political resources in the budget, and both fought to obtain the votes that gave them a slim margin of victory.

One triumph does not make a presidency, nor does it ensure that an early success will last. Every year is a new budgetary battle for the president—fresh opportunity to get Congress to do his bidding. Reagan's first eight

months of budgetary blitzkrieg and legislative accomplishment were followed by more than seven years of political conflict and budgetary stalemate. In 1994, the year after his great budget victory, Clinton suffered the greatest legislative defeat of his presidency—the failure of Congress to reform the health care system. Clinton and Congress ended the 1995 budget cycle with a protracted impasse that shut down parts of the government. The conflict resumed in subsequent years, but the two sides managed to patch up differences without surrendering their most important objectives.

▼

BOX 5-2
Role of President Clinton in Fiscal Year 1995 Budget Formulation

Remarks by OMB Director Leon Panetta:

"The President yesterday, as [Chief of Staff Mack] McLarty pointed out, completed the final decision-making process for the fiscal year 1995 budget. . . . We had, initially, a two-hour overview meeting with the President on November 29. And then, after that, spent almost 15 hours meeting with every one of the Cabinet secretaries, as well as the key agency heads to discuss their budgets. He met with 21 departments and agency heads during that process. The meetings began on December 2 [and] concluded last Friday, December 17. . . .

The meetings with department heads by a President were really unprecedented. Normally what has happened in the past is that Presidents only saw fit to meet with Cabinet members after some of the decisions had been made and only on appeals. President Clinton, however, felt it was essential that each department have the ability to present their case for their budget and then discuss the key issues with him before, not after, any final decisions were made. . . .

I would make a presentation at the beginning of the meeting that summarized the budget for that department and then addressed the major issues that demanded presidential attention. [T]he secretary was then allowed the opportunity to speak to the budget and to those issues. There was usually a question period that followed and a discussion period that followed. [T]he meetings themselves were attended by White House staff, as well as some of the NEC—National Economic Council—representatives.

The President spent a total of about six hours, then, this week [December 20 and 21] to go over the final issues [raised during the department meetings] and then made the final decisions yesterday. OMB basically went over the broad and specific issues with him on both specific departments as well as government-wide issues. And so the formal part of this process involved about 23 hours of meetings with the President.

The process now is basically a technical one because the numbers now are basically presented back to the departments and agencies. They, in turn, translate these decisions into what are literally hundreds of thousands of numbers that feed into our budget. And then [we at OMB] ultimately scrub those numbers to make sure they all fit together when we present the final budget on February 7."

Source: Office of the Press Secretary, White House, "Remarks by OMB Director Leon Panetta," December 22, 1993.

Many presidents have entered office viewing the budget as a powerful opportunity to advance their agendas; quite a few have left regarding the budget as an impediment to sweeping policy change. As they age in office, presidents perceive the budget more as an accumulation of past decisions than as a forum for making new ones.

Thus recent presidents have characteristically demanded more budget change during their first years in office than they have in later years. As the cost of meeting past commitments escalates and their political capital dwindles, presidents trim their ambitions and settle for status quo or incremental budgets.

Even when the president has early budget successes, follow-up victories may be difficult to achieve. Presidents use up political goodwill when they prod members of Congress to vote for spending cuts, as occurred in 1981, or for tax increases, as occurred a dozen years later. They cannot repeatedly demand allegiance from members who put their political careers at risk by supporting the president's budget preferences. Barely one month after winning enactment of far-reaching budget changes in the summer of 1981, Ronald Reagan was stymied when he sought another round of budget cuts. And less than one year after Congress approved his deficit reduction plan, Bill Clinton could not get Congress to reform the health care system.

Yet it is not always the case that the president's best budgetary days are behind him. Clinton recovered his political footing in 1995 and 1996 to block the efforts of congressional Republicans to restructure federal budget priorities. Clinton also had a strong role in the 1997 balanced budget agreement, which cut taxes and modestly increased domestic spending, as well as in the 1998 and 1999 appropriations end game. Clinton's continuing budgetary activism and influence was the result of many factors: he had public opinion on his side, congressional Republicans badly misread public preferences and were blamed for shutting down the government, Clinton proved to be a skillful negotiator who picked fights that he could win, and he was helped by an improving economy and a disappearing budget deficit. Clinton also effectively used the veto power to impose his own preferences on a recalcitrant Congress.

CHANGES IN PRESIDENTIAL BUDGETING

Whatever his disposition, no president can ignore the budget. Submitting the budget to Congress is one of the few tasks a president must complete each year, no matter how difficult the choices or how uncertain the outlook. The president must be attentive to how the budget is faring in Congress, and he must be prepared to intervene when salient issues are at stake. When the budget is released, the president's political standing is on the line; the media label it the Bush budget or the Clinton budget. The president's capacity to move legislation through Congress depends in some measure on how well his budget is received. "Dead on arrival" is the pundit's verdict that the president's budget carries little weight and will likely be ignored by Congress when it makes budget decisions. Through the budget, the president takes on responsibility for the performance of the economy and for policies that affect disposable income, prices, growth, and other key indicators. He cannot ignore budgetary responsibilities, even when the problems are not of his own making and the solutions are not readily at hand.

Even though all presidents must engage in budgeting, over the course of a generation there has been a fundamental change in the political status of the budget. This transformation has coincided with other developments that have weakened the chief executive's capacity to get what he wants from Congress. This weakening has its roots in Watergate and Vietnam—two failures that have been blamed on the misuse of presidential power.

During the heyday of presidential budgeting (after World War II), the annual budget served as a platform for the president's legislative program and as an authoritative statement of national policy. Every step of the way, when it appropriated money and considered tax legislation, Congress took into account what the president had requested. Although it made many changes, these tended to be small, so that the budget that came out of Congress looked pretty much like the budget sent to it. In some recent years, by contrast, the president's recommendations have been little more than opening bids in a bargaining process. Rather than revealing his true expectations at the outset, the president often submits unrealistic proposals that have no chance of adoption and whose main function is to position him for the tough negotiations at the end of the process.

This shift has resulted from such changes in federal budgeting as growing entitlements that constrain presidential initiative, tight budgets that have impelled presidents to ask Congress to cut spending and boost taxes, budget enforcement rules that limit what the president can request, greater congressional independence arising out of a long spell of divided government, increased activity by the many interest groups that monitor all stages of budgeting and offer detailed alternatives, and second-guessing of the president's budget by the Congressional Budget Office (CBO), the media, and others.

One of the most telling indicators of the changed status of the president's budget comes from the extensive use of baselines in making and scoring congressional budget actions. Before Congress used baselines, it typically made budget decisions by comparing its actions to the president's recommendations. The appropriations committees still operate in this manner, but nowadays all other congressional budget decisions are made in reference to CBO baseline projections. The baseline is completely unaffected by the president's budget. As a projection of revenue and spending, it assumes no change in policy; the baseline does not move up or down a single dollar if the president asks for more or less. The baseline is used by the budget committees in marking up the budget resolution, by authorizing committees in developing legislation and in responding to reconciliation instructions, by congressional scorekeepers in measuring the budget impact of pending or approved legislation, and in enforcing budget rules. Interest groups use the baseline to calculate whether their programs are being protected against inflation and to build a case for increased funding. It is no overstatement to assert that baselines have stolen much of the attention once accorded the president's budget.

A president can compensate for institutional weakness by investing political resources in defense of his budget. With the Democrats controlling both the legislative and executive branches, the fate of Clinton's budget in 1993 rested in their hands. Yet he had to bargain with members of his own party to secure the votes needed for passage. He fought hard for his budget that year, and despite a series of cliffhanger votes and compromises, the final version was close in its main lines to his original proposal. When the Republicans took control of Congress in 1995, Clinton was forced to negotiate with political adversaries whose budget priorities differed sharply from his own. Clinton won the 1995–96 battle of the budget by thwarting Republican efforts to cut back major social programs such as Medicare and Medicaid and winning additional spending for education and several other presidential priorities. Moreover, he had a strong role in shaping new tax legislation, and he succeeded in pinning blame on the Republicans for the temporary shutdown of some federal agencies. At the start of the battle, Clinton had a very low favorability rating in public opinion polls. By the end, a majority of Americans viewed his performance favorably. But the Republicans did not come away empty-handed, for they got Clinton to accept key portions of their budgetary agenda: a balanced budget, welfare reform, and tax cuts. Because each side could claim victory while protecting important budgetary objectives, each had a strong incentive to reach agreement despite the wide differences in budget policy.

Who wins these interbranch disputes depends on the relative political strength and bargaining skills of the two sides. Judging from Reagan's and Clinton's successes in budget negotiations, it appears that the president wins when he has a small number of attainable demands, does not allow the give and take of negotiations to dislodge him from key objectives, does a good job reading public opinion, and takes advantage of his veto power to block congressional actions that undermine his political standing. The president need not be familiar with the details of the negotiations—Reagan generally was not, Clinton was—but it is important that the president neither attempts to achieve too many objectives, nor allows the other side to redefine his objectives.

FORMULATING THE PRESIDENT'S BUDGET

Table 5-1 lists the principal responsibilities of the three sets of participants involved in preparing the executive budget: federal agencies, which request funds and carry out authorized programs; the Office of Management and Budget (OMB), which reviews agency requests, compiles the budget, and monitors congressional action and agency implementation; and the president, who has the final say on the policies set forth in the budget he submits to Congress.

Preparation of the budget typically begins in spring (or earlier) each year—at least nine months before the president transmits it to Congress, about eighteen months before the start of the fiscal year to which it pertains, and about thirty months before the close of that fiscal year. When agencies begin work on a future budget, they are also implementing the budget for the fiscal year in progress and

awaiting appropriations and other legislative decisions for the following year. In the spring of 1999, for example, most federal agencies were preparing their fiscal 2001 requests, months before they had the final results for fiscal 1999 or appropriations for fiscal 2000.

The long lead times and the fact that appropriations have not yet been made for the next fiscal year mean that agency budgets are prepared with a great deal of uncertainty about economic conditions, presidential policies, and congressional actions. Agencies cope with this uncertainty by keeping options open until late in the process, basing future budgets on past ones, and asking for more than they expect. Despite the lead times, few agencies do systematic, long-term budget planning because the same staffs that are preparing the next budget also are working on the current one. Budget preparation is a busy, deadline-driven activity, with many levels of review, enormous demands for data, and a compelling need to resolve intra- and interagency conflicts.

The length of the budget preparation cycle and the difficulty of using it as a means of establishing objectives and priorities are largely due to the bottom-up structure of budgeting. Departmental budgets usually are assembled in a decentralized manner, beginning at the lowest level of the organization capable of formulating its own request and progressing through successively higher echelons until all requests have been consolidated into a departmental budget. (Exhibit 5-1 lists the steps in preparing the budget for the National Institutes of Health.) However, some agencies provide policy guidance to operating units before getting into the details; most wait until requests have been assembled before making policy decisions. In most federal agencies, the divisions, branches, offices, and other administrative units prepare detailed estimates of expenditures for personnel, travel, supplies,

TABLE 5-1
Budget Functions of Executive Institutions

President	Office of Management and Budget (OMB)	Federal agencies
Establishes executive budget policy and submits annual budget to Congress	Operates executive budget system and advises the president on financial and other issues	Submit budget requests to OMB; appeal to the president for more funds
Submits supplemental requests, budget amendments, and updates to Congress	Issues procedural and policy guidelines to agencies	Justify president's budget recommendations before congressional committees
Signs or vetoes revenue, appropriations, and other budget-related measures passed by Congress	Issues passbacks to agencies and recommends budget levels to the president	Allot funds among subunits
Notifies Congress of proposed rescissions and deferrals	Compiles annual budget submitted to Congress	Maintain accounting systems and systems of internal control
Appoints the director of OMB and other executive officials	Reviews proposed legislation and testimony, and monitors congressional action on appropriations and other measures	Obligate funds and preaudit expenditures
Issues sequestration orders to cancel budget resources	Apportions funds and oversees implementation of the budget	Carry out activities for which funds were provided
	Scores revenue and spending legislation, as provided by the BEA	Prepare annual financial statements in accord with accounting standards
	Conducts management activities to improve efficiency of federal operations	Measure performance and develop performance-based budgets

equipment, and other items at each stage of the process. These details are reviewed, and usually revised, as the budget moves up the hierarchy. The result is that budget preparation is time-consuming and burdensome. Furthermore, budget preparation diverts managerial attention from other departmental concerns.

The bottom-up process has several characteristics that, some argue, diminish the use of budgeting as a means of establishing government policies and priorities. Since the 1960s a number of initiatives have been launched to give budgeting a more strategic and less incremental orientation. One of the most promi-

nent was the planning-programming-budgeting system (PPBS) first introduced in the Defense Department in 1961 by Robert MacNamara and prescribed for all federal agencies by President Lyndon Johnson in 1965. The most recent initiative has been under the Government Performance and Results Act of 1993 (GPRA), which directs agencies to prepare strategic and performance plans to act as guides during budget preparation. While PPBS and GPRA have numerous differences, they both seek a more top-down, output-oriented process. GPRA (more fully discussed in chapter 10) is still being phased in, so it is too early to assess its impact on federal agencies.

▶ **EXHIBIT 5-1**
National Institutes of Health Schedule for Budget Preparation

March–April	Development of preliminary budget, including submission of professional judgment budgets from ICDs (institutes, centers, divisions) to the National Institutes of Health (NIH)
May	NIH submits preliminary budget to the Public Health Service (PHS)
May	PHS initial allowances; NIH appeals and PHS final allowances
June	PHS submits department budget to the Department of Health and Human Services (DHHS)
July–August	DHHS initial allowances; PHS appeals and secretary's final allowances
September	DHHS submits budget to Office of Management and Budget (OMB)
November	OMB provides initial allowances (passback) to DHHS
November–December	DHHS appeals to OMB and president
December	OMB's and president's final policy decisions and allowances
January	DHHS and constituent units conform their budgets to presidential allowances

Source: Internal NIH memorandum.

(a) This budget calendar for the National Institutes of Health shows a bottom-up process in which lower administrative units submit requests to successively higher units. Some agencies use a more top-down approach, in which policy decisions are made at higher echelons and communicated to subordinate units, which then formulate requests consistent with these policies.

(b) The NIH budget process involves at least six levels: institutes, centers, divisions; the National Institutes of Health; the Public Health Service; the Department of Health and Human Services; the Office of Management and Budget; and the president.

(c) The basic steps at each level entail submission of the preliminary budget, issuance of allowance, appeals, and final decisions. Because of the number of levels and steps at each level, the budget cycle is started eighteen months or more before the beginning of the fiscal year.

(d) At the end of the process, DHHS and its administrative units conform their budgets to OMB and presidential decisions.

Incremental Budgeting

What GPRA has not yet accomplished and what PPBS could not do a generation ago is to wean federal budgeting away from the tendency toward incremental decisionmaking. Over the years most federal departments have budgeted on the expectation that virtually all activities funded in the current budget will be continued in the next and that program initiatives will be financed from incremental resources, not from cutbacks in existing programs. Agencies have therefore concentrated on how much more to seek for new or expanded programs and on how to respond to changes in government priorities. Agencies often propose modest savings in ongoing programs to show that they have lean, efficient operations, but this tactic is usually employed to get more money than they received for the current year.

Increments come in many sizes. The size appropriate for an ambitious agency that seeks to grow may not suit an agency that has modest budget objectives. The increases sought when a program rates high in public esteem or when increments are bountiful may be inappropriate for a low-priority program or when resources are tight. Agencies and programs do not grow uniformly, nor do they grow without interruption. Many go through periods in which funding is relatively stable, followed by growth spurts, followed by a return to stability. The spurts may be due to the entrepreneurial verve of agency officials, opportunities opened up by new legislation, shifts in public opinion, or a crisis. One of the vital skills of budgeting is to identify and exploit these opportunities by preparing budgets that suit the times.

What an agency (or one of its units) asks for influences what it gets. An agency that requests negligible increases will not get big increases but also might go through the process without OMB or Congress making significant changes. One that seeks substantial growth may get more, but at the risk of having its budget closely reviewed and revised.

Incremental budgeting requires incremental resources supplied by either a growing economy, as was the case in the 1950s and 1960s, or by deficit financing, as occurred in the 1980s. As long as the economy is growing or the government is willing to borrow, it is possible to concentrate on the increment—the extent to which next year's allocations should vary from this year's—and to spend little time reexamining past commitments and ongoing programs. When neither of these conditions suffices to cover the future cost of existing programs, incremental behavior may not be sustainable. For example, during the 1990s incrementalism became untenable in the defense budget because of a steep decline in the real resources spent on military forces. Due to the end of the Cold War and efforts to curtail federal deficits, real defense outlays dropped by one-third between 1989 and 1998, forcing the Pentagon to shed forces and close many facilities. Some critics argue that even in downsizing the Defense Department held on to its incremental mind-set, for the military did not sufficiently reconfigure its budget in response to the change in international conditions facing the United States in the post–Cold War era.

The President's Role

Where does the president fit into the agency-centered budget process? Does he have any significant input during the early stages, when agencies prepare their estimates, or is his influence concentrated at the end when the final decisions are made? In a formal sense, the answer is that the president can intervene throughout the process to communicate his priorities, give directions to agency submissions, and set limits on the amounts and things they ask for. In fact, shortly after one year's budget is sent to Congress, OMB gives each department an allowance letter that specifies the base for the next budget cycle. Nevertheless, in a bottom-up process it is inevitable that the president's main input comes in the final stages, after agencies have submitted their requests.

The extent to which the president is involved in the earliest stages has changed over the years. During the boom years of economic and program expansion, especially during the 1960s and early 1970s, OMB had a formal process, known as "spring preview," in which it developed and communicated to federal agencies presidential guidelines for the next fiscal year. OMB gave each agency dollar targets (relatively fixed in some years, elastic in others), as well as guidance on issues to be considered in that year's budget cycle. During the 1980s this process withered away, probably because of OMB and White House preoccupation with congressional budget actions and also because they did not want premature leaks of the president's budget decisions. Without the preview, agencies often commence budget work before the president's policies have been formally transmitted to them. Some presidents, such as Clinton, have issued policy directives early in the process to guide agencies in compiling their budgets; others, such as Bush, have not entered the process until agencies assembled their requests.

The lack of robust increments and limited presidential participation in early budget preparation have the potential to weaken the president's influence. When increments are plentiful, the president could intervene late in the process by allocating some or all of the additional resources to his priorities. When his principal objective is to cut spending, the president could intervene late and impose cutbacks. The former pattern generally characterized budgeting in the Kennedy-Johnson years; the latter predominated during the Reagan administration. When the president lacks incre-

ments but still seeks major program initiatives, he may find his options limited if he waits until the last minute to put his stamp on the budget.

Whatever the advantages of early presidential involvement, it is naive to assume that matters thought to have been settled by presidential guidelines at the start will remain settled through the give and take of budget negotiations. There always is some trimming needed at the end because there is always some presidential idea that needs to be accommodated in the budget. Dozens of decisions are made in the home stretch, when all the numbers have been tallied and the deadline nears for sending the budget to the printer. Defense spending typically is one of the last decisions, kept open until the final stages because the amounts are so large and billions can be quickly added or subtracted by decisions on big-ticket purchases and the size of the armed forces.

The Details of Budgeting

To budget is to compile, review, and decide many thousands of details pertaining to the operations of federal agencies, program levels, and payments to recipients of federal dollars. Even an active president, such as Bill Clinton, cannot master all of the details. Every president must focus on the relatively small number of issues that matter most to him and leave the rest to the affected agencies or OMB staff. Executive budgeting proceeds, in effect, on two tracks: one is agency-centered; the other deals with matters of interest to the president. The agency-centered process focuses on operational details: activities and projects; salaries, equipment, supplies, and other items; and the costs of programs, such as grants and transfer payments. The presidential process concentrates on proposed changes in program levels, the legislative initiatives to be included in the budget, and other policy decisions. The agency-centered process is much more detailed than the presidential one. The latter may entail several hundred decisions; the former requires thousands. The two processes overlap—many agency concerns are also of interest to the president. Nevertheless, it is useful to distinguish between the two processes because they point to an important evolution in the preparation of the executive budget. Over the years the White House has withdrawn from many details of budgeting, leaving them to the agencies or intervening only when they see an advantage in doing so. This conserves the president's time and political resources, enabling him to defer serious review of agency requests until late in the cycle, typically in November or December (as the schedule in exhibit 5-1 indicates). Late intervention reduces premature leaks of presidential decisions and enables the White House to control the spin on budget news.

Many budget issues that matter a great deal to the affected agency are of little concern to the White House. But some agency matters are inherently of ongoing interest to the president. One such matter is the total cost of operations; another is the number of employees. Recent presidents have squeezed operating expenses in order to make room within the caps for program expenditures. Staffing levels attract presidential interest because the number of employees is a popular indicator of whether the government is growing or shrinking.

The agency-centered process is time-consuming because an enormous number of details have to be filled in at each step. In 1993 the National Performance Review (NPR)— the "reinventing government" campaign led by Vice President Al Gore—proposed shortening the budget preparation cycle to make it more relevant to presidential concerns. NPR proposed that the president have a more prominent role at the start by establishing policies and priorities that would guide the agencies in

compiling their requests. But the president would have a more limited role in reviewing agencies' requests during the final stages. NPR assumed that if agencies drafted their budgets in accord with presidential instructions, there would be little need to review them at the end. Moreover, NPR recommended that agencies should draw up detailed estimates after policy decisions have been made rather than before. In this way agencies would focus on presidential objectives and program performance, not on the detailed items of expenditure.

Yet the details persist in agency budgeting. One reason is that the details are important to the agencies. Managers want to know how much they will have to spend on operations, the amount that will be available for staff resources, and whether the budget will cover price increases. Detailed budgeting is reinforced by the demands of congressional committees, especially the appropriations committees, which require extensive documentation of agency requests. The justification material submitted to these committees (discussed in chapter 9) typically contains line-item explanations of the amounts requested for salaries, supplies, and other items. Eliminating the details would affect the role of the appropriations committees and Congress in controlling federal expenditures. The issue is an old one—the power of the purse. It is not simply a matter of the amount of time spent on preparing the budget, nor of the relationship between the president and federal agencies. Agencies care about the details because they expect to be questioned by congressional committees about them.

THE OFFICE OF MANAGEMENT AND BUDGET

Most of the president's budget work is entrusted to political and career staff in the Office of Management and Budget, a 500-person agency situated in the Executive Office of the

President. OMB handles almost all the paperwork, makes most presidential budget decisions, and puts together the budget submitted to Congress. In addition, OMB leverages its budgetary power to prod federal agencies to improve their managerial practices.

The Bureau of the Budget was established in the same 1921 law that created the executive budget process. Over the past eight decades, the evolution of OMB has paralleled changes in the organization and role of the presidency. At the start, the Bureau of the Budget was placed in the Treasury Department. A modern, well-staffed presidential office had not yet emerged, and the bureau's principal task was to constrain federal spending. The bureau's staff was small, but it single-mindedly and successfully kept spending low. Then came the Depression and the New Deal, as well as a reorientation and enlargement of the president's staff. In 1939 the bureau moved into the newly established Executive Office of the President, where it was assigned overall responsibility for federal management. It also took the lead in developing the president's legislative program and in reviewing legislation to determine whether proposed measures, or ones passed by Congress, accorded with the president's priorities. After World War II it became customary for the president to prepare a legislative program in tandem with the budget. In the 1960s the bureau further expanded its portfolio of presidential responsibilities, using the budget as an instrument of economic policy and making tax and spending decisions in light of intended impacts on growth, prices, and employment.

In 1970 Richard Nixon reorganized the Bureau of the Budget into the Office of Management and Budget. While the ostensible aim was to strengthen OMB's role in coordinating government activities, the main impact was to make OMB more responsive to the president's

political interests. Before the reorganization, the agency (which then numbered 600) had fewer than half a dozen political appointees; after the reorganization, the political staff grew to as many as two dozen. Direct interaction between career staff and the White House diminished. Political appointees, who come with one president and depart with the next, now handle major policy chores.

This arrangement has persisted since the 1970s, but each president has tinkered with it to suit his style. Through it all, OMB has managed to give the president expert advice while carrying out his policy agenda. Balancing the two is not easy, especially now that OMB's judgments often are second-guessed by CBO, which has earned a reputation in Washington as being less partisan and more credible. When the two institutions disagree, media and seasoned observers generally rely on CBO's numbers, not because they have been proved more accurate, but because they have not been tainted by presidential bias (box 5-3).

Growing congressional independence in budgetary and legislative matters has affected OMB. As recently as the 1970s OMB career staff did not closely monitor congressional action on the president's budget. After submission of the budget, OMB examiners often spent considerable time with the agencies they oversaw, reviewing programs and assessing managerial strengths and weaknesses. As their work schedules allow, OMB staff still engage in these activities, but they now spend much of the time when Congress is in session monitoring the progress of appropriations bills and other measures through committees and the House and the Senate. Even as it serves the president, OMB must be attuned to what is happening in Congress. This reorientation has crowded out much in-depth policy analysis and managerial review, and it has reinforced the perception that the agency is partisan.

▼

BOX 5-3
OMB's Conflicting Roles: Neutral Competence versus Political Advice

The contemporary OMB pursues two conflicting mandates—one is to provide professional assistance to the president in preparing his budget and overseeing its implementation; the other is to articulate and promote the president's views in negotiations with Congress. The first role has been part of OMB's repertoire since its predecessor, the Bureau of the Budget, was established in 1921. The second role has emerged more recently and is a by-product of divided government, widespread conflict on budgetary matters, and the use of budget summits to resolve impasses between the White House and Capitol Hill. The first requires neutral competence—the ability to advise the president on the merits, independent of political considerations; the second plunges OMB into the maelstrom of partisan politics. The first orients OMB to the activities and finances of federal agencies; the second impels it to focus on the actions and interests of Congress.

Neutral competence requires a career staff with a long institutional memory, which carries over as one president departs and another is sworn in. The staff provides in-depth, objective assessments of federal programs, options for the president's consideration, and detailed knowledge of the organization and operations of federal agencies. OMB directors must be politically savvy, but they do not slant advice just to satisfy political interests. This professional OMB operates largely behind the scenes, leaving the job of building support for the president's programs to the spending departments.

The political role requires that a large cohort of political appointees (which did not even exist under the traditional role) depart when a new president arrives. In this role, the OMB director must actively and openly build public and congressional support for the president's policies. Political realities intrude during budget preparation. This new orientation has pulled OMB away from agencies and more toward developing substantive and procedural knowledge of Congress. Nowadays, OMB—especially its director and other OMB political appointees—has to maintain ongoing contacts with congressional leaders and rank-and-file members. The politicization is further complicated because OMB leaders must publicly advocate on the president's behalf for positions they may have recently argued against within the administration. The OMB director has acquired a political face, appearing on television and using the media to battle Congress on pending budget matters. In some cases, OMB directors have become public figures almost apart from the presidents they serve. David Stockman, Ronald Reagan's first budget director, best personified this role, but he was not the last director to build his own power base.

Source: Portions adapted from Shelley Lynne Tomkin, *Inside OMB: Politics and Process in the President's Budget Office* (M. E. Sharpe, 1998), pp. 27–29.

OMB Review of Agency Requests

No matter how attentive it is to congressional actions, OMB must devote much of its staff resources to preparing the president's budget. This involves ongoing relationships with the agencies and White House aides.

As agencies formulate their budgets, they maintain contact with the OMB examiners assigned to them. These contacts provide agencies with procedural and policy guidance in preparing their requests and inform the examiners of agency priorities and concerns. On an interpersonal level, the relationship usually is harmonious, but the two sides know they are budgetary adversaries. Agencies want more than OMB gives them, and their priorities and program assessments often differ from OMB's. But the two sides also are interdependent—agencies have information OMB wants, and OMB controls money the agencies need.

The formal side of budget preparation is based on OMB Circular A-11, which contains detailed instructions and schedules for the estimates and other material agencies submit. The technical data are too detailed to be the basis for presidential decisions, but they are used in preparing many of the schedules printed in the budget.

Agencies submit their requests to OMB in early fall. Then OMB staff and, on important issues, presidential aides review the requests. The review typically has several distinct stages: *staff review*, during which OMB examiners review the requests, consult with agency officials, and prepare recommendations; *director's review*, at which major issues are discussed, OMB examiners defend their recommendations, and the OMB director makes budget decisions; *passback*, at which agencies are notified of these decisions and have an opportunity to appeal for reconsideration; *appeals*, which are first taken to OMB, but if agreement is not reached, may be considered by the president or

certain aides; and *final decisions*, which are made up to the point that the budget documents are printed. Once they are informed of the final decisions, agencies revise their budgets to bring them in line with the president's.

The Budget and Accounting Act of 1921 bars agencies from submitting budget requests directly to Congress. This prohibition is backed by an OMB regulation (Circular A-10) that requires confidentiality in all budget requests and recommendations before the president transmits his budget to Congress. Nevertheless, internal budget documents and decisions are often leaked, sometimes by the president, who thereby controls the prerelease news. These days it is hard to keep secrets in Washington, and there are some years in which virtually all important budget decisions have been divulged in advance of the budget's release.

The format and content of the budget are partly determined by law, but the 1921 act authorizes the president to set forth the budget "in such form and detail" as he may determine. Over the past twenty years, there has been a marked increase in the political content of the budget. Not very long ago, most of the budget and its supporting documents were devoted to detailed schedules and explanations; the president's policies were highlighted in a budget message that introduced the technical details. Nowadays, much of the budget reads like a campaign document extolling the president's policies. This politicization of the budget documents mirrors the penetration of partisan politics into every corner of federal activity. Arguably, if the budget is the president's, it should put the best face on his policies and make a strong case for Congress to adopt them. However, the budget is also an account to the American people of the government's handling of its revenues and expenditures. Turning the budget into a political statement has diminished this facet of budgeting. The practice began in the 1970s, but it was greatly extended by President Clinton, who ran the White House as if it were a continuing campaign.

The budget is not the president's last word on government finance, for he is required to submit an annual update by July 15 (reflecting changes in economic conditions, congressional actions, and other developments). Moreover, the president may revise his budget any time during the year. Changes submitted before Congress has acted on the original request are treated as amendments; requests for additional funds that are made after Congress has acted on the affected appropriations bill are submitted as supplementals.

THE PRESIDENT'S BUDGET IN CONGRESS

As noted earlier, contemporary presidents must deal with a Congress that has become increasingly independent on the budget and other policy matters over the past twenty-five years. Recent presidents and their staffs have had to invest substantial time in monitoring legislative action and wooing members.

OMB tracks the progress of the president's budget through Congress, but its formal role in congressional budgeting is limited. OMB officials and the president's economic advisers appear before congressional committees to discuss overall policy and economic issues, but they generally leave discussion of particular programs to the affected agencies. Agency officials have the primary responsibility for defending the president's recommendations at appropriations hearings and other congressional forums. In the hearings, agency officials justify the president's budget, even when it diverges from their real preferences. Toward this end, OMB maintains an elaborate legislative clearance process to ensure that budget justifications, testimony, and legislative proposals

are consistent with presidential policy. But (as is discussed in chapter 9), the appropriations process is fragmented, and agencies have many informal avenues for staking out their own position on particular matters.

To get his way, the president and his staff must navigate through budget resolutions, reconciliation bills, authorization legislation, annual appropriations, tax legislation, and more. His staff must be well versed in congressional budget rules. They must be smart budget counters, mindful of how legislation is scored in enforcing these rules and of how scores can be altered through budgetary sleight of hand. They also must be good vote counters in Congress and willing to twist arms to get a winning coalition. Sometimes the president must negotiate with members of Congress, at other times he must go over their heads. He must know when to keep a safe distance and when to intervene, when to threaten a veto (or carry out the threat) and when to concede. He must know when to delegate the task of reaching agreement to others and when to act as his own budget director. The tough decisions and important details must be his call.

Political and Legislative Resources

The White House is a budget pulpit; from the Oval Office, the president has the capacity to define the terms of the budget debate. He decides which issues will be on the table, whether to seek changes in revenues and entitlements, and whether to demand program initiatives. His budget is the trigger for congressional action on these and other matters. Even when the budget is reputed to be dead on arrival, as it sometimes has been with the last three administrations, the president sets the agenda for the bargaining and legislative actions that follow. The media give the president's budget extensive coverage when it is released, policy analysts and interest groups scour its pages, and the budget, appropriations, and tax committees spring into action.

Not only does the president usually have the initiative, he can be confident that Congress will act on some of his budget proposals. Congress does not have the option of doing nothing on appropriations, and it is likely to take action pursuant to revenue proposals. But having the initiative does not ensure that the president gets his way. Every budget puts the president at risk of Congress charting its own course. To nudge legislative outcomes closer to his budget, the president must cajole a sufficient number of fence-sitting members to snatch victory from defeat. His first task is to nail down support within his own party. If, as has normally been the case over the past thirty years, he lacks a majority in one or both houses, he must reach out to swing members of the other party. The votes will not be there if they are not asked for, since members of Congress have budgetary interests that diverge from those of the president. Reagan in 1981 and Clinton a dozen years later met one-on-one with many members, mostly middle-of-the-road and conservative Democrats, whose support gave them a slim margin of victory. In both cases, journalists made much of the deals that had been cut to buy votes. In fact, presidents usually offer relatively little in exchange for votes, especially during the afterglow of their elections. During the postelection honeymoon and when his public rating is favorable, a president's most valuable resource is the predisposition of fence-sitting members to vote his way when he asks for their support. A member who meets the president before an important vote usually enters predisposed to support the president.

Some presidents have been reluctant to go one-on-one in pursuit of votes. Jimmy Carter was discomfited by this aspect of congressional-presidential relations. George Bush (who had served in the House) had a comfortable relationship with many members of Congress, but on budget matters he often stood above the fray and did not effectively exploit the advantages of his office when votes were needed. Bill Clinton, by contrast, has enjoyed this part of his job. Rather than regarding telephone calls to members as a chore, he relishes the opportunity to tell them he needs their votes and appreciates their support.

This message wears thin with repetition, which is one reason no president builds every budgetary (or legislative) disagreement with Congress into a cause célèbre. It explains why presidents tend to take their boldest budget steps early in their term and why they progressively demand less of Congress.

In addition to lobbying members of Congress, the president can rally support through adroit use of the media. Although few viewers or listeners are likely to be interested in the details of the latest budget battle, the media give the president an opportunity to paint Congress as recalcitrant and to demand action. Ronald Reagan used prime-time television with considerable effectiveness during his early years in office. He also broadcast weekend radio talks that were widely disseminated by the media on days when there normally was little solid news.

Clinton has varied his budget tactics with changes in the political lineup. In 1993, when his party still controlled Congress, Clinton's task was to persuade fellow Democrats to vote for a deficit reduction package that included tax increases and some spending cuts. To get the necessary majority, he had to provide political coverage to some Democrats who were troubled by his proposals. Clinton made two back-to-back television appearances in February 1993: the first was a brief speech that field-tested his message and primed viewers for the tax increases he proposed a few days later, and the second was a vigorous presentation of the budget plan he gave Congress. This concentrated television exposure was risky, but Clinton's gamble paid off—Congress enacted the main features of his plan. Of course, the president cannot go to the country every time a budget is pending in Congress. Presidents typically limit their television appearances to important occasions.

Presidential style makes a difference in using the budget as a pulpit. It helps if the president is comfortable in the role and an effective communicator. It also helps if the president has an upbeat disposition that enables him to bounce back from bad news and if he has the staying power to keep vital objectives in focus. For all presidents, budgeting is a grind. Before one budget is resolved, another is on the way. Few issues are fully or finally resolved. Even when they appear to be, unexpected developments often intrude, derailing budget plans and complicating negotiations. It is important, therefore, for presidents to take what they can get in each year's budget cycle and to label half a loaf as a complete victory. Few presidents have excelled more at this political art than Bill Clinton. Box 5-4 describes how he built minor concessions from Republicans in the 1998 budget battle into a political triumph.

The Whole and the Parts

Presidential influence is not spread uniformly across all facets of budgeting. The president sometimes has a stronger influence on the totals than on particular programs. His revenue proposals have a strong bearing on whether Congress will consider major changes in the tax laws; his projected budget surplus or deficit often becomes the fiscal parameters within which Congress operates. In most years since 1981, as table 5-2 indicates, Congress's budget resolution has provided for a deficit less than

(or a surplus more than) or about the same as the amount budgeted by the president. The president's budget does not legitimize deficits, but it does make it politically costly for Congress to set a higher amount. For this reason, if the president comes in with an unrealistically low deficit projection, so too will Congress.

The president's influence on the budgeted—in contrast to the actual—deficit discomfited Congress during the Reagan years. Reagan's budget was often based on unrealistically buoyant economic assumptions and on "dead on arrival" proposals to cut deeply into domestic programs. Rather than manifesting presidential impotence, Reagan's budgets skillfully positioned him for negotiations with Congress. In these negotiations and in other actions, Congress saved most of the programs the president targeted for termination, but it did so within the deficit totals he dictated. Within these totals, Congress made significant shifts in priorities, taking funds from programs Reagan wanted to expand (principally defense) and giving them to programs he wanted to shrink.

Congress also restored proposed cuts by adding to the spending totals. During the 1980s the congressional budget resolution usually allowed more total budget authority and outlays than the president had requested. In most of these years Congress made room for the additional spending by budgeting higher revenues (see table 5-2).

Reagan legitimized unrealistic budgeting as a tool of presidential power. Although Congress made many changes in his budget, the revenue and spending outcomes were closer to his preferences than they would have been had he sent up a realistic budget. But the president's tactical gains came at a high cost—they made the budget into more of a bargaining chip and undermined its status as an authoritative guide to national policy.

Both Bush and Clinton followed in Reagan's path. Year after year Bush proposed cuts that had no chance of enactment. In fact, if a cutback was proposed in one Bush budget, there was a high probability it also was in the following one and in the one after that. Clinton used more defensible economic assumptions than his predecessors, but his budgets recommended program expansions that could be accommodated within the spending caps only by playing fast and loose with the rules. In the negotiated end games that characterized budgeting in the Clinton years, the president often got some of what he wanted. If his original budget had been realistic, he might have gotten nothing.

THE VETO POWER

When the two branches' priorities diverge, even a shrewd and persuasive president may have difficulty getting his revenue and spending preferences approved. This is most likely to be the case when control of government is divided and the two parties are centered at opposite poles in the political spectrum. When this occurs Congress may disregard the president's budget and stuff appropriations bills and other budget-related matters with a slew of provisions that are contrary to his expressed policies. Over the years many presidents have complained that they are at a disadvantage because they are compelled to sign or veto the entire bill; they cannot pick and choose from among its provisions. This disadvantage is especially pronounced when spending bills are presented to them after the fiscal year has started and failure to sign the measure risks shutting down the government. To make matters worse, Congress further debilitates the veto power by wrapping multiple appropriations bills, along with substantive legislation, into an omnibus measure. To redress this imbalance of power, presidents since the Civil War have demanded line-item

veto authority, which would enable them to reject offensive provisions while signing the bill into law. In 1996 Congress gave the president a form of a line-item veto, but in 1998 the Supreme Court ruled that the line-item veto violated the Constitution.

In political relationships between the president and Congress, things are not always what they seem. The conventional all-or-nothing veto power is not inherently weak, Clinton's line-item veto power was not a genuine veto since it was not provided by a constitutional amendment, and enactment of omnibus legislation has more to do with the emergence of negotiated budgets than with congressional efforts to hoodwink or outmaneuver the president.

Presidents have a big advantage when they veto legislation; they win whenever members of their own party in Congress support them on the override vote. Although his party lacked a majority in Congress, George Bush had a sterling veto record, winning more than 30 consecutive override fights before losing one near the end of his presidency. Bill Clinton backed congressional Republicans into a political corner during the 1995–99 budget wars by vetoing some bills and threatening to veto others. Why then have recent presidents complained about the feebleness of the all-or-nothing veto that the Constitution prescribes? Part of the answer is that Congress earmarks money for projects and inserts other details that may offend the president but that do not justify a veto of the entire bill. But a big part of the answer is that few recent presidents have used their veto power effectively. In the 1980s Ronald Reagan signed omnibus appropriations bills that were chock full of provisions he did not like because he was apprehensive about shutting down the government. In any confrontation, the side that signals it is unwilling to fight loses. Clinton won because he vetoed offending bills; Reagan lost because he did not.

▼

BOX 5-4
How Bill Clinton Turned Small Disputes into a Big Victory in 1998

When the Republican-controlled Congress convened in January 1998, the leadership hoped for a calm, relatively brief session in which they and the White House would agree on appropriations, cut some taxes, and make a few changes in entitlement programs. Nine months later the two sides were once again locked in budgetary combat. They finally patched up differences in a 900-page omnibus appropriations bill that gave each side some of the things it wanted. It also gave Republicans another loss and Bill Clinton a big political triumph.

The year began with conditions favorable for budgetary harmony. Just months earlier, Clinton and Republicans hammered out a

February 2
Clinton's fiscal 1999 budget is released.

April 2
Senate passes budget resolution 57-41.

June 5
House passes budget resolution 214-206.

October 1
The fiscal year ends with a projected surplus of $70 billion.

October 7
Clinton vetoes Agriculture appropriations bill.

October 21
Clinton signs the omnibus appropriations bill into law.

November 3
Democrats gain five House seats in the midterm elections.

"balanced budget" agreement that purported to set budget policy in place through fiscal 2002. Moreover, as the session wore on, budgetary conditions turned out to be much more favorable than anticipated. Clinton's budget had projected a $10 billion deficit for fiscal 1998, but by the time the year ended, the government had racked up a $70 billion surplus.

Why, despite these conditions, did the White House and Congress lock horns? In addition, how and why did Clinton win? The answers come in two parts—Republican miscalculation and Clinton's brinksmanship. House Republicans moved slowly on the appropriations bills, miscalculating that as the elections approached, they would gain strength. They reasoned that the president's party had gained House seats in midterm elections only twice since the Civil War. The Republicans also assumed that as the surplus grew, so would congressional support for tax cuts. They took it for granted that taxpayers preferred to keep more of their earnings.

But Clinton figured that with the economy booming, most Americans would not be concerned

continued

In many conflicts the president need not actually veto a bill; threatening to do so suffices. In contrast to other recent presidents who merely suggested they would consider vetoing particular measures, Clinton said that he would and Congress revised the bill to gain his approval. It helped that Clinton often had public opinion on his side, but the important thing is that he won. Every budget victory made him stronger for the next confrontation because he had a credible veto threat.

A line-item veto would strengthen the president's hand with respect to minor details but would not make much difference on major budget issues. When Clinton signed the line-item veto into law in 1996, he claimed that it would "prevent Congress from enacting special interest provisions under the cloak of a

---

BOX 5-4
Continued

---

about taxes. Instead, they would worry about whether the Social Security system would have enough money to pay for their retirement and whether schools had enough money to do a good job of educating their children. Throughout the session, Clinton parried Republican demands with two main messages: Use the surplus to strengthen Social Security and boost education spending. Clinton had other budget priorities, but his political rhetoric was concentrated on these two popular objectives.

As the new fiscal year began and midterm elections approached, Clinton vetoed the Agriculture appropriations bill, signaling that he would be willing to shut down the government once again if Congress refused his budget demands. Republicans grew increasingly worried that they would be blamed again for a shutdown. They therefore were willing to negotiate a package deal that would resolve the outstanding budget disputes and allow Congress to adjourn.

The negotiations culminated in an omnibus appropriations bill that was fattened with budgetary goodies for both sides. Clinton got a little more for education but much less than he demanded; Republicans got more for defense and antidrug efforts. Both sides pretended that the spending increase was within the budget limits since the additional money was labeled "emergency." Clinton got Republicans to remove various riders to which he objected, including prohibiting federal funds to test or approve abortion-inducing drugs, an authorization of new roads through Alaskan wildlife sanctuaries, and a provision preventing permanent U.S. residency for 50,000 Haitian refugees. The bill was also stuffed with numerous pork barrel projects and dozens of provisions that had nothing to do with the budget but everything to do with the fact that the omnibus bill was the last opportunity to pass legislation before Congress adjourned.

Clinton proclaimed the bill a victory, and looked like a winner on television. Speaker Newt Gingrich (R-Ga.) and other Republican leaders also claimed victory, but they were hard put to say what they came away with. Four years earlier the Republicans had gained control of Congress on the pledge of cutting the budget; this year they ended up voting for spending increases. When the votes were counted on election day, two weeks after Clinton signed the omnibus bill, the president's party had gained five House seats—the first time that had happened in over 50 years. Clinton's standing in the polls was near the peak of his presidency; he had transformed relatively modest program expansions into a political triumph.

500- or 1,000-page bill." Clinton exercised the line-item veto several times before the Supreme Court ruled it unconstitutional. Inasmuch as Congress established the new power by legislation rather than constitutional amendment, it was not a genuine line-item veto. Rather, the procedures (spelled out in box 5-5) would have enabled the president to cancel portions of bills passed by Congress and

signed into law. The so-called line-item procedure applied to three types of legislation: appropriations bills, new direct spending, and revenue measures providing preferences to one hundred or fewer taxpayers. During the brief period that he had this power, Clinton used it on all three types of measures. He canceled a total of eighty-two items: seventy-nine appropriations items, two targeted tax benefits, and

TABLE 5-2

Aggregates in the President's Budget and the Congressional Budget Resolution, Fiscal Years 1981–2000

Billions of dollars

Fiscal year	Revenues		Budget authority		Outlays		Deficit/Surplus	
	President	Congress	President	Congress	President	Congress	President	Congress
1981[a]	600	614	696	697	616	614	−16	0
1982[b]	650	658	772	771	695	696	−45	−38
1983	666	666	802	822	758	770	−92	−104
1984	660	680	900	929[c]	849	859[c]	−189	−179[c]
1985	745	751	1,007	1,021	926	932	−180	−181
1986	794	796	1,060	1,070	974	968	−180	−172
1987	850	852	1,102	1,093	994	995	−144	−143
1988	917	933[d]	1,142	1,153[d]	1,024	1,041[d]	−108	−108
1989	965	964	1,233	1,232	1,094	1,100	−130	−135
1990[e]	1,066	1,066	1,339[f]	1,351/1,327[g]	1,160	1,165	−95	−100/−99[g]
1991	1,170	1,173	1,397	1,486	1,233	1,237	−63	−64
1992	1,165	1,169	1,578	1,590	1,446	1,448	−281	−279
1993[h]	1,135	1,173	1,533	1,516	1,468	1,500	−332	−327
1994	1,251	1,242	1,517	1,507	1,515	1,496	−264	−254
1995	1,342	1,338	1,537	1,541	1,518	1,514	−176	−175
1996	1,416	1,417	1,614	1,592	1,612	1,588	−197	−170
1997	1,495	1,469	1,638	1,633	1,635	1,622	−140	−153
1998	1,567	1,602	1,710	1,702	1,688	1,692	−121	−90
1999[i]	1,743	1,756/1,739	1,751	1,730/1,747	1,733	1,722/1,730	10	34/9
2000	1,883	1,876	1,781	1,754	1,766	1,735	117	141

Sources: *Budget of the United States, Fiscal Years 1981–2000; Congressional Quarterly Almanac*, 1980–89, 1991–93, 1995–97. For Congress, 1991 figures from enrolled bill, H. Con. Res. 310, 101st Cong., 2d sess., October 9, 1990; 1995 figures from *Congressional Quarterly Weekly Reports*, May 7, 1994, p. 1108; 1999 figures from H. Con. Res. 284, June 5, 1998, and S. Con. Res. 86, March 30, 1998, 105th Cong., 2d sess.; 2000 figures from enrolled bill, H. Con. Res. 68, 106th Congress, 1st session, April 15, 1999.

　a. Prior revision; this was the last year that Congress passed two budget resolutions.

　b. Reagan revision of Carter budget.

　c. Includes reserve fund items (ten programs in a special $8.5 billion fund).

　d. Includes a special tax increase for defense.

　e. Bush revision of Reagan budget.

　f. As estimated by the CBO; the document released by Bush did not contain any comprehensive information on proposed spending authority in terms used by either congressional budget or appropriations committees.

　g. The conference report included two sets of reconciliation instructions, one for each chamber. The first figure is for the House and the second figure for the Senate.

　h. Clinton revision of Bush budget.

　i. Congress failed to adopt a budget resolution; the first figure is from the House-passed resolution and the second figure is from the Senate-passed resolution.

one new direct spending provision. All told, the White House estimated $2 billion in savings from this exercise of the line-item veto. But in June 1998 the Supreme Court held that by canceling portions of a law that had been passed by Congress and signed into law by him, "the President has amended two Acts of Congress. . . . There is no provision in the Constitution that authorizes the President to enact, to amend, or to repeal statutes."

▼

BOX 5-5
The Line-Item Veto

The following procedures were established by the Line Item Veto Act (P.L. 104-130) passed by Congress in 1996 and invalidated by the Supreme Court in 1998.

1. Congress passes an appropriations bill, a bill providing new direct spending, or a "limited tax benefit" and sends the legislation to the president.
2. The president signs the measure in the same manner as he signs other bills passed by Congress. At this point, the measure is enacted into law. Steps 3 through 6 do not apply if a bill becomes law without the president's signature or by congressional override of his veto.
3. Within five days after signing the measure, the president notifies Congress that he has canceled certain spending items or limited tax benefits. The president may not cancel legislative language in an appropriations bill.
4. Within 30 days Congress may pass legislation disapproving the president's cancellation. If it fails to do so, the canceled provision ceases to have legal force or effect. Disapproval legislation would be considered under expedited procedures.
5. The president may veto the disapproval bill in the same manner as he may veto any other bill passed by Congress.
6. Congress may override the president's veto by a two-thirds vote of the House and Senate, in the same manner as it may override any presidential veto.

Source: Line Item Veto Act, P.L. 104-130.

What did the president gain when Congress gave him the line-item veto, and what did he lose when the Court took it away? Not much, despite the advantage on particular items. If the line-item veto had survived, Congress would have taken countermeasures to even the playing field. It might have written legislation so as to exempt certain provisions from the president's new veto power, or it might have taken some of his legislative priorities hostage, withholding action on them until he consented not to cancel certain provisions.

Some argue that the president lost a great deal because he cannot veto omnibus measures that contain much of the session's legislative output and many of its budget decisions. But this view does not take account of the political bargaining through which omnibus bills are assembled. These bills materialize during the final stages of the annual budget process, and Congress passes them after extensive negotiations with the president. There is much give and take at this stage, and the president gains quite a lot by wrapping separate bills into an omnibus measure. If he does not, the president has the option of vetoing the measure when there is little in it for him; he generally should refrain from exercising the veto just because there is also pork in it for members of Congress.

INFORMATION IN THE PRESIDENT'S BUDGET

In the past the structure and content of the budget documents were continued without change from one administration to the next; this is no longer the case. As a political statement, the budget is molded to fit each president's style and policies. During the Bush presidency, the budget was consolidated into a single volume that highlighted the future liabilities and fiscal risks facing the federal government. The Clinton administration split the budget into four volumes: (1) the *Budget of the United States Government*, which presents the president's proposals and revenue and spending estimates, (2) an *Appendix*, which has program and financial information for each budget account, (3) *Analytical Perspectives*, which has special cross-cutting schedules and information for budget categories such as trust funds, user charges, tax expenditures, and aid to state and local governments, and (4) *Historical Tables*, which presents annual data (back to 1940 in some cases) on revenue and spending trends.

These documents include useful budget information, as well as vast amounts of "budget spin" designed to show what the president already has accomplished or promises to achieve. The budget contains the president's budget message, which highlights major policy recommendations and changes and presents expenditure data by functions, agencies, and accounts. For each annually appropriated account, it provides the text of the current appropriation with proposed changes (exhibit 5-2), a brief description of the account's programs and performance (exhibit 5-3), a "program and financing" schedule that classifies the account into its various programs (exhibit 5-4) and specifies its financing schedule (exhibit 5-5), and a schedule of each account's objects of expenditure (exhibit 5-6). The budget also has special schedules for direct and guaranteed loans and for various business-type operations carried out by federal departments and corporations.

Although the president's budget is the most comprehensive source of information on federal finances, it may lack sufficient detail for those interested in particular programs or agencies. Additional information may be obtained from the following documents prepared by federal agencies:

— Briefing material distributed by most federal agencies to the media shortly after the president transmits his budget to Congress. Many federal agencies hold press briefings, usually on the day the budget is released or the next day, at which they provide detailed information on their programs and finances.

— Every federal agency prepares justification material for its appropriations hearings. This material (discussed in chapter 9) usually is published a few months after the hearings are held but may be obtained earlier from the agency.

— Most agencies prepare internal budgets (sometimes computer printouts) for their own use, but these are not normally made available to the public. Internal budgets are updated during the year to reflect recent developments, such as congressional actions.

CONCLUSION

For every president, budgeting balances what he wants and what he can get. The published words and numbers attest to what the president says he wants but are silent about what he will do in pursuit of his objectives and what he will settle for. How much of the budget is presidential ambition and how much is political bluster can be known only after Congress has completed its work and agencies are implementing the approved spending plans.

A review of the budgetary record of the three most recent presidents shows that each approached the annual round of revenue and spending decisions in a distinctive way. Ronald Reagan formulated budgets that he

> **EXHIBIT 5-2**
> **Appropriations Language**

Federal Funds

General and special funds:

Human Space Flight

For necessary expenses, not otherwise provided for, in the conduct and support of human space flight research and development activities, including research, development, operations, and services; maintenance; construction of facilities including repair, rehabilitation, and modification of real and personal property, and acquisition or condemnation of real property, as authorized by law; space flight, spacecraft control and communications activities including operations, production, and services; and purchase, lease, charter, maintenance and operation of mission and administrative aircraft, [$5,506,500,000] *$5,511,000,000,* to remain available until September 30, [1999: *Provided,* That of the $2,351,300,000 made available under this heading for Space Station activities, only $1,500,000,000 shall be available before March 31, 1998] *2000.*

For necessary expenses of the International Space Station, to become available on October 1 of the fiscal year specified and remain available for that and the following fiscal year, as follows: for fiscal year 2000, $2,134,000,000; for fiscal year 2001, $1,933,000,000; for fiscal year 2002, $1,766,000,000; for fiscal year 2003, $1,546,000,000; for fiscal year 2004, $350,000,000. (Departments of Veterans Affairs and Housing and Urban Development, and Independent Agencies Appropriations Act, 1998.)

Source: *Budget of the United States Government, Appendix, Fiscal Year 1999,* p. 985.

(a) This and the next four exhibits pertain to space flight activities of the National Aeronautics and Space Administration. In addition to appropriation accounts, the budget has accounts for revolving and trust funds, business operations, and credit programs.

(b) For each account funded by annual appropriations, the budget contains the text of the current appropriation. The material in brackets is proposed to be deleted; the material in italics is proposed to be added.

(c) This appropriation is somewhat unusual because the budget requests advance funding for space activities in future fiscal years. In fact, the budget proposes advance appropriations for each of the next four fiscal years. Most appropriations, however, are only for a single fiscal year.

(d) The end of the appropriations language indicates the appropriations bill in which this account appears.

▶ **EXHIBIT 5-3**
Program Description

This appropriation provides funding for human space flight activities, including development of the Space Station, the Space Station research program, and operation of the Space Shuttle. This includes support of planned cooperative activities with Russia, upgrades to the performance and safety of the Space Shuttle, and required construction projects in direct support of Space Station and Space Shuttle programs.

PERFORMANCE OBJECTIVES
Space Station.—The Space Station will be an international laboratory in low Earth orbit on which American, Russian, Canadian, European, and Japanese astronauts will conduct unique scientific and technological investigations in a micro-gravity environment. The goal of the Station is to support activities requiring unique attributes of humans in space and establish a permanent human presence in Earth orbit. The proposed budget provides multi-year funding through an advanced appropriation for the complete development of the Station with Station assembly beginning in mid-1998 and finished by the end of 2003. With the first launch to assemble this unique orbital laboratory only a few months away, the budget includes sufficient funding to keep subsequent assembly missions on schedule and provide a long-term solution to the safe return of the full complement of Station crewmembers.

Source: *Budget of the United States Government, Appendix, Fiscal Year 1999*, p. 985.

(a) For most accounts, the budget describes the activities that will be undertaken with the appropriated funds. In some cases, they also provide workload and other performance data. In this excerpt, the budget details a plan for launching a space station.

(b) OMB instructions issued pursuant to the Government Performance and Results Act require agencies to submit performance plans and reviews of past performance in conjunction with their annual budget requests. Only a small portion of this information is included in the budget. Some of this material is available via the Internet.

(c) More detailed program descriptions and performance information are included in the justification material prepared by federal agencies for the appropriations committees. This material is published as part of the appropriations hearings.

▶ **EXHIBIT 5-4**
Program and Financing Schedule: Programs and Resources

Identification Code 80-0111-0-1-252	1997 actual	1998 est.	1999 est.
Obligations by program activity:	(in millions of dollars)		
Direct Program:			
Space Station	2,088	2,273	2,272
US/Russian cooperation and program assistance	230	137	3
Payload and utilization operations	267	325	184
Space Shuttle	3,001	2,849	3,052
Reimbursable program	69	71	200
Total obligations	5,655	5,655	5,711
Budgetary resources available for obligation:			
Unobligated balance available, start of year	222	226	149
New budget authority (gross)	5,609	5,578	5,711
Unobligated balance transferred from other accounts	50	...	...
Total budgetary resources available for obligation	5,881	5,804	5,860
New obligations	−5,655	−5,655	−5,711
Unobligated balance available, end of year	226	149	149
New budget authority (gross), detail:			
Current:			
Appropriation	5,363	5,507	5,511
Transferred from other accounts	177	...	...
Appropriation (total)	5,540	5,507	5,511
Permanent:			
Spending authority from offsetting collections:			
Offsetting collections (cash)	84	71	200
Change in orders on hand from Federal sources	−15	...	...
Spending authority from offsetting collections (total)	69	71	200
Total new budget authority (gross)	5,609	5,578	5,711

Source: *Budget of the United States Government, Appendix, Fiscal Year 1999*, p. 985.

(a) The program and financing schedule has been significantly expanded. In the mid-1990s, it had four parts; it now has seven. The first three parts appear in this exhibit; the remainder are in the next.

(b) Each account has an eleven-digit identification code. The first two digits designate the agency, the next four are the account numbers, the seventh indicates the type of budget request (regular or supplemental), the eighth indicates the type of fund, and the last three designate the function in which the account is classified.

(c) These budget schedules have three columns. The first reports on the last completed fiscal year, the middle column pertains to the year in progress, and the third column shows the amounts requested for the next fiscal year.

(d) In most cases, a shift of funds between the activities listed in the first part of the schedule would require that the money be reprogrammed. "Budgetary resources" shows all available resources, including unobligated funds carried over from prior years and new appropriations. "New budget authority" provides information on total budget authority available to finance the program, regardless of source.

▶ **EXHIBIT 5-5**
Program and Financing Schedule: Financing Details

Identification Code 80-0111-0-1-252	1997 actual	1998 est.	1999 est.
Change in unpaid obligations:	(in millions of dollars)		
Unpaid obligations, start of year:			
Obligated balance: Uninvested	1,770	1,770	1,708
Orders on hand from Federal sources	48	33	33
Total unpaid obligations, start of year	1,818	1,733	1,741
New obligations	5,655	5,655	5,711
Total outlays (gross)	−5,740	−5,647	−5,674
Adjustments in expired accounts	−1	. . .	. . .
Unpaid obligations, end of year:			
Obligated balance: Uninvested	1,700	1,708	1,745
Orders on hand from Federal sources	33	33	33
Total unpaid obligations, end of year	1,733	1,741	1,778
Outlays (gross), detail:			
Outlays from new current authority	3,808	3,651	3,654
Outlays from current balances	1,865	1,925	1,820
Outlays from new permanent authority	33	71	200
Outlays from permanent balances	34	. . .	. . .
Total outlays (gross)	5,740	5,647	5,674
Offsets:			
Against gross budget authority and outlays:			
Offsetting collections (cash) from:			
Non–Federal sources	−35	−15	−11
Offsetting governmental collections	−49	−56	−189
Total, offsetting collections (cash)	−84	−71	−200
Change in orders on hand from Federal sources	15	. . .	. . .
Net budget authority and outlays:			
Budget authority	5,540	5,507	5,511
Outlays	5,656	5,576	5,474

Source: *Budget of the United States Government, Appendix, Fiscal Year 1999*, p. 985.

(a) The remaining sections of the program and financing schedule show various accounting details. "Change in unpaid obligations" relates obligations to outlays. Outlays are the difference between unpaid obligations at the start of the year plus new obligations incurred during the year minus actual or estimated unpaid obligations at the end of the year.

(b) "Outlays" indicates the outlays derived from current and permanent budget authority and from balances carried over from prior years.

(c) "Offsets" and "Net budget authority" show offsetting collections and certain accounting adjustments. The difference between net budget authority and outlays shown here and the gross amounts shown earlier is due to offsetting collections.

▶ **EXHIBIT 5-6**
Object Classification

Identification code 80-0111-0-1-252	1997 actual	1998 est.	1999 est.
Direct obligations:	(in millions of dollars)		
22.0 Transportation of things	3	3	3
23.3 Communications, utilities, and miscellaneous charges	63	63	62
24.0 Printing and reproduction	4	4	4
25.1 Advisory and assistance services	1,197	1,197	1,181
25.2 Other services	308	308	304
25.3 Purchase of goods and services from Government accounts	128	128	126
25.4 Operation and maintenance of facilities	91	91	90
25.5 Research and development contracts	3,480	3,478	3,433
26.0 Supplies and material	92	92	91
31.0 Equipment	85	85	84
32.0 Land and structures	131	131	129
41.0 Grants, subsidies, and contributions	4	4	4
99.0 Subtotal, direct obligations	5,586	5,584	5,511
99.0 Reimbursable obligations	69	71	200
99.9 Total obligations	5,655	5,655	5,711

Source: *Budget of the United States Government, Appendix, Fiscal Year 1999*, p. 986.

(a) This schedule, which accompanies every appropriation account, classifies the budgetary resources available for obligation by the major objects of expenditure. The same object classification is used by all federal agencies. The object code numbers are printed in the left margin of the schedule.

(b) For each account with personnel compensation, the budget presents summary data on the number of full-time equivalent (FTE) work years.

(c) Most agencies have some flexibility in shifting funds among object classes. However, most have ceilings on the number of FTEs and are expected by their appropriations subcommittees to implement their budgets, to the extent practicable, in accord with the object schedules. But in view of the long lead time from budget preparation to implementation, deviations from these schedules frequently occur, sometimes through the reprogramming process discussed in chapter 10, but most commonly through unilateral action by the spending agency.

knew would come out of Congress much changed from what went in. He requested a lot more for defense so that he could get more, even though Congress trimmed the increase. He demanded many of the same domestic cuts, year after year, so that the growth of many programs was slowed or halted, even though Congress restored all or most of the money. He railed against deficit spending, but he presided over gargantuan deficits that led to the Gramm-Rudman-Hollings laws enacted during his second term.

George Bush took a less ideological but more rigid posture than Reagan. Locking himself into a "read my lips, no new taxes" pledge, Bush started his presidency opposed to modest tax increases—only to be compelled by soaring deficits and the GRH targets to sign a very large tax increase. Although he also proposed domestic spending cuts, Bush distanced himself from the budget. In contrast to all post–World War II presidents, who introduced their budgets with a message outlining their policies and objectives, Bush merely sent a brief, perfunctory letter of transmittal. The real budget messages published during this period were those of Richard Darman, his budget director, who often seemed to have his own agenda.

Budgetary battles with Congress have been a recurring theme of the Clinton presidency. The first battles were with fellow Democrats who were uneasy about some of the tax increases he proposed in 1993; the later ones were with congressional Republicans who opposed his spending priorities and wanted tax cuts. Each of Clinton's battles ended in negotiation, and in each the president attained much of what he wanted. He won enactment of the deficit reduction package in 1993, blocked Republican efforts to slash taxes and certain domestic programs in 1995 and 1996, negotiated a deal with Republicans in 1997 that cut taxes, added some spending, and claimed to produce a balanced budget, and once again blocked Republican tax cuts and achieved some spending gains in 1998 and 1999. In each of his confrontations with Republicans, Clinton scored a political victory, pinning a fiscal irresponsibility label on Republicans for shutting down the government, for wanting to trim Medicare, and for refusing to go along with increases for education and some of his other priorities. Even when he got much less than he initially asked for, Clinton had no difficulty exulting in his political success.

Balancing the conflicts and tensions of budgeting seemed to come easily to Clinton, though he sometimes discomfited supporters and left others bewildered as to what he really stood for. To Clinton, balancing was not merely compromising on differences or taking a centrist position. It meant embracing seemingly clashing views by promoting government expansion while downsizing government and coopting conservative positions while advancing liberal ones. It meant taking strong steps to curtail the deficit while proposing program initiatives, and pruning government operations while extracting more tax dollars to pay for government. Budgeting by Clinton often defied conventional classifications and accommodated the constraints and opportunities of the moment. There was a streak of opportunism in Clinton's stewardship of the federal budget, but it was an opportunism that brought triumphs when the odds were stacked against him. As president, he sought new syntheses that appealed to the political middle, which wanted smaller government and more from government. Whether this was the real Clinton or the political one makes little difference; either way, it was a formula that repeatedly bested congressional Republicans.

6

The Congressional Budget Process

Shortly after the president submits his budget, Congress begins work on a budget resolution that expresses its own policies and priorities. This resolution sets forth budget totals for each of the next ten (or fewer) years and allocates spending among twenty functional categories. The resolution may also contain reconciliation instructions to change existing revenue or direct spending laws, as well as other provisions relating to the budget. In developing its budget resolution, Congress often deviates from the president's recommendations, but when the Budget Enforcement Act (discussed in chapter 4) was effective, it had to adhere to discretionary spending limits and pay-as-you-go (PAYGO) requirements.

Because it is in the form of a concurrent resolution, a budget resolution is not a law. Although both the House and Senate pass it, the resolution is not presented to the president for his signature or veto; hence it does not have statutory effect. In addition to adopting the budget resolution, Congress provides legal authority for the federal government to raise and spend money through revenue laws, appropriation acts, and other spending legislation. The purpose of the budget resolution is to establish the fiscal framework within which Congress takes these statutory actions. If everything goes according to plan, Congress's actions and the amounts actually raised and spent would conform to the levels specified in the resolution. Sometimes budget outcomes are on target or come close; other times there are significant variances. Even though Congress has enforcement tools, such as points of order, section 302 allocations to House and Senate committees, and scorekeeping reports (described later in this chapter), it sometimes enacts policies that differ from the resolution. Moreover, actual revenues and spending often diverge from the amounts set out in the resolution because of factors outside Congress's effective control (for example, the performance of the economy).

In 1998, for the first time since Congress established its own budget process a quarter of a century earlier, it failed to adopt the annual resolution. But this failure did not stop other legislative actions related to the budget. Congress appropriated funds to federal programs and agencies, and it produced a slew of authorization bills. But it did not consider reconciliation legislation, nor did it devise a comprehensive budget policy. Except for the fact that Congress produced a truly mammoth omnibus appropriation bill, 1998 was a routine budget year. No significant changes were made in the tax code, entitlement programs, or federal budget rules. The lack of a budget resolution was hardly noticed.

In some years, however, congressional budgeting has big ambitions and large conflicts. These are the years, discussed in chapter 1, when the budget resolution and the reconciliation bill dominate the legislative agenda and drive Congress to enact substantial changes in revenue and spending policy. In discussing the congressional budget process, therefore, it is necessary to distinguish between change-oriented and status quo years. In the former, the resolution hardly makes a difference; in the latter, it makes all the difference.

WHY CONGRESS HAS A BUDGET RESOLUTION

Why does Congress go through the motions of adopting a budget resolution when it still must pass separate bills that enable the government to

tax and spend? In fact, Congress operated for almost two centuries—from its first session in 1789 to 1975—without a budget resolution. During that period it made numerous financial decisions each year and acted on revenue and spending bills one at a time. But Congress did not vote on the total budget; the totals were simply the sum of its many legislative actions.

To understand why Congress established its own budget process, one must consider three questions. How did Congress manage to operate without a budget resolution in the past? Why did Congress reverse course in 1974 and create a legislative budget process? What purpose is served by having a budget resolution that lacks legal status?

Congress and budgeting do not easily fit together. Congress is inherently a decentralized institution that must, because of the basis on which members are elected, give many committees a voice in budget decisions. Fragmentation is not a legislative disorder, although it sometimes produces messy procedures and unpredictable outcomes. Rather, it is inherent in an institution in which senators come from each of the 50 states and representatives from 435 different places in America. The political job of Congress is to give voice, representation, and access to the diversity of interests in American life. In the budgetary arena Congress upholds this institutional imperative by widely distributing influence. Most members have some budgetary power by serving on one or more of the committees responsible for revenues, authorizations, and/or appropriations.

Congress's practice of taking up the many budget-related measures one at a time reinforces its decentralization. But consider the alternative—an arrangement that would give a single set of House and Senate committees control of all budget legislation. Given the size and importance of the budget, these committees would be able to leverage their power to control virtually all significant legislation. Members of these committees would influence substantive legislation, even when it was not in their committee's jurisdiction and only weakly germane to the budget. Most other members would be without a significant role or influence. Such a concentration of congressional power would not be sustainable. Eventually the rank-and-file majority excluded from budgetary power would wrest control away from the few who had it.

Budgetary fragmentation worked reasonably well in the past when Congress followed the president's lead on budget matters and jurisdiction over federal spending was concentrated in the appropriations committees. Although Congress acted on the budget in piecemeal fashion, the president's recommendations guided its actions. Every step of the way, especially in making appropriations and writing tax legislation, Congress used the president's budget as the starting point and typically made many small and incremental changes. The thousands of separate congressional decisions added up to totals that did not veer very far from the president's budget. In effect, the president served as the coordinator of congressional budget action, making it possible for a fragmented Congress to produce seemingly coordinated budget outcomes.

However, for reasons discussed in the previous chapter, the president's legislative influence sagged in the late 1960s and early 1970s. Watergate and Vietnam took a toll, as did conflict between the White House and Capitol Hill over tax increases, deficit spending, and the impoundment of appropriated funds. Impoundment was the final straw; it spurred enactment of the Congressional Budget Act (CBA) in 1974, which conceived of the budget resolution as an opportunity for Congress to stake out an independent position on the budget. For this reason the budget resolution was to be exclusively a legislative decision. The

president would not be involved, and Congress would not be beholden to his economic forecasts or policy preferences in drawing up the resolution. It would rely instead on the new Congressional Budget Office (CBO) for information and analysis.

Relations with the president were not Congress's only concern in establishing its own budget process. During the decade before CBA, congressional control of spending became increasingly difficult. The appropriations committees, which once had jurisdiction over virtually all federal spending, were unable to block the rising tide of entitlements and other backdoor methods that shifted jurisdiction to authorizing committees. As entitlements gained budgetary prominence, it became evident that Congress could not control total federal spending through annual appropriation decisions. It needed a broader process that encompassed all expenditures—one that linked revenue and spending. The budget resolution was to be that coordinating device. It covers all federal spending, regardless of committee jurisdiction, and requires Congress to make explicit decisions on total revenue and spending, budget priorities, and the deficit.

But in devising a comprehensive budget process, Congress had to ensure that legislative power remained dispersed. CBA balanced budgetary integration and legislative fragmentation by layering the budget resolution on top of existing authorizations, appropriations, and revenue processes. The coexistence of an integrated budget process and decentralized revenue and spending processes has greatly complicated congressional budgeting. All revenue and spending set in the budget resolution is also in the jurisdiction of other congressional committees. The resolution is advisory; the work of other committees is legislative. The resolution deals with aggregates and a small number of major spending categories; other committees get into the details and make specific program decisions. Implementing the "big picture" of the resolution depends on the actions of authorizing, appropriations, and revenue committees. As a fiscal framework, the resolution is highly important when it controls what others do and is unimportant, even irrelevant, when it does not. In some years the resolution has a lead role in framing the legislative agenda and in determining how much is raised and spent. In other years it merely ratifies the status quo.

In the quarter of a century that Congress has been producing budget resolutions, the process has rarely been the same two years in a row. Not only has the timing of Congress's actions differed, so too has the content and length of these measures they have become political variables which expand and contract to suit the current Democratic or Republican agenda. The Democrat's fiscal 1995 resolution covered five years and sought few changes in budget policy. With Republicans winning control of Congress for the first time in 40 years, the fiscal 1996 resolution demanded more than $1 trillion in revenue and spending changes. A seven-year time frame was selected because the resolution targeted fiscal 2002 as the first year in which the budget would be balanced. The fiscal 1997 resolution covered six years and curtailed the budgeted savings; the fiscal 1998 resolution reverted to a five-year horizon with modest policy objectives. The fiscal 2000 resolution was stretched to ten years because the Republican majority wanted to show deep tax cuts. Because tax cuts are scored against the baseline, the longer period covered by the resolution, the bigger the reported size of the cuts. For the fiscal 2001 resolution, Republicans cut the length covered by the resolution in half from ten to five years because they wanted to show smaller tax cuts (so as to demonstrate that the cuts would not touch the Social Security

surplus). Like just about everything else in budgeting, each year is a different story because of changes in budget and political conditions and in relationships of party leaders, other committees, and the budget committees.

The history of the budget process tells us that Congress cannot abide major changes in policy each year—trying to do so would provoke partisan conflict, congest the legislative calendar, and strain relations between the budget committees and other congressional committees. But it is also the case that Congress cannot accept stand-pat budget policies year after year. Election results, pressure from the White House, emerging spending demands, concern about the deficit, and recently, fights over how to dispose of surpluses have impelled Congress to use the budget resolution as a platform for redirecting government policies. "Big bang" years in congressional budgeting have tended to be followed by relatively quiet years. Congress enacted major budget changes in 1990, had status quo budget resolutions in 1991 and 1992, launched another round of policy changes the following year, sought few changes in 1994, tried to enact truly significant budget legislation in 1995 (but stirred up so much conflict that some federal departments were shut down for lack of funds), and settled for more modest legislation the next several years.

The extent to which the budget resolution seeks change can be measured by the scope of its reconciliation instructions. A resolution that does not contain reconciliation merely accommodates the status quo; one that has such instructions seeks to change existing law. The broader the scope of reconciliation—the more committees subjected to it and the more dollars involved—the greater the importance of the resolution in setting Congress's agenda and revising budget policy.

Paradoxically, the budget resolution was intended to manifest congressional independence, but in some reconciliation years it has been an instrument of presidential power. In 1981 Ronald Reagan seized control of the congressional budget process to win far-reaching changes in revenue and spending laws. Bill Clinton did much the same in 1993. These presidential triumphs, a dozen years apart and serving very different political objectives, have been among the most salient accomplishments of congressional budgeting. In practice, the resolution reflects the interdependence of the two branches. Congress can pass any resolution it wants, but to enact its proposals, Congress must win the president's acquiescence. The wider the disagreement between the two branches, the more they have to reach out to one another to bridge their differences. When they fail to do so, not only is the congressional budget process at risk, but the continuing operation of government is also in jeopardy.

In both status quo and policy initiative years, Congress uses the budget resolution as the basis for allocating budget authority and outlays among House and Senate committees. This "section 302" process (described later in the chapter) sets the budgetary boundaries within which congressional committees operate. Ideally, for the resolution to serve this purpose, it should be adopted in a timely manner—before committees begin work on appropriations and other budget-related matters. Although the official timetable of the congressional budget process calls for adoption of the budget resolution by April 15, table 6-1 shows that this deadline is often missed by a few weeks and sometimes by months. In some years Congress has adopted the resolution after the fiscal year had started and some appropriation bills already had been enacted. Delay in the resolution is a barometer of budgetary conflict. In some years disagreement has been so deep and pervasive that it has been hard to assemble a majority in support of the resolution. However, before 1998 the House and Senate almost always managed to eke out a majority.

TABLE 6-1
Adoption Dates for the Budget Resolution, Fiscal Years 1976–2001[a]

Fiscal year	Date of adoption	Days after deadline
1976	May 14	1
1977	May 13	0
1978	May 17	2
1979	May 17	2
1980	May 24	9
1981	June 12	28
1982	May 21	6
1983	June 23	39
1984	June 23	39
1985	October 1	139
1986	August 1	78
1987	June 27	73
1988	June 24	70
1989	June 6	52
1990	May 18	33
1991	October 9	176
1992	May 22	37
1993	May 21	36
1994	April 1	0
1995	May 12	27
1996	June 29	75
1997	June 13	59
1998	June 5	51
1999	not adopted	. . .
2000	April 15	0
2001	April 13	0

Sources: *Congressional Quarterly Almanac*, 1975–97; *Congressional Quarterly Weekly Reports*, April 17, 1999, p. 881; April 15, 2000, p. 885.

a. The dates pertain to the first budget resolution for fiscal years 1976 through 1982, and to the annual resolution for subsequent years. Before fiscal 1987 Congress was supposed to adopt the resolution by May 15; since then the scheduled adoption date has been April 15.

Box 6-1 discusses the breakdown in the process in 1998 and suggests that the resolution was as much a victim of indifference as of conflict. With the federal budget balanced for the first time in a generation, and with House and Senate budget committee leaders divided on the appropriate strategy for dealing with the new situation, Congress opted for inaction.

BOX 6-1
The Budget Resolution That Wasn't: Republicans Fighting Republicans

Both the House and the Senate passed budget resolutions for fiscal 1999, but the two chambers could not agree on a final version. This was the first time since the congressional budget process began that Congress failed to complete its budget work. It should not have turned out this way, for Republicans controlled both the House and Senate. Furthermore, just a year earlier they had negotiated a deal with the president that cut taxes, increased some spending, and promised a balanced budget in fiscal 2002. In 1998, however, a strong economy and bull stock market produced a revenue surge that helped liquidate the budget deficit. But politicians demonstrated that they can quarrel just as much over how to spend a surplus as they can on how to get rid of a deficit, and Republicans showed that they could fight each other with as much zeal as when they battle Democrats.

Even before Congress started work on the budget resolution, Bill Clinton made two astute moves that put congressional Republicans on the defensive and split their ranks. The first, in the 1998 State of the Union Address, was a four-word demand—"save Social Security first"—which put Republicans on notice that the president would oppose using the looming surplus for tax cuts. Clinton did not offer any concrete proposals for strengthening Social Security, but his démarche had the effect of portraying tax cuts as undermining the viability of the Social Security system. His second ploy, in his fiscal 1999 budget, was to use $65 billion in tobacco money (that would come either from a tax on cigarettes or from tobacco litigation) to offset additional spending that he proposed on education and other social programs. The fact that the offset breached budget rules (separating discretionary expenditures from direct spending and revenues) did not hinder Clinton, for he was able to depict the issue as tobacco versus kids.

These two issues—tax cuts and tobacco money—became fault lines in Congress when the House and Senate worked on the budget resolution. Senate Budget Committee Chair Pete Domenici (R-N. Mex.) put together a status quo resolution that contained a token tax cut, re-

continued

STRUCTURE AND CONTENT OF THE BUDGET RESOLUTION

A budget resolution has three types of provisions: budget aggregates and functional allocations, as required by the CBA; optional reconciliation instructions, inserted at the budget committees' discretion (since 1980, when reconciliation was first used, most resolutions have contained reconciliation instructions, but their form and scope have varied); and "sense of the Congress" statements and other nonbinding provisions, included in most resolutions, which give members an opportunity to go on record concerning federal budget issues.

Budget Aggregates

CBA requires four main aggregates (exhibits 6-1 and 6-2):

— total revenue and the amount by which the total should be changed;

— total new budget authority and outlays;

— the deficit or surplus; and

— the public debt.

These totals do not include the receipts and outlays of the Social Security trust funds that are, by law, off budget. As a result, when the unified federal budget ran a surplus in the late 1990s, the budget resolution continued to show a deficit. The Senate, but not the House, separately sets

BOX 6-1
Continued

jected Clinton's spending initiatives, and held discretionary spending to approximately the level set in the caps. After some internal battles among Republicans, Domenici got the Senate to pass his resolution unaltered on a mostly party line vote, 57-41, on April 2. He was aided by Senate rules that require a 60-vote approval for the tax cuts that some Republican colleagues wanted.

House Republicans delayed work on the budget resolution, hoping that buoyant revenue estimates would bolster their case for tax cuts. CBO progressively raised the estimated surplus, from $8 billion in March to $63 billion just three months later. House Budget Committee Chair John Kasich (R-Ohio) decided to craft a resolution that would appeal to the conservative wing of the party to enhance his prospects of winning the Republican presidential nomination in 2000. Kasich's proposal had $70 billion in tax cuts, $150 billion in spending reductions, and abolition of one or more Cabinet departments. On June 5 his resolution squeaked through the House on a 216-204 vote.

Once the deadline for adopting the resolution passed, the appropriations committees began marking up their spending bills. More important, Congress passed a costly transportation bill that added tens of billions of dollars to federal spending (see box 8-2) and made a mockery of the House Budget Committee's cutback efforts.

In conference, the House and Senate budget resolutions were poles apart. The Senate had tobacco money but no reconciliation instructions; the House had reconciliation but no tobacco money. The Senate did not curb spending or include major tax cuts; the House had both. Kasich wanted an issue more than he wanted a budget resolution; Domenici, one of Congress's leading advocates of biennial budgeting, preferred inaction over a resolution that would reopen budget wounds. De facto, Domenici got a two-year budget when the conference broke up without a resolution. Kasich got an issue, but not what he had hoped for. His proposed spending cuts evaporated and were replaced, as box 5-4 chronicles, by sizable spending increases.

forth Social Security revenues and outlays in the resolution. From time to time, Congress has altered the treatment of Social Security in the budget, and it is likely to do so again.

CBA requires members of Congress to vote on, and thereby take responsibility for, budget totals. If there were no resolution, the totals would simply be the arithmetic sum of past decisions, new legislation, current appropriations, and the impact of economic conditions on revenues and expenditures. Voting on total outlays and the deficit has been onerous for many members, who are in the position of endorsing budget outcomes they do not favor. The public debt limit has also been a

hard vote. The limit is largely symbolic, for it does not effectively control the amount the government borrows or owes. Nevertheless, because law limits the total debt, Congress must periodically pass legislation raising the limit. It must do so even when there is a surplus because money borrowed from Social Security and other trust funds is included in the statutory limit on the public debt. To ease the political burden, the House has a special procedure whereby passage of the budget resolution is also deemed to pass the debt limit legislation. The Senate does not have a comparable procedure. Hence senators must vote twice: once on the budget resolution and again on raising the statutory debt limit.

▶ **EXHIBIT 6-1**
Budget Aggregates: Revenue and Budget Authority

The following budgetary levels are appropriate for the fiscal years 2000 through 2009:

(1) FEDERAL REVENUES.—For purposes of the enforcement of this resolution—

(a) The recommended levels of Federal revenues are as follows:

Fiscal year 2000: $1,408,082,000,000.
Fiscal year 2001: $1,434,837,000,000.
Fiscal year 2002: $1,454,757,000,000.
Fiscal year 2003: $1,531,512,000,000.
Fiscal year 2004: $1,584,969,000,000.
Fiscal year 2005: $1,648,259,000,000.
Fiscal year 2006: $1,681,438,000,000.
Fiscal year 2007: $1,735,646,000,000.
Fiscal year 2008: $1,805,517,000,000.
Fiscal year 2009: $1,868,515,000,000.

(b) The amounts by which the aggregate levels of Federal revenues should be changed are as follows:

Fiscal year 2000: $0.
Fiscal year 2001: –$7,810,000,000.
Fiscal year 2002: –$53,519,000,000.
Fiscal year 2003: –$31,806,000,000.

Fiscal year 2004: –$49,180,000,000.
Fiscal year 2005: –$62,637,000,000.
Fiscal year 2006: –$109,275,000,000.
Fiscal year 2007: –$135,754,000,000.
Fiscal year 2008: –$150,692,000,000.
Fiscal year 2009: –$177,195,000,000.

(2) NEW BUDGET AUTHORITY.—For purposes of the enforcement of this resolution, the appropriate levels of total new budget authority are as follows:

Fiscal year 2000: $1,426,720,000,000.
Fiscal year 2001: $1,455,785,000,000.
Fiscal year 2002: $1,486,875,000,000.
Fiscal year 2003: $1,559,079,000,000.
Fiscal year 2004: $1,612,910,000,000.
Fiscal year 2005: $1,666,657,000,000.
Fiscal year 2006: $1,698,214,000,000.
Fiscal year 2007: $1,753,326,000,000.
Fiscal year 2008: $1,814,537,000,000.
Fiscal year 2009: $1,874,778,000,000.

Source: *Conference Report on the Budget Resolution: Fiscal Year 2000*, H. Rept. 91, 106th Cong., 1st sess., 1999, pp. 2–3.

(a) The first part of a budget resolution sets forth total revenues, the amounts by which revenues are to be changed, new budget authority, outlays, the deficit or surplus, and the public debt. The revenues and budget authority totals in the fiscal 2000 budget resolution are displayed here.

(b) These totals do not include the revenues and outlays of the Social Security trust funds. In comparing budget data from different sources, one should ascertain whether Social Security is included. The totals published in the president's budget usually include Social Security; hence, comparison with the aggregates in the budget resolution may require an adjustment for Social Security.

(c) Revenue changes may be either increases or decreases, but they cover only changes due to legislation, not those resulting from changes in the volume of economic activity or in the behavior of taxpayers.

(d) This and subsequent budget resolutions set final budget aggregates and functional allocations for ten years. The previous practice established targets for five years.

EXHIBIT 6-2
Budget Aggregates: Outlays, Deficit, and Debt Limit

(3) BUDGET OUTLAYS.—For purposes of the enforcement of this resolution, the appropriate levels of total budget outlays are as follows:

Fiscal year 2000: $1,408,082,000,000.
Fiscal year 2001: $1,434,837,000,000.
Fiscal year 2002: $1,454,757,000,000.
Fiscal year 2003: $1,531,512,000,000.
Fiscal year 2004: $1,583,753,000,000.
Fiscal year 2005: $1,639,568,000,000.
Fiscal year 2006: $1,667,838,000,000.
Fiscal year 2007: $1,717,042,000,000.
Fiscal year 2008: $1,781,865,000,000.
Fiscal year 2009: $1,841,858,000,000.

(4) DEFICITS OR SURPLUSES.—For purposes of the enforcement of this resolution, the amounts of the deficits or surpluses are as follows:

Fiscal year 2000: $0.
Fiscal year 2001: $0.
Fiscal year 2002: $0.
Fiscal year 2003: $0.
Fiscal year 2004: $1,216,000,000.
Fiscal year 2005: $8,691,000,000.
Fiscal year 2006: $13,600,000,000.
Fiscal year 2007: $18,604,000,000.
Fiscal year 2008: $23,652,000,000.
Fiscal year 2009: $26,657,000,000.

(5) PUBLIC DEBT.—The appropriate levels of the public debt are as follows:

Fiscal year 2000: $5,628,400,000,000.
Fiscal year 2001: $5,708,500,000,000.
Fiscal year 2002: $5,793,500,000,000.
Fiscal year 2003: $5,877,400,000,000.
Fiscal year 2004: $5,956,300,000,000.
Fiscal year 2005: $6,024,600,000,000.
Fiscal year 2006: $6,084,600,000,000.
Fiscal year 2007: $6,136,500,000,000.
Fiscal year 2008: $6,173,900,000,000.
Fiscal year 2009: $6,203,400,000,000.

Source: *Conference Report on the Budget Resolution: Fiscal Year 2000*, H. Rept. 91, 106th Cong., 1st sess., 1999, p. 3–4.

(a) The outlay amounts in the budget resolution are estimates; actual outlays depend on the rate that budget authority and other budget resources are spent. The Budget Enforcement Act imposed limits on discretionary outlays, as explained in chapter 4.

(b) These aggregates exclude Social Security. If Social Security were included, the budget resolution would show a surplus for all years listed here. The budgeted surplus would grow from $142 billion in fiscal 2000 to about $473 billion in fiscal 2009. The actual surplus, if any, depends on both congressional actions and the performance of the economy.

(c) For each of the outyears covered by the resolution (2001–09), Congress will adopt a new budget resolution, undoubtedly revising these totals and other entries. The fiscal 2009 amounts will be revised at least nine times (assuming Congress adopts a budget resolution each year).

(d) Each year's increase in the public debt is greater than that year's budgeted deficit. The main reason for this discrepancy is that the public debt includes money borrowed from trust funds, including Social Security funds. Amounts borrowed from these funds are included in the public debt; they are excluded from a separate measure, "debt held by the public." The latter amount is about $2 trillion less than the public debt. This $2 trillion represents the balances held in various trust funds.

Functional Allocations

The budget resolution allocates total new budget authority, outlays, direct loans, and loan guarantees among the twenty budget functions listed in exhibit 6-3 (two functional categories, Allowances and Undistributed Offsetting Receipts, are not exhibited here). Each function is divided into a number of subfunctions, and each budget account is assigned to a subfunction. The last three digits in an account's identification code represent the subfunction in which it is classified. Although the subfunctions express Congress's budget priorities, they do not bind the appropriations committees in recommending funds for federal programs and agencies. As the section 302 allocations (discussed later in the chapter) have become more important as the basis for Congress's internal budget control, the functional allocations have receded in importance.

Functional allocations must add up to the corresponding budget aggregates. This rule of consistency is strictly enforced; it bars members of Congress from proposing increases or decreases in functional amounts without also proposing adjustments in the budget totals. The requirement of arithmetic consistency is fundamental to budgeting, but in politics consistency is not always easy to achieve. Public opinion polls generally show that Americans want bigger programs and a smaller budget. They favor reductions in total federal spending but oppose reductions in particular programs. They prefer larger allocations to the various budget functions but encourage cutbacks in government spending. Arithmetic consistency means that elected politicians may not do what the voters want. Some members of Congress resolve the contradictions in public opinion by voting to raise functional allocations while opposing the budget resolution on the grounds that total spending is too high.

The budget resolution does not allocate funds among specific programs or accounts; doing so would trespass on the jurisdiction of the spending committees. The lack of line-item detail in the budget resolution complicates its passage, for members cannot readily take credit for earmarking funds to particular programs. Congressional rules require members to vote on budget resolutions without getting credit for spending on popular programs and often without knowing how much particular programs will get. Although the resolution does not mention programs, the committee report accompanying it often specifies the program assumptions underlying the functional allocations (exhibit 6-4). In some years the budget committees' reports have recommended or provided specified amounts for particular programs. But the amounts are not binding, and the appropriations committees may disregard them. However, to the extent that the functional allocations reflect consensus or majority sentiment in Congress, they may influence the appropriations committees' actions. Since appropriators value their independence, it is rare that they implement all the budget resolution's expectations.

Finally, the budget resolution often contains provisions that either express nonbinding sentiments or attempt to influence budget policy. For example, the fiscal 1998 resolution specified discretionary spending limits for each of the next six years, prescribed how revenue from the sale of government assets should be accounted for in the budget, and established reserve funds to cover possible legislation. The resolution also contained more than two dozen "sense of the Congress" (or of the House or Senate) statements expressing views on budget issues. One of these called for a change in baseline scoring practices, another for legislation authorizing the sale of loan assets held by the federal government, and a third for tax cuts to benefit working families.

▶ EXHIBIT 6-3
Functional Allocations in the Fiscal Year 1999 Budget Resolution

(in billions of dollars)		1998	1999	2000	2001	2002	2003
050 National Defense	BA	267.7	270.5	274.3	280.8	288.6	296.8
	O	268.1	265.5	268.0	269.7	272.1	279.8
150 International Affairs	BA	15.2	14.6	14.3	15.1	15.2	15.2
	O	14.1	14.2	14.7	14.5	14.5	14.4
250 Science, Space, and Technology	BA	18.0	18.3	17.8	17.7	17.3	17.0
	O	17.7	17.9	17.9	17.6	17.4	17.0
270 Energy	BA	0.5	0.6	0.6	0.5	0.4	0.4
	O	1.0	0.3	. . .	−0.2	−0.4	−0.4
300 Natural Resources and Environment	BA	24.2	23.4	23.3	23.0	22.9	22.9
	O	23.0	23.4	23.5	23.4	23.0	22.9
350 Agriculture	BA	11.8	12.0	11.6	10.3	10.2	10.4
	O	10.8	10.5	9.9	8.7	8.5	8.8
370 Commerce and Housing Credit:	BA	7.9	4.2	15.5	14.7	15.6	14.9
Total (on-budget and off-budget)	O	1.3	3.2	10.4	10.4	11.8	11.7
400 Transportation	BA	46.0	51.5	51.8	52.1	51.4	52.0
	O	42.5	42.8	44.7	45.7	45.8	46.9
450 Community and Regional Development	BA	8.7	8.7	7.9	7.6	7.6	7.6
	O	11.2	10.9	9.7	8.9	8.1	8.1
500 Education, Training, Employment, and Social Services	BA	61.3	63.0	63.3	64.5	64.9	68.4
	O	56.1	61.0	62.7	63.8	63.7	67.1
550 Health	BA	136.2	145.8	152.6	161.5	170.1	181.2
	O	132.0	143.7	151.6	160.4	169.9	181.1
570 Medicare	BA	199.2	210.3	221.8	239.4	251.2	273.4
	O	199.7	210.9	221.1	242.3	248.8	273.6
600 Income Security	BA	229.5	243.3	257.3	268.5	279.2	289.8
	O	234.7	248.1	259.4	266.7	274.2	282.4
650 Social Security	BA	378.9	394.7	412.0	430.9	451.9	474.5
Total (on-budget and off-budget)	O	379.1	394.9	412.0	430.9	451.9	474.5
700 Veterans' Benefits	BA	42.6	42.8	43.4	44.8	46.2	48.2
	O	42.5	43.3	44.0	45.2	46.6	48.6
750 Administration of Justice	BA	25.1	25.8	24.5	24.5	24.7	25.0
	O	22.5	24.6	24.9	24.8	24.3	24.2
800 General Government	BA	14.5	14.4	13.9	13.6	13.4	13.5
	O	14.3	13.4	13.8	13.8	13.6	13.5
900 Net Interest:	BA	245.1	247.3	242.7	236.7	230.5	225.5
Total (on-budget and off-budget)	O	245.1	247.3	242.7	236.7	230.5	225.5

Source: *Concurrent Resolution on the Budget: Fiscal Year 1999*, S. Rept. 170, 105th Cong., 2d sess., 1998, pp. 65–66.

(a) The functional categories group together related programs. A single function may cover programs funded in several appropriations acts and carried out by various federal agencies. Total budget authority and outlays are allocated among twenty budget functions; the sum of these allocations must equal the corresponding budget aggregates.

▶ **EXHIBIT 6-4**
Program Assumptions Underlying the Functional Allocations

Function 750: Administration of Justice

For discretionary spending the Committee-reported resolution assumes $25.2 billion in budget authority and $24.0 billion in outlays for 1999. This represents an increase of $1.0 billion in budget authority and $2.4 billion in outlays, a 4.0 percent and an 11.3 percent increase respectively over 1998. The discretionary spending increase includes $5.8 billion in budget authority and $5.4 billion in outlays for the Violent Crime Reduction Trust Fund (VCRTF) programs. Compared to 1998, this funding represents a 5 percent increase in budget authority and an 8 percent increase in outlays for VCRTF. The 1999 Committee-reported resolution is $0.4 billion in budget authority above and $0.2 billion in outlays below the BBA. It is $0.8 billion in budget authority and $0.6 billion in outlays above the freeze. The Committee resolution assumes the following policy options to achieve the recommended funding levels.

The resolution fully funds the VCRTF with $5.8 billion in budget authority and $5.4 billion in outlays. It assumes current policy funding for the Local Law Enforcement Block Grants, which were terminated under the President's proposal, and it assumes $1.4 billion will be available for completion of the Community Oriented Policing Services program (Cops on the Beat). The President assumes the program will have fulfilled its objectives in 1999 and requests no additional funds beyond next year. The Committee also recommends increased funding over the baseline for juvenile crime reduction programs by $100 million in 1999, a 43 percent increase over 1998, for a total increase of $1.5 billion in budget authority over five years.

Source: *Concurrent Resolution on the Budget: Fiscal Year 1999*, S. Rept. 170, 105th Cong., 2d sess., 1998, p. 44.

(a) Program assumptions are not included in the text of the budget resolution. Members, however, insert the assumptions' underlying function allocations in committee reports on the budget resolution because they want to know what the allocations portend for the programs they are interested in, and they want to create a legislative history that may influence future budget decisions.

(b) This excerpt pertains to Function 750 Administration of Justice; it provides the detailed assumptions made by the Senate Budget Committee in its report on the fiscal 1999 budget resolution. The committee also made assumptions for the other budget functions, as did the House Budget Committee in its report on the resolution. In some years the House committee makes detailed assumptions, while the Senate committee only offers general comment. For 1999, however, the reverse occurred; the House Budget Committee did little more than describe each function, while the Senate committee made detailed program assumptions.

(c) Although these assumptions do not bind other committees, to the extent they manifest a consensus on future spending, they may influence subsequent congressional action on appropriations and other measures. It is highly unlikely, however, that the appropriations committees will comply with all of the program assumptions. Doing so would indicate their subservience to the budget committees.

These types of statements serve as substitutes for legislative action; they enable members to go on record for or against certain matters, even when no legislation is forthcoming. Some of these statements have appeared in the budget resolution year after year.

The Budget Committees

The House and Senate budget committees are responsible for developing the budget resolution and shepherding it through their respective chambers. The resolution can originate in either the House or Senate, in contrast with revenue bills, which must originate in the House, or appropriation bills, which until the late 1990s always did. In most years there is extensive consultation between the two committees before they mark up the resolution.

The budget committees appear to be like other congressional committees, with their own jurisdiction, membership, and staffs. But they are different—their jurisdiction is very circumscribed and very broad. The budget resolution and reconciliation bills are their only legislative products: the former cannot become a law, and the latter must be assembled without changing the substantive provisions that other committees insert. They keep busy year-round monitoring budget developments and the work of other committees. Occasionally, they issue reports on topical budget issues, but they do not produce legislation dealing with these issues.

The budget committees are both powerful and weak—powerful because they can initiate sweeping changes in federal tax and spending policy and weak because they are dependent on other committees to carry these changes through the legislative labyrinth. They are strong when the budget resolution propels changes in policy, weak when the resolution merely accommodates the status quo. When

they were established in 1974, there was fear that they would become congressional bullies, forcing other committees to produce legislation against their will. After a quarter of a century, it should be apparent that these committees are only as strong as the House and Senate are willing for them to be. As Congress's budget mood changes from year to year, so too does the legislative standing of the budget committees.

Fear that the budget committees would become too powerful was especially pronounced in the House, where liberals were concerned that the fiscal discipline imposed by the new congressional budget process would be used as a club against social programs. To ease these fears, CBA limited service on the House Budget Committee to two consecutive Congresses (this was later increased to three Congresses) and assigned more than half the seats to members of the House Appropriations and Ways and Means Committees and to the majority and minority leadership. These provisions were designed to deter members from using the Budget Committee as a power base; they could make a splash, but not a career, on the committee. The Senate Budget Committee does not have a comparable limitation, and some of its leaders have used the committee to enhance their legislative careers.

Over the years the budget committees have evolved into instruments of the House and Senate party leaderships. Rather than operating autonomously (as most committees do), the budget committees shape the resolution to reflect the preferences of the majority party's leaders in Congress. They consult with Democratic or Republican leaders before drafting the resolution and rely on the leadership to win its passage. Several factors account for the strong role of party leaders in determining the resolution's policy orientation.

First, the budget resolution covers a broad swath of legislative issues: it deals with defense, agriculture, transportation, and just about every other area of legislative activity. Congress's budget posture affects most major legislation, and there inevitably are disputes between the budget committees and others over the priority and dollars to be accorded to particular areas. Party leaders often iron out differences among the committees and settle disputes over both aggregates and functional allocations.

Second, the budget resolution is one of the most partisan matters Congress takes up each year. What is at stake is not just the legislative preferences of one or another committee, but the Republican budget or the Democratic budget. When the president is of the other party, as has been the case for all but half a dozen years since the congressional budget process was inaugurated, the resolution is seen as Congress's alternative budget policy. Only party leaders can represent the range of views needed to formulate and defend the party's position on the budget.

Finally, because of party line voting and fissures within Democratic and Republican ranks, in many years it has been hard to assemble a majority in favor of the budget resolution. Party leaders make deals and apply pressure to get the resolution through the House and Senate. In lining up the votes, they have gained a strong voice in determining the orientation and content of the budget resolution.

FORMULATING THE BUDGET RESOLUTION

The budget committees cannot mark up the budget resolution in a normal legislative manner. Although the resolution is a brief document, it touches the interests of virtually all House and Senate committees. The resolution is the budget committees' business, but it also happens to be the business of the revenue, appropriations, and most authorizing commit-

tees. It is not enough that the budget committees comprehend the budget and its policy implications; they must also know what other committees care about. They hold hearings and rely on CBO data and reports as well as on "views and estimates" submitted by other committees. But their most important sources of information come from informal, behind-the-scenes discussions with party leaders, committee chairs, and rank-and-file members. These discussions deal with big issues (such as changes in tax levels and legislative initiatives), but they also fill in some of the program detail that is of interest to members of Congress but missing from the resolution.

CBO's baseline provides a useful starting point for preparing the resolution. It enables the budget committees to focus on policy changes rather than on the myriad line items that constitute the budget. CBO also produces an annual *Economic and Budget Outlook* that projects the budget on the basis of economic assumptions over the next ten years. In assisting the budget committees, CBO must be within easy reach but remain distant. It must get involved with estimates and analysis but maintain its independence from the partisan fray. Balancing these conflicting pressures is not always easy, for as much as Congress depends on CBO for reliable data, CBO depends on Congress to use the information it provides. Once in a while the strife and tensions of congressional budgeting pressure CBO to compromise its independence. But over the years it has nonetheless steadfastly maintained its reputation as a supplier of objective information. Box 6-2 contains excerpts of correspondence in which CBO Director June O'Neill rebuffed demands by House Republican leaders in 1998 that her agency provide more optimistic revenue estimates to bolster their case for including a tax cut in the budget resolution. O'Neill held her ground, thereby reinforcing CBO's reputation as an independent, nonpartisan source of budgetary advice and information.

By mid-March each year, committees submit their views and estimates on budgetary matters in their jurisdiction to the budget committees. An excerpt from one such report appears in exhibit 6-5. These documents are supposed to alert the budget committees to the plans and preferences of other committees; over the years they have become less revealing and less useful. Although a few committees treat this report as an opportunity to lay out their legislative agenda or to comment on the president's budget, many have come to regard it as one of the things they have to do to get through the annual budget cycle. Because the views and estimates are prepared early in the session, most committees avoid locking themselves into specific budgetary or legislative positions. Instead, they practice defensive budgeting—seeking to derail presidential recommendations they oppose while keeping congressional options open for opportunities that may materialize later in the session. Most committees prefer informal channels of communications to advise the budget committees of their preferences and to obtain assurance that their interests are protected in the resolution.

Budget committee chairs use the period between the hearings and the markup to develop the majority party's position on budget issues and to consult with others on their preferences. The chairs usually convene their committees to mark up the resolution after reaching an understanding in the majority party. In 1998, however, House Budget Chair John Kasich (R-Ohio) drafted a resolution calling for a new round of spending cuts without first obtaining consensus in Republican ranks. The ensuing friction and disarray delayed adoption of the resolution and contributed to Congress's failure

to complete its budget work. In the House, the Budget Committee's preresolution consultations have always been partisan. In the Senate, during the early years of the process the chair reached out to the minority party in an effort to broaden support for the resolution. In the 1990s, however, partisanship drove a wedge between Democrats and Republicans on the Senate Budget Committee.

The markup is organized around the "chairman's mark," a document that proposes the aggregates, functional allocations, and other provisions to be included in the resolution. If agreement among majority party members has been secured in advance and everything goes according to script, the committee will ratify the chair's proposal with almost all Democrats voting on one side and almost all Republicans on the other. The committee may alter the chair's mark, but doing so can be difficult because the markup is usually conducted under "budget neutral" rules, which require proposed spending increases to be offset by proposed cuts or by increasing the totals.

Although the resolution does not itself mention programs, much of the discussion at markup concerns particular programs. In committee, members often try to obtain assurance that the amount allocated for a particular function can accommodate the programs in which they are interested. These discussions create a legislative history that might make the difference later in the year when appropriations are decided.

FLOOR ACTION

House and Senate rules and practices guide debate on the budget resolution. In the House, the Rules Committee usually devises a "special rule" (in the form of a simple House resolution), which, once approved, sets the terms under which the budget resolution is consid-

---

BOX 6-2
CBO Independence: Challenge and Defense

CBO's role in developing baseline projections and scoring the budgetary impact of legislation sometimes places it into conflict with members of Congress. Members often try to influence CBO's estimates behind the scenes, but it is rare that disputes break out into the open. However, in 1998, as this exchange of letters indicates, House Speaker Newt Gingrich (R-Ga.) and CBO Director June O'Neill clashed on the accuracy of CBO's revenue projections. At stake were Republican claims that a projection of higher revenues (and therefore a bigger surplus) would strengthen their case for tax cuts. Although CBO had increased its original revenue projection for fiscal year 1999 by $72 billion, the Republican leadership argued that this estimate should have been raised by a greater amount.

The first salvo was fired by House Republican leaders in a letter to Rep. James Walsh (R-N.Y.), who chaired the House Legislative Branch Appropriations Subcommittee. Implied in this was the threat that if CBO was not more accommodating in revenue estimates, its appropriations would be cut:

"We are deeply concerned about the increasing evidence that the Congressional Budget Office (CBO) is utterly unable to predict consistent and accurate future revenues or even the fiscal implications of changes in budget policy. Because of these failures, I urge you to direct the CBO to address these shortcomings immediately.

While forecasting is an inexact science and there is some logic to being cautious, the CBO's low estimates have been consistently wrong—and wrong by a country mile. Currently, the CBO is estimating that real GDP growth will be a slow 2.1 percent over the long-term. Yet over the past 16 years the average GDP growth has been 3.0 percent, in line with the entire post World War II period. In the past, this understatement of GDP growth by 1 percent per year on average resulted in dramatic overestimates of the budget deficit and underestimates of the growing surplus. Comparing the CBO's 1998 deficit estimate from May 1996 to that of May 1998 shows a massive difference of $275 billion—from a $222 billion *deficit* to a $53 billion *surplus*.

continued

---

ered. Typically, the rule allows the minority party to offer a substitute resolution and may also permit amendments on particular provisions. The minority never gets its way, for party lines are sharply drawn in the House, where (as table 6-2 shows) Democrats and Republicans have almost always taken the opposite position on passage of the resolution. In most years the majority party has supplied almost all the votes needed to pass the resolu-

tion; it can count on little or no help from the minority. This condition prevailed in the 1970s and 1980s, when the Democrats were the majority in the House, and it persisted in the late 1990s, when the Republicans had majority status. Regardless of which party is the majority, it often encounters deep fissures within its ranks on budget policy. For years the Democrats had difficulty bridging differences between the liberal and conservative wings of

BOX 6-2
Continued

These forecasts are the foundation upon which Congress crafts legislation. Congress should not be put in a position of relying upon incorrect information. The CBO must address this problem. If it does not, I believe we must review the structure and funding for the CBO in this appropriations cycle."

CBO Director June O'Neill responded two weeks later, upholding CBO's objectivity and independence in budget work:

"It is important that we understand your concerns so that we can respond to them. We at CBO take our obligation to the Congress and to the country very seriously. We understand how important it is to produce state-of-the-art and unbiased estimates, projections, and studies with the highest degree of accuracy possible. CBO staff—a well-trained group of professionals—work hard to do so. . . .

Estimating errors, even large ones, can never be eliminated given the complexity of the federal government's budget, which is greatly affected by the economy here and abroad and by numerous other factors that are difficult, if not impossible, to predict exactly. With total revenues and outlays each approaching $1.7 trillion, even very small percentage deviations from CBO's projected amounts can easily swing budgetary outcomes by tens of billions of dollars. . . .

We have particularly emphasized the uncertainty involved in economic and budget forecasting in our twice-yearly reports to the Congress on the economic and budget outlook. We have also taken steps to provide the Congress with an early-warning mechanism that will signal when actual receipts and outlays are deviating from our estimates for the current fiscal year. . . ."

Sources: Letter from Republican Leaders to Chair of the House Legislative Branch Appropriations Subcommittee, James Walsh (R-N.Y.), Washington, June 9, 1998; excerpts from a letter to Speaker Newt Gingrich (R-Ga.) from CBO Director June O'Neill, Washington, June 23, 1998.

the party. More recently, Republicans have had difficulty balancing the preferences of those in its ranks who want to downsize government and those who prefer the status quo.

The situation was different in the Senate during the early years of the congressional budget process, when bipartisan cooperation facilitated adoption of the resolution (as table 6-3 shows). Partisanship emerged when the Republicans gained control of the Senate in 1981

and has persisted in most years since. In some recent years every minority party senator has voted against the resolution, requiring the majority party to shop among its own members for the necessary votes. Senate rules limit debate on the resolution to fifty hours, thus precluding filibusters and other dilatory tactics.

In both the House and Senate, amendments must preserve the arithmetic consistency of the resolution. An amendment changing any func-

▶ **EXHIBIT 6-5**
Views and Estimates Report

I am extremely concerned with proposals in the President's budget relating to assistance to state and local law enforcement. State and local law enforcement assistance programs, funded largely through the Office of Justice Programs (OJP) and its constituent offices, are a major component of the overall Department of Justice Budget. For FY 1999, OJP funding is estimated by the President's proposed budget to be $4.678 billion, or 22.3 percent of the Department's $20.92 billion proposed budget. . . .

As in past years, however, the President's budget request includes unwise programmatic and funding recommendations which, if adopted by the Congress, would put at risk programs vital to the hard-forged partnership between the federal government and state and local governments to combat crime across the nation. Indeed, the President proposes a $485 million cut in OJP funding, a reduction of 9.3 percent from FY 1998. The recent gains of state and local law enforcement in the fight against violent crime are fragile, and we ought not risk present tentative successes with unwise budget cuts and the adoption of untested programs. . . .

I strongly recommend that the Budget Committee reject the President's juvenile crime proposal, and adopt instead a budget resolution based on the provisions of S. 10, the Hatch-Sessions Violent and Repeat Juvenile Offender Act of 1997. This legislation, which the Senate will consider in the coming months, includes a $500 million block grant for state and local accountability based juvenile crime reduction efforts, as well as reform and reauthorization of key JJDPA programs such as the Part B state formula grants, the Part D Gang Free Schools and Communities programs, and the Part G mentoring program.

Source: Excerpts of a letter from Chair of the Senate Judiciary Committee, Orrin Hatch (R-Utah), in *Concurrent Resolution on the Budget: Fiscal Year 1999*, S. Rept. 170, 105th Cong., 2d sess., 1998, pp. 132–34.

(a) Section 301(c) of the Congressional Budget Act provides for each House and Senate committee to report to the budget committee of its chamber its views and estimates on budgetary matters within its jurisdiction. These views and estimates are sometimes published by the House or Senate Budget Committee in the report on the resolution. The excerpts shown here are from the Senate Judiciary Committee's views on the fiscal 1999 budget resolution.

(b) There is no standard practice concerning the views and estimates. Some committees offer only perfunctory comments—others go into detail on programs and budgets. For example, the Senate Energy and Natural Resources Committee submitted a three-line report that endorsed a balanced budget and stated that it did not expect to report any legislation that would create unfunded mandates. The Senate Governmental Affairs Committee, by contrast, prepared a 15-page letter.

(c) This excerpt, like many other views and estimates reports, comments on proposals in the president's budget, indicating areas of agreement and disagreement. Few committees comment on all programs in their jurisdiction.

TABLE 6-2
House Votes on Adoption of the Budget Resolution, by Party, Fiscal Years 1976–2001[a]

Fiscal year	Total		Democrats		Republicans	
	Yes	No	Yes	No	Yes	No
1976	200	196	197	68	3	128
1977	221	155	208	44	13	111
1978	213	179	206	58	7	121
1979	201	197	198	61	3	136
1980	220	184	211	50	9	134
1981	225	193	203	62	22	131
1982	270	154	84	153	186	1
1983	219	206	63	174	156	32
1984	229	196	225	36	4	160
1985	250	168	229	29	21	139
1986	258	170	234	15	24	155
1987	245	179	228	19	17	160
1988	230	192	230	19	0	173
1989	319	102	227	24	92	78
1990	263	157	157	96	106	61
1991[b]	218	208	218	34	0	174
1992	261	163	243	17	18	145
1993[c]	215	201	214	44	0	157
1994	243	183	242	11	0	172
1995	223	175	222	11	0	164
1996	238	193	8	191	230	1
1997	226	195	5	190	221	4
1998	333	99	132	72	201	26
1999	216	204	3	194	213	9
2000	221	208	4	205	217	2
2001	211	207	2	201	208	5

Sources: *Congressional Quarterly Almanac*, 1975–98; *Congressional Record*, March 25, 1999, p. H1780; March 23, 2000, p. H1401.

a. Votes are on adoption of the budget resolution in the House, not on the conference report. For fiscal 1976 through fiscal 1982, Congress adopted two or more resolutions; for those years, the votes shown here are on the first resolution. When the president's party does not control the House, a "no" vote is in support of the president. Since 1992 Rep. Bernard Sanders (I-Vt.) is included in the total but not in the breakdown by parties. Since 1992, Independents are included in the total but not in the breakdown by parties.

b. A second budget resolution was passed on October 9; the votes shown here are for the first resolution.

c. The House passed two budget resolutions, Plan A and Plan B; the votes shown here are for Plan A.

tional allocation must make reciprocal adjustments in other parts of the resolution. This rule, in combination with PAYGO and the discretionary spending caps, made it difficult to win adoption of floor amendments increasing expenditures or cutting revenues.

WHY THE RESOLUTION IS RARELY ADOPTED ON SCHEDULE

In the final stages of the budget resolution process, a conference committee resolves differences between the House and Senate versions. As shown by the entries in table 6-1,

TABLE 6-3
Senate Votes on Adoption of the Budget Resolution, by Party, Fiscal Years 1976–2001[a]

Fiscal year	Total Yes	Total No	Democrats Yes	Democrats No	Republicans Yes	Republicans No
1976	69	22	50	4	19	18
1977	62	22	45	6	17	16
1978	56	31	41	14	15	17
1979	64	27	48	8	16	19
1980	64	20	44	5	20	15
1981	68	28	49	6	19	22
1982	78	20	28	18	50	2
1983	49	43	3	41	46	2
1984	50	49	29	17	21	32
1985	41	34	1	31	40	3
1986[b]	50	49	1	45	48	4
1987	70	25	38	6	32	19
1988	56	42	53	0	3	42
1989	69	26	44	6	25	20
1990	68	31	38	17	30	14
1991	Voice vote					
1992	Voice vote					
1993	54	35	36	15	18	20
1994	54	45	54	2	0	43
1995	57	40	55	0	2	40
1996	57	42	3	42	54	0
1997	53	46	0	46	53	0
1998	78	22	37	8	41	14
1999	57	41	3	41	54	0
2000	55	44	1	44	54	0
2001	51	45	0	43	51	2

Sources: *Congressional Quarterly Almanac*, 1975–98; *Congressional Record*, March 25, 1999, p. S3432; April 7, 2000, p. S2429.

a. Votes are on adoption of the budget resolution in the Senate, not on the conference report. For fiscal 1976 through fiscal 1982, Congress adopted two or more resolutions; for those years, the votes shown here are on the first resolution. When the president's party does not control the Senate, a "no" vote is in support of the president.

b. Vice President George Bush voted "yes" to break the tie.

adoption of the conference report often occurs long after the CBA deadline. The original target was May 15; in the mid-1980s Congress moved it one month earlier but since then it has been even more laggard than before.

Deadlines are missed because members often have more reasons to vote against the resolution than for it. It is easier to vote against big deficits than for them, easier to vote for individual spending items than for spending totals, easier not to vote on the public debt limit than to vote for a $5 trillion debt. Deadlines are missed because nothing stops if the budget resolution is behind schedule or even if it is not adopted. Congress still makes appropriations and federal agencies continue to operate.

Getting the budget resolution adopted is a political ordeal. Republicans have one plan for disposing of the surplus or dealing with the deficit; Democrats have another. The president presents his priorities; Congress has others. Debate on the budget sets one wing of each party against another, the House against the Senate, the parts against the whole, the preference for smaller government against the push for bigger programs, the tax cutters against the debt cutters. The budget resolution is not a law, but it may spawn more strife than if it were. It is a symbol of what divides the parties, of what Americans want from and think is wrong with government, and of failures of will and leadership. If it were a law, and federal revenue and spending were dependent on it, the resolution would have to be enacted. Missing statutory deadlines matters in ways that missing symbolic ones does not.

Until 1998 the budget was a conflict that had a resolution. One way or another, Congress managed to produce a budget resolution, in one case almost half a year after the official deadline. The actual adoption dates suggest a patternless process, budgeting without predictable routines. Some years the resolution made it through only because enough members felt that having a congressional budget was better than not having one. In 1998 a majority just did not care enough to have a resolution. Quite probably, this will not be the last time Congress fails to complete its budget work.

THE RECONCILIATION PROCESS

Reconciliation is the procedure Congress uses to bring revenue and direct spending under existing laws into conformity with the levels set in the budget resolution. The process has two distinct phases: issuance of reconciliation

instructions in the budget resolution and enactment of a reconciliation bill (or bills) changing revenue and spending laws. Two separate procedures are needed because the budget resolution cannot change laws.

Reconciliation is an optional process. Although it has been used frequently since 1980, its scope has varied. As explained earlier, it is used most extensively in years in which major changes are made in budget policy and not at all in years when status quo budgets are adopted.

Reconciliation begins with instructions in a budget resolution directing designated committees to report legislation that changes existing law. Exhibit 6-6, taken from the fiscal 1998 resolution, shows the instructions the House and Senate used. The instructions have three components: they name the committees directed to recommend legislation, they specify the amounts by which existing revenue or direct spending laws are to be changed, and they usually set a deadline by which the committees are to recommend legislation implementing the changes. The Senate and House issue separate instructions to their committees, allowing each chamber to fine-tune the text to its own practices. The instructions usually cover the same fiscal years specified in the budget resolution but do not specify how the changes are to be made or the programs affected—these details are left to the discretion of the committees receiving the instructions.

The number of designated committees indicates the scope of the year's reconciliation process. Because of their jurisdiction over taxes and major entitlements, the House Ways and Means and the Senate Finance Committees are always among the designated committees. In a few years (1981 and 1995 are leading examples), just about every committee with direct spending jurisdiction was drawn into the reconciliation process. Reconciliation instructions

▶ **EXHIBIT 6-6**
Reconciliation Instructions

SENATE INSTRUCTIONS

(a) *Reconciliation of Spending Reductions*—Not later than June 13, 1997, the committees named in this subsection shall submit their recommendations to the Committee on the Budget of the Senate. After receiving those recommendations, the Committee on the Budget shall report to the Senate a reconciliation bill carrying out all such recommendations without any substantive revision.

(1) *Committee on Agriculture, Nutrition, and Forestry*—The Senate Committee on Agriculture, Nutrition, and Forestry shall report changes in laws within its jurisdiction that provide direct spending (as defined in section 250(c)(8) of the Balanced Budget and Emergency Deficit Control Act of 1985) to increase outlays by not more than $300,000,000 in fiscal year 2002 and by not more than $1,500,000,000 for the period of fiscal years 1998 through 2002.

(2) *Committee on Banking, Housing, and Urban Affairs*—The Senate Committee on Banking, Housing, and Urban Affairs shall report changes in laws within its jurisdiction that reduce the deficit $434,000,000 in fiscal year 2002 and $1,590,000,000 for the period of fiscal years 1998 through 2002.

HOUSE INSTRUCTIONS

(1) *Committee on Agriculture*—The House Committee on Agriculture shall report changes in laws within its jurisdiction that provide direct spending such that the total level of direct spending for that committee does not exceed: $34,571,000,000 in outlays for fiscal year 1998, $37,008,000,000 in outlays for fiscal year 2002, and $179,884,000,000 in outlays in fiscal years 1998 through 2002.

(2) *Committee on Banking and Financial Services*—The House Committee on Banking and Financial Services shall report changes in laws within its jurisdiction that provide direct spending such that the total level of direct spending for that committee does not exceed: –$8,435,000,000 in outlays for fiscal year 1998, –$5,091,000,000 in outlays for fiscal year 2002, and –$32,743,000,000 in outlays in fiscal years 1998 through 2002.

Source: *Concurrent Resolution on the Budget: Fiscal Year 1998*, H. Con. Res. 84, 105th Cong., 1st sess., 1997, pp. 14 and 16.

(a) Separate instructions, with different wording, are issued for House and Senate committees. These instructions cover five fiscal years (1998–2002). The wording is changed frequently, and it is common for the text of one year's instructions to differ materially from the prior year's language.

(b) Both the House and Senate set June 13, 1997, as the deadline for committees to submit recommended changes in law; this was barely one week after the conference report on the budget resolution was adopted. While the tight deadline is often missed, it does influence the behavior of affected committees, leading them to recommend financial changes rather than fundamental program revisions.

are not issued to the appropriations committees or to authorizing committees whose jurisdiction is limited to discretionary programs. Additionally, by law, reconciliation may not be used to legislate changes in Social Security.

The dollar amounts in the resolution are computed with reference to the CBO baseline. The changes specified in the instructions are the amounts by which revenues or spending are to be changed from baseline levels. These computations are based on assumptions about the future levels of revenue and spending under current law and the impact of the changes that would ensue from new legislation. Hence the savings that reconciliation generates are assumed savings; the actual savings often diverge, sometimes significantly.

The instructions do not specify how the dollar changes are to be realized or how the programs are to be altered. Mentioning programs in the instructions would violate the legislative division of labor between the budget committees and other congressional committees. This relationship gives the budget committees control of money and authorizing committees control of programs. Reconciliation would break down if the budget committees became so powerful that they could dictate which programs and laws should be altered. Nevertheless, the instructions are based on assumptions concerning the programs reconciliation will affect. Voting on the instructions in the budget resolution is not a pig-in-a-poke exercise in which members of Congress blindly endorse spending changes without awareness of what these changes are likely to be. As noted earlier, program assumptions often are set forth in budget committees' reports on the resolution. Like other assumptions linked to the resolution, these are typically based on understandings worked out in advance between the budget committees and the committees of jurisdiction.

Even when they are published, the program assumptions are not binding. Each committee has discretion to decide on the legislative changes to be made in complying with the instructions. Committees sometimes fall a bit short of the mark, producing less than 100 percent of the targeted savings, but it is rare that a committee ignores or significantly shortchanges the instructions. The budget committees monitor compliance, but even when they find that a committee has not followed the instructions, they cannot unilaterally change the committee's recommendations. When (as is usually the case) more than one committee in the House or Senate is subject to reconciliation, the legislative changes are sent to the budget committee, which consolidates the proposals into an omnibus bill. CBA bars the budget committees from making substantive revisions in the legislation that the committees of jurisdiction send to them. This restriction pertains even when the proposed legislation fails to meet the dollar targets specified in the reconciliation instructions. As a last resort, the budget committee can take the fight to the floor. In the House, it needs a cooperative Rules Committee to offer an amendment to the legislation, as it cannot act unilaterally.

Consolidating the legislative work of many committees into an omnibus reconciliation bill serves several purposes. First, it simplifies the task of coordinating the various pieces of legislation and monitoring their compliance with the instructions. Rather than congest the legislative calendar with numerous bills, the House and Senate take them up in an omnibus measure. Second, all committees subject to reconciliation are treated alike; no committee has to be concerned that Congress might enact the savings it has proposed but not act on the cutbacks proposed by other committees. Finally, consolidating the legislation in an omnibus bill transforms the vote in the House from cutting particular programs into saving the surplus or reducing the deficit. This is not the case when program elements are voted on separately.

Sometimes, however, Congress deems it advantageous to split reconciliation into two or more bills. It did so in 1982 and 1996—years of intense conflict between Democrats and Republicans on budget policy. By splitting various components into separate measures, the House and Senate voted on provisions that had broad support, leaving other items to their own fate. In 1995 the Republican-controlled Congress produced an omnibus reconciliation bill that packaged Medicare cutbacks, tax cuts, and many other provisions into a single measure. President Clinton vetoed that bill and accused Republicans of using cuts in Medicare to pay for tax reductions that would benefit upper income earners. To avoid being attacked again, Republicans devised three separate reconciliation bills the following year; Congress passed the one that reformed federal welfare programs but did not act on the other two dealing with Medicare and taxes.

In most years reconciliation is considered as a package, under rules and procedures that restrict the time available for debate and opportunities to amend the measure. Budget rules require that amendments be revenue-neutral—that they not increase the deficit nor reduce the surplus. To satisfy this restriction, an amendment reducing revenues or increasing spending must contain offsets. The House takes up the reconciliation bill pursuant to a special rule (drafted by the Rules Committee) that specifies which amendments may be considered. Despite the enormous size of some reconciliation bills—the 1995 version covered more than fifteen hundred pages—the Rules Committee typically permits consideration of fewer than half a dozen amendments. One of these usually is a substitute bill offered by the minority party.

In most years the House passes the reconciliation bill compiled by the budget committee with few or no changes.

The Senate allows only twenty hours of debate on the reconciliation bill, which works out to only twelve minutes per member. In some years this amounts to less than one minute per page. When the twenty hours are up, the Senate votes on the bill, including pending amendments, without further debate.

The net effect of the special House and Senate rules is that once the process is initiated by instructions in the resolution, the implementing legislation is passed. The only time that instructions did not lead to a reconciliation act was in 1995, when President Clinton vetoed the omnibus bill compiled by congressional Republicans.

Because there is a strong probability that a reconciliation bill will pass once it is initiated, it is an attractive vehicle for provisions that are unrelated to the budget. In response to this problem, the Senate adopted the "Byrd rule," which restricts the inclusion of extraneous matter in a reconciliation bill. According to this rule, a provision is extraneous if it does not change revenues or outlays, increases outlays or decreases revenues for a committee not in compliance with its reconciliation instructions, is outside the jurisdiction of the committee that inserted the provision, has outlay or revenue provisions that are merely incidental to nonbudgetary items, or would increase future deficits. The Byrd rule may be waived by a three-fifths vote of the Senate. Because of the rule's complexity, its application depends on parliamentary interpretation. The rule has blocked provisions that some may have deemed relevant to deficit reduction while permitting others that have had little impact on the deficit. In 1993, House-passed provisions establishing a procedure for reviewing entitlement expenditures were struck from the bill in the Senate on the grounds that they were not germane to deficit reduction. In 1996, however, the Senate parliamentarian ruled that tax cuts that would have caused the deficit to rise did not violate the Byrd rule.

Reconciliation procedures are cumbersome because they must balance divergent perspectives and interests. Congress's impulse to legislate drives it to expand programs; its need to budget drives it to contract them. The budget committees have a fiscal outlook; authorizing committees have a programmatic perspective. The budget committees control the budget resolution, which targets savings. Authorizing committees control the reconciliation bill; they select the programs. Reconciliation would be a lot simpler if the budget committees did the whole job, but such an unbalanced arrangement would not be sustainable.

Balance comes at some cost. Reconciliation is a leaky process in which not all the savings promised at the start are achieved at the end. Its tight timetable discourages committees from making truly significant changes in affected programs. Instead, reconciliation puts a premium on short-term fixes that enable Congress to come close to the dollar targets without genuine retrenchment. Since its inauguration in 1980, reconciliation has claimed almost $2 trillion in deficit reduction, almost $1 trillion (over ten years) in 1990 and 1993 alone. Yet few programs have been terminated or significantly altered through this process. Over the years Medicare has been the most "reconciled" federal program, yet not a single major benefit available in 1980 is unavailable two decades later.

With a balanced budget, reconciliation may have a new use in the years ahead. Its procedure can be applied to either raise or cut taxes and spending. In the past it was applied almost exclusively to deficit reduction. In the future, if sur-

pluses persist, it may be used to decide whether excess federal money should be returned through tax cuts or spent on program expansions.

ENFORCING CONGRESSIONAL BUDGET DECISIONS

Achieving the outcomes set forth in the budget resolution depends on the actions of Congress and the president, the performance of the economy, and the accuracy of the estimates and assumptions on which the resolution is based. Some critical variables lie beyond Congress's direct control. When economic conditions—growth, employment, inflation, and interest rates—vary from the forecast, so too do actual federal revenues and spending. Budget results also veer off mark if program assumptions, such as the number of participants in entitlement programs, are faulty.

The budget resolution is enforced in terms of new legislation, for this is the only variable Congress directly controls. These appear in the policy changes column in table 6-4. In every year until 1993 the actual deficit was higher than the level set in the budget resolution; in every year since 1993 the actual deficit has been lower. Throughout the period, unbudgeted policy changes added to the deficit, though by lesser amounts than were added by economic changes and estimation errors. Although policy initiatives increased the deficit in fifteen of the nineteen years since 1980, the increases generally were modest and were smaller in the 1990s than in the previous decade. Various enforcement mechanisms promoted legislative compliance, including revenue floors and spending ceilings, the allocation of budget shares to committees (and control of the legislation they produce), cost estimates and scorekeeping reports, and various points of order to block legislation that violates budget rules.

TABLE 6-4
CBO Computation of Differences between Budgeted and Actual Deficits, by Cause, Fiscal Years 1980–98[a]

Billions of dollars

Fiscal year	Policy changes	Economic conditions	Estimation errors[b]	Total change in deficit
1980	13	4	19	36
1981	28	1	29	58
1982	–12	76	9	73
1983	22	59	11	92
1984	15	3	–14	4
1985	23	15	–16	22
1986	16	11	22	49
1987	–15	15	6	6
1988	9	8	29	46
1989	17	–20	20	17
1990	20	49	50	119
1991	–19	32	2	15
1992	12	25	–26	11
1993	12	9	–93	–72
1994	11	–21	–40	–50
1995	2	2	–15	–11
1996	25	–48	–40	–63
1997	–5	–37	–89	–131
1998	7	–71	–96	–160
Mean	12	8	2	15
Average[c]	15	26	33	54

Source: Congressional Budget Office, *The Economic and Budget Outlook: Fiscal Years 2000–2009*, January 1999, table B-3, p. 107.

a. Budgeted deficit is the deficit set forth in the first or only budget resolution adopted for the fiscal year.

b. CBO designates estimation errors as technical differences.

c. The average disregards whether the differences are positive or negative.

Revenue Floors and Spending Ceilings

During the quarter century of congressional budgeting, enforcement rules have been tightened and new points of order added. The original budget resolution process enforced ceilings on total budget authority and outlays and established a floor for total revenue. CBA bars consideration of any measure that breaches the revenue or spending aggregates. This prohibition applies only to the totals; there is no restriction on measures that would cause functional allocations to be exceeded.

It did not take long for the shortcomings of this arrangement to become apparent. When only the totals are enforced, legislation can proceed as long as there still is room in the budget, even if the inevitable effect would be to cause violations later in the fiscal year. Once the totals are violated, however, no spending legislation could proceed—not even measures that had been assumed in the budget resolution. Of course, Congress would not allow coveted legislation to be blocked just because total spending had been exceeded. At times, Congress has stopped minor bills, but it has never applied the rule against important bills such as regular or supplemental appropriations.

In budgeting, the totals are not effective enforcement tools. This lesson, which was learned when congressional budgeting was inaugurated in the 1970s, was relearned when the Gramm-Rudman-Hollings Act sought to control the deficit in the 1980s. Totals do not provide a reliable basis for control because there is an inherent tension between them and the various parts of the budget. As has already been mentioned, most Americans want the totals to be smaller and the parts to be larger; they want more programs and less government. Unless the pressure for more programs is contained, it is difficult to constrain the totals (even when Congress passes laws such as Gramm-Rudman-Hollings that purport to limit the deficit). The totals do not hold because program advocates are stronger than the guardians of the budget. It does not take much daring for those who want more money to disable or outmaneuver aggregate controls. They can ignore or waive the rules, play fast and loose with the numbers to make it appear that spending is lower than it actually is, frontload spending cuts and backload the increases, and use other bookkeeping tricks to get what they want while pledging fidelity to budget discipline.

Committee and Subcommittee Allocations

Although revenue and spending totals are still controlled, nowadays Congress relies principally on allocations to committees and appropriations subcommittees to enforce its budget decisions. These allocations, required by section 302 of the Congressional Budget Act, recognize that Congress operates through its committee system. To effectively limit spending, it is necessary that each committee be given a budget for the legislation in its jurisdiction. The basic rule is that committees cannot generate more spending than has been allocated to them in the budget.

Section 302 prescribes a two-step procedure. First, the spending totals in each budget resolution are allocated among House and Senate committees, then the appropriations committees subdivide the amounts allocated to them among their subcommittees. This procedure forms a chain of control that links individual appropriations to the budget totals. The amounts allocated to committees cannot exceed the budget authority and outlay aggregates in the budget resolution, the amounts distributed to appropriations subcommittees cannot exceed the amount available to the parent committees, and the budget authority and outlays provided or ensuing from appropriation bills cannot exceed the amount available to the relevant appropriations subcommittee.

The House and Senate budget committees take the first step, a section 302(a) allocation, which is usually incorporated in the statement of managers that accompanies the conference report on the budget resolution. Although budget committees make these allocations, they are based on assumptions and understandings developed in formulating the resolution. By the time the budget committees mark up the resolution, committees have a good idea of the amounts that will be allocated to them. Allocations are made to the appropriations committees and to authorizing committees that have direct spending jurisdiction; section 302 allocations are not made for discretionary authorizations. The new budget authority and outlays allocated to committees may not exceed the corresponding totals in the budget resolution.

The House and Senate budget committees have different allocation practices. The House committee (as exhibit 6-7 shows) allocates amounts to each committee for each Budget Enforcement Act category and distinguishes between the "current level" (spending under existing law) and "discretionary action" (spending that will ensue from new legislation, including annual appropriations). The House also divides each committee's allocation among the functional categories in the budget resolution. But these are not binding on the affected committees. In addition to section 302 allocations for the next fiscal year, the House Budget Committee issues less detailed allocations for the next five years.

The Senate Budget Committee avoids detailed allocations. It does not distinguish between current level and discretionary action, nor does it allocate by functions. Instead, it gives each committee lump sums for budget authority, outlays, and entitlements funded in annual appropriations (as exhibit 6-8 shows).

After the appropriations committees receive their allocations, they subdivide their amounts among their subcommittees in a section 302(b) report (discussed in chapter 9). When an appropriation is considered in the House or Senate, the budget authority and outlays resulting from the bill are compared to the relevant subcommittee's allocation. A point of order can be raised against a measure that exceeds its section 302(b) allocation.

▶ **EXHIBIT 6-7**
Section 302 Allocations to House Committees

Fiscal Year 1998	Budget Authority	Outlays	Entitlement Authority
House Veterans Affairs Committee	(in millions of dollars)		
Current level (enacted law)			
700 Veterans benefits and services	1,358	1,440	22,196
Subtotals	1,358	1,440	22,196
Discretionary action (assumed legislation)			
700 Veterans benefits and services	−224	−224	327
Subtotals	−224	−224	327
Committee totals	1,134	1,216	22,523
House Ways and Means Committee			
Current level (enacted law)			
500 Education, training, employment, and social services	0	0	6,935
550 Health	50	39	0
570 Medicare	231,519	231,654	226,966
600 Income security	65,068	63,790	23,509
650 Social security	8,148	8,148	0
750 Administration of Justice	493	481	0
800 General government	450	453	0
900 Net interest	366,612	366,612	366,612
950 Undistributed offsetting receipts	−85	−85	0
Subtotals	672,255	671,092	624,022
Discretionary action (assumed legislation)			
550 Health	0	0	400
570 Medicare	−6,500	−6,500	0
600 Income security	582	582	0
Subtotals	−5,918	−5,918	400
Committee totals	666,337	665,174	624,422

Source: *Conference Report on the Budget Resolution: Fiscal Year 1998*, H. Rept. 116, 105th Cong., 1st sess., 1997, pp. 139–43.

(a) The House and Senate budget committees make separate allocations to the committees of their respective chambers. The two committees have different formats and contents.

(b) In addition to budget authority and outlays, the House Budget Committee allocates entitlement authority to authorizing committees that have legislative jurisdiction. Entitlement authority includes mandatory programs funded by current or permanent appropriations.

(c) "Current level" refers to spending that is pursuant to existing law; "discretionary action" refers to legislation changing direct spending laws and new appropriations. The term "discretionary" has a different meaning in the Budget Enforcement Act rules (discussed in chapter 4).

(d) The functional amounts shown under each committee's allocation are not binding, and deviations from them are not subject to a point of order.

▶ **EXHIBIT 6-8**

Section 302 Allocations to Senate Committees

(in millions of dollars)	Direct spending jurisdiction		Entitlements funded in annual appropriations act	
Committee	Budget Authority	Outlays	Budget Authority	Outlays
Appropriations			0	0
General Purpose Discretionary	531,771	536,700	0	0
Violent Crime Reduction Trust Fund	4,500	5,554	0	0
Highways	0	24,574		
Mass Transit	0	4,117		
Mandatory	321,502	304,297	0	0
TOTAL	857,773	875,242	0	0
Agriculture, Nutrition, and Forestry	10,843	7,940	26,696	9,419
Armed Services	49,327	49,433	0	0
Banking, Housing, and Urban Affairs	4,676	(1,843)	0	0
Commerce, Science, and Transportation	8,420	5,774	721	717
Energy and Natural Resources	2,336	2,258	40	63
Environment and Public Works	36,532	2,041	0	0
Finance	683,333	676,384	156,910	157,096
Foreign Relations	9,354	11,976	0	0
Governmental Affairs	59,501	57,941	0	17
Judiciary	4,759	4,235	234	234
Labor and Human Resources	9,023	8,363	1,309	1,309
Rules and Administration	114	289	0	0
Veterans' Affairs	1,106	1,381	23,667	23,540
Indian Affairs	151	150	0	0
Small Business	0	(155)	0	0
Unassigned to Committee	(310,297)	(293,097)	0	0
TOTAL	1,426,931	1,408,292	209,577	192,378

Source: *Conference Report on the Budget Resolution: Fiscal Year 2000*, H. Rept. 91, 106th Cong., 1st sess., 1999, p. 65.

(a) As required by section 302 of the Congressional Budget Act, the Senate Budget Committee allocates budget authority, outlays, and entitlement spending to Senate committees for the next fiscal year. It also allocates total spending for the next five and ten years to each committee. Only the allocation for the next fiscal year is shown here.

(b) "Direct spending" has a different meaning in this context from the meaning it has in the PAYGO rules discussed in chapter 4. Here it includes all spending controlled by committees; in PAYGO, it covers spending by committees other than the appropriations committees.

(c) "Entitlements funded in annual appropriations" includes programs such as Medicaid and food stamps that receive annual appropriations. These programs are included both in the amounts allocated to the appropriations committee as well as in the amounts allocated to affected authorizing committees.

(d) In the Senate, legislation exceeding either the budget authority or outlay allocation to the committee of jurisdiction may be subject to a point of order that can be waived only by a three-fifths vote of the membership.

SCORING AND SCOREKEEPING

Enforcing congressional budget rules requires information on the budgetary impact of pending or passed legislation and on the status of the budget. The first type of information is known as scoring, the second as scorekeeping. Scoring pertains to a particular measure, scorekeeping to the cumulative impact of past and current legislation on the budget. Scoring is done by CBO, which prepares cost estimates of legislation reported by House and Senate committees (exhibit 6-9). These estimates are especially important in assessing the budgetary impact of open-ended entitlement legislation. Scorekeeping reports are issued on an irregular basis, much less frequently than was the practice in the early years of congressional budgeting. A sample of one such report—the current level report—appears in exhibit 6-10. It compares congressional action affecting the budget with the amounts set forth in the budget resolution.

Scorekeeping is not just an informational exercise; its most important use is in ruling on points of order against pending legislation. Since 1975 Congress has come to rely heavily on procedural and substantive points of order to enforce budgetary rules. The original process was permissive: it operated on the notion that Congress should be allowed to take any budgetary action it wanted, provided that it was informed on the financial implications of its actions. Procedural points of order were devised to ensure that Congress complied with budget rules. For example, it is out of order to consider revenue or spending legislation before adoption of the budget resolution.

As the deficit mounted in the 1980s, Congress decided that it needed tougher enforcement mechanisms. The use of reconciliation to bring existing revenue and spending laws in line with the resolution was an important step in this direction. Congress also tightened enforcement by enacting discretionary spending caps and PAYGO rules for direct spending and revenues. Through these and other changes, Congress shifted from procedural enforcement to substantive rules—from the notion that it should be free to adopt any budget resolution that a majority preferred to the notion that its budget actions must conform to preset policy guidelines. The procedural requirements have been continued, but the current emphasis is on ensuring that Congress adheres to BEA, the budget resolution, and section 302 allocations. As part of this shift, budget information is now used to score congressional action, not merely to inform Congress on the status of the budget.

Section 302 bars the House and Senate from considering any measure that would cause an appropriations subcommittee's allocation to be exceeded. In the House, points of order can be waived by a special rule that is voted on before consideration of the measure to which it pertains; such rules need only a majority to pass. In the Senate, however, many budgetary points of order can be waived only by a three-fifths vote (60 votes) of the membership (some of these are listed in box 6-3). In light of the party lineup in the Senate, neither Democrats nor Republicans can waive affected budget rules without obtaining some support from the other side. The effect has been to give each party a veto on revenue and spending initiatives and to impel them to negotiate budget agreements that satisfy both parties.

One reason that the Senate is stricter in enforcing budget rules is that the Senate Budget Committee, with its permanent committee assignments, is stronger than the House Budget Committee (whose members must leave the committee after several terms). The Senate Budget Committee is more likely to fight for institutional power; the House Budget Committee is inclined to accommodate other committees. The various points of order and super-majority rules give the Senate Budget Committee a strong voice in determining

▶ **EXHIBIT 6-9**
CBO Cost Estimate

Federal Employees Health Care Protection Act of 1998 (H.R. 1836) would modify the administration of the Federal Employees Health Benefits (FEHB) program, transfer the health coverage of retirees and certain active employees of the Federal Deposit Insurance and the Board of Governors of the Federal Reserve to the FEHB program, and raise the pay of certain physicians employed by the federal government. CBO estimates that the legislation would reduce direct spending by $54 million and federal revenues by $7 million over the 1999–2003 period. Consequently, pay-as-you-go procedures would apply to the legislation. In addition, CBO estimates that implementing H.R. 1836 would increase discretionary outlays by $30 million over the 1999–2003 period, assuming appropriation of the authorized amounts. . . .

(in millions of dollars)	1998	1999	2000	2001	2002	2003
Changes in direct spending						
FDIC:						
Budget authority	0	0	0	0	0	0
Outlays	0	160	−14	−15	−18	−20
FEHB:						
Budget authority	0	−178	6	7	8	10
Outlays	0	−178	6	7	8	10
Total Changes in Direct Spending:						
Budget authority	0	−178	6	7	8	10
Outlays	0	−18	−8	−8	−10	−10
Changes in revenues						
FEHB Coverage for Federal Reserve:						
Revenues	0	−11	1	1	1	1
Spending subject to appropriation						
Spending on Physicians Comparability Allowance Under Current Law						
Budget authority	27	27	27	27	14	0
Outlays	27	27	27	27	14	1
Proposed changes:						
Authorization level	0	7	9	9	5	0
Outlays	0	7	9	9	5	a
Spending on Physicians Comparability Allowance Under H.R. 1836						
Authorization level	27	34	36	36	19	0
Outlays	27	34	36	36	19	1

a. Less than $500,000.

Source: *Federal Employees Health Care Protection Act of 1997*, S. Rept. 257, 105th Cong., 2d sess., 1998, pp. 11–12.

(a) The Congressional Budget Act requires CBO to prepare five-year cost estimates of all public bills (other than appropriations bills) reported by House or Senate committees. These estimates usually are published in the report accompanying each measure. The cost estimate exhibited here affects direct spending, revenues, and discretionary authorizations.

(b) The cost of direct spending and revenue legislation is estimated in reference to baseline projections. Thus the estimates shown here are the estimated changes from baseline levels. The estimate for discretionary spending, which is subject to appropriations, assumes that the appropriation will equal the authorized amount.

▶ EXHIBIT 6-10
Scorekeeping Report

Congressional Budget Office
Washington, DC, July 30, 1998.
Hon. Pete V. Domenici,
Chairman, Committee on the Budget,
U.S. Senate, Washington, DC.

Dear Mr. Chairman: The enclosed report for fiscal year 1998 shows the effects of Congressional action on the 1998 budget and is current through July 28, 1998. The estimates of budget authority, outlays, and revenues are consistent with the technical and economic assumptions in the 1998 Concurrent Resolution on the Budget (H. Con. Res. 84). This report is submitted under Section 308(b) and in aid of Section 311 of the Congressional Budget Act, as amended. . . .

Sincerely,
June E. O'Neill
Director.

The Current Level Report for the U.S. Senate Fiscal Year 1998, 105th Congress, 2nd Session, as of Close of Business July 28, 1998

	Budget Resolution H. Con. Res. 84	Current level	Current level over/ under resolution
On-budget	(in billions of dollars)		
Budget Authority	1,403.4	1,387.2	−16.2
Outlays	1,372.5	1,374.4	1.9
Revenues:			
1998	1,199.0	1,198.0	−1.0
1998–2002	6,477.7	6,480.7	3.0
Deficit	173.5	176.4	2.9
Debt Subject to Limit	5,593.5	5,451.7	−141.8
Off-budget			
Social Security Outlays			
1998	317.6	317.6	0.0
1998–2002	1,722.4	1,722.4	0.0
Social Security Revenues			
1998	402.8	402.7	−0.1
1998–2002	2,212.1	2,212.3	0.2

Note: Current level numbers are the estimated revenue and direct spending effects of all legislation that Congress has enacted or sent to the President for his approval. In addition, full-year funding estimates under current law are included for entitlement and mandatory programs requiring annual appropriations even if the appropriations have not been made. The current level of debt subject to limit reflects the latest U.S. Treasury information on public debt transactions.

Source: *Congressional Record*, daily ed., August 31, 1998, p. S9694.

(a) The Congressional Budget Act requires the House and Senate Budget Committees to issue scorekeeping reports on the status of the congressional budget. These committees insert CBO reports into the *Congressional Record* from time to time; there is no fixed schedule. The CBO report takes the form of a "current level" letter, with accompanying tables, addressed to each budget committee chairman.

(b) Scorekeeping reports are used principally in determining whether a pending measure would violate section 311 of the Congressional Budget Act by causing total budget authority or outlays to exceed, or total revenues to fall below, the levels set in the budget resolution.

(c) As used here, "current level" includes both new legislation enacted during the session and revenue or spending resulting from existing law. The scorekeeping reports take account only of legislation passed by Congress; they do not take into account pending measures, not even those whose enactment is expected.

(d) These scorekeeping reports deal only with budget totals, not with functional or committee allocations. See exhibit 9-2 for a report pertaining to section 302(b) committee allocations.

BOX 6-3
Selected Senate Budget Rules Requiring 60 Votes to Waive a Point of Order

- Consideration of appropriations before the appropriations committee has filed a section 302(b) report.
- Consideration of a measure providing budget authority or outlays in excess of the committees' section 302(a) or (b) allocation.
- Consideration of a budget measure for a fiscal year before adoption of the budget resolution.
- Consideration of amendment to a reconciliation bill that is not deficit neutral.
- Inclusion of extraneous matter in a reconciliation bill (Byrd rule).
- Consideration of a budget resolution that would exceed the discretionary spending limits.
- Inclusion of Social Security legislation in a reconciliation bill.
- Revenue or direct spending legislation that would increase the deficit for the first year, years 1 through 5, or years 6 through 10.

Source: Senate Budget Committee, *The Congressional Budget Process: An Explanation,* 104th Cong., 2d sess., S. Prt. 70, December 1996.

---

whether proposed legislation is admissible under the budget rules. The relatively lax House budget rules, and the ease with which they can be swept aside, reflect the strength of its leadership and the weakness of its Budget Committee.

The differences between the two chambers on budget matters are also rooted in institutional culture. The rules of the House are designed to facilitate the passage of legislation that the majority party favors and its committees produce; the Senate's accommodate more floor amendments and are designed to produce a less partisan outcome. When it is unified, the majority party in the House can remove any rules barrier to floor action on a bill while also thwarting the legislative ambitions of the minority. The House majority often waives budget rules, especially when the violations are procedural. It also waives substantive points of order when the violation is deemed to be minor or technical, or when the leadership is determined to have its way. Because it does not restrict floor amendments and is more vulner-

able than the House to proposals that would breach budget rules, the Senate has to be more circumspect in considering budget legislation. The ease with which members can filibuster or otherwise block action has acculturated the Senate to behave in a less partisan manner. The 60-vote requirement dictates that both parties cooperate when the Senate faces proposals that would violate budget rules.

CONCLUSION

During its quarter of a century, the congressional budget process has been frequently remade—either through formal changes in the rules or informal adaptation. At the outset there were two budget resolutions a year, at least one too many for those in Congress who did not want to vote repeatedly on the deficit and other difficult matters. By the early 1980s the second resolution was discarded, and the surviving resolution was transformed from a target into a constraint. In line with this new arrangement, Congress shifted reconciliation from the end of the annual budget cycle to the beginning. It stretched the period covered by the resolution from one year to three, then to five, and recently to ten. It tinkered with the legislative calendar by accelerating action on the budget resolution, and permitting House consideration of appropriations bills after May 15, even without adoption of the resolution.

The budget resolution has played many roles. In some years it has rubber-stamped previous decisions; in others it has taken the lead in recasting budget policy. Often the resolution has accommodated the demands of revenue and spending committees; sometimes it has challenged them. Once the budget committees largely controlled the resolution; now these committees have nominal jurisdiction, with much budget policy being dictated by party leaders or developed in negotiations with the president. Over the years the president has moved from being an outsider to being a vital participant in changing congressional budget policy. He does not have a formal veto power over the resolution, but he can block implementing legislation.

The variability of the budget resolution manifests weakness and instability in the process. Even after 25 years the resolution has not earned a secure niche in Congress. Each year, it is only as important as Congress wants it to be, only as relevant as the budget committees are. The resolution is a strange breed, more than a symbolic statement but less than a law. Nothing stops if Congress fails to adopt it, and nothing has to be changed if the numbers prove faulty or if they are overtaken by economic circumstance. The budget cannot be ignored, but neither is it always followed.

In this makeshift environment, the congressional budget process has attracted contradictory reform proposals. Some would weaken or do away with the budget resolution; others would strengthen it. Abolishing it, along with the budget committees and the budget rules that have accreted over the years, would return Congress to the pre-1974 situation, in which the totals were added up without anyone having to vote on them. The case for terminating the congressional budget process rests on the argument that it has spawned confusion, complicated Congress's budget work, and has not effectively controlled federal spending. Some critics have argued that the process has weakened presidential responsibility and has spurred increased spending.

The problem with abolishing the budget process is that doing so would not return Congress to the old status quo. The appropriations committees now control a much smaller share of federal spending, and entitlements consume a much larger share. Without a budget process, there would be no reconciliation mechanism, eliminating the most effective means available to Congress to curb entitlements and impel revenue changes. Perhaps the budget committees, shorn of a role in making legislative policy, could serve as monitors of the fiscal behavior of other congressional committees. Yet it is doubtful they would be effective in an advisory role. Perhaps party leaders could make budgetary policy, for this is a role to which they have gravitated over the years. But they would not likely enforce budgetary discipline with the same single-mindedness that the budget committees have.

The congressional budget process is a malleable tool. It served Congress during the decades of high deficits and assisted Congress in balancing the government's books in the late 1990s. If it survives, it will be because the process enables Congress to set the policies and priorities it wants, not because it prevents a legislative majority from working its will.

7

Revenue Legislation

In any year, almost all revenues derive from permanent law, not from current legislative decisions. Congress has the option of doing nothing and allowing existing law to continue or of revising the tax code to change either the volume of revenues or the incidence of taxation. In the years that the president's budget and Congress's budget resolution do not propose significant changes, these documents do little more than estimate the receipts from existing tax laws. In other years, when one or both branches seek to change the amount collected or the distribution of the tax burden, revenue policy is among the most controversial features of the budget.

Two variables are important in defining the process and politics of revenue legislation. One is whether the aim is to raise or lower tax rates; the other is whether the president or Congress initiates proposed changes. When deficit reduction was the priority, as it was from 1982 through 1993, legislation to increase revenues was usually a prominent part of the reconciliation package. When the budget moved to a surplus in the late 1990s, controversy flared over whether to lower the tax burden. Even when tax issues are on the back burner, Congress considers some revenue measures, tinkering with a few tax provisions or extending some expiring provisions.

In some years Congress takes up major tax legislation on its own initiative. This typically occurs when tax reduction is in vogue, but it also occurred in 1982 (the second year of the Reagan presidency), when Senate Republicans were alarmed by the growing budget deficit and pushed through tax increases to reverse some of the revenue losses enacted the previous year. Two aborted congressional initiatives took place in 1995 and 1999, when Republican leaders sought to cut taxes in the face of strong opposition from President Clinton, who vetoed the legislation sent to him. The most common pattern, however, is for Congress to act only after the president has proposed major changes in revenue legislation. For example, in 1993 Clinton prodded Congress to enact tax increases as part of a deficit reduction package. Once Congress becomes involved, it usually exercises considerable independence, altering the volume or composition of taxes to suit its preferences. Even when it meets the president's revenue target, Congress does so in its own manner.

Two intrinsic features of tax policy propel congressional independence: tax policy directly affects most Americans, and it is controversial. Revenue legislation is intensively lobbied and closely monitored by affected interests, which actively use their political clout to influence the outcome. Members of the tax-writing committees (the House Ways and Means and the Senate Finance Committees) often receive more campaign money from political action committees than do the members of any other congressional committees. With the money comes pressure to benefit certain taxpayers by changing the tax code.

During the high deficit era, Congress frequently boosted federal revenues. When the president took the initiative by proposing the increases, he gave Congress political cover to raise taxes. But the growing budget surpluses of the late 1990s emboldened congressional leaders to take the initiative in seeking tax cuts. Both types of action—tax increases and cuts—

spark conflict between the president and Congress, between the major political parties, and sometimes between the House and Senate as well. Getting tax legislation through Congress can be a difficult chore but one that has been accomplished frequently during the past two decades (table 7-1). Often the task has been eased by treating revenue legislation as an opportunity to benefit particular interests or taxpayers. Just about every tax bill that makes it through Congress contains tax breaks, even measures whose ostensible purpose is to increase federal revenue. With increases and decreases combined in the same measure, producing tax legislation is almost always a redistributive activity in which some gain and others lose. The winners and losers are selected through complex legislative procedures and political maneuvers that often produce gargantuan bills, which revise hundreds of sections of the tax code.

Two centuries ago Americans revolted against taxation without representation; nowadays many do not even like taxation with representation. Yet the federal government has an enormous need for revenues to finance the many programs that Americans want. As difficult as the task is, Congress and the president have devised a tax system that raises more than $1.8 trillion a year. Two centuries ago tax disputes were settled in battle; today's disputes are settled through political action and legislative procedures.

REVENUE LEGISLATION IN CONGRESS

The Constitution grants Congress the power to levy taxes but says little about how to exercise this power. One of its few requirements is that revenue legislation must originate in the House. This sequence—first the House, then the Senate—has given rise to differences in the way the two chambers handle revenue mea-

TABLE 7-1
Major Tax Legislation, 1980–97

Billions of dollars

Year	Legislation	Estimated revenue impact[a]
1980	*Omnibus Budget Reconciliation Act* First use of the reconciliation process	+4 (one year)
1981	*Economic Recovery Tax Act* Enacted six months after Ronald Reagan became president; indexed major features of the individual income tax	–749 (five years)
1982	*Tax Equity and Fiscal Responsibility Act* Initiated by the Senate; repealed some of the tax breaks enacted the previous year	+98 (three years)
1983	*Social Security Amendments* Increased revenue for Social Security system, which was on the brink of insolvency	+165 (seven years)
1984	*Deficit Reduction Act* Revenue gains and spending cuts were packaged together in a reconciliation bill	+51 (four years)
1986	*Tax Reform Act* Designed to be revenue-neutral; lowered rate on highest individual income tax bracket from 50 to 28 percent; revenue loss offset by eliminating many tax expenditures	+11 (one year)
1987	*Budget Reconciliation Act* Canceled Gramm-Rudman-Hollings sequestration of $23 billion	+23 (two years)
1989	*Omnibus Budget Reconciliation Act* Included approximately $10 billion in spending cuts	+6 (one year)
1990	*Omnibus Budget Reconciliation Act* Contained the Budget Enforcement Act, which introduced new controls on revenue and spending legislation	+137 (five years)
1993	*Omnibus Budget Reconciliation Act* Raised highest individual tax rate to 39.6 percent	+240 (five years)
1997	*Taxpayer Relief Act* Part of the balanced budget agreement between the president and Congress; expanded several major tax expenditures; estimated revenue loss much higher after first five years	–95 (five years)

Sources: *Congressional Quarterly Almanac*, 1980–97.

a. Revenue impact estimated at time of enactment; actual revenue impact usually diverges from these estimates. The number of years in parentheses is the number of years covered by the estimate.

TABLE 7-2
House Ways and Means Committee: Pre-Reform and Post-Reform

Pre-reform (before 1975)	Post-reform (since 1975)
Democratic members of Ways and Means appointed Democratic members of other committees.	Committee appointments are made by Democratic Steering and Policy Committee; Ways and Means no longer has a role.
Ways and Means had complete jurisdiction over Medicare and Medicaid.	Medicare Part B is shared with Energy and Commerce Committee (now the Commerce Committee), which also has complete jurisdiction over Medicaid.
No subcommittees. All legislation was developed and marked up by the full committee, which thereby kept controversial matters off the congressional agenda.	Ways and Means is required to have at least six subcommittees, though major tax legislation is still considered by the full committee.
The committee was small, with only 25 members. It was dominated by a coalition of Republicans and conservative Southern Democrats.	Committee was enlarged to 37 members, and the ratio of Democrats to Republicans was increased from 15-10 to 25-12. In the 106th Congress the ratio was 23 Republicans to 16 Democrats.
Almost all markups were closed. Staff was small and controlled by the chair.	Most markups are held in open session (though premarkup in party caucuses is closed). Staff was increased but is still mostly controlled by the chair.
Most bills reported by the committee were considered in the House under a closed rule that barred floor amendment.	Most bills are considered under a limited rule that permits designated floor amendments.

sures. However, the congressional budget process and pay-as-you-go (PAYGO) rules have narrowed the differences, and the House and Senate now often behave similarly.

In the House

Almost all tax measures begin their legislative journey in the House Ways and Means Committee—a panel whose vast jurisdiction covers Social Security, trade legislation, unemployment benefits, and some health programs. Reforms that swept through the House in the 1970s greatly affected this committee; it is much less independent and powerful than it was before the reforms. Some of the changes are listed in table 7-2, which compares the pre-reform and post-reform Ways and Means Committee.

The full committee generally develops major revenue legislation; subcommittees may handle minor matters. At one time the Ways and Means Committee shielded itself from lobbyists by marking up legislation behind closed doors. House rules now require it (and other committees) to conduct business in the open unless it expressly votes to meet in executive session. Openness has exposed Ways and Means to more intense political pressure, but the chair sometimes brokers deals in private and then convenes the committee to approve the bargains that have already been struck. Ways and Means once thrived on bipartisan cooperation; Democrats and Republicans worked together to produce legislation that commanded overwhelming support on the floor. But bipartisanship was attacked by reformers who saw it as the means by which a conservative coalition of Republicans and Southern Democrats controlled tax legislation and blocked consideration of measures that liberal Democrats favored. The reformers broke the conservative hold on the committee by enlarging Ways and Means and changing the ratio of Democrats to Republicans. Since the 1970s the committee has been polarized (as has the House as a whole), and voting often splits along party lines.

Heightened partisanship has been accompanied by an increase in the frequency and size of tax legislation. It has been common for issues decided one year to be reconsidered one or two years later, and for Congress to change hundreds of sections of the tax code in a single bill. Partisanship has also reduced the committee's insularity and independence, making it more susceptible to outside influence. Ways and Means does not have a completely free hand in initiating and drafting tax legislation: it must be mindful of party leaders' preferences, the revenue levels set in the budget resolution, and the reconciliation instructions. Much of what the committee produces by way of revenue legislation is at the behest of other congressional actors, in particular the Speaker of the House and the House Budget Committee. Ways and Means still enjoys great latitude in the details of legislation, but external pressures often drive overall policy. In response to these pressures, the majority party members on Ways and Means usually caucus in advance of formal committee meetings to hammer out legislation that comports with their party's position.

After Ways and Means reports a bill, it seeks a rule (in the form of a House resolution) that prescribes the terms and conditions under which the measure is considered on the floor. The Rules Committee, which the Speaker controls, has three basic options. One is to write a closed rule, which bars floor amendments and forces members to approve or reject the entire measure. Another option is to draft an open rule, which permits members to offer any amendment. The third is to compose a limited rule, which permits consideration of designated amendments. Ways and Means used closed rules routinely from the 1950s until the early 1970s, during the eighteen-year reign of Chair Wilbur Mills (D-Ark.). This procedure gave Ways and Means enormous leverage, and it almost always got the House to pass the legislation that it reported. Nowadays the House often changes some parts of reported measures and rarely permits closed rules on tax legislation.

Because use of open rules on revenue bills is unworkable, the House rarely employs them. Operating under open rules, the House can disregard the compromises crafted in committee and rewrite legislation from scratch. This makes for wonderful political theater but not for sound legislation. Open rules encourage members, for whom the next election is always less than two years away, to turn a measure raising revenue into one that cuts taxes.

Most tax legislation is considered these days under a limited rule, which enables the majority party to decide which amendments the House may consider. Typically the majority crafts the limited rule to permit amendments that improve the bill's chance of passing; it blocks amendments that might split or embarrass their party. The House must approve the rule drafted for a bill before it takes up the measure. Those opposing the legislation try to defeat the rule. If they succeed, the bill will not be considered unless a new rule has been drafted and approved. After the rule is approved, the House acts on the bill and any permitted amendments. Once the rule passes, it is almost always the case that the bill also passes.

▼

BOX 7-1
Senate Initiative on Revenue Legislation: The 1982 Tax Increase

Barely one year after he signed a massive tax cut into law, President Ronald Reagan signed the Tax Equity and Fiscal Responsibility Act (TEFRA), which increased federal revenue by an estimated $98 billion over three years. TEFRA was an extraordinary policy reversal that bypassed normal legislative procedures and was enacted without any House consideration of the measure before the conference report. TEFRA was cobbled together in the Senate, taken to conference, and passed with little House influence on its final provisions.

1981
August 13
Reagan signs tax cuts into law ($749 billion over five years).

1982
July 23
Senate passes, 50-47, tax increase bill.

August 19
Conference report passes House, 226-207, and Senate, 52-47.

September 3
Reagan signs TEFRA into law.

The Congress that enacted TEFRA was split along party lines. The Democrats had a majority in the House, and the Republicans had the Senate and the White House. In 1981 this political lineup spawned a bidding war between House Democrats and the president as to who could produce the bigger tax cuts. When the bidding ended, Reagan was the winner, but his triumph soon presented the president with a political quandary: how to deal with an escalating budget deficit that was far higher than he had estimated earlier in the year. Reagan's solution, presented in a September 24, 1981, television address was to propose that $22 billion be raised by eliminating "abuses and obsolete incentives in the tax code."

Inasmuch as this proposal came late in the legislative session, Congress did not act on it. Reagan renewed his call for revenue enhancements early in the next session, but House Ways and Means Committee chair Dan Rostenkowski (D-Ill.) refused to act. He feared that House Democrats would be blamed for increasing taxes, and he did not want another bidding war with the White House.

That would have been the end of the matter were it not for the determination of Senate Finance

continued

In the Senate

Senate work on revenue measures begins in the Finance Committee, whose legislative jurisdiction is even broader than that of its House counterpart. Although the Senate is supposed to wait until the House has completed action, it sometimes gets around this requirement by stripping a minor House-passed bill (such as a measure renewing an expiring tariff) of all text except the enacting clause and then substituting its own revenue provisions. Box 7-1 describes one of the most prominent Senate initiatives: a 1982 tax increase that the president did not propose and was not included in any House-passed legislation. Although this procedure did not adhere to the spirit of the constitutionally prescribed sequence, it did follow the strict letter of the re-

**BOX 7-1
Continued**

Committee Chair Robert Dole (R-Kans.) to do something about the deficit. Dole negotiated the deals and compromises between committee Republicans and the White House that enabled him to draft a bill that would pass on a straight party line vote.

But how could the bill be reported? The House had not acted, and the Constitution requires it to initiate revenue legislation. Dole's solution was to attach his committee's tax increases to a minor revenue bill that the House had passed late in the previous session. The enlarged bill passed the Senate without any Democratic support.

Action then shifted to the House, which could have been expected to produce its own bill so as to position itself for the ensuing conference with the Senate. But Ways and Means Committee Democrats, still fearful that they would be tarred as tax increasers, opted to go straight to conference. The conferees then hammered out a final bill based almost entirely on the Senate-passed version.

By this time, there were deep fissures in the Republican ranks—especially in the House—where the midterm elections were only a few months away. With the Republicans split, the bill needed substantial Democratic support in the House to be enacted. House Democrats could no longer remain on the sidelines, but they would not supply the needed votes until they got three political protections. First, the House took up the conference report under a closed rule that precluded separate votes on controversial provisions. Second, Reagan promised to give Democrats who supported the bill letters thanking them for their votes. And finally, each party produced a majority of its House members in support of the conference report.

As a revenue raiser, the 1982 measure had relatively little impact on the deficit, which soon passed the $200 billion mark. But it had a lingering impact on subsequent legislation and on political fortunes. The bill set a precedent for political sleight of hand that remained through the 1980s; revenue enhancements were not to be treated as tax increases. TEFRA earned Senator Dole the label "tax collector for the welfare state," a stigma he could not shake off among some Republican voters when he ran for president fourteen years later, in 1996. As for Ronald Reagan, he signed the 1982 tax increase without comment and went on to sign more than half a dozen additional increases before leaving office. Yet he is remembered as the tax-cutting president.

quirement. Federal courts have consistently refused to pass judgment on the legality of congressional procedures; hence tax legislation initiated by the Senate is valid law.

In most cases, the Senate takes up tax measures only after the House has acted. For decades, this sequence differentiated the Senate's behavior from the House's. Considering the bill first, the House was constrained by

strict rules that limited members' ability to vote for tax cuts or to give breaks to favored interests. Tax legislation that passed the House was adorned with few amendments and had almost no extraneous provisions. The Senate outcome was altogether different. In both the Finance Committee and on the floor, senators added numerous amendments that awarded tax breaks and other benefits. At times, hundreds of amendments were added—a process that came to be known as "Christmas treeing" the bill. It was not uncommon for the Senate to turn a House bill that raised revenue into one that reduced revenue.

These amendments gave the Senate considerable advantage vis-à-vis the House in the ensuing conference convened to resolve differences in the two chambers' bills. It is widely understood on Capitol Hill that tax bills, more than other types of legislation, are rewritten in conference. Much of what the House or Senate passes may be cast aside by the conferees, who sometimes insert provisions that were not in either chamber's revenue measure. When the conference drafts the final bill, Senate conferees use many of their added provisions as bargaining chips to extract concessions from the House. Because of this, the conference report often hews more closely to the Senate's position.

PAYGO RULES

As detailed in the next section, the PAYGO rules prescribed by the Budget Enforcement Act of 1990 changed the Senate's incentive to add provisions to revenue bills, as well as other aspects of tax legislation. The basic rule (which was more fully discussed in chapter 4) is that congressional action on revenue and direct spending legislation should not add to the budget deficit nor diminish the surplus. Legislation reducing federal revenues must be offset by an increase in revenues or a decrease in direct spending. If Congress fails to fully offset the net revenue loss, funds must be sequestered from certain direct spending programs.

In enforcing PAYGO, congressional scorers must distinguish between baseline revenues deriving from existing laws and changes in revenues resulting from new legislation. Congress is not required to offset a drop in revenues resulting from changing economic conditions,

nor may it use an increase in revenues resulting from improved economic circumstances to offset legislated revenue losses. However, Congress is required to offset projected decreases resulting from new legislation.

The North American Free Trade Agreement (NAFTA), which Congress approved in 1993, illustrates how PAYGO works. At the time it was considered, NAFTA was estimated to reduce tariffs and increase direct spending by $2.7 billion over its first five years. Some NAFTA proponents argued that it would actually increase tax collections by stimulating trade and increased economic activity, but assumptions about the overall macroeconomic impact were not included in the official estimates. Hence they had no bearing on Congress's need to find $2.7 billion in offsets. Although PAYGO does not require that the NAFTA legislation itself offset the $2.7 billion—the offsets could have been included in other revenue or direct spending bills passed by Congress—it would not have been possible to muster a majority in support of the measure unless it contained the offsets. The administration first proposed to generate additional revenue by doubling customs fees and adjusting other charges. However, House Republicans, whose votes were needed to pass NAFTA, labeled the proposal a tax increase and threatened to vote against it. The administration then negotiated a compromise in which most of the additional revenue came from bookkeeping changes in several taxes, with only a small increase in customs fees. Once the agreement was reached on satisfying the PAYGO rules, a sufficient number of Republicans voted for NAFTA to pass it in the House.

When Congress acted on NAFTA, it lacked certain knowledge of the legislation's future budgetary impact. Knowledgeable people, using slightly different assumptions, can come up with widely divergent estimates. The 1990

Budget Enforcement Act decrees that Office of Management and Budget (OMB) estimates are determinative in scoring legislation and enforcing PAYGO rules. In practice, however, Congress relies on Congressional Budget Office (CBO) estimates when it is considering legislation—even when they diverge significantly from OMB's figures. But once revenue legislation has been enacted, OMB issues an official score, which determines whether the requirements have been met.

OMB and CBO often differ because they use different assumptions about the future behavior of taxpayers in response to changes in tax rules. Scoring is often routine, with little dispute about the assumptions used and the estimates deriving from them. Sometimes, however, conflict between the president and Congress or between Democrats and Republicans complicates the scoring of tax policy. When this occurs, scoring becomes a weapon one side or the other uses to promote or impede legislation. During the Bush administration, for example, the president argued that reducing capital gains tax rates would increase federal revenue by spurring owners to sell long-held assets. Using different assumptions, however, CBO advised Congress that a lower tax rate would reduce federal revenue over a five-year period. At one level, this was a technical argument, where experts who had information on the past actions of taxpayers disagreed on how their behavior might change in response to future rate changes. At another level, it was a political dispute between protagonists who differed over tax policy; each side used the assumptions that supported its position. Because Congress relied on CBO, its projection that lower rates would lose revenue doomed the legislation. But this was not the end of the matter; the dispute flared in every subsequent session until Congress reduced capital gains rates in 1997.

IMPACT OF PAYGO ON CONGRESSIONAL BEHAVIOR

During the decade it has been in effect, PAYGO has affected both actions of Congress and the revenue legislation it has produced. Some of the effects have been procedural; many have been substantive.

PAYGO has diminished the Senate's advantage in going second on tax legislation. It is now less practicable for the Senate to "Christmas tree" tax bills by inserting revenue-losing provisions as bargaining chips for the conference. Every step of the way, senators must be mindful of whether a proposal would cause a drop in revenue. Senate-passed tax legislation must be deficit (or surplus) neutral. All revenue losses must be offset, even if the revenue loss is incidental to the bill's main objectives. In 1998, for example, the Senate Finance Committee reported a bill that restricted certain practices that the Internal Revenue Service used to enforce tax laws. Although the legislation did not aim to change federal revenues, it was scored as causing an $18 billion loss over five years. Before reporting the bill, the Finance Committee had to devise offsets that satisfied PAYGO but were not perceived as tax increases. Approximately half of the offset came from cutting taxes, but in the complex world of PAYGO these were scored as a revenue gain.

PAYGO has impelled both the House and the Senate to play the offsets game—that is, to include revenue-raising provisions whose sole purpose is to make room for tax cuts. Gaming the process occurs because neither chamber or party relishes the task of voting for tax increases. Accordingly each seeks revenue enhancements while avoiding the blame for raising taxes. In this game, timing is important. When the revenue change takes effect and when it expires strongly influence the score accorded legislation. Another tactic is to exploit the fact that scoring covers a finite period—typically five or ten years.

What happened earlier or is projected to happen after this period has no bearing on the score.

One popular timing ploy is to extend an expiring tax. For example, the federal tax on airline tickets expired in 1996, was renewed for a brief period that year, and then renewed again (in a somewhat different form) the following year. In contrast to a permanent tax, which is scored as a revenue increase only once, a temporary tax is scored whenever it is renewed. The reverse of this game is to structure tax cuts so that they are effective for only a portion of the scored period, thereby reducing the amount that has to be offset.

Congress has become adept at turning long-term revenue losers into short-term (five- to ten-year) revenue gainers. The trick is to structure the tax law so that more money flows into the Treasury during the first part of the scored period and the majority of revenue loss occurs during the last part. A good example of this device was the 1996 legislation that contained a variety of breaks for small businesses, which were estimated to cause a $10 billion loss over five years and $20 billion loss over ten years. A portion of the required offsets was obtained by temporarily suspending a 15 percent surcharge on certain distributions from pension funds. This tax cut was scored as a revenue producer because it gave taxpayers an incentive to withdraw money from their pension funds. In so doing, they would not pay the 15 percent surcharge, but they still would be subject to ordinary income taxes, which would result in a revenue increase during the scored period. Although there would be revenue loss after this period, it did not affect the score. Congress used a similar tactic in 1998 legislation that reformed the internal revenue system.

TAX EXPENDITURES

The old practice of "Christmas treeing" revenue bills and the new practice of structuring revenue legislation to get a favorable score indicate that Congress does not simply view such legislation as a means of generating revenue: it also is an opportunity to give benefits to certain firms or households through adjustments in the tax code. These benefits appear in the budget as *tax expenditures*, a term defined in law as revenue losses resulting from deductions, exemptions, credits, and other exceptions to the normal tax structure. Tax expenditures are breaks and loopholes that reduce the tax liabilities of certain taxpayers.

Tax expenditures are means by which the federal government pursues certain public objectives. They may be regarded, as the term denotes, as alternatives to direct spending and other policy instruments. A preferential rate on capital gains aims to stimulate investment, deducting mortgage interest payments from taxable income promotes home ownership, credits for child care expenses enable parents to work outside the home. The government can also promote these objectives through grants (which are budgeted as expenditures) rather than through tax breaks. It can provide cash subsidies to homebuyers (or owners), to families whose parent or parents work outside the home, or to firms that invest in physical or human capital. The budget facilitates comparison of direct and tax expenditures by classifying both into functional categories, but there is relatively little explicit trading off between the two types of expenditures.

The budget publishes two slightly different measures of tax expenditures/revenue losses and outlay equivalents. The first measures the revenue forgone by the government; the second measures the direct spending that would be required to give taxpayers the same out-of-pocket income. The budget lists more than one hundred tax expenditures; each of the fifty largest has annual revenue losses in excess of $1 billion. Table 7-3 lists the largest tax ex-

TABLE 7-3
Major Tax Expenditures: Estimated Revenue Losses, Fiscal Years 1996 and 2001

Billions of dollars

Tax expenditure	Revenue forgone	
	1996	2001
Exclusion of employer pension plan contributions and earnings	59.0	92.4
Employer contributions for medical insurance and medical care	66.6	80.6
Mortgage interest on owner-occupied homes	54.2	60.9
Deduction of certain state and local taxes	28.8	42.4
Preferential capital gains tax rate	6.2	41.8
Accelerated depreciation	20.9	32.8
Rebasing of capital gains at death	29.5	28.2
Charitable contributions	24.2	26.6
Interest on public purpose bonds	12.7	23.2
State and local property taxes	15.7	23.1
Child credit[a]	. . .	19.5
Capital gains exclusion on home sales	17.9	19.1
Social security benefits for retired workers	17.4	18.9
Interest on life insurance savings	11.2	16.1
Individual retirement account contributions and earnings	6.4	16.0

Sources: *Budget of the United States Government, Analytical Perspectives: Fiscal Year 1996*, table 5-6, p. 64; *Budget of the United States Government, Analytical Perspectives: Fiscal Year 2001*, table 5-3, p. 117.
a. The child credit was enacted in 1997.

penditures in the fiscal 2001 budget and compares their estimated revenue losses with those reported five years earlier. Most of the major tax expenditures have been in effect since the early years of the federal income tax, but some (such as the earned income credit, individual retirement accounts, and the child credit) were enacted in the 1970s or later.

Despite the availability of budgetary information on tax expenditures, Congress does not have a formal mechanism for substituting between them and direct expenditures. The two types of spending are likely to be in the jurisdiction of different committees and are usually considered in different types of legislation. Trade-offs between annual appropriations and tax expenditures are impeded by budget enforcement rules, which subject appropriations

to discretionary spending caps and tax expenditures to PAYGO requirements.

Tax expenditures are a form of entitlement. Like the entitlements that appear in the direct spending part of the budget, they generally are governed by permanent legislation, are not normally reviewed by Congress each year, are not controlled by the appropriations process, and grow in response to exogenous factors without any congressional action. The estimated revenue loss from exclusion of employer contributions for medical insurance and care rose automatically from $67 billion in 1996 to $81 billion five years later. During the same period, the loss from exclusion of employer contributions to pension plans grew from $59 billion to $92 billion (see table 7-3). As a form of entitlements, tax expenditures can be altered by

Congress through reconciliation legislation or ordinary revenue measures. But if Congress does nothing, the volume of tax expenditures, like the cost of other entitlements, depends on requirements already mandated in law.

RATES VERSUS BREAKS: THE 1980s VERSUS THE 1990s

Virtually every deficit reduction package enacted since 1980 (the major exception was 1981) has curtailed some tax expenditures. In these bills and other revenue legislation, the real trade-off has been between tax breaks and tax rates: the more breaks in the tax codes, the higher the rates have to be to meet revenue targets.

The rates versus breaks contest played out very differently in the 1990s than it did in the previous decade. The 1980s began with more than a dozen individual tax brackets, the highest of which was 70 percent on certain types of income. In 1981, President Ronald Reagan's first year in office, Congress enacted a 25 percent cut (over three years) in income taxes, indexed the tax brackets (they have been adjusted each year since 1985 for changes in consumer prices), reduced the top rate on "unearned" income (investment income such as dividends) from 70 percent to 50 percent, and introduced or expanded tax breaks. This last group included accelerated depreciation of assets, a tax credit for research and development expenses, an increase in individual retirement accounts, a reduction in estate taxes, exclusion of some interest income, and an increase in the child care tax credit. The 1981 Economic Recovery Tax Act decreased revenue both by lowering rates and by increasing breaks. At the time it was enacted, the law was estimated to reduce federal revenues by $749 billion over the next five years. Although some of these breaks were eliminated the next year, that law

reduced fiscal 1990 revenue by an estimated $323 billion.

This was the high-water mark for tax breaks in the 1980s. During the remainder of the decade, Congress passed and Republican presidents signed almost a dozen tax increases, which chipped away at the breaks while steeply reducing tax rates. The first step in this direction was taken in a 1982 law that increased federal revenue by an estimated $98 billion over three years. The law curtailed various corporate tax preferences, repealed provisions that let firms sell unused tax breaks, mandated that a portion of interest and dividend income be withheld, and cut back other tax preferences (see box 7-1). Congress also trimmed some tax breaks through reconciliation legislation enacted in 1984, 1986, 1987, and 1989. But the biggest shift from breaks to lower rates was made by the Tax Reform Act of 1986—a measure whose main purpose was to simplify the tax code, not to change the amount of federal revenue. Congress decided that this legislation should be revenue-neutral, which compelled it to trade off rates and breaks. The only way it could lower the former was to eliminate some of the latter. The 1986 tax reform collapsed the fourteen individual tax brackets into two and lowered the top rate from 50 percent to 28 percent. It also reduced effective tax rates by increasing the personal exemption as well as the standard deduction for taxpayers who do not itemize deductions. These rate reductions were paid for by eliminating the deduction for state and local sales taxes, raising the capital gains tax rate, phasing out the deduction for consumer interest payments, taxing unemployment benefits, and making numerous other adjustments in tax expenditures.

The rates versus breaks pattern was very different during the 1990s. The highest individual income tax rate was raised from 28 percent to 39.6 percent, and corporate income tax rates (which were reduced in 1986) were also raised. Congress passed rate increases in 1990 when Republican George Bush was in the White House and again in 1993 when Democrat Bill Clinton was president. These laws made many relatively minor adjustments in tax expenditures, but the 1997 balanced budget agreement (discussed in chapter 2) added a handful of major breaks: a new individual retirement account (Roth IRA) that allows tax-free distribution of pension funds, education tax credits and education savings accounts, a new tax credit for children, deductibility of student loan interest payments, lower capital gains rates, increases in estate tax exemptions, full deductibility (phased in over a number of years) of health insurance premiums paid by self-employed taxpayers, and many other revenue-losing provisions. The estimated revenue losses were $95 billion during the first five years, $275 billion over ten years, and vastly higher amounts beyond that period.

Why the reversal in the rates versus breaks trade-off? The answer comes in at least three parts and is indicative of how the political climate and budget behavior changed from one era to the next: changes in public perception of tax breaks, a difference in the importance of the deficit on the political agenda, and the introduction of PAYGO budget rules.

First, there was a shift in public sentiment on taxes. In the 1980s, supply-side arguments that high marginal tax rates lower saving, investment, and output carried the day. Even liberal Democrats joined the bandwagon for lower tax rates, though some were motivated more by their dislike of tax breaks than by their acceptance of the new economic doctrine. In the 1990s, by contrast, the supply-side position lost favor, and there was growing concern that high-income earners had not paid their fair share. The widening income

gap—low-income households losing ground and high earners reaping the dividends of an expanding economy—contributed to this shift in political sentiment. In fact, virtually all the rate increases enacted during this decade were imposed on upper-income taxpayers, who bore a rising share of the income tax burden.

Second, there was a more sustained effort to curtail the deficit during the 1990s than there was in the previous decade. In the 1980s the White House was occupied by presidents who were less concerned about reducing the deficit than about reducing the tax burden. Although Reagan did sign many tax increases into law, most were small, and the additional revenue was obtained by closing loopholes, not by across-the-board tax increases. Reagan's only big tax increase was the 1982 legislation, which he was persuaded to accept on the expectation that each dollar of increased revenue would be matched by three dollars of spending cuts. When the expected spending cuts did not materialize (because it was not possible to get Congress to enact such deep cutbacks), Reagan felt cheated and resolved not to sign any other tax increases. He grudgingly relented from time to time, only agreeing to as little new revenue as he could get away with.

Presidential behavior has been very different since Reagan left office. Bush promised "no new taxes," but his own aides maneuvered him into accepting a large tax increase when it became apparent that the Gramm-Rudman-Hollings deficit targets would be breached; if this were to occur, the required sequestration would have had dire consequences for many federal programs, including defense. Furthermore, Congress would not agree to a new budget deal unless it included hefty tax increases. As noted in chapter 5, Bush generally distanced himself from budgetary matters, which gave his aides broad scope to negotiate a package that contradicted his oft-stated position and thereby damaged his political career. Clinton's tax increase was enacted on his initiative, and he had to fight a reluctant Congress to get it. Bush's increase took effect during a recession, Clinton's at the start of an economic boom. Bush left office long before the deficit had receded; Clinton continued in office as the deficit vanished.

Finally, PAYGO narrowed the options open to Congress in dealing with revenues. The requirement that revenue losses be offset biased congressional action against broad rate cuts and in favor of targeted tax breaks. In contrast to rate cuts, which lose substantial revenue because they benefit most taxpayers, the losses from breaks can be limited by targeting particular taxpayers or by structuring them in ways that defer the revenue loss beyond the scored period. This is exactly what Congress did in 1997 when it accommodated costly tax breaks within the PAYGO budget constraint.

TRENDS IN FEDERAL REVENUE

Annual revenues reached $100 billion in 1963; less than thirty years later (in 1990), they exceeded $1 trillion. Very early in the new century, they will pass the $2 trillion mark. These revenue increases have been driven principally by inflation and economic growth—not by tax legislation. Federal revenues are elastic; they grow automatically as the economy expands and as personal and corporate incomes rise.

Despite their relentless rise, until recently, federal revenues moved within a narrow band as a proportion of the gross domestic product (GDP). In 1960 they totaled 17.8 percent of GDP and in 1996, 18.9 percent. During this period there was much less variability in revenues than in outlays. The gap between the highest and lowest ratios of revenue to GDP was 2.7 percentage points; the spread on the

expenditure side was more than twice as wide, at 6.3 percentage points.

Revenue stability was due to legislative action, not to happenstance. If Congress had not acted, revenues would have been propelled upward by inflation, which boosts nominal incomes, and by economic expansion, which raises real incomes. In the past, Congress periodically responded to rising revenue trends by lowering tax rates or increasing breaks. Thus when budget receipts soared from 17.2 percent of GDP in 1976 to 19.6 percent in 1981, Congress cut tax rates and indexed individual income tax brackets to the rate of inflation. Revenues then receded to 17.5 percent of GDP in 1986, only slightly higher than they had been a decade earlier.

Like PAYGO, indexation narrowed Congress's legislative options. Before indexation, when Congress compensated for rising tax yields it typically redistributed the tax burden, giving more reductions to some taxpayers than to others. This arrangement enabled both branches to take credit for reducing taxes, even though some taxpayers may not have been fully compensated for inflation. However, high inflation during the 1970s exposed politicians to blame for allowing tax burdens to float upward. Inasmuch as the legislative response lagged inflation, there usually was a period during which tax burdens were above the trend line.

Indexation (which took effect in 1985) enables the president and Congress to avoid the blame for inflation-induced tax increases. The adjustment is swift and automatic, but it is not complete because not all relevant features of the tax system have been indexed. Indexation also means that politicians no longer have the expedient option of reducing nominal tax rates to compensate for inflation. Instead their role has often been to raise taxes in order to curtail the budget deficit. In fact, since enact-

TABLE 7-4
Federal Revenues, by Source, as Share of Total Receipts and GDP, by Decade, 1960–2000

Revenue source	1960	1970	1980	1990	1998	2000[a]
Percentage of total receipts						
Individual income taxes	44.0	46.9	47.2	45.2	48.1	48.6
Corporate income taxes	23.2	17.0	12.5	9.1	10.1	9.8
Social insurance taxes	15.9	23.0	30.5	36.8	33.5	33.2
Excise taxes	12.6	8.1	4.7	3.4	3.9	3.5
All other receipts	4.2	4.9	5.1	5.4	4.4	4.8
Percentage of GDP						
Individual income taxes	7.8	8.9	8.9	8.1	9.6	9.9
Corporate income taxes	4.1	3.2	2.4	1.6	2.0	2.0
Social insurance taxes	2.8	4.4	5.8	6.6	6.7	6.8
Excise taxes	2.3	1.5	0.9	0.6	0.8	0.7
All other receipts	0.8	0.9	1.0	1.0	0.9	1.0
Total receipts	17.8	19.0	18.9	18.0	20.0	20.4

Source: *Budget of the United States Government, Historical Tables, Fiscal Year 2001*, table 2.2, pp. 29–30, and table 2.3, pp. 31–32.
a. Estimated.

ment of indexation, Congress has passed more than a dozen revenue-raising measures. No broad tax reductions have been enacted since indexation took effect, though Congress has occasionally redistributed the tax burden (as it did in the Tax Reform Act of 1986). The targeted tax cuts enacted in 1997 significantly reduced the taxes paid by certain earners, but the overall impact on federal revenues was much more modest (at least during the first five years) than its proponents and opponents claimed. According to official estimates, the 1997 legislation will reduce total federal revenues by only about 1 percent during its first five years. Unlike previous tax cuts, which reduced revenue as a percentage of GDP, the revenue-to-GDP ratio continued to rise after the 1997 legislation.

Arguably, indexation has reoriented revenue legislation from stabilizing and redistributing tax burdens to producing more revenue. Partly because of indexation, bureaucrats cut taxes and politicians raised them during the 1990s.

This role reversal enabled the government to generate revenues in excess of the levels realized in the past. Federal revenues soared from 18.0 percent of GDP in 1990 to 20.0 percent in 1999 and an estimated 20.4 percent in 2000 (table 7-4). Before 1999, the only time federal revenues exceeded 20 percent of GDP was during World War II. If these revenues had been the same share of GDP in 1999 as they averaged during the 1980s, the budget would have incurred a $100 billion deficit rather than being in surplus.

Regardless of which party controls Congress in the early years of the new millennium, the surplus, if it persists, will change the terms of the tax policy debate. Pressure will build to return some of the excess revenue to taxpayers. If the economy weakens and the deficit returns, Congress will face pressure to cut taxes to stimulate the economy. Two factors, however, impede business-as-usual tax cuts. One is that PAYGO does not distinguish between a surplus and a deficit; in both situations revenue losses must be offset. The other is that politicians face pressure to reserve some or all of the surplus for the Social Security system, which will have to cope with an aging U.S. population early in the next century. Despite these factors, if they are determined to cut taxes, Congress and the president will find a way out of the PAYGO constraints and the Social Security predicament.

SOURCES OF FEDERAL REVENUE

Over the years there has been both stability and change in the composition of federal revenues. Individual income taxes have been a stable revenue source for an extended period, accounting for about 47 percent of total receipts since 1960, as well as a fairly stable percentage of GDP (table 7-4). But the portion of revenues derived from corporate income taxes is currently a third less than what it was after World War II (although it edged up a bit during the 1990s). The share from social insurance taxes (for Social Security and Medicare) has more than quadrupled since the war, while excise taxes have dropped to less than 4 percent of total revenues.

One cause of the decline in corporate taxes is the reductions in the marginal tax rates on business; another has been relatively low profits. Corporate profits amounted to 10 percent of GDP in 1960; in 1990 they were 7 percent. Greater reliance on debt financing, generous tax breaks, and more aggressive tax avoidance practices may have also contributed to the decline in corporate tax revenues. Whatever the reasons, corporations paid more than 40 percent of their profits as taxes in 1960 but less than 25 percent in 1990. Proceeds from this source have increased during the 1990s as profits improved, but taxes continued to decline as a percentage of profits.

The increase in social insurance taxes has

been accompanied by higher spending on Social Security and Medicare. Note, however, that the rise in the share of revenue coming from these taxes was smaller in the 1980s than in the two preceding decades and that social insurance taxes are expected to account for a smaller proportion of total federal revenue in 2000 than they did a decade earlier. This reversal of the long-term trend may appear surprising, as an aging population will require more government spending on pensions and health care. While it is true that the amount collected from social insurance has continued to rise, the Social Security and Medicare trust funds will nonetheless face serious financial imbalances once the baby boom generation retires. Why has the government not boosted social insurance taxes to shore up the financial condition of these funds?

A powerful clue comes from the data presented in table 7-5, which are drawn from CBO calculations. The table shows that in 1995, 38 percent of all taxpayers paid more Social Security taxes than income taxes. With the employer's share of social insurance taxes added in, the percentage almost doubles to 73 percent. The relative burden of social insurance taxes is highest for the lowest-income taxpayers. Payroll taxes exceeded income taxes for 99 percent of those earning less than $10,000 and for 92 percent of individuals and families in the lowest income quintile.

Not surprisingly, taxpayer resistance to higher social insurance taxes has increased as these taxes have taken a bigger bite out of their paychecks. From 1950 until 1990, Congress frequently raised the social insurance tax rate, boosting it from 1.5 percent each for employees and employers at the start of this period to 7.65 percent each at the end. All told, there were twenty tax rate increases during this forty-year stretch, on average one every other year (table 7-6). Since 1990 the tax rate has re-

TABLE 7-5
Individuals and Families Whose Payroll Taxes Exceed Their Income Taxes, by Cash Income and Income Quintiles, 1995

Percent

	Employee share	Employee and employer share
Cash income (dollars)		
0 to 10,000	99	99
10,000 to 20,000	69	91
20,000 to 30,000	46	81
30,000 to 40,000	34	78
40,000 to 50,000	25	74
50,000 to 75,000	14	71
75,000 to 100,000	6	52
100,000 to 200,000	3	20
200,000 or more	3	4
All incomes	38	73
Quintile		
Lowest	92	97
Second	48	82
Middle	31	77
Fourth	16	72
Highest	5	37
All quintiles	38	73

Source: Congressional Budget Office, "Estimates of Federal Tax Liabilities for Individuals and Families, by Income Category and Family Type," memorandum, May 1998, tables 8 and 13.

TABLE 7-6
Social Insurance Tax Rate and Maximum Taxable Earnings, Employed and Self-Employed People, 1937–99[a]

Percent unless otherwise designated

Year	Employee tax rate[b] (percent)	Self-employed tax rate (percent)	Maximum taxable earnings[c] (dollars)
1937–49	1.0	...	3,000
1950	1.5	...	3,000
1951	1.5	2.25	3,600
1954	2.0	3.0	3,600
1957	2.25	3.375	4,200
1960	3.0	4.5	4,800
1962	3.125	4.7	4,800
1963	3.625	5.4	4,800
1966	4.2	6.15	6,600
1967	4.4	6.4	6,600
1969	4.8	6.9	7,800
1971	5.2	7.5	7,800
1973	5.85	8.0	10,800
1978	6.05	8.1	17,700
1979	6.13	8.1	22,900
1981	6.65	9.3	29,700
1982	6.7	9.35	32,400
1984	7.0	14.0	37,800
1985	7.05	14.1	39,600
1986	7.15	14.3	42,000
1988	7.51	15.02	45,000
1990	7.65	15.3	51,300
1999	7.65	15.3	72,600

Source: Social Security Administration, *Social Security Bulletin: Annual Statistical Supplement: 1999*, table 2.A3, p. 99.
a. This table only includes the years in which the rates were changed (except for 1999).
b. The same percentage is paid by the employer.
c. From 1966, when Medicare was first implemented, until 1990, taxable earnings for the hospital insurance contribution were the same as the earnings base for Social Security. During 1991–93, maximum taxable earnings were higher for the hospital insurance contribution than for Social Security. Since 1994 the hospital insurance tax has been levied on all earnings, while Social Security has been capped at the amounts shown in this column.

mained unchanged, though the maximum earnings on which the tax is imposed climbed from $51,300 to $72,600 in 1999. Raising the maximum taxable wage base affects only those workers whose earnings exceed the previous base. Since most employees earn less than the maximum taxable earnings, the increase does not affect them.

Resistance to raising the social insurance tax rate may compel politicians to rely on other measures to sustain the Social Security and Medicare trust funds. If this resistance persists, social insurance taxes will account for a declining share of future federal revenues, in

TABLE 7-7
Federal Funds Receipts by Decade, 1960–2000

Measure	1960	1970	1980	1990	2000[a]
Federal funds receipts as percent of GDP	14.6	14.2	12.9	11.2	13.2
Federal funds receipts as percent of total receipts	81.8	74.2	67.8	61.6	63.8
Federal funds receipts as percent of federal funds outlays	101.1	91.6	80.9	65.1	94.7
Net interest as percent of federal funds receipts[b]	9.1[c]	10.0	15.0	29.0	17.9
Gross interest on the public debt as percent of federal fund receipts	12.1[c]	13.5	21.3	41.6	28.9

Source: *Budget of the United States Government, Historical Tables, Fiscal Year 2000*, table 1.2, pp. 21–22, table 1.4, pp. 25–26, and table 3.2, pp. 50–64.
  a. Estimated.
  b. Net interest is gross interest paid by the government minus the interest earned by trust funds and other federal entities.
  c. Data for 1962.

contrast to the period before the 1990s, when these taxes provided a rising share of revenues.

Social insurance taxes are earmarked to particular uses; they do not finance the general expenses of government. However, the government borrows from the balance in the Social Security trust fund (and in other trust funds), paying prevailing interest rates and using the money to finance the overall budget. Earmarking has decreased the federal funds portion of revenues that is available for the general purposes of government. (Federal funds also include a small amount of earmarked revenue, which is deposited into special funds. In the discussion here, the terms "federal funds" and "general funds" are used interchangeably, even though the former includes some earmarked revenue.) Federal fund revenues dropped steeply from almost 15 percent of GDP in 1960 to only 11 percent in 1990 (table 7-7). At the start of the 1990s, federal funds accounted for only 62 percent of total receipts, compared with 82 percent three decades earlier. Federal fund receipts financed all general outlays in 1960, but by 1990 they covered only about two-thirds of federal fund expenditures, with the remainder financed by borrowing. During the same period, net interest payments soared from less than 9 percent of general receipts to

29 percent. This share was even greater when computed in terms of gross interest, almost all of which is paid by the general fund.

These trends strongly indicate that the deficit problem, which persisted until the late 1990s, was due to inadequate general fund revenues. The general fund pays for national defense, interest charges, the operating expenses of virtually all federal agencies, most grants to state and local governments, and the hundreds of federal programs that do not have earmarked revenue. By the early 1990s, general expenditures exceeded $1 trillion dollars a year, but general revenues were $350 billion less. This shortfall was greater than the consolidated budget deficit because a portion of the deficit was offset by trust fund surpluses that exceeded $100 billion later in the decade. In fact, if general revenue had been the same share of GDP in the early 1990s as it was thirty years earlier—before Medicaid, food stamps, head start, and other multibillion dollar programs were established—the federal budget would have been close to balance.

The sharply different financial condition of the general fund compared with trust funds has its roots in the American dislike of being taxed to pay for government. Historically, taxes have been somewhat more acceptable when the proceeds are earmarked for specific purposes such as highways, Social Security, and Medicare. Although opposition to general taxes certainly is not new—throughout most U.S. history, major increases in these taxes occurred only in wartime—the deterioration in the general fund suggests that enacting tax increases to pay for the expenses of government became more difficult in the 1970s and 1980s. Factors that may have contributed to the erosion of general taxation include decreased confidence in government, protracted conflict between the president and Congress over tax policy, increased attentiveness of interest groups to revenue legislation, and indexation of individual income taxes.

Viewed in this historical context, the 1990 and 1993 income tax increases were an anomaly. In neither case was the United States at war, nor was there a significant upswing in public approval of government performance. Despite this, Congress and the president agreed to boost general revenues because of growing alarm over the size of the deficit. In both years, tax increases were not formulated in free-standing legislation but as part of a deficit-reducing reconciliation package negotiated by the president and congressional leaders. Moreover, most of the additional revenue came from high-income taxpayers. The vast majority of taxpayers were not affected by increases in marginal tax rates, the removal of the cap on the Medicare tax base, and the phase-out of certain exemptions and deductions. In fact, by the end of the 1990s, millions of low- and moderate-income households had lower effective income tax rates than they had at the start of the decade. By concentrating the tax increases on a sliver of taxpayers, Congress and the president were able to defuse political opposition.

The 1990 and 1993 actions improved the condition of the general fund, which received most of the new revenue. In an extraordinary reversal of budget trends, general revenues grew more rapidly during the 1990s than general outlays. These revenues were approximately $500 billion higher at the end of the decade than they had been at the start, but general outlays rose by less than $300 billion. Just as deterioration in general fund revenues led to the high deficit era, the recent recovery in these revenues made it possible to incur budget surpluses. If general fund revenues weaken again for any reason, budget deficits will return.

WHO PAYS FEDERAL TAXES?

In considering revenue legislation, Congress is not only concerned with the amount of money the government collects but also with the distribution of the tax burden among segments of the population. Calculating the incidence of federal taxes is a complex and controversial task—it entails assumptions about how taxes paid by others (such as the employers' share of social insurance taxes and corporate income taxes) affect particular income earners, such as workers and shareholders. It stirs disputes about the definition of income and requires that the impact of the many preferences and special provisions in the tax code be measured.

The nominal income tax rate American taxpayers use in preparing their returns is not an accurate measure of actual tax burdens. These rates do not indicate how preferences and breaks reduce taxable income or the taxes actually paid. The two principal measures used in calculating actual tax burdens are taxes as a percentage of adjusted gross income and the effective tax rate. The former covers only income that is subject to taxation; the latter is a broader measure that covers all cash income but excludes noncash income such as in-kind benefits from government and health care premiums

TABLE 7-8
Shares of Adjusted Gross Income and Individual Income Taxes, by Income Class,
1989, 1992, and 1996

Income class[b] (dollars)	Share of adjusted gross income[a] (percent)			Share of individual income taxes[a] (percent)			Income taxes as percent of adjusted gross income[a]		
	1989	1992	1996	1989	1992	1996	1989	1992	1996
0 to 10,000	3	3	3	0	0	−1	−0.2	−1.5	−5.8
10,000 to 20,000	8	9	8	2	2	1	3.4	2.8	1.1
20,000 to 30,000	10	10	10	6	6	5	7.6	7.8	7.6
30,000 to 50,000	20	21	19	16	16	14	10.3	10.2	10.3
50,000 to 75,000	21	21	19	19	19	17	12.0	11.7	12.1
75,000 to 100,000	11	11	11	13	12	12	14.6	14.3	14.7
100,000 to 200,000	13	12	13	17	17	17	17.9	17.4	18.2
200,000 to 500,000	7	7	8	11	12	14	22.7	23.2	25.3
500,000 to 1,000,000	3	3	3	5	6	7	24.1	25.8	30.1
1,000,000 or more	5	5	7	10	11	15	24.4	26.8	31.7

Source: Congressional Budget Office, "Estimates of Federal Tax Liabilities for Individuals and Families, by Income Category and Family Type," memorandum, May 1998, tables 2 and 3.
   a. Includes refunds of the earned income tax credit.
   b. Adjusted gross income in constant 1996 dollars.

paid by employers. The effective tax rate is calculated by dividing total cash income into the amount of taxes paid. For example, a person making $100,000 a year who pays $10,000 in federal income taxes has an effective tax rate of 10 percent. The effective tax rate is negative when taxpayers receive refunds from the government in excess of the taxes they paid.

Table 7-8 shows that the individual income tax is highly progressive. At all income levels, those who earn more pay a higher percentage of their income in taxes than those who earn less. Moreover, the income tax became more progressive during the 1990s. At the lowest income level, taxpayers paid −0.2 percent of their income in individual income taxes in 1989 but had a −5.8 rate in 1996. In dollar terms, those making $10,000 averaged a $20 payment from the government in 1989 but $580 in 1996. At the other end of the income spectrum, the average millionaire paid $244,000 in federal income taxes in 1989 and $317,000 in 1996.

The steepening progressivity of the income tax has had a great deal to do with the revenue surge experienced by the government during the 1990s. As noted earlier in this chapter, the highest marginal tax rate was increased during this decade from 28 percent to 39.6 percent. During this period, upper-income earners gained ground, earning a higher share of national income, while low-income earners lost ground. In effect, the government muddled through to a policy in which the winners were more heavily taxed on their gains while the losers were taxed less. Arguably, this was a fortuitous combination of good economic and social policy, for it allowed markets to function efficiently and allowed for some redistribution of income. It also suggests, however, that continuing the boom in federal revenues will depend upon sustained financial gains by upper-income taxpayers.

The adjusted income data on which table 7-8 is based are a narrow measure of relative tax burdens because they leave out social in-

TABLE 7–9
Effective Tax Rates for All Individuals and Families, by Cash Income

Cash income (dollars)	Individuals and families (millions)	People (millions)	Average pretax income (dollars)	Effective tax rates (percent)				
				Total	Individual income	Social insurance	Corporate income	Excise
0 to 10,000	16.3	27.9	6,030	7.6	−3.2	6.3	0.6	3.9
10,000 to 20,000	19.3	37.5	14,900	11.6	−0.3	8.3	1.3	2.3
20,000 to 30,000	16.0	34.3	24,800	17.0	4.0	9.6	1.6	1.7
30,000 to 40,000	13.7	32.7	34,700	20.0	6.6	10.3	1.6	1.4
40,000 to 50,000	10.8	28.7	44,700	22.1	8.1	11.1	1.5	1.3
50,000 to 75,000	16.3	47.9	61,200	23.9	9.7	11.5	1.6	1.1
75,000 to 100,000	7.6	23.1	86,000	25.9	11.9	11.2	1.9	0.9
100,000 to 200,000	6.0	18.4	132,000	27.8	14.5	9.1	3.6	0.6
200,000 or more	1.8	5.1	491,000	35.3	22.5	3.5	8.9	0.3
All incomes	109.6	258.8	45,700	24.7	11.3	9.2	3.2	1.1

Source: Congressional Budget Office, "Estimates of Federal Tax Liabilities for Individuals and Families, by Income Category and Family Type," memorandum, May 1998, table 4.

surance taxes and nontaxable income. Both of these items are included in table 7-9, which shows effective tax rates on all cash income. Social insurance taxes are inherently nonprogressive because they are levied at a flat rate and the Social Security portion is imposed only up to the maximum earnings listed in table 7-6. Middle-income taxpayers earning between $30,000 and $100,000 have a higher effective social insurance tax rate than do individuals and families with cash income in excess of $100,000. But in considering the overall progressivity of the Social Security system, it is appropriate to take into account the benefits government pays out. Social Security replaces a higher percentage of the lifetime earnings of low-income workers. The more one makes, the lower the percentage one gets back from Social Security. Moreover, the earned income tax credit, which was significantly expanded during the 1990s, compensates low-income earners for all or a portion of their social insurance taxes.

Even with social insurance and other taxes factored in, the effective tax rate is higher for each income class than for the next lower class. Low-income earners bear a heavier burden in excise taxes but a much lower one in corporate income taxes. The total effective tax rate on individuals and families with cash income in excess of $200,000 is more than double the rate on those making $20,000 to $30,000.

The progressivity of the tax system pertains to vertical equity—the taxes paid by people who differ in the amounts they earn. Economists are also concerned with horizontal equity—the taxes people earning the same amount pay. The myriad preferences and breaks in the tax code impair horizontal equity, as they are not evenly distributed among taxpayers or among those with similar incomes. Consider two families, each earning $100,000 a year: one owns a home, the other rents; one has capital gains, the other does not; one has a pension fund, the other does not. In these and numerous other ways, the two taxpayers are differentiated in the income taxes they pay. One family might have a $5,500 tax bill; the other might pay only $2,000. Tax expenditures are the great unequalizer of the federal tax system, for they are not evenly distributed across or within income ranks. To ameliorate some of the inequity, Congress has established an alternative minimum tax that requires taxpayers who benefit from certain tax preferences to pay more taxes than would be required by the normal rates.

USER CHARGES

The federal government collects more than $140 billion a year in user charges. These charges differ from taxes in that they are levied on recipients of particular benefits or services, or on activities that the government regulates. The government, in the exercise of its sovereign powers, collects taxes; it collects user fees in carrying out business-type activities. In contrast to taxes that are accounted for as budget receipts, most user fees are budgeted as offsetting collections.

CBO has identified four types of user charges. The largest category consists of fees individuals or businesses pay for goods and services the government provides. These typically resemble business transactions in that the payer voluntarily obtains the good and services. These fees include the premiums paid for participating in the Medicare part B program, purchases of postal services, and charges for using federal parks.

The second category consists of charges paid for activities the government regulates. These transactions are partly voluntary because they can be avoided by not engaging in the regulated activities. They include copyright and patent fees, and licenses required as a condition for engaging in certain activities.

Third, certain taxes are levied on beneficiaries of federally provided goods and services. But unlike most user fees, they generally are budgeted as tax receipts, not as offsetting collections. Benefit charges include taxes on airline tickets and on gasoline.

Finally, liability-based charges are imposed on various activities to compensate for damage to the environment or injury to those affected by the activities. These charges usually are earmarked to trust funds set up to remedy the harm or compensate those injured by it. Taxes on coal mining compensate miners afflicted with black lung disease (or their survivors), taxes on vaccines compensate those injured by measles shots or other prescribed vaccinations, taxes on crude oil finance the cleanup of oil spills and provide compensation for damages resulting from them.

Since the mid-1980s Congress and the president have viewed user charges as a means of generating additional revenue. Before then, the prevailing policy was to charge beneficiaries the cost of providing goods or services. A 1952 statute expressed the sense of Congress that benefits and services provided by federal agencies "shall be self-sustaining to the full extent possible." But the law also provided that fees should be fair and equitable and should take into account the public interest. The implementing guidelines issued by OMB provided for user charges to be imposed only for special benefits available to identifiable recipients.

The Consolidated Omnibus Budget Reconciliation Act of 1985 expanded user fees to cover not only the cost of providing services but also some or all of the federal agency's operating expenses. For example, the law directed the Nuclear Regulatory Commission to recover one-third of its annual operating expenses; the 1990 reconciliation legislation raised the target to 100 percent. Other agencies that have been directed to recover all or a portion of operating costs include the Customs Service, the Patent and Trademark Office, and the Food and Drug Administration.

Efforts to curtail the budget deficit and budget enforcement rules have stimulated increases in user charges. The rules distinguish between discretionary and mandatory user fees. The former are authorized and made available in appropriations acts and are scored as offsetting collections. They enable Congress to make an equivalent amount of additional appropriations. Mandatory fees authorized in substantive legislation, however, do not affect the amount that may be appropriated. This distinction gives the president and Congress a strong incentive to structure user fees so that they are classified as discretionary. Some groups complain that various user fees have been set above the amounts required to recover costs and that the excess revenue has been spent on other federal programs.

OFFSETTING COLLECTIONS

Offsetting collections reduce budget authority or outlays by an equivalent amount. For example, $50 million of offsetting collections credited to an account reduce budget outlays in that account by $50 million. Most user charges are scored as offsetting collections, as are income from the sale of assets, interest earned by federal entities, and certain flows of money between federal accounts or funds.

When is a receipt budgeted as revenue and when is it accounted for as an offsetting collection? The basic rule, laid down by the President's Commission on Budget Concepts in 1967, is that activities "essentially governmental in character, involving regulation or compulsion, should be reported as receipts," but that business or market-oriented activities should be offset against expenditures. This is not a clear-cut distinction, as evidenced by the manner in which Medicare part B premiums are budgeted. Until 1983 these premiums were recorded as receipts; since then they have been budgeted as offsetting collections. These premiums, which amount to more than $20

billion a year, are still recorded as receipts in the national income and product accounts.

Classifying revenue as an offsetting collection rather than as a receipt does not affect the size of the deficit or surplus because it reduces total revenue and spending by equal amounts. But it can affect the consideration of legislation under the budget enforcement rules. Revenue that is classified as a receipt is included in the PAYGO part of the budget; revenue classified as an offsetting collection is sometimes treated as discretionary, in which case it may affect the amount available for appropriation.

CONCLUSION

Congress processes revenue legislation in much the same manner as it did two hundred years ago. These measures still originate in the House, and the House Ways and Means and Senate Finance Committees still have virtually exclusive jurisdiction. But there have been important changes—some impelled by the proliferation of budget rules, some by the growth of earmarked and trust fund revenues. Revenue legislation is now formulated in the context of a budget resolution and often is enacted in a reconciliation bill. Tax measures must abide by budget enforcement rules that limit the amount of revenue loss enacted. Indexation and big deficits in the 1980s and 1990s changed the characteristic congressional revenue action from reducing taxes to raising them. Behavioral differences between the House and Senate have been narrowed, and the Senate is sometimes the more constrained chamber in considering tax legislation.

Additional changes in the revenue process are likely in the years ahead, especially as Congress deals with the budgetary impact of an aging population. Despite the urgings of economists and others who argue that stable, predictable tax policy contributes to national efficiency, revenue legislation will continue to be active on the congressional agenda. Future legislation will change the amounts the government collects and redistribute the tax burden. Whether the budget is in surplus or deficit, Congress will take up proposals to cut taxes. And whether Democrats or Republicans control the House and Senate, Congress will produce legislation cutting taxes for some groups.

Tax rates versus tax breaks will continue to be a point of contention, and the more Congress legislates on this subject, the more complex the tax code will become.

If the past is any guide, tax legislation will be cyclical: rates will be raised, then reduced, reduced and then raised again. There is no such thing as equilibrium in taxes; there is only the legislative impulse to tinker with the tax code.

8

Authorizing Legislation

Congress has two distinct processes for establishing and funding federal programs and agencies. One leads to the enactment of *authorizing legislation*, which establishes the legal basis for the operation of federal agencies and programs. The other culminates in the *appropriation of money*, which enables agencies to incur obligations and expenditures. These steps are usually taken in separate measures, but sometimes they are combined in direct spending legislation. The distinct actions are prescribed by House and Senate rules, which bar unauthorized appropriations and the insertion of legislation into appropriation bills. Although the rules are sometimes waived or disregarded and allow for certain exceptions, they define the boundaries of authorizing legislation and appropriation measures.

The distinction between the two types of measures was incorporated into House rules in the 1830s and into Senate rules two decades later; it is now codified as House Rule XXI and Senate Rule XVI. However, the practice predates the establishment of Congress and was probably adapted from the British Parliament. The First Congress, which convened in 1789, understood that substantive legislation would not be combined with appropriations. It thus passed one law establishing the War Department and another law appropriating funds to this department and other newly established agencies. The separation of authorizations and appropriations was placed in the rules decades later, in response to the frequent insertion of riders and other legislative provisions in appropriation bills.

House Rule XXI provides that "an appropriation may not be reported in a general appropriation bill . . . for an expenditure not previously authorized by law." It also provides that "a provision changing existing law may not be reported in a general appropriation bill. . . ." Note that these restrictions apply only to general appropriations bills. Through House precedents, a continuing resolution (providing stopgap funding for agencies that have not yet received regular appropriations) is not a general appropriation bill. Hence it may contain both unauthorized appropriations and substantive legislation.

Senate Rule XVI provides that the "Committee on Appropriations shall not report an appropriation bill . . . proposing new or general legislation." It also bars appropriations that are not "made to carry out the provisions of some existing law. . . ." But the Senate rule is not as strictly enforced as the House one. The Senate allows more exceptions and has procedures that enable it to insert legislation in appropriation bills. Box 8-1 highlights some of these instances from the 1990s.

Nineteenth century debates in the House and Senate indicate two reasons for separating authorizations and appropriations. One was a concern that conflict over legislation would impede the flow of funds to federal agencies. The other was that the urgency of funding ongoing agencies would impel Congress to enact ill-considered legislation in appropriations bills. Both concerns have contemporary relevance for Congress. Conflict over legislation, not disputes over the amount that should be made available, is the usual cause when there is protracted delay in enacting appropriations. Moreover, many provisions that probably would not be enacted on their own have been enacted in appropriations bills.

TYPES OF AUTHORIZING LEGISLATION

Authorizations represent the exercise of the legislative power accorded to Congress by the Constitution. (At one time, what is now referred to as authorizing legislation was referred to simply as legislation.) In exercising its legislative power, Congress can place just about any kind of provision in an authorization. It can prescribe what an agency must or may not do in carrying out assigned responsibilities. It can spell out the agency's organizational structure and its operating procedures. It can grant an agency broad authority or restrict its operating freedom by legislating in great detail. Authorizing measures do not have a uniform structure—some are only one or two pages long, a few run to hundreds of pages. Some are divided into titles, others into chapters; most are subdivided into sections. Some enable agencies to obligate money; most do not.

The broad scope and variety of authorizing measures contribute to the considerable confusion about them. The term authorization is part of the problem, for it has several meanings in federal budgeting. An authorization law looks in two directions: inward to Congress, where it serves as a license for the House and Senate to consider appropriations, and outward to federal agencies, where it serves as a license for them to operate. To sort out the different types of measures and their functions, it is necessary to distinguish between discretionary authorizations and direct spending, as well as between substantive legislation and the authorization of appropriations. The distinctions affect both the legal status of authorizing legislation and the manner in which Congress handles it.

Discretionary Authorizations and Direct Spending Legislation

Budget enforcement rules distinguish between discretionary authorizations, which do not

FIGURE 8-1
Authorizing Legislation

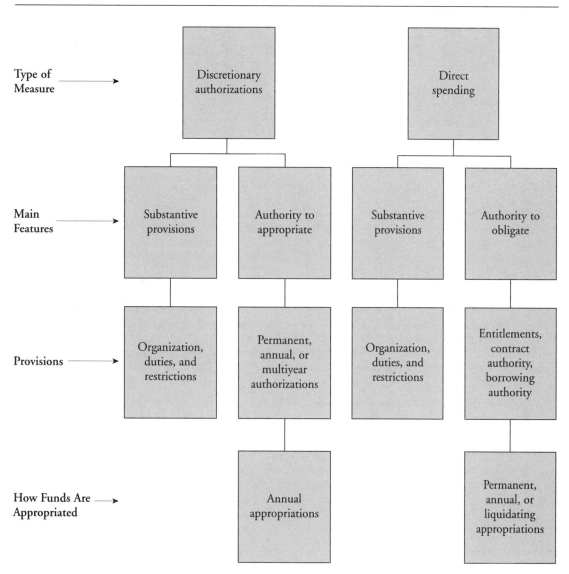

Type of Measure →

Main Features →

Provisions →

How Funds Are Appropriated →

provide budget resources, and direct spending legislation, which provides budgetary resources or enables the affected agency to obligate funds. Figure 8-1 diagrams the contents of both types of legislation, which contain substantive legislation specifying such matters as the organization and duties of the agency.

However, they differ in their relationship to appropriations. Discretionary authorizations provide authority to appropriate; direct spending provides authority to obligate.

This difference can be further clarified by referring to table 8-1, which shows the sequence of four key steps in federal budgeting:

▼

BOX 8-1
Democrats versus Republicans: Fighting over Legislation in Appropriations Bills

The prohibition against legislation in appropriations is not strictly enforced by Congress, which often inserts relatively minor legislation in appropriations bills. During the 1990s, however, the volume and significance of such legislation increased to the point where entire laws were sometimes enacted in appropriations acts.

Senate Republicans removed restrictions to legislation in appropriations bills in 1995 by overturning a parliamentary ruling on Rule XVI. Four years later the roles were reversed, and Republicans voted to restore the bar against legislation in appropriations bills, while Democrats voted to permit legislation. Both times the parties were motivated by short-term considerations, but their actions had long-term consequences for Congress.

Round One: Republicans Disable Rule XVI

During Senate consideration of a supplemental appropriations bill on March 16, 1995, Senator Kay Bailey Hutchinson (R-Texas) offered an amendment to nullify certain court orders concerning the Endangered Species Act and to prohibit the Fish and Wildlife Service from using appropriated funds to determine that particular species were endangered. Senator Harry Reid (D-Nev.) raised a point of order that the amendment was legislation in an appropriations act, and the chair sustained the point of order. Senator Hutchinson appealed this ruling, and the ruling was rejected 42-57. Following this vote, the Senate parliamentarian let it be known that he would no longer advise the Senate to enforce Rule XVI.

Round Two: Democrats Use Appropriations Bills to Force Action on Legislation

With Rule XVI disabled, there was no impediment in the Senate to inserting legislation in appropriations bills. Senate Democrats, led by Minority Leader Tom Daschle (D-S.Dak.), realized that they now had a clear path to wrest control of the legislative calendar from Republicans. By long-standing tradition, the majority leader decides which bills the Senate should consider. This role enables the majority party to block legislation the minority wants. Senator Trent Lott (R-Miss.) actively deployed this power when he became majority leader in 1996. In response, his Democratic counterpart, Senator Daschle, boldly attached controversial legislation favored by his party but opposed by Republicans to pending appropriations bills. In one case he added minimum wage legislation, in another a bill regulating health care organizations. Rather than take

continued

authorizations, appropriations, obligations, and outlays. The second and third steps are reversed in the two types of measures: in discretionary spending, appropriations precede obligations; in direct spending, authorizations precede obligations. The action that immediately precedes obligations defines the type of measure. Although this distinction might appear to be merely a technical matter, it has important political and legislative consequences. Enabling federal agencies to incur obligations in advance of appropriations shifts legislative power from the appropriations committees to authorizing committees. The appropriations committees have the upper hand in controlling discretionary spending; authorizing com-

▼

BOX 8-1
Continued

up these and other measures on Democratic terms, Senator Lott pulled various appropriations bills from the Senate floor, delaying their passage and risking a government shutdown. The impasse ended, not surprisingly, with Republicans agreeing to take up Democrat-supported measures and Democrats withdrawing the legislation they had attached to appropriations bills.

Round Three: Republicans Restore Rule XVI
With the Democrats gaining the upper hand despite their minority status, Senator Lott reversed course in July 1999, offering a motion to restore Rule XVI. During the debate, he vented his frustration on how action on appropriations had been stymied:

> "Every Senator dumps his out basket on the floor of the Senate with every amendment he or she has ever dreamed of . . . [and] whole bills or major amendments are offered on the floor of the Senate to appropriations bills . . . where the committees have not been allowed to act, where the committee chairman has not had any input. It is time to bring this process under control."

Senator Daniel Moynihan (D-N.Y.), nearing the end of an illustrious twenty-four-year career in the Senate, bemoaned that when Rule XVI was vitiated "a century or more of fixed senatorial practice crashed and burned and has been burning all around us ever since. Our government became incomprehensible. . . . The authorizing committees are gradually being marginalized and have no role." When debate ended, the Senate by a 53-45 party-line vote restored Rule XVI. However, too much had changed since 1995 for the Senate to fully restore the old practice.

Rule XVI only bars legislation in the form of Senate amendments to appropriations bills. From the time this rule was devised more than a century ago until the late 1990s, these "amendments" included both changes made by the Senate Appropriations Committee to House-passed spending bills and floor amendments. The reason, explained in the next chapter, is that when the House acts on appropriations bills first, the Senate does not produce its own bill but merely amends the House-passed version. But when the Senate Appropriations Committee reports a bill before the House has completed action, as has often been the case since the late 1990s, it does so in the form of an original bill, not an amendment. The net effect is that the Rule XVI prohibition does not apply to legislation added by the Senate Appropriations Committee to any spending bill initiated by the committee. The rule continues to apply, however, to floor amendments.

mittees have the lead role in determining the amount of direct spending. Throughout this book, the term *authorizing legislation* generally refers to discretionary programs. Although direct spending is also provided in authorizing legislation, the differences in budget rules and legislative procedures dictate that it be labeled differently.

Substantive Legislation and Authorization of Appropriations

Authorizing legislation typically has two main components, corresponding to the characteristics mentioned earlier. Looking outward to federal agencies, it contains substantive provisions that prescribe the terms and conditions under which they operate. Looking inward to Con-

TABLE 8-1

Comparison of Sequence for Discretionary and Direct Spending

Discretionary	Direct
1. Authorization	1. Authorization
2. Appropriation	2. Obligation
3. Obligation	3. Appropriation
4. Outlay	4. Outlay

gress, it authorizes the making of appropriations. The two components are usually combined in the same measure, as in the legislation shown in exhibit 8-1, establishing the Office of AIDS Research and authorizing appropriations for that office. The "authorized to be appropriated" language is the formula used to indicate that the rules requiring authorization before appropriation have been satisfied. For reasons explained shortly, while Congress sometimes appropriates funds to agencies whose "authorized to be appropriated" language has expired, it does not appropriate funds for programs lacking substantive provisions.

Temporary and Permanent Authorizations

Authorizing legislation—both the substantive provisions and "authorized to be appropriated" language—is permanent unless the law expressly limits its duration. The permanent provisions continue in effect until they are repealed or amended by new authorizing legislation. (However, an appropriations act and any substantive legislation in it is effective for only a single fiscal year unless the act expressly provides a longer period of effectiveness.) In many areas of federal activity, the permanence of authorizing law obviates the need for new legislation. Of course, even when authorizations are permanent, Congress has the option of writing new law on the subject.

Although the substantive provisions are al-

most always permanent, the "authorized to be appropriated" language often pertains to a specific fiscal year. These authorizations of appropriations may be permanent, annual, or multiyear (an example of these three types of authorizations is in exhibit 8-2). *Permanent authorizations* do not mention specific years and continue in effect until Congress changes them. These authorizations typically are for "such sums as may be necessary"; they do not mention amounts of money. An agency having a permanent authorization only needs to obtain annual appropriations to continue in operation. *Annual authorizations* are for a single fiscal year and usually for a fixed amount of money. Under House and Senate rules, these authorizations have to be renewed every year in order for appropriations to be made. All Congress is required to do is extend the "authorized to be appropriated" provision for another fiscal year. In practice, however, Congress often uses the reauthorization to legislate changes in substantive law. *Multiyear authorizations* are typically in effect for two to five years and have to be renewed when they expire. These provisions often authorize escalating amounts for each fiscal year.

Until the 1960s, virtually all authorizations of appropriations were permanent. But most programs established over the past four decades have had annual or multiyear authorizations, and many older programs have been converted from permanent to temporary status. It is important to keep in mind that even when a program or agency is put on temporary authorization, substantive law governing its operations continues to be permanent.

There are two main reasons for the trend toward temporary authorization, which correspond to the two functions of authorizing legislation. First, a temporary authorization gives Congress and its committees of jurisdiction

► **EXHIBIT 8-1**
Basic Features of Authorization Acts

ESTABLISHMENT OF AGENCY

SEC. 2351. ESTABLISHMENT OF OFFICE

(a) IN GENERAL.—There is established within the National Institutes of Health an office to be known as the Office of AIDS Research. The Office shall be headed by a director, who shall be appointed by the Secretary.

DUTIES AND FUNCTIONS

(b) DUTIES.—

(1) INTERAGENCY COORDINATION OF AIDS ACTIVITIES.—With respect to acquired immune deficiency syndrome, the Director of the Office shall plan, coordinate, and evaluate research and other activities conducted or supported by the agencies of the National Institutes of Health. In carrying out the preceding sentence, the Director of the Office shall evaluate the AIDS activities of each of such agencies and shall provide for the periodic reevaluation of such activities.

AUTHORIZATION OF APPROPRIATIONS

(d) FUNDING.—

(1) AUTHORIZATION OF APPROPRIATIONS.—For the purpose of carrying out AIDS activities under the Plan, there are authorized to be appropriated such sums as may be necessary for each of the fiscal years 1994 through 1996.

Source: *National Institutes of Health Revitalization Act of 1993*, P.L. 103-43.

(a) These excerpts illustrate the basic elements of authorizations: establishment of federal agencies or programs, specification of the agency's duties and functions (including any restrictions), and authorization of appropriations. The first two of these are referred to in the text as substantive legislation.

(b) Authorizing legislation does not always prescribe how an agency should be organized. But the trend has been to specify major organizational units in law, as shown here for the National Institutes of Health.

(c) There has also been a trend to spell out the agency's functions in detail. Only a few of the duties assigned to the Office of AIDS Research are displayed here.

(d) The office was given temporary (three-year) indefinite authorization of "such sums as may be necessary." Typically, temporary authorizations are for definite amounts.

▶ **EXHIBIT 8-2**
Examples of Duration of Authorization to Appropriate

PERMANENT

(d) AUTHORIZATIONS.—For fiscal year 1990, and each fiscal year thereafter, there are authorized to be appropriated such sums as may be necessary to carry out the provisions of this section.

ANNUAL

(a) IN GENERAL.—There are authorized to be appropriated to the Secretary of Veterans Affairs for fiscal year 1995—
  (1) $379,370,000 for the major medical facility projects authorized in subsections (a), (b), and (c) of section 201; and
  (2) $15,800,000 for the major medical facility leases authorized in section 201(a).

MULTIYEAR

(a) IN GENERAL.—The following sums are authorized to be appropriated out of the Highway Trust Fund (other than the Mass Transit Account):
  (1) INTERSTATE MAINTENANCE PROGRAM.—For the Interstate maintenance program under section 119 of title 23, United States Code, $3,427,341,000 for fiscal year 1998, $3,957,103,000 for fiscal year 1999, $3,994,524,000 for fiscal year 2000, $4,073,322,000 for fiscal year 2001, $4,139,630,000 for fiscal year 2002, and $4,217,635,000 for fiscal year 2003.

Sources: *Global Climate Prevention Act of 1989*, S. 1610, as passed Senate, 101st Cong., 1st sess., 1998; *Veterans Health Programs Extension Act of 1994*, P.L. 103-452; and *Transportation Equity Act for the 21st Century*, P.L. 105-178.

(a) The three examples shown here differ in the period covered by the authorization of appropriations. The first example is of a permanent authorization. It has no time limit, and under the rules, Congress can make annual appropriations without any new authorizing legislation. Permanent authorizations usually are indefinite (no dollar limit) and authorize "such sums as may be necessary."

(b) Annual authorizations must be renewed each year, unless Congress terminates the program or makes unauthorized appropriations. Annual authorizations usually authorize definite amounts for the fiscal year. In annually reauthorized programs, there is usually little difference between the authorized and appropriated amounts.

(c) Multiyear authorizations, for two or more years, often specify escalating amounts with higher amounts authorized for the next year than for the prior year. In these cases, the subsequent appropriation is often much lower than the authorization.

frequent opportunities to review agency activities and to make changes as they deem appropriate. Congress boosts its oversight and control when it lacks confidence in the agencies, as happened after the Watergate scandal, when Congress shifted the Justice Department and intelligence agencies to temporary authorization. Second, congressional committees seek temporary authorizations to increase their legislative influence, especially with respect to the amounts subsequently appropriated to federal agencies. Some temporary authorizations itemize the amounts for particular projects and activities. Notice, for example, the breakdown of authorizations for the National Institute of Standards and Technology in exhibit 8-4 (page 176). Although the amount authorized does not determine the amount that is appropriated—under the rules, the appropriation can be as much as or less than the authorization—there is often a close correspondence between the two. This is particularly so in annually authorized programs, where the appropriation typically exceeds 90 percent of the authorized level. Inasmuch as both the annual authorization and the annual appropriation are enacted in the same session and under the same political and budgetary conditions, the authorization strongly influences the subsequent appropriation. The annual defense authorization and appropriation acts exemplify this pattern.

The link tends to be considerably weaker in multiyear authorizations because these typically specify escalating amounts for each fiscal year. Since appropriations are made one year at a time, there is often a widening gap between the authorized and appropriated resources. Moreover, committees that specialize in multiyear authorizations, such as the House Committee on Education and the Workforce, tend to become strong advocates for their programs, leading them to give more weight to program needs than to budget conditions. The gap between authorized and appropriated levels has spurred some interest groups to demand full funding for their programs, by which they mean that Congress should appropriate the amounts promised in authorizations.

Congress often sets aside (or ignores) its rules and makes authorized appropriations for programs whose "authorized to be appropriated" language has expired. As mentioned earlier, an appropriation in excess of the authorized amount is also deemed to be unauthorized. In fact, unauthorized appropriations have become commonplace. There were 247 programs whose authorization had expired, some more than a decade earlier, that received appropriations for fiscal year 2000 (the largest such programs are listed in table 8-2). Congress made $121 billion in unauthorized appropriations for that year for nondefense discretionary programs; this amounted to approximately 40 percent of all nondefense discretionary spending. During the 1990s, national defense has been the only major area whose expiring authorizations have consistently been renewed year after year. In many other areas, Congress has skipped the authorization process and continued federal programs by providing them with annual funding. As the list in table 8-2 shows, some prominent programs have been continued despite their lack of a current authorization—including veterans' medical care, NASA space activities, the Department of Justice, federal aviation operations, and the Customs Service.

In most cases, unauthorized appropriations are fully available for obligation and expenditure. The main exception is when there is a statutory bar, such as in the middle entry of exhibit 8-3, against the obligation or use of unauthorized funds. When Congress appropriates money for programs whose "authorized to be appropriated" provision has expired, the funds are spent according to the permanent substan-

TABLE 8-2
Major Federal Programs with Expired Authorization of Appropriations, Fiscal Year 2000ᵃ

Billions of dollars

Program	Last fiscal year authorized	Fiscal 2000 appropriation
Veterans' medical care	1998	19.0
Justice Department	1980	14.2
NASA	1993	8.7
Local educational grants and Even Start	1999	8.7
International security and economic assistance	1987	8.3
National Institutes of Health	1996	7.0
Federal Aviation Operations	1999	5.4
Community development block grants	1994	4.4
U.S. Coast Guard	1999	4.0
Energy supply programs	1984	3.8
Substance abuse and mental health	1994	2.7
Water pollution control grants	1994	2.2
Airway facilities improvements	1999	2.1
National Institute of Justice	1994	1.9
U.S. Customs Service	1992	1.8
Innovative education strategies	1999	1.7

Source: Congressional Budget Office, *Unauthorized Appropriations and Expiring Authorizations*, January 7, 2000.

a. This annual report, required by law, lists all programs that received appropriations for the current fiscal year, even though their authorizations have expired.

tive laws in effect. Congress, however, rarely makes appropriations for programs that lack substantive legislation. Doing so would infringe on the authorization process and would leave the affected agency without statutory guidance on how the funds are to be spent.

AUTHORIZING LEGISLATION IN CONGRESS

There is no prescribed legislative path for authorizations. Some originate in the House, others in the Senate. Many are considered by only one committee in each chamber; some are jointly or sequentially referred to two or more committees.

Authorizing legislation defines the jurisdiction of most House and Senate committees. Most of the work of congressional committees involves their authorizing responsibilities; for most members of Congress, legislative influence derives from their service on these committees. Table 8-3 shows the authorizing committee jurisdiction of selected programs, and it indicates that the House and Senate do not have parallel authorizing committee structures. Moreover, authorizing committees differ greatly in legislative activity and output. Some have robust agendas and produce significant legislation each session; others are inactive and go through long spells without much legislative productivity. The active committees tend to have jurisdiction over programs with temporary authorization or matters of current interest. The strength of committee leadership also makes a difference, as does the extent to which changes in budget policy that arise through the reconciliation process affect the matters in a committee's jurisdiction.

▶ **EXHIBIT 8-3**
Examples of Reauthorization Requirements in Law

RESTRICTION ON APPROPRIATION

(b) No funds may be appropriated after December 31, 1960, to or for the use of any armed force of the United States for the procurement of aircraft, missiles, or naval vessels unless the appropriation of such funds has been authorized by legislation enacted after such date.

RESTRICTION ON OBLIGATION

(a)(1) Notwithstanding any provision of law enacted before the date of enactment of the State Department/USIA Authorization Act, Fiscal Year 1975, no money appropriated to the Department of State under any law shall be available for obligation or expenditure with respect to any fiscal year commencing on or after July 1, 1972—

   (A) unless the appropriation thereof has been authorized by law enacted on or after February 7, 1972; or

   (B) in excess of an amount prescribed by law enacted on or after such date.

RESTRICTION ON APPROPRIATION FOR UNAUTHORIZED PROJECT

Notwithstanding any other provisions of this Act—

(1) no amount appropriated pursuant to this Act may be used for any program deleted by Congress from requests as originally made to either the Committee on Commerce, Science, and Transportation of the Senate or the Committee on Science, Space, and Technology of the House of Representatives;

(2) no amount appropriated pursuant to this Act may be used for any program in excess of the amount actually authorized for that particular program by section 4 (a), (b), and (d). . . .

Sources: *Military Construction Authorization Act of 1959*, P.L. 86-149; *Department of State/USIA Authorization Act, Fiscal Year 1975*, P.L. 93-475; and *NASA Authorization Act, Fiscal Year 1992*, P.L. 102-195.

(a) The first of the three excerpts shown here was the genesis of annual authorization for the Defense Department. When the department was established, it had a permanent authorization. Annual authorization was initially applied to certain procurement expenditures; since then it has been extended to the entire department. Inasmuch as the bar is only against appropriations, the funds would be available for expenditure if appropriations were made for unauthorized programs.

(b) The second example is the provision of law that converted the State Department from permanent to temporary authorization. In this case, unauthorized appropriations may not be used because the bar is against obligation, unless the appropriation act expressly waives the prohibition.

(c) The final example is from an annual authorization act for the National Aeronautics and Space Administration. Once again, there is a bar against using unauthorized appropriations, but in this instance (unlike the previous example) it pertains only to that year's appropriations.

TABLE 8-3
House and Senate Authorizing Committee Jurisdictions for Selected Programs[a]

Program	House committee	Senate committee
Food stamps	Ways and Means	Agriculture, Nutrition, and Forestry
School lunch	Education and the Workforce	Agriculture, Nutrition, and Forestry
Civil service	Government Reform and Oversight	Governmental Affairs
Social Security	Ways and Means	Finance
Veterans' pensions	Veterans' Affairs	Veterans' Affairs
Medicaid	Commerce	Finance
Medicare–Part A	Ways and Means	Finance
Medicare–Part B	Commerce	Finance
NASA	Science	Commerce, Science, and Transportation
National Institutes of Health	Commerce	Labor and Human Resources
National Science Foundation	Science	Labor and Human Resources
Highways	Transportation and Infrastructure	Commerce, Science, and Transportation
Maritime Administration	Resources	Commerce, Science, and Transportation
National parks	Resources	Energy and Natural Resources

Sources: *House Manual*, 104th Cong., 2d sess., H. Doc. 272; *Senate Manual*, 104th Cong., 1st sess., S. Doc. 2.

a. The authorizing jurisdictions of House and Senate committees are not parallel. Thus a House committee may be paired with a Senate committee on some matters but not on others. (The jurisdiction of House and Senate appropriations subcommittees is identical.) On major legislation, two or more House or Senate committees may claim jurisdiction. For example, the House Commerce Committee and the House Ways and Means Committee share Medicare jurisdiction. Since the House has more committees than the Senate, it has more overlapping jurisdictions. When two or more committees have jurisdiction over portions of the same bill, the measure may be assigned to them concurrently (multiple referral) or sequentially. In the case of sequential referral, after the first committee has completed its work, the remaining committees are usually given a deadline by which to report the bill.

Two other factors affect authorizing activity in Congress. One is the extent to which the White House takes the lead in proposing programs and funds are available to pay for them; the other is the capacity of the House or Senate to act on legislation its committees produce. Authorizing activity was relatively low during the 1980s, when President Reagan sought to curtail many domestic programs and chronic deficits ruled out major legislative initiatives. Nevertheless, some committees continued to generate streams of legislation. The House and Senate armed services committees produced annual authorizing legislation covering the Defense Department; the House Ways and Means Committee and the Senate Finance Committee (which have broad authorizing jurisdiction in addition to their responsibilities in tax policy) formulated important legislation concerning health, trade, and Social Security.

There has been a steep decline in the volume of laws enacted by Congress. When Dwight Eisenhower was president in the 1950s, each two-year Congress produced as many as 1,000 public laws. In the 1990s Congress has averaged only about half as many. The factors accounting for this trend include conflict within Congress, differences between Capitol Hill and the White House, closer monitoring of congressional action by interest groups (which guard against legislation adverse to their interests), the tendency to view legislation in terms of its budgetary impact, and the proclivity of Congress to package legislation into broad, program-oriented bills.

The trend has affected the way most authorizing committees work. In some sessions, much of the year's legislation has been folded into an omnibus reconciliation or appropriations bill. The process feeds on itself—the more difficult it is to pass ordinary legislation, the more committee chairs and others in Congress seek a vehicle on which their stalled measure can ride to enactment. The upshot is a stunted authorizations process in which some bills make it through on their own, some are enacted as parts of other measures, and some do not get enacted.

THE RELATIONSHIP OF AUTHORIZATIONS AND APPROPRIATIONS

It is a basic rule of federal law that appropriated funds are to be spent according to the terms set in authorizing law. Appropriations determine the amounts available for expenditure; authorization acts determine how the money is spent. In practice, however, the relationship is not always clear-cut, and there may be considerable friction between the two types of congressional action. Some authorizations provide budget authority; most appropriations acts contain substantive law. Differences in the reports filed by the relevant authorizing and appropriations committees sometimes further complicate the relationship.

There has been intermittent conflict between the two sets of committees since the appropriations committees were established during the Civil War era. At times appropriators have been dominant, using their control of the purse to influence the course of legislation. At other times authorizers have had the upper hand, using their much larger numbers to outvote the appropriations committees when their jurisdictions and interests clash. One of the purposes of the House and Senate rules is to diminish conflict by walling off the appropriations and authorizations process from one another. Despite the rules, however, the committees often get in each other's way—the appropriations committees by inserting legislative provisions in their bills, the authorizing com-

mittees by providing budget resources in their legislation. Other factors have also altered the division of legislative work: extensive earmarking of funds, an increase in direct spending, and the insertion of appropriation-forcing language in authorizing legislation. Legislation in appropriations bills is discussed in the next chapter; other practices generating conflict between authorizations and appropriations are considered in the remainder of this chapter.

Earmarks in Legislation and Reports

Authorizing legislation is as general or as detailed as Congress makes it. When it is general, as was once the usual practice, affected agencies have considerable discretion in spending appropriated funds. When authorizing legislation details exactly how agencies operate and funds are spent, however, the possibility of conflict with the preferences of the appropriations committees escalates. Since the 1970s there has been a pronounced trend toward greater specificity in authorizing legislation, many of which earmark amounts for specified projects or activities, as displayed in exhibit 8-4.

Authorizing committees are not the only earmarkers; the appropriations committees also specify how funds are to be spent. As chapter 9 shows, the appropriations committees extensively earmark funds and dictate other conditions in the reports that accompany their spending bills. Quite often, the itemizations in authorizing legislation differ from those set forth in appropriations bills or reports. One frequent source of friction between the two sets of committees is the appropriation of funds for unauthorized projects or activities. In 1993, for example, fighting broke out into the open when the House Transportation Appropriations Subcommittee earmarked more than $300 million to fifty-eight highway projects that had not been included

▶ **EXHIBIT 8-4**
Earmarked Authorizations

Sec. 2. AUTHORIZATIONS OF APPROPRIATIONS FOR SCIENTIFIC AND TECHNICAL RESEARCH AND SERVICES.

(a) LABORATORY ACTIVITIES—There are authorized to be appropriated to the Secretary of Commerce for the Scientific and Technical Research and Services laboratory activities of the National Institute of Standards and Technology—

  (1) $278,563,000 for fiscal year 1998, of which—

    (A) $38,104,000 shall be for Electronics and Electrical Engineering;

    (B) $18,925,000 shall be for Manufacturing Engineering;

    (C) $31,791,000 shall be for Chemical Science and Technology;

    (D) $30,372,000 shall be for Physics;

    (E) $50,914,000 shall be for Material Science and Engineering;

    (F) $13,404,000 shall be for Building and Fire Research;

    (G) $47,073,000 shall be for Computer Science and Applied Mathematics;

    (H) $19,376,000 shall be for Technical Assistance; and,

    (I) $28,604,000 shall be for Research Support. . . .

(b) LIMITATIONS ON APPROPRIATIONS—No sums are authorized to be appropriated to the Director of the National Institute of Standards and Technology for fiscal years 1998 and 1999 for the activities for which sums are authorized by this Act, unless such sums are specifically authorized to be appropriated by this Act. . . .

Sec. 10. NOTICE.

(a) NOTICE OF REPROGRAMMING—If any funds authorized by this Act are subject to a reprogramming action that requires notice to be provided to the Appropriations Committees of the House of Representatives and the Senate, notice of such action shall concurrently be provided to the Committee on Science of the House of Representatives and the Committee on Commerce, Science, and Transportation of the Senate.

Source: *National Institute of Standards and Technology Authorization Act of 1997*, H.R. 1274, as passed House, 105th Cong., 1st sess., 1997.

(a) Some authorizing measures, such as the one excerpted here, earmark amounts for specific programs and activities. Extensive earmarking increases the likelihood of conflict between the authorizing and appropriations committees.

(b) An appropriation in excess of an earmarked amount is an unauthorized appropriation. Section (b) in the exhibit reinforces this rule by limiting appropriations to the amounts specifically authorized for particular projects. However, an appropriation in excess of the authorized amount may be used.

(c) A shift of funds among activities in the same account is known as a reprogramming. Section 10(a) above requires the authorizing committees to be notified of any such reprogramming. Reprogramming is more fully discussed in chapter 10.

in authorizing legislation passed by Congress two years earlier. This precipitated a bitter clash between the subcommittee and the Public Works and Transportation Committee and delayed enactment of the transportation appropriations bill for many months. This battle between authorizers and appropriators is chronicled in box 8-2. It turned out to be only one round in an ongoing turf battle in Congress over who should control billions of dollars of transportation money. The next round was played out in 1997 and 1998 and is discussed in box 8-3.

Appropriation-Forcing Language

Discretionary authorizations do not enable agencies to incur obligations or spend money: the authorized funds are available only to the extent provided in appropriations acts. But authorizing committees sometimes expand their budgetary influence by inserting appropriation-forcing language in legislation. In some instances, the authorizing legislation stipulates that not less than a certain amount of appropriated funds shall be made available for a particular purpose. In others, it bars spending appropriated funds for activities that the appropriations committees favor unless a threshold amount is also appropriated for activities that the authorizing committees favor. The appropriations committees are not legally required to provide the threshold amount, but if they do not, funds appropriated for their preferred activities might become unavailable.

Dealing with Conflicts

Several principles guide the resolution of conflicts between authorizations and appropriations, but application of the principles hinges on the precise wording of the statutes in question. One principle is that legislation in an ap-

propriations act is valid law, even when it is enacted in disregard of House or Senate rules. Substantive provisions in appropriations acts generally have the same legal status as provisions enacted in authorizing legislation. One major difference, however, is that in contrast to authorizing law, which is permanent unless the law expressly limits its period of effectiveness, appropriations are effective for only one fiscal year unless the text of the law gives it a longer duration. In practice, most legislation in appropriations bills is effective for a single fiscal year but is reenacted annually.

The second principle is that appropriations can repeal or amend authorizing law, but only if this action is done expressly or in a manner that manifests Congress's intent to revise or terminate the earlier law. Whenever possible, laws that seem to conflict are to be interpreted in ways that reconcile their intent or effect. Suppose, for example, that Congress passes legislation that bars an agency from spending unobligated funds but then makes an unauthorized appropriation to the agency. On the surface, this may appear to be a collision between two laws—one providing money, the other barring its use. But an alternative explanation may resolve the conflict; in making the appropriation Congress conditioned its availability on enactment of authorizing legislation. Because repeal of a statute must be explicit or manifest, it has become common to insert "notwithstanding any other provision of law" into legislation. This language is designed to ensure that the new law prevails, regardless of any previous enactment to the contrary.

Even without this language, when two laws conflict, the more recent statute governs. Inasmuch as the normal sequence is for appropriations to follow authorizations, direct conflict between the two usually results in the application of appropriations law. Complications may arise if one of the laws passes Congress

▼

BOX 8-2
Authorizations versus Appropriations: Who Controls Transportation Money?

In 1991 Congress earmarked $6.2 billion in contract authority (over six years) to more than 600 highway and mass transit projects. Two years later, the House Transportation Appropriations Subcommittee tried to redirect $300 million of this money to 58 different projects—many of which happened to have been in the home state of the subcommittee's new chair, Representative Bob Carr (D-Mich.). He argued that the reallocations were based on economic and environmental criteria, but it turned out that more than half of the earmarked money would have gone to states that had members on his subcommittee.

On June 24, 1993, Carr's subcommittee requested that the Rules Committee grant a blanket waiver of House Rule XXI, which prohibits unauthorized appropriations. This request was opposed by Representative Norman Mineta (D-Calif.), the new chair of the Public Works and Transportation Committee, who complained that the appropriation infringed on his committee's jurisdiction. Four days later, the Rules Committee sided with Mineta, making it likely that the disputed projects would be struck from the bill by a point of order.

On June 29, Speaker Tom Foley (D-Wash.) tried to broker a deal in which the Public Works Committee would report a new bill authorizing the disputed projects, after which the House would take up the appropriations bill. But Mineta refused to go along, arguing, "I'm not a rubber stamp; the Public Works Committee is not a rubber stamp." The next effort at compromise came in July, when the leadership proposed a new procedure for handling disputes between the two committees. However, Mineta insisted that his committee must have the final say on disputed projects. Carr refused to concede veto power to Public Works, insisting that "any policy that impacts on money is of interest to us and is within our jurisdiction."

To break the impasse, which blocked House passage of the transportation appropriations bill for months, Carr's subcommittee drafted a new bill, which reclassified the disputed projects. On September 23, when the House was finally set to vote on the bill, nearly all of the disputed projects had been removed. The bill passed by a vote of 312-89, giving Mineta a clear victory and stymieing the appropriators' raid on authorization jurisdiction.

Why did the battle take place, and why did the Public Works Committee win? The protagonists were new to their posts, they were not familiar with the informal means of working out accommodations, and each wanted to prove his mettle. Moreover, the projects added by the appropriations subcommittee were to be funded by taking money from previously authorized projects, not by providing more for transportation. This set up a zero-sum conflict between the two committees.

The authorizers won for two main reasons. First, with 63 members, Public Works was the largest committee in the House. Moreover, the authorizers drew support from members of other House committees who felt that Appropriations had overstepped its jurisdiction and had become too powerful. But this was not the last round in the battle, for as exhibit 8-2 shows, the appropriation committees have other powers in their legislative arsenal. The next round occurred four years after the Carr-Mineta confrontation, when the multiyear transportation program came up for reauthorization. The stakes were much higher this time and many of the combatants were different, but once again the battle lines were drawn in the House between the authorization and appropriation committees.

BOX 8-3
The 1998 Washington TEA Party: Revenge of the Transportation Committee

Weighing in at 500 statute pages, the Transportation Equity Act for the 21st Century (TEA-21) is no ordinary law. It was the product of prolonged budgetary strife between the House Transportation Committee and the Appropriations Committee. One facet of this conflict (recounted in box 8-2) revolved around highway projects; an even bigger battle pertained to control of the Highway Trust Fund—the more than $20 billion collected each year from taxes on gasoline and other products. Each side had its power base—the Transportation Committee had its own trust fund, and the Appropriations Committee had its annual spending bills. Each had allies—Transportation could count on support from many in Congress who had highway or mass transit money earmarked to their states or districts; Appropriations made common cause with the budget committees and the White House, both of which wanted to constrain this area of spending.

1997
May 21
Shuster's amendment to the fiscal 1998 budget resolution fails, 214-216.

September 30
ISTEA, set to expire, is extended for six months.

1998
March 27
Shuster's new bill is reported in the House.

April 1
TEA-21 passes the House, 337-80.

April 2
TEA-21 passes the Senate amended, by unanimous consent.

May 22
TEA-21 conference report passes the Senate, 88-5, and the House, 297-86.

June 9
Clinton signs TEA-21 into law.

Periodically, the Transportation Committee produced a law, such as the Intermodal Surface Transportation Efficiency Act of 1991 (ISTEA), in which the trust fund money was allocated according to its preference. The Appropriations Committee would then limit the amount that could be obligated each year. Rep. Bud Shuster (R-Pa.), the tough chair of the Transportation Committee, vowed that this time would be different. He would get revenge by passing a bill that granted his committee full control of the trust fund and eliminated the appropriators' role in transportation funding.

His chance came when ISTEA's six-year authorization was scheduled to expire. Without a new authorization, the flow of highway money from Washington to the states would stop. Just about everyone in Congress took it for granted that there would be a new transportation bill in 1997. What they did not know was whether the appropriators or authorizers would dictate its terms. When Clinton signed TEA-21 in 1998, there was no doubt who had won; the law was an unqualified victory for the Transportation Committee, which got more money and more control through Shuster's shrewd legislative maneuvers.

Shuster's first move was to enlarge his committee to 73 members—making it the largest in Congress. Members were eager to volunteer for seats on the committee, confident that their loyalty would be amply rewarded with money for their districts. His second ploy was to demand

continued

▼

BOX 8-3
Continued

that the fiscal 1998 budget resolution be amended to add $12 billion for transportation. This demand put House Republican leaders in a quandary, since they had just signed a deal with the president that was thought to have settled budget issues for the next several years. Despite this, Shuster pressed forward with his amendment, but an all-out effort by the leadership produced just enough votes to narrowly defeat it. However, the Transportation Committee would not be subdued by a single vote. "We'll be back," Shuster warned.

This close call convinced party leaders that Shuster's demands would have to be accommodated. They negotiated a brief extension of ISTEA, promising Shuster that he would get favorable treatment the following year. This delay played into Shuster's hand, for 1998 was an election year, and members could be counted on to vote for local projects. Moreover, by 1998, the previous year's balanced budget deal was no longer news, and the surging surplus made it feasible to spend money without appearing to bust the budget. With adoption of the fiscal 1999 budget resolution delayed (discussed in box 6-1), transportation advocates had a clear field to demand more money without being constrained by budget decisions.

Shuster exploited these advantages to produce his dream bill, which proposed $217 billion over six years for highway and mass transit programs (including $9 billion on 1,467 specified projects). Rather than resorting to the usual stealth methods for funding members' projects, Shuster explicitly listed all of them in the text of the bill—a display of the heady combination of money and power. This was ten times the number of projects in a highway bill Reagan vetoed in 1987 and nearly three times more than the Democratic Congress distributed in the 1991 ISTEA. The bill moved the highway trust fund off-budget and beyond the reach of the Appropriations Committee's control. To gain legislative backing, the bill included such provisions as a subsidy for ethanol producers, which drew support from corn producing states.

When the House took up his bill, Shuster set forth his budget philosophy in plain terms: "Spend the revenue coming in [the highway trust fund]. This is honesty in budgeting. If we are not going to spend the revenue coming in, then we should reduce [highway] taxes." The bill sailed through the House unaltered.

But Shuster still had three hurdles: the Senate, the president, and the need to offset the additional spending. The Senate version had less spending, fewer earmarks, and did not disturb existing budget rules and relationships. But the House-Senate conference reached enough compromises to enable the bill to pass both chambers. One compromise kept the highway trust fund on-budget but built a "firewall" around the fund that ensured reductions in highway or mass transit spending would not be used for increased spending in other programs. Clinton criticized the bill but stopped short of explicitly threatening a veto. In due course, the price for support from the White House became known—a stricter drunken driver standard. Clinton accepted this concession because his bargaining power was limited and he knew that Congress would not sustain a veto. The offsets required by budget rules were a bit complicated; an estimated $18 billion was needed. Most of this was realized by curtailing disability payments to veterans for smoking-related ailments.

Its victory thus achieved, TEA-21 should bring at least six years of budgetary peace in the transportation arena. But if the past is any indication, this is a conflict that does not have a final chapter.

first but is signed by the president after the other. This situation occurred in 1992, when Congress inserted different provisions in the defense authorizations and appropriations acts. Legal counsel representing Congress argued that the "last law prevails" rule is determined by the sequence of legislative action. The White House took the position, however, that this rule should be applied on the basis of the sequence in which the bills become law.

Conflict between authorizations and appropriations also arises from differences in the reports that accompany these bills. As is discussed in the next chapter, the appropriations committees usually express legislative intent in their reports, not in the text of their bills. By contrast, authorizing committees express much of their legislative intent in the bills themselves. When an authorization law and an appropriations report collide, legal rules may clash with political expedience. On strictly legal grounds, the authorization should take precedence, but the affected agency may nevertheless feel impelled to abide by the dictates of the appropriations report. If it does not, it risks being penalized in the next round of appropriation decisions.

DIRECT SPENDING LEGISLATION

Authorization law provides or effectively controls more than half the budget resources federal agencies spend. This type of authorization is termed "spending authority" by the Congressional Budget Act and "direct spending" by the BEA; it sometimes is referred to as "backdoor spending." The terms are not precisely synonymous, but they are sufficiently similar to be used interchangeably, except when the specific provisions of law pertaining to them are being discussed. *Direct spending* is the term preferred here because it distinguishes this type of measure from *discretionary authorizations*.

The classification of an expenditure as direct or discretionary depends on which committee controls it. Appropriations committees control discretionary spending; all other spending is classified as direct because it is directly controlled by authorizing committees. Direct spending includes entitlements funded in annual appropriations acts because eligibility criteria and payment schedules set in authorizing law are what determine the amounts spent. For example, although annual appropriations finance Medicaid, expenditures for Medicaid are classed as direct spending because the authorizing law determines the amount to be spent.

Entitlements are the most prominent form of direct spending. Direct spending takes several other forms, including *borrowing authority* (provisions authorizing agencies to spend borrowed funds), *contract authority* (provisions authorizing agencies to incur obligations in advance of appropriations), and *authority to forgo the collection of user fees* or certain other charges. The Congressional Budget Act bars Congress from considering new contract or borrowing authority legislation unless this authority is made effective only to the extent provided in appropriations acts. However, trust funds, such as the Highway Trust Fund, are exempted from this restriction. Exhibits 8-5 and 8-6 provide examples of entitlement and contract authority.

Entitlements are a form of direct spending that give eligible recipients a legal right to payments from the government. The government is obligated to make such payments even if the budget and appropriation acts do not provide sufficient funds. Most entitlement laws are open-ended—they do not specify or limit the amount to be spent. Instead they spell out eligibility criteria and establish a formula for computing the size of payments. The total paid depends on the number of

▶ **EXHIBIT 8-5**
Entitlement Programs

ENTITLEMENT LEGISLATION

ENTITLEMENT TO HOSPITAL INSURANCE BENEFITS

Sec. 266. (a) Every individual who—

(1) has attained the age of 65, and

(2) is entitled to monthly insurance benefits under section 202 or is a qualified railroad retirement beneficiary, shall be entitled to hospital insurance benefits under part A of title XVIII for each month for which he meets the condition specified in paragraph (2), beginning with the first month after June 1966 for which he meets the conditions specified in paragraphs (1) and (2).

PERMANENT APPROPRIATION

Sec. 1817. (a) There is hereby created on the books of the Treasury of the United States a trust fund to be known as the "Federal Hospital Insurance Trust Fund" (hereinafter in this section referred to as the "Trust Fund"). The Trust Fund shall consist of such amounts as may be deposited in, or appropriated to, such fund as provided in this part. There are hereby appropriated to the Trust Fund for the fiscal year ending June 30, 1966, and for each fiscal year thereafter, out of any moneys in the Treasury not otherwise appropriated. . . .

ANNUAL APPROPRIATION

For payment to the Federal Hospital Insurance and the Federal Supplementary Medical Insurance Trust Funds, as provided under sections 217(g) and 1844 of the Social Security Act, sections 103 (c) and 111 (d) of the Social Security Amendments of 1965, section 278 (d) of Public Law 97-248, and for administrative expenses incurred pursuant to section 201 (g) of the Social Security Act, $62,953,000,000.

Sources: *Social Security Amendments of 1965*, P.L. 89-97; and *Omnibus Consolidated and Emergency Supplemental Appropriations Act for Fiscal Year 1999*, P.L. 105-277.

(a) These entries pertain to Medicare: the first provision established entitlement to Medicare, the second made a permanent appropriation to the Medicare Health Insurance Trust Fund, and the third made an annual appropriation to the Medicare Supplementary Medical Insurance Trust Fund.

(b) The Congressional Budget Act defines entitlements as authority "to make payments (including loans and grants), the budget authority for which is not provided for in advance by appropriations acts, to any person or government if, under the provisions of law containing such authority, the United States is obligated to make such payments to persons or governments who meet the requirements established by such law."

(c) When an entitlement has a permanent appropriation and is financed through a trust fund, as in the case of the Health Insurance Trust Fund, all receipts of the trust fund become available for obligation without further action by Congress. Hence the receipts of these trust funds are scored as budget authority.

▶ EXHIBIT 8-6
Contract Authority

AUTHORIZING LEGISLATION

(1) OUT OF HIGHWAY TRUST FUND—There shall be available from the Highway Trust Fund (other than the Mass Transit Account) the following sums:

(A) NATIONAL MAGNETIC LEVITATION PROTOTYPE DEVELOPMENT PROGRAM—For the national magnetic levitation prototype development program under this section $5,000,000 for fiscal year 1992, $45,000,000 for fiscal year 1993, $100,000,000 for fiscal year 1994, $100,000,000 for fiscal year 1995, $125,000,000 for fiscal year 1996, and $125,000,000 for fiscal year 1997.

LIMITING APPROPRIATION

None of the funds in this Act shall be available for the planning or execution of the National Magnetic Levitation Prototype Development program as defined in subsections 1036 (b) and 1036 (d)(1)(A) of the Intermodal Surface Transportation Efficiency Act of 1991.

LIQUIDATING APPROPRIATION

For grants and payment of obligations incurred in carrying out the provisions of the High Speed Ground Transportation program as defined in subsections 1036(c) and 1036(d)(1)(B) of the Intermodal Surface Transportation Efficiency Act of 1991, including planning and environmental analyses, $7,118,000, to be derived from the Highway Trust Fund and to remain available until expended: *Provided,* That none of the funds in this Act shall be available for the implementation or execution of programs the obligations for which are in excess of $5,000,000.

Sources: *Intermodal Surface Transportation Efficiency Act of 1991,* P.L. 102-240; and *Department of Transportation and Related Agencies Appropriations Act for Fiscal Year 1996,* P.L. 104-50.

(a) This exhibit shows the often-fractious relationship between authorizations and appropriations. The first entry, from the 1991 transportation authorization act, provided contract authority to the national magnetic levitation prototype development program for each of the subsequent six years. The phrase "there shall be available" enables an agency to incur obligations in advance of appropriations. The amounts made available by this act were to rise from $5 million in 1992 to $125 million in 1996 and 1997.

(b) The middle entry, drawn from the fiscal 1996 transportation appropriations act, imposed a limitation on obligating funds for the magnetic levitation program. In fact, it barred the use of any funds for this program. Without the limitation on obligations, $125 million would have been available from the authorization; the limitation in the appropriation act reduced this to zero.

(c) The final entry is of a liquidating appropriation, which is made to pay off obligations incurred pursuant to contract authority provided in authorizing legislation. A liquidating appropriation does not provide additional resources nor does it change the amount that may be obligated.

(d) No liquidating appropriation was needed for the magnetic levitation program because the limitation in the middle entry barred any obligations for this purpose.

those eligible and the amount each person is entitled to receive.

Some entitlements (such as Social Security) have permanent appropriations—the mandated payments are made without annual congressional action. Most entitlement programs, however, go through the annual appropriations process, although Congress does not really control them at this stage. If the amount appropriated is not sufficient, Congress has to provide supplemental funds. A few entitlements are formally contingent on appropriations, but the control is not effective. The law authorizing the food stamps program, for example, specifies that the amount spent shall be limited by annual appropriations. But food stamp spending has never been constrained by appropriations decisions, and the BEA classifies this program as direct spending.

The Growth of Direct Spending

Chapter 2 discussed the transformation of the federal budget from a means of financing government agencies and programs into a means of financing American families and households. Whatever the reasons for this transformation, it has resulted in a steady expansion of the share of the budget defined as direct spending.

Although the growth in direct spending has been remarkable, more than two-thirds of these expenditures have been in three areas: Social Security, interest on the public debt, and Medicare and Medicaid. With the exception of Medicaid, almost all the growth in these expenditures has resulted from pre-1980s legislation, not from new congressional action. In fact, Congress has taken repeated, though relatively modest, steps since 1980 to cut these expenditures. The cuts have been achieved through reconciliation bills, not through the PAYGO process. PAYGO is effec-

tive in stemming spending increases due to new legislation; it is not effective in dealing with increases generated by existing law.

The rise in direct spending has had an enormous impact on federal outlays and congressional operations. It has made the control of federal spending more difficult than was the case when discretionary authorizations and annual appropriations governed most of the budget. It has put Congress in the politically uncomfortable position of having to vote for spending cuts rather than increases. Furthermore, it has made the budget more sensitive to changes in economic conditions.

The surge in direct spending has, by definition, shifted budgetary power in Congress from the appropriations committees to certain authorizing committees. Although the appropriators still have vast budgetary power—the $500 billion in annual spending that they control is a lot of money by anyone's count—they review a shrinking percentage of total expenditures. The growth in direct spending has been propelled by efforts of various authorizing committees to augment their power by freeing programs in their jurisdiction from the control of appropriators. This is not to say, however, that direct spending programs are exempt from recurring congressional scrutiny. Some are, while others are not—Social Security has been; Medicare has not.

BEA, which walls off the discretionary portions of the budget from direct spending programs, has slowed the raid on appropriations committees' control. Under current rules, legislation converting a discretionary program into an entitlement would have to be fully offset in accordance with PAYGO procedures. Although PAYGO has made it difficult to legislate new or expanded entitlements, it is highly unlikely that direct spending will shrink as a share of the federal budget in the years ahead. Even if new direct spending programs are not added, the aging of the U.S. population will impel future increases in spending on pensions and health care—the two biggest direct spending programs.

CONCLUSION

In its first decade, the Budget Enforcement Act had a mixed impact on the authorizations process. It did not directly influence discretionary authorizations, which Congress can enact for any amount. Nevertheless, because the caps constrained discretionary spending, Congress was less inclined that it once was to authorize programs at amounts well in excess of appropriated levels. BEA placed formidable legislative obstacles in the way of new entitlements, but it did not control spending resulting from existing law. New direct spending legislation had to run the gauntlet of PAYGO rules, but increases caused by past legislation were not limited, even when they exceeded budgeted levels.

BEA moderated budgetary conflict between the appropriations and authorizing committees. Each operated according to its own rules and in its own orbit. If direct spending exceeded budgeted levels, Congress still could appropriate as much as was allowed by the discretionary caps. Moreover, the rules made it difficult to convert discretionary spending into direct spending or to take money from one category and spend it on the other. But the rules were not airtight and not self-enforcing—they did not put an end to conflict between authorizers and appropriators. On a number of occa-

sions, Congress raided PAYGO accounts to spend more on discretionary programs than the caps allowed. On other occasions, it simply manipulated the rules to obtain more spending than would otherwise be permitted.

Conflict between authorizers and appropriators is inherent in an institution that looks at the same issues through both program and financial perspectives, and in which the two sets of committees have different members. Sometimes conflict breaks out in the open, as occurred in both 1993 and 1997–98 on transportation programs. Most often, however, it is waged behind the scenes and fought over relatively small amounts of money—earmarks, unauthorized projects, and the like. From time to time, reformers have proposed to simplify congressional procedures by merging the authorization and appropriation functions in a single set of committees. Although Congress has shown little interest in restructuring its committee system along these lines, it has merged the authorization and appropriation processes for direct spending. For all practical purposes, the authorizing committees control direct spending. As this part of the budget has expanded, the relative jurisdiction of the appropriations committees has shrunk in relative size. The appropriations committees accepted spending caps in the 1990s as part of a quid pro quo that protected their jurisdiction against new raids by authorizing committees. Despite some continuing skirmishes, the bargain was maintained for a decade, enabling appropriations committees to hold on to control of one-third of federal spending.

9

The Appropriations Process

A n appropriations act is a law passed by Congress that enables agencies to incur obligations and the Treasury to make payments for designated purposes. Congress's power to appropriate derives from the Constitution, which provides that "no money shall be drawn from the Treasury but in consequence of appropriations made by law." An agency may not spend more than the amount appropriated to it, and it must use available funds only for the purposes, and according to the terms, that Congress sets. Over the past few decades, appropriations have also come to be regarded as mandates that agencies carry out prescribed activities by spending the funds appropriated to them. Impoundment rules (discussed in the next chapter) that restrict the president's power to delay or withhold the expenditure of funds reflect this newer concept of appropriations. Executive discretion is now limited by appropriations in two ways: by imposing a ceiling on the maximum and a floor on the minimum that may be spent.

Although appropriations provide legal authority for outlays, with few exceptions the amounts set forth in appropriations acts pertain to budget authority. They make money available for obligation; they do not specify the amounts to be disbursed during the fiscal year. In contrast to most states and local legislatures, which appropriate to cover cash payments, Congress does not normally require that appropriations be spent in the fiscal year for which they are made. In many cases, outlays occur years after the appropriation is enacted. This practice provides agencies with funding for activities (such as procurement and construction) that span a number of years, but it weakens the ability of the appropriations process to control short-term outlays.

The Constitution does not require annual appropriations, but since the First Congress in 1789, the practice has been to appropriate each year. From time to time, Congress has been urged to adopt a biennial budget (to make appropriations every other year) as many state legislatures do. But the appropriations committees have resisted such proposals, preferring the short-term control that comes from annual action to the longer-term perspective that might be gained from biennial decisions. Change does not come easily to the appropriations committees; appropriators hold on to traditions even when external conditions change. Nevertheless, strong pressure has built up in recent years to shift from an annual to a biennial appropriations cycle, and at this writing Congress appears at the brink of adopting this change. The implications of biennial appropriations are discussed in the concluding chapter.

Appropriations must be obligated during the fiscal year for which they are provided, unless (as often happens) Congress expressly makes the money available for a longer period. In contrast to authorizing legislation, which is presumed to be permanent, an appropriations act and any substantive provisions in it expire at the end of the fiscal year—unless the text makes them permanent or effective beyond the fiscal year. The annual nature of appropriations explains why Congress often reenacts the same or similar provisions (such as restrictions on using federal money to pay for abortions) year after year.

TYPES OF APPROPRIATIONS ACTS

The Constitution does not prescribe the type of measure in which appropriations are made. Ap-

propriations can be inserted in any law, but the practice that predates the Constitution is that appropriations are made in acts that are distinct from other types of legislation. This distinction is codified in House and Senate rules.

Congress produces four types of appropriations. *Regular appropriations* provide budget authority for the upcoming fiscal year, or if it has already started, for the year in progress. *Supplemental appropriations* provide additional budget resources when the regular appropriation is deemed insufficient or for activities the regular appropriation does not fund. *Continuing appropriations* (usually referred to as continuing resolutions because they are enacted as joint resolutions rather than as bills) fund agencies that have not received regular appropriations by the start of the fiscal year. *Permanent appropriations* (usually enacted in substantive legislation) become available without current action by Congress. Because of the rise in interest charges, Social Security, and other expenditures financed by permanent appropriations, only about half of federal spending requires new appropriations.

Thirteen regular appropriations bills—never more or less—are fixed in congressional tradition (table 9-1). However, the number of supplementals and continuing resolutions (CRs) varies from year to year. For example, in 1993 there were three supplementals and three continuing resolutions, while in the following year there were two supplementals and no continuing resolutions. Jurisdiction over these measures is vested in the House and Senate appropriations committees, each of which is divided into thirteen parallel subcommittees. Each paired House and Senate subcommittee handles one regular appropriations bill, as well as the portions of supplementals and continuing resolutions pertaining to matters in its jurisdiction.

In the 1990s the number and size of supplementals were affected by the discretionary spending caps, which limited the amounts that could be appropriated each year. At the same time that they constrained ordinary supplementals, which added funds for ongoing activities, the caps spurred Congress to enact emergency supplementals for extraordinary expenses that it did not anticipate when it enacted the regular appropriation. By the time Congress took up a supplemental, just about all the money available within the caps had been spent through regular appropriations. Nevertheless, Congress still manages to make room for supplemental spending. One ploy is to designate the additional spending as emergency; another is to offset the additional funds by rescinding idle resources that would not be spent anyway. In the early 1990s, when the budget enforcement rules were new, Congress used the emergency designation sparingly and provided supplemental funds for genuine emergencies, such as the 1994 California earthquake. But as the decade wore on, Congress and the president became less inhibited in using the emergency escape clause.

The discretionary caps weakened the distinction between regular and supplemental appropriations. In enforcing the caps, it made no difference whether the funds were provided in a regular or supplemental bill; what mattered was whether the spending was designated as emergency. Under these rules, supplemental spending must be within the caps if not designated for emergencies; regular appropriations must be outside the caps if they are designated for emergency purposes. Putting this new logic into practice induced Congress to make supplemental appropriations in regular appropriations acts. The omnibus appropriations act for 1999 offered the best example of this approach. In addition to regular appropriations, it provided $15 billion for "emergency supplemental appropriations" plus another $6 billion in "emergency appropriations." By packaging emer-

TABLE 9-1
The Thirteen Regular Appropriations Acts

Agriculture–Rural Development–Food and Drug Administration
Commerce–Justice–State–Judiciary
Department of Defense
District of Columbia
Energy and Water Development
Foreign Operations
Interior Department
Labor–Health and Human Services–Education
Legislative Branch
Military Construction
Transportation Department
Treasury–Postal Service–General Government
Veterans Affairs–Housing and Urban Development–Independent Agencies

gency supplementals in the omnibus bill, Congress made room in the same measure for more regular appropriations while staying within the caps. If this practice does take hold, Congress may make more supplemental appropriations in the future but have fewer supplemental bills.

Because of recurring delays in enacting appropriations, Congress typically passes one or more continuing resolutions each year. However, the incidence of these measures is so varied that it is hard to discern a pattern. Congress passed fourteen CRs for fiscal 1996 but none for the previous or subsequent fiscal years. The scope, duration, and number of these measures depend on the intensity of budgetary conflict within Congress and between it and the president, as well as on the extent to which the continuing resolution is used as a vehicle for enacting substantive legislation.

In some years more than half of the regular appropriations bills have been folded into an omnibus measure together with vast amounts of legislation. Omnibus bills represent a strong break with the tradition that each appropriations bill be enacted separately. Other important deviations are discussed in the next section.

TRADITION AND CHANGE

In describing the appropriations process, it is necessary to distinguish between the way things have been done over the years and the recent changes that have uprooted or challenged long-established practices.

From afar, the appropriations process does not appear to be much different than it was in the past. The appropriations committees initiate their work in response to the president's budget. Each bill is in the jurisdiction of a single subcommittee that operates largely independently of other subcommittees and the full committee. Each bill is structured on the basis of accounts, and agency officials appear at subcommittee hearings to justify their budget requests.

But a closer look reveals changes in the world of appropriations. Once the appropriations committees controlled virtually all federal spending; now they have effective jurisdiction over only one-third. Once they had no rival in Congress for determining how much was spent on the programs in their jurisdictions; now they must reckon with budget resolutions and (in some years) preset spending caps. Once they worked almost entirely behind closed doors; now they mark up almost all bills in the open. Moreover, in 1999 C-SPAN was allowed to broadcast conference committee negotiations on a supplemental appropriation for the first time. Once authorizing legislation did not specify the amounts authorized to be appropriated; now many such measures do. Once just about every appropriations bill was enacted by the start of the fiscal year; now many—in some years most—are not. These and other breaks with tradition are spelled out in table 9-2.

For generations, tradition was centered in the House Appropriations Committee. Much more than its Senate counterpart, the committee was bound by norms and practices that in-

sulated it from pressures within Congress and from changes in the role and scope of government. House Appropriations was the custodian of the spending process: it initiated all spending bills, its members spent long days reviewing spending plans, it operated in a bipartisan manner, and it took pride in guarding the Treasury against federal agencies' demands for more money. Members on House Appropriations rarely served on any other committee; Appropriations was their sole committee assignment. They did not legislate, advocate, or evaluate programs, nor did they prepare budgets; they only appropriated money.

For decades, tradition was a buffer against change. Over time, however, it weakened the Appropriations Committees by rendering them less malleable and less responsive to congressional demands. To understand how traditional practices once sheltered the appropriations process and now undermine its effectiveness, the evolution of appropriations in Congress must be reviewed.

Congress had an appropriations process for three-quarters of a century before it had appropriations committees. But from the start, the notion was branded into the political mind-set of the appropriators that their job was to restrain the spending ambitions of executive agencies, not to legislate. Appropriators were to decide how much the agencies, established through previous congressional decisions, should spend.

Early in the history of the appropriations process, it became apparent that spending pressures did not emanate only from the executive branch but that they also came from members of Congress who favored particular expenditures. The appropriators were also pressured to add legislative provisions to their bills. To ward off these internal pressures, the House (in the 1830s) and the Senate (in the 1850s) adopted rules against unauthorized appropriations and

TABLE 9-2
Tradition and Change in the Appropriations Process

Traditional practice	Current practice
Committee	
Had jurisdiction over virtually all federal spending	Has jurisdiction over only one-third of spending
Experienced members from relatively safe districts appointed to the committee[a]	Many junior members, often from swing districts, selected[a]
Exclusive committee; members had no other major committee assignment[a]	Many appropriations members serve on other House committees[a]
High bipartisan cooperation; many bills passed with overwhelming majorities	Partisan conflict; many bills passed on party line votes[a]
Party leaders had no role in committee decisions	Party leaders often have lead role in making appropriations decisions
Procedures	
Thirteen separate appropriations bills	Regular appropriations often enacted in omnibus appropriations
House originated all appropriations bills	Some bills originate in Senate
Small amount of legislation inserted in appropriations bills	Appropriations often contain vast amounts of legislation
Decisions made in executive session	Bills marked up in open session
All (or almost all) appropriations enacted by the start of the fiscal year	Many (in some year most) appropriations bills enacted after the fiscal year started
Spending/Control	
Authorizing legislation rarely specified amounts authorized to be appropriated	Authorizing legislation often specifies amounts authorized to be appropriated
Appropriations committees were not constrained in the total appropriated	Total constrained by section 302(a) allocations and discretionary spending caps
Subcommittees decided spending amounts independently of one another	Subcommittee decisions coordinated by section 302(b) allocations
OMB gave little formal attention to appropriations process	OMB monitors appropriations bills and prepares statements of administration policy on each bill
No procedure for assessing whether appropriations bills are within budget	OMB prepares seven-day letter scoring each appropriations bill enacted into law
Appropriations only limited expenditure, they did not mandate that funds be spent	Appropriations also mandate that available resources be spent

a. Applies only or predominately to the House Appropriations Committee.

legislation in appropriations bills. Though they have been modified over the years, these rules still define the basic relationship between appropriations and other congressional activity. More importantly, they set appropriations apart from just about everything else Congress does. The need for these rules was a harbinger of things to come. Congress makes of the ap-propriations process what it wants, and it often redefines the relationship between appropriations and other legislative business.

The demands of the Civil War and the expansion of government impelled the House to establish a separate Appropriations Committee in 1865; the Senate followed suit three years later. The new committees' perceived duty was twofold: to take a knife to federal spending and to resist the entreaties of those inside and outside Congress who wanted to spend more. There then ensued a fifty-year war between the appropriations and legislative committees. The former won the first round when the House adopted the Holman Rule, authorizing the Appropriations Committee to insert legislation retrenching expenditures in its bills. The latter retaliated by seizing jurisdiction over various spending bills, beginning with the pork-laden rivers and harbors bill and ending with control of half of the appropriations bills.

The contest between spenders and guardians is never-ending; economic conditions and the mood of the country as much as the internal rules of Congress determine the balance of power between the two. By the end of World War I, sentiment had shifted in favor of the appropriators. Federal spending ballooned more than twenty-five-fold during the war years, big deficits emerged, and Congress was receptive to demands for fiscal discipline. It passed the Budget and Accounting Act of 1921, which enlisted presidential power on behalf of spending control. The president was thus made an ally of the appropriations committees; together they would constrain the spending demands of federal agencies and congressional committees. To enforce the new controls, Congress returned jurisdiction of all spending bills to the appropriations committees.

This was the environment in which tradition hardened in the House Appropriations Committee. The world of appropriations was cloistered and patterned. The committee did not consider any spending demands until the president submitted his budget. Then it held hearings but invited only agency officials to testify. Agencies prepared justification books that focused on the extent to which the amount requested differed from the previous year's appropriation, and the committee pre-

pared reports that focused on the extent to which the amount it recommended differed from the previous appropriation and the president's request. The committee did not compare the appropriation to the amount authorized. In many cases, it did not even know how much had been authorized.

As guardian of the Treasury, the House Appropriations Committee sheltered itself from the spending pressures that buffeted Congress. It recruited members from safe districts, put them through a long apprenticeship, had them work long hours poring over agency requests and reviewing spending details with agency witnesses, and taught them how to give agencies what they needed while cutting their requests. The long hours and closed process molded members into a cohesive, nonpartisan group that rarely aired differences to outsiders. Appropriations staff were part of this small community. They typically were recruited from federal agencies, not from other congressional committees, or from the ranks of political campaigners and law school graduates. Appropriations staff paid attention to what agencies did and maintained close relations with agency budget staff. Periodically, Appropriations and agency staff went on retreat to guzzle beer, play cards, and trade war stories.

Appropriations bills were structured distinctively, by accounts rather than sections, and most of the committee's intent was encased in report language and not in the bill. Senate amendments were numbered in a way that often made it difficult for outsiders to follow the action. When conferees met to resolve House-Senate differences, they convened in a small room that was barely big enough to seat all of them plus the one or two staff who kept the tally sheets. This was a world in which government talked to itself—everybody else was a stranger.

This closed world could not survive the enlargement of government ushered in by the

New Deal and World War II, and further expanded by Great Society legislation in the 1960s. Authorizing legislation took on a new look; it was broader, more programmatic, and in many cases sought to influence the amount appropriated or to bypass the appropriations process. As they held on to tradition, the appropriations committees became increasingly dysfunctional. The account structure was poorly aligned with federal programs and activities. It had an annual perspective, but Congress was determined to establish long-term commitments through income transfer programs, such as Social Security and Medicare. Appropriators protested the raid on their jurisdiction, but they were too weak to resist the expansion of entitlements. They railed against "backdoor spending," a term invented by appropriators to convey the notion that spending through authorizing legislation was illicit. They continued to hold onto tradition, even though it left them with a shrinking jurisdiction.

In the post–Vietnam/Watergate era, reformers seeking a more open, responsive institution attacked congressional tradition. Rule changes forced all committees to open their doors. In the House, the ratio of Democrats to Republicans on Appropriations was increased, giving the committee a more liberal orientation. The Democratic Caucus was given a voice in selecting House Appropriations subcommittee chairs. Furthermore, voting procedures in the House were changed to permit recorded votes in the Committee of the Whole, where appropriations bills and much other legislation are considered.

The insulation of the appropriations process was further undermined by the Congressional Budget Act of 1974, which established House and Senate budget committees to police congressional action on revenue and spending legislation. The clear message was that the appropriations committees did not effectively control federal spending. Much spending was outside their jurisdiction, and appropriations bills were not adequately related to one another, or to total spending, revenues, and the deficit.

The appropriations committees now had to operate within budget constraints set by others. Over time these constraints were codified in budget enforcement rules and in procedures (discussed later in this chapter) that divide discretionary funds among the thirteen subcommittees. Impoundment procedures, also enacted in 1974, were another blow to tradition, for they gave statutory recognition to the reality that as much as Congress limits what agencies spend, it wants them to spend what it appropriates.

The weakening of tradition has made the appropriations process more similar to other congressional activities and much less insulated from the political tides affecting Congress. The appropriations process is more permeable than it once was, although it still stands apart from other legislative activities. The loss of tradition is reflected in a number of conditions, such as partisan strife, tardy enactment of appropriations bills, recourse to omnibus bills, Senate initiative on appropriations bills, the weakening of subcommittee independence, increased legislation in spending bills, and the enlarged role of party leaders.

Congress is conflicted by the need to make appropriations and the difficulty of doing so. The need to complete action pushes the appropriations process to the center, but the polarization of Congress pushes it to the extremes. The problem is more pronounced in the House, where partisanship is more strident. In the traditional relationship between the two chambers, the House Appropriations Committee starts the process. If the House does not complete its work on time, neither does the Senate. The House Appropriations Committee used to be a unifying institution in

Congress; now it is a polarizing force. It is the forum to which many partisan legislative disputes are brought when there are no other avenues for resolution. Rather than being walled off against conflict, the appropriations process in the House has become a conduit for amplifying and spreading friction and for forcing action on other issues at the expense of stalemating appropriations bills.

This tendency did not begin in the 1990s, but it picked up momentum with the Republican takeover of the House in 1995. Even before he was sworn in as Speaker, Newt Gingrich (R-Ga.) demanded that each appropriations subcommittee chair pledge fealty to the Republican legislative agenda. Republican party leaders preempted many decisions that the appropriations committees traditionally had made, such as the insertion of controversial riders and the timing of various actions, and thus further ensnared appropriations in partisan strife. From 1996 through 1999, final appropriation decisions were made in summit negotiations between party leaders and the president or his aides. Sometimes appropriations committee leaders were consulted; often they were not.

The pent-up anger of the House Appropriations Committee, provoked by its loss of independence, burst into the open in an extraordinary letter sent by Chairman Robert Livingston (R-La.) to Speaker Gingrich on November 6,1998—three days after that year's midterm elections and one day before Gingrich announced his resignation from Congress (box 9-1). Livingston demanded that he be empowered to run the Appropriations Committee "without being subject to the dictates of any other Member of Congress" and that he "be the final authority to determine the content of legislation within the Appropriations Committee, and the schedule under which legislation is produced, without inter-ference." Livingston's plea was a throwback to a lost legislative world in which the appropriations committees operated according to their own rhythm, largely indifferent to the tides of change in Congress and the nation. That world can be rebuilt only by distancing the work of appropriations from the political context in which budgets are made.

THE APPROPRIATIONS COMMITTEES AND THEIR SUBCOMMITTEES

Despite attrition in jurisdiction and independence, the appropriations committees are among the most coveted assignments in Congress. In both the House and Senate, members actively campaign for these posts by calling on party leaders, getting senior members to intervene on their behalf, and pointing to the political or geographical strengths they would bring to the committee.

These committees are powerful because they control the portion of federal spending that is subject to annual congressional action. The more than $500 billion in discretionary money that they control is, by a wide margin, the largest pool of dollars over which Congress has recurring influence. This is the part of the budget on which money is spent because of current rather than past decisions. Almost all the rest is governed by statutory rules that continue in effect unless Congress changes them. Appropriating $500 billion of discretionary money requires legislative action; spending $1 trillion of mandatory money can be done with congressional inaction. The appropriations committees' legislative prominence derives not only from the huge pot of money they control, but also from the small amounts they dole out to particular projects.

In many regards, the appropriations committees resemble other congressional committees. Seniority determines influence, subcom-

▼

BOX 9-1
Appropriations versus Party Leadership

The following excerpts are from a letter sent by House Appropriations Committee Chair Robert Livingston (R-La.) to Speaker Newt Gingrich (R-Ga.) on November 6, 1998:

In consideration of the deep respect and friendship that I hold for you, I have set forth herewith a list of requirements that I believe are critical and vital to the success of the 106th Congress. In order for the majority to complete its work and demonstrate that we can properly govern, I believe it imperative that you acknowledge and agree to these suggested changes in House procedure, without exception:

1. I, as Chairman of the Appropriations Committee, shall run the Committee as I see fit and in the best interest of the Republican majority, with full consultation with the Leadership, but without being subject to the dictates of any other Member of Congress.
2. That I be the final authority to determine content of legislation within the Appropriations Committee, and the schedule under which legislation is produced, without interference.
3. That all future budget resolutions be completed for House approval between April 15 and April 30, and that thereafter all appropriations bills are free to proceed with or without a Budget Resolution, for completion in the House of Representative by the end of June of every calendar year. The Senate will be urged to do likewise so that all conferences can be completed before the August break of each calendar year.
4 I, as Appropriations Chairman, shall be present in all Leadership discussions of the budget affecting Appropriations matters. No decisions on Appropriations issues will be made within the context of budget negotiations without consultation (not necessarily approval) with me.
5. There will be no amendment in Rules or Law affecting Appropriations jurisdiction without my approval.
6. No Member or Subcommittee Chairman will be removed from my committee or from their post on my committee without my approval. . . .
9. Members should not be assigned to Committees 'because of their districts.' Fragile Members are afraid to cast tough votes, and that inhibits the passage of credible legislation.
10. No Republican will be assigned to the Appropriations Committee without my approval.
11. No Member should hold more than 5 subcommittees without waivers, and waiver should never be issued except under the strictest of conditions or dire emergency or importance. No Member of the Appropriations Committee shall serve on any Committee or Subcommittee other than that of the Budget Committee. . . .
13. I, as Chairman of the Appropriations Committee, during last minute negotiations with Democrats or with representatives of the White House on all appropriations bills, will make all final decisions, but with full consultation with the leadership.
14. There should be weekly meetings with Democrats to last no more than one hour, and I as Chairman of the Appropriations Committee should be included. . . .
16. The Speaker shall insist that the Senate concur and conform to our expedited schedule on Appropriations and budget, with the understanding that should either house fail to pass an appropriations bill by July 30, that the respective bill which has been passed by the remaining House of Congress will become the actionable vehicle for conference.

mittees conduct hearings, and staff draft bills and reports. The full committee takes up each bill after the relevant subcommittee has completed its work. Bills go from the committee to the floor, and disagreements between the House and Senate versions are worked out in conference. But the differences are more illuminating.

The two critical distinguishing characteristics are the bounded jurisdiction of the appropriations committees and the near certainty of congressional action. On almost every House and Senate committee, the most important decisions each year revolve around setting a legislative agenda and deciding which issues and bills are to be taken up. In the case of appropriations, these decisions are predetermined by jurisdiction. These committees must dispose of the thirteen regular appropriations bills and of continuing resolutions made necessary by failure to complete the regular bills on time. The committees have some discretion in deciding whether to report supplemental spending bills, but almost all of their agenda is set for them in advance. Just about every other congressional committee must be concerned with whether the House and Senate will take up the measures it reports and whether disagreements between the two chambers will be worked out in conference. The appropriations committees do not have any such doubts; they have absolute certainty that their spending bills will be enacted. They may not know when each bill will be considered or whether all the regular appropriations will be enacted by the start of the fiscal year. They also may not know whether the thirteen bills will be enacted in normal fashion (one at a time) or will be combined in an omnibus bill. But they do know that theirs is "must-pass" legislation—one way or another, all the work will be completed.

The special status of the annual spending bills shapes the behavior and operations of the appropriations committees. As noted previously, these have been among the least partisan committees in Congress, markedly less divided along party lines than the budget committees. Over the years, even when Democrats and Republicans disagreed on budget policy and spending priorities, they usually joined ranks in passing appropriations bills. The money these committees distributed muted their partisanship—Democrats and Republicans each got funds for their projects and constituencies, giving members from each party strong incentive to vote for appropriations. For fiscal 1994, for example, tables 9-3 and 9-4 show that all passed the Senate by lopsided margins or voice vote and all but two passed the House by large margins, in contrast to that year's budget resolution, which was opposed by all House and Senate Republicans.

These tables also reveal that in recent years the Senate has come to rely more upon voice votes, while partisanship has become more pronounced in the House. In fact, partisan strife was so intense and widespread that for fiscal 1996, none of the regular appropriations bills were enacted on time (table 9-5). Moreover, Congress and the president fought over the terms of continuing resolutions, as evident in the veto of the second CR, and federal agencies were shut down for several weeks. The conflict over fiscal 1996 appropriations is one of the truly extraordinary political stories of our time; its causes and implications are discussed in box 9-2. The unthinkable happened—Congress failed to complete action on "must pass" appropriations, and many government operations were suspended. The protracted impasse and forced closing of federal agencies are additional indications that the old order on appropriations has broken down.

In normal times, the appropriations committees excel at turning big policy disputes into routine matters of a little more or a little less money. Historically, appropriating has

TABLE 9-3
House Votes on Passage of Appropriations Acts, Selected Fiscal Years[a]

Bill	1994		
	Total	Democrats	Republicans
Agriculture	304-119	239-13	64-106
Commerce-Justice-State	327-98	244-6	82-92
Defense	325-102	230-24	95-77
District of Columbia	213-211	200-50	12-161
Energy and Water	350-73	248-4	101-69
Foreign Operations	309-111	202-47	107-63
Interior	278-138	227-17	50-121
Labor-HHS-Education	305-124	237-18	67-106
Legislative Branch	224-187	217-24	6-163
Military Construction	347-67	223-18	123-49
Transportation	312-89	219-15	92-74
Treasury-Postal Service	263-153	227-18	35-135
VA-HUD	313-110	236-16	76-94

Source: *Congressional Quarterly Almanac*, 1993, 1995, and 1998.

a. The votes listed here are on passage of the bill in the House, not on adoption of the conference report. Representative Bernard Sanders (I-Vt.) is included in the total, but not in the breakdown by parties. However, in most instances, he voted with the majority of Democrats.

TABLE 9-4
Senate Votes on Passage of Appropriations Acts, Fiscal Years 1994–96[a]

Bill	1994		
	Total	Democrats	Republicans
Agriculture	90-10	53-3	37-7
Commerce-Justice-State	87-13	54-2	33-11
Defense	voice	voice	voice
District of Columbia	70-29	52-3	18-26
Energy and Water	89-10	51-4	38-6
Foreign Operations	88-10	52-3	36-7
Interior	voice	voice	voice
Labor-HHS-Education	82-17	52-3	30-14
Legislative Branch	85-7	48-3	37-4
Military Construction	voice	voice	voice
Transportation	90-9	54-2	36-7
Treasury-Postal Service	73-27	54-2	19-25
VA-HUD	91-9	53-3	38-6

Source: *Congressional Quarterly Almanac*, 1993–95.

a. The votes listed here are on passage of the bill in the Senate, not on adoption of the conference report.

1996			1999		
Total	Democrats	Republicans	Total	Democrats	Republicans
313-78	120-63	193-14	373-48	173-25	199-23
272-151	66-129	206-21	225-203	28-175	197-27
294-125	85-105	209-19	358-61	149-47	209-13
224-191	31-155	193-35	214-206	3-194	211-11
400-27	175-23	225-3	405-4	187-0	217-4
333-89	133-57	200-31	255-161	69-126	186-34
244-181	31-166	213-14	245-181	38-162	207-18
219-208	6-189	213-18	b	b	b
337-87	110-85	227-1	235-179	36-158	199-20
319-105	125-74	194-30	396-10	179-7	216-3
361-61	144-50	217-10	391-25	193-2	197-23
216-211	15-181	200-30	218-203	26-169	192-33
228-193	27-165	201-27	259-164	54-145	205-18

b. This bill was not voted on until the conference report for the omnibus fiscal 1999 appropriations bill, H.R. 4328; the votes on its adoption were 333-95: Democrats 170-31 and Republicans 162-64.

1995			1996		
Total	Democrats	Republicans	Total	Democrats	Republicans
92-8	56-0	36-8	95-3	45-0	50-3
voice	voice	voice	voice	voice	voice
86-14	54-2	32-12	voice	voice	voice
68-32	49-7	19-25	voice	voice	voice
91-8	54-1	37-7	voice	voice	voice
84-9	51-2	33-7	91-9	42-4	49-5
voice	voice	voice	92-6	41-4	51-2
87-13	55-1	32-12	b	b	b
voice	voice	voice	voice	voice	voice
84-2	50-0	34-2	84-10	35-8	49-2
91-9	55-1	36-8	98-1	44-1	54-0
72-27	50-5	22-22	voice	voice	voice
86-9	51-2	35-7	55-45	1-45	54-0

b. This bill was included in an omnibus appropriations act for fiscal 1996; it was not voted on separately. The omnibus bill, H.R. 3019, passed 79-21, with Democrats 40-7 and Republicans 39-14.

TABLE 9-5
House and Senate Passage Dates of Appropriations Bills, Fiscal Year 1996[a]

Regular appropriations	Passage		Conference report approved		President		Omnibus bill
	House	Senate	House	Senate	Signed	Vetoed	
Agriculture	7/21	9/20	10/12	10/12	10/21		
Commerce-Justice-State	7/26	9/29	12/6	12/7		12/19	4/26/96
Defense	9/7	9/5	11/16	11/16	[b]		
District of Columbia	11/2	9/22	. . .	. . .			4/26/96
Energy and Water	7/12	8/1	10/31	10/31	11/13		
Foreign Operations	7/11	9/21	. . .	. . .	[c]		
Interior	7/18	8/9	12/13	12/14		12/18	4/26/96
Labor-HHS-Education	8/4	. . .	. . .	. . .			4/26/96
Legislative Branch	6/22	7/20	9/6	9/22		10/3	
(Legislative Branch II)	10/31	11/2	11/10	11/10	11/19		
Military Construction	6/21	7/21	9/20	9/22	10/3		
Transportation	7/25	8/10	10/25	10/31	11/15		
Treasury-Postal Service	7/19	8/5	11/15	11/15	11/19		
VA-HUD	7/31	9/27	12/7	12/14		12/18	4/26/96

Source: *Congressional Quarterly Almanac*, 1995–96.

a. All dates listed without the year pertain to calendar 1995.

b. Became law without signature on December 1.

c. This bill was attached to the continuing resolution, HR 2880, which was signed into law on January 26, 1996.

meant making decisions at the margins for programs and agencies already in operation, not questioning whether the programs and agencies should continue or whether the government should make fundamental changes in policy. If members of Congress want to review the role of government in alleviating malnutrition around the world, the appropriate forum might be the agriculture or foreign relations committees. These committees have little (if any) must-pass legislation; they usually have as much time as they want to probe an issue, even if it means that action will be delayed to next year or later. But the appropriations committees must act. Over the years, they have done so by narrowing controversial issues to marginal spending questions: how much higher or lower should appropriations be to combat hunger? Should the amount be more or less than the president requested? Which countries should get more and which less?

The division of labor among the thirteen pairs of appropriations subcommittees also facilitates the passing of appropriations bills. The independence and prominence of these subcommittees goes back to the early decades of the twentieth century. Each subcommittee is a fiefdom that guards its jurisdiction and has its own operating style. All the work of each parallel set of subcommittees revolves around a single appropriations bill; it does not produce any legislation other than its bill and supplementals or continuing resolutions related to the bill. There has been no shift whatsoever in subcommittee jurisdictions since the 1970s. Although Speaker Gingrich redrew the boundaries of various authorizing committees in 1995, he did not touch Appropriations and its subcommittees.

Work and power on Appropriations are concentrated in the subcommittees. Except for a brief overview session, the subcommittees con-

▼

BOX 9-2
From Revolution to Shutdown: The 1995–96 Battle of the Budget

When Republicans gained control of Congress in the 1994 midterm elections, they took it for granted that they were elected to change the way things were done in Washington and that President Clinton would be unable to impede their revolution. Favoring big rather than incremental changes, Republican leaders sought to use appropriations bills as a vehicle for enacting their agenda by inserting significant changes in substantive law. However, they underestimated Clinton's willingness to use his veto power. The result was a massive breakdown of the appropriations process; many spending bills were delayed for more than half a year, and portions of the government were shut down twice. In an attempt to keep the government operating, a record thirteen continuing resolutions were enacted.

The fight started over efforts to reduce spending levels; it ended without much spending being changed. The early rounds were over congressional efforts to rescind previous appropriations; the final rounds were over congressional efforts to enact new appropriations. While this was the first budget clash between Clinton and congressional Republicans, it was not the last one in which Clinton emerged victorious.

Republicans passed a budget resolution in June 1995 that proposed to sharply reduce the size of the federal government. In addition to deep cuts in discretionary programs, their plan made room for hundreds of billions of dollars in tax cuts (over seven years) by curtailing Medicare, Medicaid, and other social programs. Because the president has no formal role in the budget resolution, Clinton could not impede adoption of the Republican version. However, almost half a year later in December 1995, Clinton derailed Congress's budget revolution by vetoing the reconciliation bill that would have enacted many of the proposed tax and entitlement changes.

1995

June 29
House, 239-194, and Senate, 54-46, pass conference report on budget resolution.

October 1
Fiscal 1996 begins; first continuing resolution enacted the previous day.

November 14
First partial government shutdown follows veto of second CR.

November 17
House, 237-189, and Senate, 52-47, pass conference report on reconciliation bill.

November 20
Government reopens.

December 6
Clinton vetoes reconciliation bill; only seven appropriations bills enacted thus far.

December 16
Second partial government shutdown ensues.

December 18
Two appropriations bills vetoed; another is vetoed the next day.

1996

January 6
Government reopens.

April 25
House, 399-25, and Senate, 88-11, pass conference report on the omnibus appropriations bill for fiscal 1996; Clinton signs the bill April 26.

continued

▼

BOX 9-2
Continued

After passing the budget resolution, Republicans moved ahead on the fiscal 1996 appropriations, producing spending bills with even deeper cuts than those originally assumed by the budget resolution. Both long-held Democratic priorities and Clinton's pet initiatives were targeted. But the appropriations process was delayed by these efforts to shrink the government, and by the time the new fiscal year started, only two of the regular spending bills had been sent to the president. Congressional Republicans were forced to break their "no continuing resolutions" pledge and pass one to prevent a government shutdown.

At this point, Republicans believed they held the advantage and that Clinton would capitulate to their demands. They did not expect him to risk shutting down the government by vetoing a continuing resolution. House Appropriations Chair Robert Liv-

Continuing Resolutions, 1995–96

| | President | | |
Number	Signed	Vetoed	Expiration
First	9/30/95		11/13/95
Second		11/14/95	(12/1/95)
Third	11/19/95		11/20/95
Fourth	11/20/95		12/15/95
Fifth	12/22/95		1/3/96
Sixth	1/4/96		1/25/96
Seventh	1/6/96		9/30/96[a]
Eighth	1/6/96		1/26/96[a]
Ninth	1/6/96		1/26/96
Tenth	1/26/96		3/15/96
Eleventh	3/15/96		3/22/96[a]
Twelfth	3/22/96		4/3/96
Thirteenth	3/29/96		4/24/96
Fourteenth	4/24/96		4/25/96

a. These expiration dates applied to the majority of the programs; additional continuing resolutions were necessary for the other programs.

ingston (R-La.) confidently asserted that the president has "to accept actions that must be taken to accomplish the desires expressed by the American people last November." Certain they would win, Republicans presented Clinton with a rider-laden continuing resolution. The president vetoed the measure, forcing federal agencies that lacked appropriations to close their doors. Although the federal government had been closed nine times previously, none of the shutdowns had lasted for more than three days. While it was Clinton's veto that forced the shutdown, he was not blamed for the impasse; Republicans were. Both sides finally negotiated a new temporary continuing resolution that reopened the government and gave each side some of its most

continued

duct all appropriations hearings. Each has its own staff, produces its own bill, maintains year-round relations with agencies in its jurisdiction, and operates independently of the other subcommittees. The chairs of the subcommittees are commonly referred to as cardinals, in recognition of the authority each exercises in his or her domain. Their power comes from tradition, control of the purse strings, their capacity to

channel funds to favored activities and areas, and the deference accorded them by executive officials and members of Congress. Traditionally, each cardinal has had considerable autonomy in running the subcommittee, free from interference by the full committee chair or party leaders. Tenure on the subcommittee, not full committee seniority, usually determines who becomes a cardinal. For example, Barbara

BOX 9-2
Continued

salient demands. Clinton agreed to a tax cut and the goal of a balanced budget in seven years. In exchange, Republicans agreed to protect important Democratic priorities.

But this respite in the budget war did not bring lasting peace. House Republican leaders linked action on appropriations to tax and spending cuts they sought in the vetoed reconciliation bill. Clinton stood his ground, declaring, "I won't yield to these threats. . . . I won't be forced into signing a budget that violates our values." Clinton brokered a deal with Speaker Newt Gingrich (R-Ga.) and Senate Majority Leader Robert Dole (R-Kans.) on a new continuing resolution that would avert another shutdown. However, Republican freshmen in the House refused to accept the deal, and parts of the government closed for three weeks. Dole claimed that "Clinton's fingerprints" were "all over the shutdown," but the public again blamed the Republicans.

As weeks of budgetary impasse stretched into months, both sides hardened their positions. House Budget Committee Chair John Kasich (R-Ohio) stated the Republican case for staying the course: "If you don't worry about getting beaten up, you can do great things." But when Congress reconvened in 1996, Republicans acknowledged that their confrontational strategy had failed; it was time to reopen the government and keep it open by passing the remaining appropriations bills. After further delay and several more continuing resolutions, the five remaining appropriations were folded into an omnibus measure that finally cleared Congress in April and was quickly signed into law.

House Republicans had misinterpreted the 1994 election and the attitudes of most Americans. They also underestimated Clinton's steely use of the veto power and determination to get his way. Senate Republican leaders were reluctantly drawn into the fight and sensed that budgetary brinksmanship would lead their party into a quagmire. On the other side, Clinton and congressional Democrats never wavered in protecting their priorities; they rescued programs slated for elimination and forced Republicans to drop most of the controversial riders. Throughout, Clinton managed to sidestep blame, portraying himself as committed to a balanced budget and to keeping the government open. The 1996 election results cemented Clinton's victory—he defeated Dole in the presidential race, and Republicans lost seats in the House.

Mikulski (D-Md.) was appointed chair of the Veterans Affairs–Housing and Urban Development Subcommittee during her first term in the Senate, even though she was outranked in seniority by others on the committee. During the 1970s House Democrats decreed that appropriations subcommittee chairs would be selected by the party caucus, in the same manner as the chairs of all committees. At the time, no other House subcommittees were subjected to this special procedure.

One of the distinctive features of the appropriations process is the perfect jurisdictional alignment of the House and Senate committees and their subcommittees. Every federal program and agency has an identical niche in the House and Senate appropriations bills. Despite the parallel structure, the House and Senate committees are different institutions. The House Appropriations Committee has twice as many members as its Senate counterpart, most of whom do not serve on any other major committee. Representatives on Appropriations are expected to concentrate on committee work, to master the details of programs and spending in their subcommittee's jurisdiction, and to view legislative issues from the perspective of Appropriations. However, every member of the Senate Appropriations Committee concurrently serves on one or more authorizing committees. These other obligations limit the amount of time senators can devote to Appropriations. More important, many senators fill two conflicting roles—they are both program advocates and spending controllers. Sometimes the conflicts are in the same program area, when senators serve on both an authorizing committee and the appropriations subcommittee that deals with the same subject. Senator Richard Russell (D-Ga.) chaired the Armed Services Committee at the same time that he chaired the Defense Appropriations Subcommittee; Senator John Stennis (D-Miss.) also held both these posts at the same time. More recently, Senator J. Bennett Johnston (D-La.) concurrently chaired the Energy and Natural Resources Committee and the Energy and Water Appropriations Subcommittee.

Multiple committee assignments divide the loyalties of those serving on Senate Appropriations and diminish the time they devote to the committee's work. Senators who serve on several committees inevitably bring their authorizing interests and perspectives to the appropriations process. Some dominate an issue in the Senate (and occasionally throughout Congress) by virtue of their commanding position on both the authorizing committee and the Appropriations Committee.

Until the mid-1990s the sequence of congressional action also differentiated the House and Senate appropriations committees. Although the Constitution is silent on the matter, by precedent going back to the First Congress, appropriations bills originated in the House. When its action follows the House's, the Senate does not produce its own bill, but instead it amends the House-passed appropriations by inserting the Senate's changes. Then the conference committee resolves the differences in the measures passed by the two chambers. This sequence, and the time demands of multiple committee assignments, spurred the Senate to concentrate on matters still in dispute after the House had completed its work. Agencies would "reclama"—that is, appeal to Senate Appropriations to give them more money than was voted by the House or make other changes in the House-passed bill. Its role as a court of appeals typically resulted in the Senate appropriating more than the House provided.

The discretionary spending caps narrowed the behavioral differences between the House and Senate committees. The caps limited the additional funds the Senate could provide after the House had completed its work. The House has usually appropriated up to the allowable limit, putting the Senate in the politically awkward position of having to cut some programs in order to provide more money for others. The Senate Appropriations Committee adapted to the new situation by reporting some of its bills before the House has acted. When this occurs, Congress preserves the notion that the House acts first by inserting the Senate version into the bill subsequently passed by the House. The reality is, however, that two centuries of tradition have been overturned.

PROCEDURES AND POLITICS OF COMMITTEE ACTION

In contrast to authorizing committees, which typically take up legislation in response to the

TABLE 9-6
Timetable of Appropriation Actions[a]

February	**President submits his budget to Congress**
	This initiates the appropriations process; appropriations committees rarely act without a presidential request
February	**Full appropriations committees sometimes conduct brief overview hearings**
	These are the only full committee hearings. In some recent years, the committees have forgone these hearings
February/March	**Each agency submits justification material**
	These documents are printed in the agency hearings, and they offer a detailed explanation of the agency's budget request
February/April	**Subcommittee hearings held**
	House appropriations subcommittee hearings usually are held first, followed shortly thereafter by Senate subcommittee hearings
May/July	**Section 302(b) allocations made by the appropriations committees**
	These allocations to the subcommittees must precede floor consideration of appropriations bills
May/July	**The chair's mark (optional)**
	Each subcommittee chair issues a "mark" recommending amounts for the accounts in the subcommittee's jurisdiction
May/July	**Subcommittee markup**
	Each subcommittee marks up its bill and drafts a report explaining its decisions and providing guidance to affected agencies
May/July	**Full committee reports the bill**
	Full committee normally makes only minor changes (if any) in the bill prepared by the subcommittee
May/July	**House floor action**
July/August	**Senate floor action**
September/October	**Conferences and final passage**

a. While the steps in this schedule occur every year, the timing of actions may vary from the timetable shown here.

introduction of a bill, the appropriations committees initiate their work in response to a request by the president for money. These committees rarely act on their own initiative or pursuant to legislative proposals by members of Congress. In fact, a bill does not even exist during the early stages of the appropriations process; usually, an appropriations bill is introduced when the committee is about to report the measure. Often the bill is introduced, referred to committee, and reported on the same day. Despite the absence of a bill, however, there is considerable activity concentrated around hearings, the allocation of discretionary budget resources among the thirteen subcommittees, markup, and drafting of the report that accompanies the bill. These stages in the appropriations process are listed in table 9-6.

Hearings

In some years, soon after the president sends his budget to Congress, each appropriations committee conducts overview hearings at which the director of the Office of Management and Budget (OMB) and others testify concerning overall budget policies and priorities. These are the only sessions in which OMB is formally involved (other than in hearings on its own appropriation) and the only hearings the full committees hold. In some years, the appropriations committees skip the overview hearings altogether.

Each agency justifies its budget before its appropriations subcommittee. Before the hearings, agencies prepare justification material that compares the president's budget request with the previous appropriation and explains variances between the two. Each subcommittee dictates the format and content of the justification material, but it is common for the spending agencies to break down their budgets into discrete line items and activities and to justify changes from the previous budget. Exhibit 9-1 shows one type of information included in many agency justification books.

During the hearings and subsequent negotiations, OMB relies on agency officials to uphold the president's budget, even when it differs from their own preferences. Of course, there are ways of prying information from agencies regarding what they really want. Although they are not permitted to volunteer such information, agencies may do so in response to questions—some of which may be prearranged—from subcommittee members. Behind the scenes, OMB enforces fidelity to the president's budget by reviewing agency testimony (which is submitted to it in advance) and monitoring the hearings and other action on the appropriations bills. OMB also intervenes at various stages to notify the appropriations committees of any objections the president may have to pending measures.

Most of the testimony is by agency officials, many of whom carefully prepare for the hearings by reviewing detailed briefing books, the previous year's appropriation, and reports. A few agency heads stage mock hearings, at which they are questioned by staff on matters that the subcommittee may raise. In large agencies, the top official is accompanied at the hearings by an entourage of aides who are prepared to provide on-the-spot information in response to questions from members. At most hearings, the testifying agency is given interrogatories—questions for the record—to which it must respond within a few days.

Do the hearings make a difference in appropriations outcomes? Probably some, but not all that much. Informal contact with appropriations committee members and staff are more important in shaping congressional decisions than the formal hearings. Why then do agencies invest so much care and effort in the hearings? One reason is that a poor appearance can damage an agency's case. Agency witnesses are schooled in proper behavior at the hearings. They must be deferential to members of Congress and not challenge them, even when they feel mistreated. They must be responsive to all questions, and they must supply such additional information as is requested. But it is not only the agency's budget that is on trial at the hearings; its officials are also under examination. How they come through the ordeal has a bearing on the extent to which appropriators have confidence in their performance and trust their numbers. Hearings matter because they are rituals that test the agency's mettle. They also matter because they transmit to agencies the concerns and interests of members. Moreover, they put agencies on notice that, even though they may get just about all that was requested, Congress controls the purse.

Section 302(b) Allocations

Although the hearings process is decentralized, with each subcommittee arranging its own schedule and examining the witnesses who appear before it, a subcommittee cannot formally mark up its bill until it has received a section 302(b) allocation from the full committee. This allocation limits the total budget authority and outlays available to each subcommittee for all accounts in its jurisdiction. When Congress adopts the annual budget res-

> **EXHIBIT 9-1**
> **Agency Justification of Appropriations Request**

Smithsonian Institution
Salaries and Expenses
Summary of FY 1998 Change

FY 1997 Appropriation	$318,492,000
FY 1998 Increases/Decreases:	
Non-Recurring Costs	(835,000)
Mandatory Costs Increases	10,353,000
Program Increases—	
Smithsonian Astrophysical Observatory	1,225,000
New Facilities Support	4,362,000
Collections Information Systems	960,000
FY 1998 Request	$334,557,000

Mandatory Increases for Sustaining Base Operations
The Smithsonian Institution seeks additional funds for costs for which increases are beyond its control. These costs result from legislatively-mandated pay increases; escalating costs of library materials; utilities, communications and postage; and rent. The Institution requests an increase of $10,353,000 for the mandatory costs shown below.

Salary and Related Costs:	
Annualization of FY 1997 Pay Raises	$1,833,000
Proposed FY 1998 Pay Raises	4,678,000
Federal Employees' Retirement System	100,000
Subtotal, Salary and Related Costs	$6,611,000
Extraordinary Inflation for Library Materials	$334,000
Utilities, Communications, and Postage	3,198,000
Rental of Space	210,000
Total	$10,353,000

Source: *Department of the Interior and Related Agencies Appropriations for Fiscal Year 1998*, hearings before the House Interior Department Appropriations Subcommittee, 105th Cong., 1st sess., pp. 294 and 297.

(a) Each agency requesting appropriations submits detailed justifications to the appropriations subcommittees with jurisdiction over its budget. The justifications are published as part of the subcommittee's hearings.

(b) Each subcommittee prescribes the form of the material submitted to it; this exhibit displays the traditional format, which concentrates on proposed increases or decreases from the previous year's appropriation. As is the case here, the request is usually higher than the previous appropriation. The justifications highlight increases or decreases because these increments are what the appropriations committees traditionally have focused on in reviewing spending requests.

(c) Since the mid-1990s, some subcommittees have reformatted the budget justifications to focus on total spending rather than incremental changes, and on outputs and objectives rather than inputs and items of expenditure.

olution, the budget committees allocate budget resources to each House and Senate committee with jurisdiction over discretionary or direct spending. All discretionary spending is allocated to the appropriations committees, which also receive allocations for entitlements funded in the appropriations bills. Each appropriations committee then issues a section 302(b) report subdividing its budget resources among the thirteen subcommittees. The sum allocated to all subcommittees may not exceed the amount available to the full committee. House and Senate rules bar floor consideration of spending measures before the appropriations committees have filed the required section 302(b) report. Excerpts from one such report appear in exhibit 9-2.

This report is not simply a formality. Preparing it involves decisions on the relative priority of federal programs, as represented by subcommittee jurisdictions. The process triggers two rounds of zero-sum competition—first between subcommittees and then among the accounts in each subcommittee's jurisdiction. More for one subcommittee means less for another; more for one account means others will get less. The 302(b) allocations have impelled the appropriations committees to coordinate their subcommittees' spending plans. The subcommittees can no longer act wholly independently of one another—they cannot be indifferent to total spending nor to the amounts available to other subcommittees. Before one subcommittee marks up its bill, all subcommittees must be informed through the 302(b) procedure of how much they have to spend.

Dividing the discretionary spending pie among competing subcommittees combines political judgment and interpersonal contact. In each chamber, the chair of the appropriations committee leads the process. The chair usually consults with the subcommittee chairs, probing the amounts they want or might settle

for, proposing allocations to the subcommittees and gauging reactions, and calling the committee together to approve the section 302(b) report only when informal agreements have been reached. Appropriations staff play an important but confidential role in developing a data base for the allocations and in negotiating understandings that might then be taken to committee members for their approval.

The House Appropriations Committee aims to issue its 302(b) report in May, and the Senate committee usually does so in June, but the subcommittees cannot wait this long to start preparing their spending bills. Although they might not have exact figures, the subcommittees have ballpark numbers long before the formal allocations are issued. The effect is to move up appropriations decisions to an earlier stage; the budget fate of many programs is sealed months before formal appropriation decisions are made.

There are, however, two ways by which programs obtain more money later in the process. One is through revision in the section 302(b) report; the other is through budgetary negotiations between the president and Congress. The appropriations committees may revise the 302(b) report at any time during the year, provided that the total allocated to the thirteen subcommittees remains within budget limits. Typically, the reports are updated periodically to take into account conference committee decisions and other developments affecting spending levels. However, since 1996 the section 302(b) reports have also been revised to reflect budgetary agreements between the White House and Capitol Hill that generate more appropriations than were contemplated under the original section 302(b) allocations. In some cases, these agreements have made room for additional spending by designating some items as emergency, in others by using various resources to offset the additional spending, and

▶ **EXHIBIT 9-2**
Section 302(b) Allocations to Appropriations Subcommittees

(in millions of dollars)

Subcommittee	Discretionary		Mandatory	Total
	General Purpose	Crime Trust Fund		
Agriculture-Rural Development-Food and Drug Administration				
Budget authority	13,751	. . .	35,048	48,799
Outlays	12,997	. . .	35,205	49,202
Commerce-Justice-State-Judiciary				
Budget authority	25,968	5,259	522	31,749
Outlays	25,548	3,434	532	29,514
District of Columbia				
Budget authority	835	. . .	. . .	835
Outlays	537	. . .	. . .	537
Energy and Water Development				
Budget authority	20,793	. . .	. . .	20,793
Outlays	20,893	. . .	. . .	20,893
Foreign Operations				
Budget authority	12,800	. . .	44	12,844
Outlays	13,060	. . .	44	13,104
***				
Emergency Reserve				
Budget authority	246	. . .	. . .	246
Outlays	259	. . .	. . .	259
Grand Total				
Budget authority	521,002	5,500	277,312	803,814
Outlays	549,706	3,592	278,725	832,023

Source: *Revised Subdivision of Budget Totals for Fiscal Year 1998*, H. Rept. 260, 105th Cong., 1st sess., 1997, pp. 2–3.

(a) It is not in order to consider appropriations bills until the appropriations committee files a section 302(b) report subdividing the amounts available to it among its thirteen subcommittees. The appropriations committee may revise these allocations by filing a new report.

(b) The amounts allocated to the subcommittees may not exceed the total allocated to the appropriations committee.

(c) The format of this report corresponds to the categories established by the Budget Enforcement Act. The appropriations committees control discretionary spending; authorizing committees control mandatory spending. The mandatory amounts shown here are entitlements funded in annual appropriations.

(d) The Crime Trust Fund is itemized separately with its own suballocation; the appropriations committees cannot use this money for any other purpose.

in still others by deferring spending to the next fiscal year. A fair appraisal of the section 302(b) allocations is that while they are not airtight, they have had a constraining effect on total discretionary spending.

Subcommittee Markup

Markups are sessions at which subcommittees (or committees) review and report legislation. In the appropriations process, the subcommittee markup is particularly important because the full committee rarely makes major revisions in the bill referred to it. (Technically, only committees report legislation; subcommittees refer legislation to the full committee.) Moreover, the subcommittee drafts the report that accompanies the appropriation bill. It, too, is reported by the full committee with little or no change.

Because of the section 302(b) allocations, almost all appropriations decisions have been made by the time the subcommittee markup begins. These decisions usually are distilled in the "chairman's mark," a document distributed by the chair at, or shortly before, the markup that recommends amounts for each account in the bill. The chair's mark usually spends just about all the funds available under the subcommittee's 302(b) allocation, leaving rank-and-file members little opportunity to add funds for favored programs. Hence members have an incentive to notify the chair of their preferences in advance, since the markup is usually too late to influence subcommittee decisions.

Most subcommittee markups are conducted under rules requiring budget neutrality—an amendment increasing one account must also propose offsetting cuts in other accounts. This rule diminishes explicit competition among programs for scarce appropriations, but trade-offs are sometimes made

during markup. These are most likely in subcommittees that have sprawling jurisdiction over programs whose only affinity is that they are funded in the same appropriations bill. Competition for money has been especially intense in the VA-HUD subcommittee, which has jurisdiction over veterans' programs, space exploration, housing and urban development, environmental programs, the National Science Foundation, and other federal agencies.

In addition to setting appropriations levels, the markup approves provisions in the appropriations bill and the text of the accompanying report. As will be discussed later in the chapter, these provisions are often among the most controversial features of appropriations bills. Some provisions earmark funds to particular purposes, others limit the use of appropriated funds, and still others contain legislation changing existing law. The limitations and legislative provisions tend to sharpen partisan conflict on subcommittees. Between 1995 and 1998, Republican efforts to limit enforcement of various environmental laws split the House VA-HUD Appropriations Subcommittee. Although these provisions did not survive the legislative gauntlet, they damaged subcommittee cohesion and delayed enactment of appropriations.

Subcommittees do not closely review report language during markup, but they may take up controversial matters brought to their attention. Sometimes, controversy is resolved by moving disputed provisions from the appropriations bill to the committee report.

Full Committee Markup

The appropriations committees may revise the bills and reports the subcommittees prepare, but they rarely make major changes. Their markup usually occurs only a few days before the House and Senate take up the spending bill—often the committee completes work on more than one bill in a single meeting. Normally, the appropriations committees review each bill to ascertain whether it is within the section 302(b) allocation and to make a few adjustments in amounts and report language to reflect their preferences. Overall, however, an informal rule of reciprocity pervades full appropriations committee markups. Members defer to the judgment of the subcommittee of jurisdiction in the expectation that when their subcommittee's bill is taken up, others will defer to them.

Incrementalism

Although they often miss deadlines, the appropriations committees regard the timely completion of their work as a measure of their effectiveness. To do so, they traditionally limited the conflict inherent in the allocation of money among competing claims. In most appropriations cycles, their main behavioral rule was that appropriations should vary only incrementally from the previous year's level. Ongoing programs should be continued, cuts in existing programs should be avoided or minimal, and increases should be modest and broadly distributed among an array of programs.

Making incremental decisions requires that the appropriations committees review each request with reference to the amount provided for the previous year. These committees are the only major congressional budget makers who do not explicitly use baselines to measure the financial impact of their actions. Baselines are grounded on assumptions about future conditions; the appropriators rely instead on actual amounts: the current year's appropriation and the president's request for the next year. By rejecting baseline projections, the committees strengthen their control of incremental resources. Suppose, for example, that inflation for the next year is estimated at 3 percent, but

the appropriations committees recommend nominal increases of 2 percent for particular programs or accounts. If baselines were used, this decision would be scored as a cutback; in appropriations it is counted as an increase, even though it does not fully compensate for expected inflation.

Since the appropriations committees behave incrementally, they focus on nominal year-to-year spending changes at all stages of the process—from the preparation of justification material, through hearings, to markup and committee reports. For most subcommittees, the agencies' justification material highlights the arithmetic difference between the previous appropriation and the budget request. Only rarely do agencies justify their entire request. In normal times, when the president asks for more than was appropriated for the current year, his request and the previous appropriation form the boundaries within which most appropriations decisions fall. That is, most appropriations have been higher than the previous year's level and below the president's budget.

Incremental outcomes are not happenstance. Every step of the way, account by account, the appropriations committees calculate how much the amounts they are providing are more or less than the previous appropriation and the president's request. In fact, as exhibit 9-3 shows, they often publish the arithmetic difference between their actions and these two reference points in the committee reports. They need these calculations to do their own work.

From the vantage point of the appropriations committees, incremental decisions have several compelling advantages. They reduce conflict over spending and facilitate the timely enactment of appropriations. They reduce the legislative workload by enabling the committees to concentrate on changes at the margins

▶ **EXHIBIT 9-3**
Incrementalism in the Appropriations Process

HOUSE REPORT

MEDICAL AND PROSTHETIC RESEARCH

Fiscal year 1999 recommendation	$310,000,000
Fiscal year 1998 appropriation	272,000,000
Fiscal year 1999 budget request	300,000,000
Comparison with fiscal year 1998 appropriation	+38,000,000
Comparison with fiscal year 1999 budget request	+10,000,000

SENATE REPORT

AMOUNT OF NEW BUDGET (OBLIGATIONAL AUTHORITY)

Amount of bill as reported to Senate	$93,331,942,030
Amount of appropriations to date, 1998	88,392,163,000
Amount of budget estimates, 1999	94,081,470,705
Under estimates for 1999	749,528,675
Above appropriations for 1998	4,939,779,030

HOUSE COMPARATIVE STATEMENT

Agency and Item	Appropriated, 1998 (enacted to date)	Budget estimates 1999	Recommended in bill	Bill compared with appropriated 1998	Bill compared with budget estimates 1999
VETERANS HEALTH ADMINISTRATION					
Medical Care	16,487,396,000	16,392,975,000	16,211,396,000	−276,000,000	−181,579,000
Delayed equipment obligation	570,000,000	635,000,000	846,000,000	+276,000,000	+211,000,000
Total	17,057,396,000	17,027,975,000	17,057,396,000	. . .	+29,421,000
(Transfer to general operations)	. . .	. . .	(−23,000,000)	(−23,000,000)	(−23,000,000)
Medical collections guarantee	15,000,000	. . .	. . .	−15,000,000	
Medical care cost recovery collections:					
Offsetting receipts	−543,000,000	−558,000,000	−558,000,000	−15,000,000	. . .
Appropriations (indefinite)	543,000,000	558,000,000	558,000,000	+15,000,000	. . .
Total Available	(17,600,396,000)	(17,585,975,000)	(17,615,396,000)	(+15,000,000)	(+29,421,000)
Medical and prosthetic research	272,000,000	300,000,000	310,000,000	+38,000,000	+10,000,000

Sources: *Departments of Veterans Affairs and Housing and Urban Development, and Independent Agencies Appropriations Bill for Fiscal Year 1999*, H. Rept. 610, pp. 14 and 127, and S. Rept. 216, p. 1, 105th Cong., 2d sess., 1998.

(a) In their reports, the appropriations committees often compare the amounts recommended with the current year's appropriation and the president's budget request.

(b) All three of these entries have five lines or columns. While the sequence is different in the House and Senate entries, the five entries convey the same information: the current appropriation, the president's request, the committee's recommendation, the arithmetic difference between the committee recommendation and the current appropriation, and the arithmetic difference between the recommendation and the president's request.

(c) The appropriations committees do not use baseline projections in calculating the budgetary impact of their actions. These committees avoid baselines, which depend on assumptions about future conditions, and rely instead on the amounts actually appropriated or requested.

rather than on the total request. They often enable the committees to take credit both for cutting the budget (below the president's request) and increasing expenditures (above the previous level). In view of the preference of most Americans for smaller government and bigger programs, the capacity of the appropriators to satisfy both sentiments is no small political feat.

Incrementalism has been the unseen hand that coordinates the decentralized appropriations process. When most appropriations fall between current spending and the president's budget, the appropriations committees can be confident that the total of all their decisions will also be between these reference points (see exhibit 9-3). Over the years, incrementalism has enabled the appropriations committees to produce seemingly coordinated outcomes without trespassing on the autonomy of the subcommittees.

Incrementalism depends on a cooperative president, who by asking for more enables the appropriations committees to give more while taking credit for cutting back. This condition did not prevail during the 1980s, when Ronald Reagan demanded deep cuts in many established programs. Although he got his way at first, the appropriations committees quickly regrouped and managed to spend more on domestic programs while staying within the president's budget by trimming some of the additional resources he sought for defense. Reagan's unwillingness to play by incremental rules generated intense conflict and delayed the enactment of appropriations bills. George Bush also confronted Congress on the budget by proposing domestic cutbacks, but he did not have Reagan's early success. By the end of his term, Bush took a more accommodating stance on budgetary increments, accepting spending increases while attacking Congress for spending too much.

During the 1990s, congressional Republicans' efforts to cut federal spending and the discretionary caps undermined incrementalism. Table 9-7 compares the appropriations reported by the House Appropriations Committee in 1995—the year in which Republicans gained control of Congress—with the amounts appropriated the previous year. Hundreds of programs and accounts were slashed below previous levels, leading to an impasse that was broken only after a partial shutdown of government and restoration of many of the cuts. The table also shows that in the following year, House Republicans adopted a more conciliatory approach. Since then they made feeble efforts to cut some domestic programs, but after working out differences with the Senate and the White House, the appropriations usually have been close to or above the previous year's level.

The discretionary spending caps had an uneven impact on incremental behavior. Each time the new caps were enacted (in 1990, 1993, and 1997), they made room for additional spending in the years immediately ahead but tightened spending totals in the last years to which the limits applied. If these caps were strictly applied, there would have been robust increments in some years and cutbacks in others. But Congress, with cooperation or pressure from the president, managed to escape the harsh austerity implied by the caps. In some years, it reset the caps to allow additional spending; in others it used bookkeeping tricks and the emergency escape route to appropriate more than the caps specified.

Projects and Pork

In making appropriations, subcommittee members do more than look at past budgets, the president's numbers, and agency justifications. They also listen to other members of

TABLE 9-7
Accounts for Which the House Appropriations Committee Recommended Increases or Decreases, Fiscal Years 1996 and 1997[a]

Percent

	Fiscal year 1996 recommendations					
	Compared with FY1995 appropriation			Compared with president's request		
Bill	Increase	Decrease	No change	Increase	Decrease	No change
Agriculture	33	38	29	11	66	23
Commerce	36	47	17	6	83	11
Energy and Water	25	73	2	12	69	19
Foreign Operations	25	59	16	8	77	14
Interior	16	71	12	4	80	16
Labor-HHS	24	73	3	6	74	20
Transportation	25	57	18	7	57	36
Treasury	19	66	15	7	68	25
VA-HUD	15	56	29	8	64	28
Average percentage	24	60	16	8	71	21

Sources: House Appropriations Committee, *Comparative Statement of New Budget (Obligational) Authority for 1995 and Budget Estimates and Amounts Recommended in the Bill for 1996,* 104th Cong., 1st sess., selected reports, and House Appropriations Committee, *Comparative Statement of New Budget (Obligational) Authority for 1996 and Budget Estimates and Amounts Recommended in the Bill for 1997,* 104th Cong., 2d sess., selected reports.

Congress (especially colleagues on the appropriations committees) who want money earmarked to projects in their districts or states. Subcommittees typically receive more of these requests than they can accommodate, but they satisfy enough of them to give the appropriations bill a solid base of support in the full committee and on the floor.

The normal practice is to earmark funds in committee reports rather than in the appropriations bill; exhibit 9-4 shows earmarks in one such report. The subcommittee chair, consulting with the ranking minority member, usually has the final say over the projects, but widely shared distributive norms guide the process. First, subcommittee members get the biggest prizes, with full committee members next in line. Second, the process is usually bipartisan; both Republicans and Democrats

bring home some benefits. Third, members who request and receive earmarked funds are expected to vote for the appropriations bill. The operative norm is "do not ask for money if you do not support the bill."

Each subcommittee has its own notions about how much earmarking is appropriate. For years, the two largest appropriations bills moved in opposite directions on this issue. The Labor, Health and Human Services, and Education bill was relatively pork-free; the Defense bill was crammed with earmarks. Representative Bill Natcher (D-Ky.), the longtime chair of the Labor-HHS subcommittee until his death in 1994, did not like earmarks and allowed few in his bill. Defense, however, has been a pork barrel for generations because it funds thousands of military installations and companies. If pork is, as some pundits have quipped, spending with a

Fiscal year 1997 recommendations					
Compared with FY1996 appropriation			Compared with president's request		
Increase	Decrease	No change	Increase	Decrease	No change
33	37	30	2	58	40
47	42	11	5	80	15
32	58	10	16	62	22
17	49	34	10	51	39
36	36	28	11	53	36
53	44	3	7	75	18
34	35	31	10	52	38
47	30	23	18	39	43
45	26	29	14	53	33
38	40	22	10	58	32

a. Table does not include Defense, District of Columbia, Legislative Branch, or Military Construction appropriations bills. The figures include various special types of accounts such as working capital funds, trust funds, estimated loan levels, liquidation and rescission of contract authorizations, and limitations on direct loans, obligations, borrowing authority, and administrative expenses.

zip code attached, there are far more zip codes in defense appropriations than in any other bill.

There are cycles in Congress's appetite for pork. When Republicans took control of Congress in 1995, many vowed that they would purge appropriations bills of earmarks, which they believed built congressional coalitions in favor of higher appropriations. Conservatives produced studies showing that the longer a member serves in Congress, the more inclined she or he is to vote for appropriations bills. They reasoned that many members who enter Congress determined to cut federal spending are coopted to support higher spending by the pork that their seniority earns. But after a few years of boasting that their spending bills had fewer earmarks, congressional Republicans succumbed to the temptation of using their legislative power for political advantage. When it comes to doing

good for one's state or district, differences between Democrats and Republicans vanish.

Hardly anyone has a nice thing to say about earmarked appropriations. The president and executive agencies do not like earmarks because they narrow agency discretion in using funds. Authorizing committees profess not to like the practice because they would rather have the earmarks in their own bills. Members of Congress who do not get what they regard as a fair share of the money complain that the practice is wasteful and corrupt. Many who come away winners claim to abhor the volume of pork distributed through the appropriations bills but justify their actions by saying that everybody else is earmarking funds, and they have to look after the interests of their states and districts. The news media and critics of Congress see corruption and vote buying behind earmarked projects.

▶ **EXHIBIT 9-4**
Earmarks in Appropriations Committee Reports

The conference agreement includes $500,000 to provide 3 years of support for the Chippewa Falls Area Unified School System, Wisconsin after school program, $400,000 to provide 3 years of support for the Wausau School System, Wisconsin after school program; $350,000 for the New Rochelle School System after school program; $100,000 for the New York Hall of Science, Queens, New York after school program; $300,000 for the Bay Shore Community Learning Wellness and Fitness Center for Drug Free Lifestyles in Bay Shore, New York; $400,000 for the Green Bay Public School System, Wisconsin after school program; $2,500,000 for an after school anti-drug pilot program in the Chicago Public Schools; $25,000 for Louisville Central Community Centers Youth Education Program to support after-school programming; and $25,000 for Canaan's Community Development Corporation in Louisville, Kentucky for the Village Learning Center after school program. . . .

State of Louisiana.—The conference agreement includes $11,000,000 for buses and bus-related facilities for the State of Louisiana to be distributed as follows: Baton Rouge, $200,000; Jefferson Parish, $350,000; Lafayette, $425,000; Louisiana DOTD, including the purchase of vans, $650,000; Monroe, $450,000; New Orleans, $8,075,000; Shreveport, $400,000; state infrastructure bank, transit account, $350,000; and St. Tammany Parish, $100,000.

Commonwealth of Virginia.—The conference agreement includes $10,000,000 for the Commonwealth of Virginia for buses and bus facilities, of which $5,955,000 shall be distributed as follows: Falls Church electric bus facilities, $650,000; Manassas Transit Depot park and ride lot expansion, $280,000; Potomac and Rappahannock Main Street Station, $2,000,000; Stringfellow Road/Interstate 66 park and ride lot improvements, $1,000,000; and Warrenton Circuit Rider, $25,000.

State of Wisconsin.—The conference agreement includes $12,875,000 for the State of Wisconsin, of which $4,875,000 shall be distributed as follows: $2,075,000 for the Appleton, Green Bay, Shawano, Menominee Tribe and Oneida Tribe; $1,000,000 for the LaCross, Onalaska, Prairie DuChien, Rice Lake, Viroqua and Ho Chuck Nation; $300,000 for Ashland, Chippewa Falls, Eau Claire, Ladysmith, Marchfield, Rhinelander, Rusk County, Stevens Point, Wausau and Wisconsin Rapids; $1,000,000 for the Milwaukee intermodal facility rehabilitation; and $500,000 for the Waukesha transit center. In addition, $4,000,000 is provided for Milwaukee County.

Source: *Omnibus Consolidated and Emergency Supplemental Appropriations for Fiscal Year 1999*, H. Rept. 825, 105th Cong., 2d sess., 1998, pp. 1311 and 1441-2.

(a) The appropriations committees often earmark funds to designated projects or activities. Agencies are expected to comply with the earmarks, as well as with other guidance issued by the appropriations committees.

(b) The education earmarks displayed here were among many hundreds included in the Omnibus Appropriations Act for fiscal 1999. Note the small amounts of most of these earmarks and the much larger amount for Chicago public schools. This Chicago earmark may be due to the fact that chair of the House Departments of Labor, Health and Human Services, and Education Appropriations Subcommittee, John Porter (R), is from Illinois.

(c) The transportation earmarks went to bus systems in forty-six states and totaled more than $500 million.

Earmarks flourish because members of Congress would rather decide where appropriations are to be spent than let executive officials makes the decisions. They survive periodic reform campaigns because the chief political value of serving on Appropriations is to bring home the bacon, not to guard the Treasury. The appropriations committees earmark because a spending bill with projects spread across the country is easier to pass than one without them. Earmarks flourish in good times when incremental resources are plentiful and, it seems, even more in hard times when the budget is tight.

Though the amounts may appear to be very large to ordinary citizens, in budgetary terms, earmarks are relatively inexpensive—many dozens can be crammed into a tight appropriations bill. Five hundred projects averaging $1 million each would total less than one-tenth of a percent of discretionary spending and less than one-thirtieth of a percent of all federal spending. When funds are scarce, pork is prized because it may be the only benefit that members can bring home.

Programs, by contrast, are expensive because they typically provide nationwide (rather than local) benefits. Consider, for example, a proposal to improve public education by subsidizing school linkups to the Internet. Even if such a program were started modestly, with only $100 allotted per student, the total cost would exceed $5 billion. Suppose, however, that instead of a national program, a member had $1 million earmarked to a school in her district for an Internet demonstration project. In the political arithmetic of budgeting, $100 per student may be too expensive while $1 million for one school is affordable.

To argue that earmarking is relatively inexpensive is not to justify the practice or to claim that all the money is well spent. But neither should one conclude that the enormous size of the federal budget is due to pork; it is due to the expensive program commitments undertaken by the government.

PROCEDURES AND POLITICS OF HOUSE AND SENATE ACTION

The House normally takes up each appropriations bill within a few days after it has been reported. Box 9-3 lists the main steps in House action on appropriations. This sequence is followed for all the regular appropriations bills but differs from that used for some other types of legislation.

Because appropriations bills are privileged for floor consideration, the House can consider them without first obtaining a special rule through the Rules Committee. Nevertheless, most appropriations come to the floor under a special rule waiving one or more of the standing rules, such as the rule against unauthorized appropriations. The House first adopts the special rule (exhibit 9-5), then takes up the appropriations bill.

Special rules on appropriations bills are usually open; they do not restrict floor amendments. During the 1990s, however, the legislative branch appropriations bill was sometimes considered under a closed rule that precluded amendments. The majority party resorted to this tactic to block the minority from offering amendments that might embarrass it.

During House consideration, the subcommittee chair (who manages the bill on the floor) or the budget committee may advise the chamber whether the budget authority and outlays deriving from the bill are within the section 302(b) allocation to the subcommittee; exhibit 9-6 shows one such statement. Appropriations bills rarely exceed the section 302(b) allocation—doing so would indicate that the appropriations committee has violated Congress's budget policy. Occasionally, the bill ex-

▼

BOX 9-3
Sequence of House Actions on Appropriations Measures

Special Rule
Although appropriations bills are privileged and the House can consider them at any time, the House normally considers them under special rules (in the form of a simple House resolution) waiving certain points of order, such as those arising out of the rule barring unauthorized appropriations.

Committee of the Whole
After the House adopts the rule, it takes up the appropriations bill in the Committee of the Whole rather than in the House itself. The Committee of the Whole has a much smaller quorum requirement than that of the House.

General Debate
The floor managers—the chair and ranking minority member of the relevant appropriations subcommittee—open debate on the bill. Opening statements may also be made by the chair of the Appropriations Committee, who may advise the House on the overall status of appropriations bills, and by the chair of the Budget Committee, who may comment on whether the bill conforms to the subcommittee's section 302(b) allocation.

Amendments
Regular appropriations bills are usually considered under an open rule that does not preclude consideration of any floor amendments. An amendment must be offered in a timely manner, when the portion of the bill to which it pertains is being considered. (An exception to this requirement is made for amendments pertaining to two or more parts of the appropriations bill, whose amounts are completely offsetting.)

Points of Order
Points of order (which also must be timely) may be raised either against the bill reported by the Appropriations Committee or a floor amendment. In the House, it is rare for the ruling of the chair on a point of order to be challenged.

Limitations
Floor amendments inserting certain limitations into an appropriations bill may be offered only after consideration of funding levels has been completed. At this point, it is in order to move that the Committee of the Whole "rise and report." If the motion is adopted, there may be no opportunity to offer limitation amendments.

Final Passage
After the Committee of the Whole reports, final consideration is before the House. Under certain circumstances, the House may reconsider amendments adopted in the Committee of the Whole, but it usually concurs with the previous vote.

▶ **EXHIBIT 9-5**
Special House Rule on Appropriations Bills

H. RES. 194
In the House of Representatives, U.S.,
July 24, 1997.

Resolved, That at any time after the adoption of this resolution the Speaker may, pursuant to clause 1(b) of rule XXIII, declare the House resolved into the Committee of the Whole House on the state of the Union for consideration of the bill (H.R. 2203) making appropriations for energy and water development for the fiscal year ending September 30, 1998, and for other purposes. The first reading of the bill shall be dispensed with. General debate shall be confined to the bill and shall not exceed one hour equally divided and controlled by the chairman and ranking minority member of the Committee on Appropriations. After general debate the bill shall be considered for amendment under the five-minute rule. Points of order against provisions in the bill for failure to comply with clause 2 or 6 of rule XXI are waived. During consideration of the bill for amendment, the Chairman of the Committee of the Whole may accord priority in recognition on the basis of whether the Member offering an amendment has caused it to be printed in the portion of the Congressional Record designated for that purpose in clause 6 of rule XXIII. Amendments so printed shall be considered as read. The Chairman of the Committee of the Whole may: (1) postpone until a time during further consideration in the Committee of the Whole a request for a recorded vote on any amendment; and (2) reduce to five minutes the minimum time for electronic voting on any postponed question that follows another electronic vote without intervening business, provided that the minimum time for electronic voting on the first in any series of questions shall be fifteen minutes. At the conclusion of consideration of the bill for amendment the Committee shall rise and report the bill to the House with such amendments as may have been adopted. The previous question shall be considered as ordered on the bill and amendments thereto to final passage without intervening motion except one motion to recommit with or without instructions.

Source: *A resolution providing for consideration of the bill (H.R. 2203) making appropriations for Energy and Water Development for the fiscal year ending September 30, 1998, and for other purposes,* H. Res. 194, as passed House, 105th Cong., 1st sess., 1997.

(a) Although appropriations bills are privileged in the House and may be taken up at any time, the practice is to consider them pursuant to a special rule (in the form of a House resolution) waiving certain points of order that would otherwise apply. The House acts first on the rule and then considers the appropriations bill.

(b) The rule exhibited here waives points of order on unauthorized appropriations and legislation in an appropriations bill. Note that the waivers pertain to the entire measure; at times special rules are drafted so as to protect specified portions of the bill.

(c) This is an open rule: it does not restrict floor amendments, but it permits the chair to give priority to members whose amendments have been printed in advance in the *Congressional Record.*

> **EXHIBIT 9-6**
> **Section 302(b) Scoring Statement**

MR. DOMENICI. Mr. President, the final appropriations measure that the Congress passed before adjournment was H.R. 2267, the Commerce, Justice, State, and the Judiciary appropriations bill for the fiscal year 1998. I today submit a table displaying the Budget Committee scoring of the final bill.

The conference agreement accompanying the bill provides $31.7 billion in budget authority and $21.2 billion in new outlays to operate the programs of the Department of Commerce, the Department of Justice, the Department of State, the Judiciary, and related Federal agencies for fiscal year 1998.

When outlays from prior-year budget authority and other completed actions are taken into account, the bill totals $31.8 billion in budget authority and $29.5 billion in outlays for fiscal year 1998. The final bill is within the revised Senate subcommittee's section 302(b) allocation for both budget authority and outlays. The bill is $7 million in budget authority and $77 million in outlays below the Senate subcommittee's 302(b) allocation.

SENATE BUDGET COMMITTEE'S SCORING OF H.R. 2267
FISCAL YEAR 1998 COMMERCE–JUSTICE–STATE APPROPRIATIONS

	Defense	Non-defense	Crime	Mandatory	Total
		(in millions of dollars)			
Budget Authority					
Section 302(b)	298	25,757	5,225	522	31,802
Bill	298	25,750	5,225	522	31,795
Difference	0	−7	0	0	−7
Outlays					
Section 302(b)	342	25,285	3,401	532	25,560
Bill	340	25,211	3,400	532	29,483
Difference	−2	−74	−1	0	−77

Source: Adapted from the *Congressional Record*, daily ed., December 15, 1997, S12722.

(a) During or after debate on an appropriations bill, the chair of the House or Senate Budget Committee may provide a comparison of the amounts in the bill to the relevant subcommittee's section 302(b) allocation. In this case, the comparison was provided by Senate Budget Committee Chair Pete Domenici (R-N.Mex.) after the appropriations bill was passed.

(b) The budget committees are the official scorers of budget action for Congress; their analysis is authoritative in ruling on points of order concerning violations of the section 302(b) limits. However, OMB is the official scorer for determining whether Budget Enforcement Act rules have been breached.

(c) As is the case here, the Budget Committee statement usually reports that the appropriations bill is within the subcommittee allocation. Note that the bill uses almost all of the budget authority and outlays available to the subcommittee.

(d) The "score" is broken down into four categories: defense, non-defense, crime, and mandatory, which correspond to the classifications used to enforce the Budget Enforcement Act.

ceeds the allocation for technical rather than substantive reasons. When this occurs, the House usually waives the point of order.

Section 302 rules inhibit the passage of floor amendments that would change the amounts appropriated. As reported by committee, spending bills are usually at or slightly below the levels allowed by section 302(b). Amendments boosting appropriations above the 302(b) allocation may be blocked by points of order—those reducing budget authority or outlays may be challenged on the grounds that the reported levels are consistent with congressional budget decisions. The only other option is to transfer funds from one account to another within the section 302(b) limits. Transfer amendments rarely win because those whose programs would lose resources strongly oppose them.

Despite these impediments, amendments cutting appropriations below the level that section 302 allows may prevail when an economizing mood takes hold on Capitol Hill. However, because of an anomaly in budget rules, amendments that purport to cut appropriations may not actually accomplish what they set out to do. The reason is that the section 302 process has two linked, but separate, limitations: one on total discretionary spending, the other on spending deriving from each subcommittee's appropriations. A successful floor amendment that cuts an appropriations bill below the subcommittee limit does not itself change the limit on total discretionary spending. Consequently, the resources saved by the floor amendment can be recycled through the section 302 process to be spent on other appropriations. When Republicans took control of the House in 1995, they dealt with this situation by devising a "lockbox" rule that lowers the discretionary caps by an amount equal to the savings. For example, an amendment cutting $100 million from an appropriations bill would automatically reduce that year's caps by $100 million. The Senate did not adopt such a rule, and in the final budget negotiations the House has often set aside the lockbox in order to reach agreement on appropriations.

Before voting on an appropriations measure, the House may be advised of concerns raised by the White House or OMB. This advice takes the form of a statement of administration policy (SAP) (exhibit 9-7). Each statement specifies the administration's concerns as the appropriations bill moves through the House and Senate. SAPs are normally issued at seven stages of congressional action: House Appropriations subcommittee markup, House Appropriations Committee markup, House consideration, Senate subcommittee action, full committee markup, Senate consideration, and conference committee. The SAP comments on items in the most recent version of the appropriations measure that the administration finds objectionable. It is carefully worded and structured to signal the intensity of the administration's objections and the extent to which the bill may provoke a presidential veto. Before the Clinton presidency, it was rare for the SAP to state outright that the president would veto appropriations bills with objectionable provisions. Instead, it averred that the president's advisers would recommend a veto. By not overtly declaring that he would veto the bill, the SAP opened the door to negotiation and compromise. Bill Clinton, however, changed the formula when he confronted Republican efforts to trim domestic spending and to attach restrictive riders to appropriations bills. Rather than hinting at a veto, SAPs declared his intention to veto appropriations bills if funding was not restored or the riders were not removed.

SAPs are a relatively recent innovation in federal budgeting. They were introduced in the 1980s in response to protracted conflict be-

▶ **EXHIBIT 9-7**
Statement of Administration Policy

(This statement has been coordinated by OMB with the concerned agencies)

This Statement of Administration Policy provides the Administration's views on H.R. 4194, the Departments of Veterans Affairs and Housing and Urban Development, and Independent Agencies Appropriations Bill, FY 1999, as reported by the House Appropriations Committee. Your consideration of the Administration's views would be appreciated.

The Administration appreciates efforts by the Committee to accommodate certain of the President's priorities within the 302(b) allocation. However, the allocation is simply insufficient to make the necessary investments in programs funded by this bill. As a result, critical programs are not funded or are underfunded, in particular, key Presidential priorities such as funding for National Service, Superfund, and climate change. Furthermore, the Administration is very concerned that the Committee has included problematic language regarding the Kyoto Protocol and other issues. Finally, the Administration understands that an amendment may be offered to include unacceptable provisions now contained in H.R. 2, such as income targeting. If the bill were presented to the President without responding to these concerns, the President's senior advisors would recommend that he veto the bill. . . .

Below is a discussion of our specific concerns with the Committee bill. We look forward to working with the House to resolve these concerns as the bill moves forward . . . .

Source: Office of Management and Budget, *Statement of Administration Policy on H.R. 4194—the Departments of Veterans Affairs and Housing and Urban Development, and Independent Agencies Appropriations Bill for Fiscal Year 1999*, July 15, 1998, p. 1.

(a) A statement of administration policy (SAP) is issued for each annual appropriations bill at the start of congressional action. The exhibited SAP was issued before the House Rules Committee considered the rule for the bill. Sometimes, the SAP is placed in the *Congressional Record* and referred to during debate on the measure.

(b) Each SAP specifies administration objections to provisions in the appropriations bill. The objections may pertain to funding levels or to substantive language. The first part of the SAP (exhibited here) provides general objection to the bill; subsequent sections detail concerns about particular accounts or provisions.

(c) The SAP sometimes states that the bill will be vetoed if objectionable provisions are not remedied. More frequently, it is usually the formula employed here: "The President's senior advisors would recommend that he veto the bill." This language conveys a strong threat, for it indicates that both the director of OMB and the president's political aides have agreed to recommend a veto.

TABLE 9-8
Which Chamber Acted First on Appropriations Bills, Selected Fiscal Years

Bill	1994		1998		1999	
	Reported	Passed[a]	Reported	Passed[a]	Reported	Passed[a]
Agriculture	House	House	House	same day	Senate	House
Commerce-Justice-State	House	House	Senate	Senate	Senate	Senate
Defense	House	House	Senate	Senate	Senate	House
District of Columbia	House	House	Senate	House	Senate	House
Energy and Water	House	House	Senate	Senate	Senate	Senate
Foreign Operations	House	House	Senate	Senate	Senate	Senate
Interior	House	House	House	House	Senate	House
Labor-HHS-Education	House	House	House	Senate	House	[b]
Legislative Branch	House	House	Senate	Senate	Senate	House
Military Construction	House	House	House	House	Senate	House
Transportation	House	House	House	House	Senate	Senate
Treasury-Postal Service	House	House	Senate	Senate	Senate	Senate
VA-HUD-Independent Agencies	House	House	House	House	Senate	Senate

Source: *Congressional Quarterly Almanac*, 1993, 1997, and 1998.

a. This refers to which chamber first passed each bill, not on adoption of the conference report.

b. The bill was not voted on until the conference report, which the House voted on first.

tween the president and Congress on budgetary matters. Prodded by its director, David Stockman, to pay more attention to what Congress does to the president's budget, OMB established SAPs as a means of monitoring congressional action and communicating administration concerns. SAPs do not displace the give and take between presidential aides and legislators, but they indicate a more formal, distant relationship between the president and Congress—one that impels the White House to put its differences down on paper and to threaten vetoes. In fact, SAPs often set the stage for negotiations that lead to resolution of differences and enactment of appropriations. Sometimes, however, the process breaks down, and the vetoes turn from threats into reality.

Senate Action

In discussing Senate work on appropriations, one must distinguish between the traditional sequence in which the House acts first and re-cent variations in which the Senate takes the initiative and produces appropriations bills before the House does (table 9-8). In both cases, Senate appropriations subcommittees conduct hearings, recommend appropriations, draft report language, and prepare the bill for floor consideration. The main difference is that when the Senate goes first, it produces an entirely new bill; when it follows the House, the Senate amends the House-passed bill. These amendments are numbered sequentially and inserted in the bill at the point where the change is made (exhibit 9-8). In numbering Senate amendments, there is no difference between changes the Senate Appropriations Committee makes and those adopted on the floor; both are inserted at the relevant point in the House-passed bill. Immediately following each numbered amendment, the Senate bill lines out language in the House bill that the Senate deleted and italicizes language not in the House bill that the Senate added.

When it acts first, the Senate produces its

▶ **EXHIBIT 9-8**
Senate Amendments to House-Passed Appropriations Bill

9	ADDITIONAL HIGHWAY PROJECTS
10	Appalachian Corridor Improvement Project
11	For 80 percent of the expenses necessary to continue
12	construction on (130) ~~Kentucky Corridor B~~ *West Virginia*
13	*Corridor L* of the Appalachian Development Highway System,
14	as authorized by section 1069(y) of Public Law 102-240 (131)
15	~~$3,800,000~~ *$62,200,000.*
16	(132) ~~CUMBERLAND GAP TUNNEL PROJECT~~
17	~~For 80 percent of the expenses necessary for the~~
18	~~Cumberland Gap Tunnel Project, as authorized by~~
19	~~1069(c) of Public Law 102-240, $10,000,000.~~
20	(133) *PITTSBURGH BUSWAY*
21	*For 80 percent of the expenses necessary for the*
22	*Pittsburgh Busway, as authorized by section 1069(e) of Public*
23	*Law 102-240, $28,000,000.*

Source: *Department of Transportation Appropriations Act, Fiscal Year 1994*, H.R. 2750, as passed Senate, with numbered amendments, 103rd Cong., 1st sess., 1993, p. 40.

(a) In the traditional sequence, the House completes action on an appropriations bill before the Senate considers the measure. In this sequence, the Senate does not initiate its own appropriations bill. Instead, it amends (in committee or on the floor) the House-passed bill.

(b) The numbers in parentheses designate Senate amendments (changes) to the House-passed bill. The amendments are numbered sequentially and are referred to in the conference report on the appropriations bill (see exhibit 9-9).

(c) The lined-out text immediately following the numbered amendment is language in the House-passed bill struck by the Senate; the italicized text is language inserted by the Senate. The remaining text is House-passed language to which the Senate made no changes.

(d) When the Senate passes an appropriations bill before the House, it waits for the House to complete action, then inserts its bill as a single amendment to the entire House bill.

(e) When the appropriations bill exhibited here was being considered, the House Appropriations Committee was chaired by a member from Kentucky, who inserted money for his state. The Senate Appropriations Committee was chaired by a member from West Virginia, who deleted the Kentucky earmark and inserted a much larger amount for his state. This is an example of how members position themselves for the conference at which final decisions are made.

own bill but holds it until the House has completed its version. When the House is done, the entire Senate-passed bill is inserted as a single amendment to the House bill. In this way, the prerogative of the House to initiate appropriations is preserved, even though the Senate acted first.

Senate hearings on appropriations are not as extensive as those held by the House, but the Senate does not routinely defer to the House's actions. Whether it goes first or second, the Senate's appropriations often differ significantly in amounts and other provisions from the House's. When an appropriations bill goes to conference, there are likely to be more than one hundred differences between the two versions. Some of the differences are "bargaining chips," which one of the chambers uses to strengthen its position in conference; others represent real disagreements.

In acting on appropriations, as on other measures, the Senate places few restrictions on members' freedom to offer floor amendments. But it does present tough hurdles to provisions, whether in the reported bill or proposed on the floor, that would violate section 302 limits. The Senate restrictions are more stringent than those the House applies, but they can be waived by a three-fifths vote. Overall, however, Senate debate on appropriations bills is less structured than in the House; the main steps in the Senate process are listed in box 9-4.

After both the House and Senate pass an appropriations bill, a conference committee is convened to resolve differences between the two versions. When the traditional sequence is followed, the conferees work out differences on each of the numbered Senate amendments (exhibit 9-9). When the Senate acts first, the conferees go through each of the accounts to iron out disagreements. Either way, appropriations bills cannot become law until the House and Senate pass them in identical form. Some-

times the conferees report that certain matters are in disagreement, even though they have resolved all differences. These are technical, not actual, disagreements, which require a separate vote in the House and Senate after the conference report has been approved.

As with other legislation, appropriations bills are presented to the president after Congress completes action on them. The president has the option of signing or vetoing the entire measure; he cannot veto portions of appropriations bills (the line-item veto is discussed in chapter 5). Before Congress finalizes an appropriations bill, it usually resolves many of its differences with the president. Consequently, by the time Congress completes work on an appropriations bill, it may have a strong expectation that the president will sign the measure, even if he does not approve of all the items in it. However, some recent presidents have vigorously wielded the veto to block appropriations bills at variance with their priorities. Bill Clinton was especially successful in using the veto to strengthen his bargaining power vis-à-vis Congress.

When appropriations are enacted, there is an additional requirement that is not imposed on any other type of legislation. OMB must send Congress a report within seven days estimating the budget authority and outlays in the act and comparing its estimates with those of the Congressional Budget Office (CBO). These estimates have been used in enforcing the discretionary spending limits (exhibit 9-10).

SUPPLEMENTAL AND CONTINUING APPROPRIATIONS

Supplemental appropriations and continuing resolutions take a route similar to that of regular appropriations bills. There is no fixed number of these measures, but some are passed in every session of Congress.

▼

BOX 9-4
Sequence of Senate Actions on Appropriations Measures

Waiver Motion (Optional)

The Congressional Budget Act bars consideration of revenue or spending measures that would violate certain substantive or procedural budget rules—for example, the rule against considering these measures until the budget resolution has been adopted. The Senate may set aside these rules by unanimous consent or by adopting a waiver motion.

Time Limitation Agreement

Appropriations bills and other major legislation are often considered in the Senate under a time limitation agreement (also referred to as a unanimous consent agreement), which specifies the time set aside for debate, amendments to be considered, and sometimes when voting will take place on final passage. The majority leader usually proposes the time limitation agreement after consultation with the minority leader and other interested senators.

Managers' Statements

The chair and ranking minority member of the relevant appropriations subcommittee provide an overview of the bill, including comparison with the previous appropriation and with the president's request.

Committee Amendments

Changes recommended by the Senate Appropriations Committee to the House-passed bill are usually voted on en bloc (all together) and approved by voice vote. This procedure pertains only when the Senate takes up an appropriations bill the House already passed.

Floor Amendments

The entire appropriations bill is open to floor amendment at any time. However, the time limitation agreement sometimes specifies the sequence in which amendments are to be considered.

Points of Order

Points of order may be raised at any time during consideration of the bill. When a point of order is raised that an item is legislation in an appropriations bill, another member may raise the defense of germaneness. If the Senate decides that the item is germane, the original point of order fails.

Final Passage

After all amendments are disposed of (or when the time arrives for voting on final passage, stipulated in the time limitation agreement) the Senate votes on the bill. Some appropriations bills are agreed on by voice—rather than recorded—vote.

▶ **EXHIBIT 9-9**
Conference Report: Traditional Sequence (Senate Amends House-passed Appropriations Bill)

The committee of conference on the disagreeing votes of the two Houses on the amendments of the Senate to the bill (H.R. 2750) "making appropriations for the Department of Transportation and related agencies, for the fiscal year ending September 30, 1994, and for other purposes," having met, after full and free conference, have agreed to recommend and do recommend to their respective Houses as follows:

That the Senate recede from its amendments numbered 28, 37, 40, 42, 43, 58, 61, 63, 64, 81, 82, 83, 84, 85, 113, 115, 117, 123, 146, 152, 153, 161, 162, 165, 166, 169, 170, 173, 174, 178, 179, 181, 183, 184, and 187.

That the House recede from its disagreement to the amendments of the Senate numbered 18, 19, 20, 22, 24, 25, 39, 44, 49, 55, 69, 75, 76, 77, 78, 79, 80, 86, 87, 89, 94, 95, 96, 97, 105, 108, 112, 116, 119, 120, 121, 126, 141, 148, 151, 156, 157, 160, 164, and 167, and agree to the same.

Amendment number 27:

That the House recede from its disagreement to the amendment of the Senate numbered 27, and agree to the same with an amendment, as follows:

In lieu of the sum proposed in said amendment insert: $2,570,000,000; and the Senate agree to the same.

Amendment numbered 30:

That the House recede from its disagreement to the amendment of the Senate numbered 30, and agree to the same with an amendment, as follows:

In lieu of the sum proposed in said amendment insert: $327,500,000; and the Senate agree to the same.

Source: *Conference Report on Appropriations for the Department of Transportation and Related Agencies for Fiscal Year 1994*, H. Rept. 300, 103rd Cong., 1st sess., 1993, p. 1.

(a) In the traditional sequence, when the House passes its bill first, the conference report references the Senate amendments to the House-passed bill. To interpret the conference report, it is therefore necessary to have a copy of the Senate-passed bill. As shown in exhibit 9-8, the Senate-passed bill contains both the House text and the Senate amendments.

(b) When the Senate initiates an appropriations bill, the conference report provides the full text agreed to by the conferees.

(c) The conference resolves House-Senate differences on appropriations bills in four ways, three of which are exhibited here. It can drop the Senate amendments (as it does here for amendments 28, 37, 40, and so on), it can accept the Senate amendments (as it does here for 18, 19, 20, and so on), it can devise a compromise by adopting new language (as it does here for 27 and 30), or it can report certain amendments in technical disagreement.

(d) Amendments are designated in technical disagreement even though the conferees have actually reached an agreement to avoid a point of order on the conference report. These amendments usually are adopted by the House and Senate immediately after they approve the conference report.

▶ EXHIBIT 9-10
OMB Seven-Day Report on Appropriations Acts

Estimates Contained in P.L. 105-276,
FY99 Veterans Affairs, Housing and Urban Development, and
Independent Agencies Appropriations Act (in millions of dollars)

Fiscal Year 1999	Budget Authority	Outlays
Non-defense Discretionary Spending		
OMB Estimate	69,941	79,412
CBO Estimate	69,914	80,364
Total Difference	27	−952

Scorekeeping Differences:

FHA and Special Risk Insurance Negative Subsidy	−18	59

OMB and CBO have different estimates of the negative subsidy that this program generates. CBO estimates fewer receipts ($125 million) and thus scores a higher net cost ($167 million). OMB estimates higher receipts ($143 million from the program) and thus a lower net cost ($149 million). This results in a $7 million difference in new outlays. CBO also estimates lower outlays from prior-year balances than does OMB ($66 million difference).

GSE Default Loss Protection Provision	41	41

The bill includes a provision which would relax restriction on Freddie Mac's ability to buy mortgage with low down payments. CBO and OMB project a loss of revenue from increased use of mortgage interest deduction as a result of this provision. CBO scores the projected revenue loss as mandatory ($4 million in FY99 and a total of $215 million through FY03. Consistent with scorekeeping rule 3, OMB scores the entire loss ($41 million) as discretionary.

Source: Adapted from Office of Management and Budget, *Budget Enforcement Act Report for H.R. 4194 (Veterans Affairs, Housing and Urban Development, and Independent Agencies Appropriations Act, FY99)*, table 4, pp. 7–10.

(a) Within seven days after enactment of an appropriations act, OMB must submit a report to Congress estimating the budget authority and outlays provided or derived from the measure. These estimates are based on the economic and technical assumptions used in the most recent budget. The estimates presented in the seven-day report have been used in enforcing the discretionary caps and in determining whether funds should be sequestered.

(b) A central feature of this report is an explanation of differences in CBO and OMB estimates. These scoring differences are usually minor, but they sometimes can spell the difference between a determination that spending is within or above the discretionary caps. It is not enough that OMB report differences between the two estimates; it must also identify the factors that account for discrepancies.

(c) The seven-day report exhibited here shows a small net difference between CBO and OMB budget authority estimates, but a much larger difference in outlays. This is a common pattern; most budget authority amounts are specified in the appropriations act, but outlay estimates are derived from spendout rates—that is, estimates of how fast new budget authority will be spent.

Supplementals are prepared by the subcommittees with jurisdiction over the programs to be funded, but not on their initiative alone and usually with more coordination than befits regular appropriations. As previously noted, section 302 allocations preclude the subcommittees from acting on their own, without regard for whether the additional funding can be accommodated within budget limits. Compiling a supplemental entails decisions on the scope of the bill, the amount of additional resources that should be provided, whether some or all of the supplemental funding should be designated as emergency, and whether emergency spending should be offset by cutbacks in other areas. Resolving these questions may entail negotiations within Congress and with the White House that range across the jurisdictions of the subcommittees whose programs are targeted for supplemental appropriations.

Since the 1980s, continuing resolutions frequently have been used to provide interim or full-year funding, and their scope has been much broader than it was in earlier periods. The traditional CR, which has been enacted intermittently for more than a century, is a brief, temporary measure that lists the programs or agencies that have not yet received their regular appropriations, provides a continuing rate of funding (usually the lower of the previous year's appropriation or the president's budget request), is scheduled to expire within days or weeks, and has a few technical provisions made necessary by its temporary status (exhibit 9-11). In contrast, some contemporary continuing resolutions are omnibus measures that fund all or many of the regular appropriations, are in effect through the fiscal year, specify amounts for each account in the same manner as is done in regular appropriations acts, have significant amounts of substantive legislation, and contain other provisions normally found in regular appropriations. The traditional CR is a few pages long; the omnibus version may run for hundreds of pages. In some years, Congress enacts a series of brief, traditional CRs, each one only providing stopgap funding, and a final omnibus CR covering the remainder of the fiscal year. This omnibus measure is, in effect, a vehicle for enacting the regular appropriations.

Several characteristics of CRs make them ripe for conversion into omnibus measures. First, under House precedents they are deemed not to be general appropriations bills. Hence the rules against unauthorized appropriations and legislation in appropriations bills do not apply. Just about anything can be placed in a continuing resolution without drawing a point of order. Second, the manner in which these measures are considered—under imminent threat of government shutdown—makes them ideal vehicles for enacting legislation that would not become law under other circumstances. Third, omnibus continuing resolutions are usually hammered out in summit negotiations between the White House and Congress. There is a lot of confusion and give and take, with each side accepting provisions the other wants on condition that some of its preferences are included. The upshot is a bloated CR that few in Congress profess to like but few vote against.

Many observers consider massive CRs evidence of the breakdown of the regular appropriations process. The problem, however, lies not in appropriations procedures but in sustained and intense conflict over budget policy. Omnibus continuing resolutions enable the president and Congress to agree on appropriations through extraordinary procedures when normal means do not suffice. If an era of surpluses were to bring budgetary peace to Washington, continuing resolutions would become less common and more modest in size.

▶ **EXHIBIT 9-11**
Continuing Resolution

Joint Resolution
Making continuing appropriations for the fiscal year 1999, and for other purposes.

Sec. 101. (a) Such amounts as may be necessary under the authority and conditions provided in the applicable appropriations Act for the fiscal year 1998 for continuing projects or activities including the costs of direct loans and loan guarantees (not otherwise specifically provided for in this joint resolution) which were conducted in the fiscal year 1998 and for appropriations, funds, or other authority would be available in the following appropriation Acts:

1) the Agriculture, Rural Development, Food and Drug Administration, and Related Agencies Appropriations Act, 1999;

2) the Departments of Commerce, Justice, and State, the Judiciary, and Related Agencies Appropriations Act, 1999; . . .

Sec. 103. Appropriations made by section 101 shall be available to the extent and in the manner which would be provided by the pertinent appropriations Act. . . .

Sec. 104. No appropriation or funds made available or authority granted pursuant to section 101 shall be used to initiate or resume any project or activity for which appropriations, funds, or other authority were not available during the fiscal year 1998. . . .

Sec. 106. Unless otherwise provided for in this joint resolution or in the applicable appropriations Act, appropriations and funds made available and authority granted pursuant to this joint resolution shall be available until: (a) enactment into law of an appropriation for any project or activity provided for in this joint resolution; or (b) the enactment into law of the applicable appropriations Act by both Houses without any provision for such project or activity; or (c) October 9, 1998, whichever first occurs.

Source: *Continuing Appropriations for Fiscal Year 1999*, P.L. 105-240.

(a) A continuing appropriations act is enacted in the form of a joint resolution for agencies that have not received a regular appropriation for the fiscal year. Although it is often referred to as a continuing resolution (CR), it has the same legal status as a bill. It may be in effect for only part of the fiscal year or for the remainder of the year.

(b) The continuing resolution lists the regular appropriations covered by it. This continuing resolution, for fiscal 1999, covered twelve of the thirteen regular appropriations acts.

(c) Most continuing resolutions are temporary measures that expire on the date specified in the CR, or are superseded by enactment of the regular appropriations act. This CR was in effect for nine days, from the start of the fiscal year through October 9. When it expired, another temporary continuing resolution was enacted.

(d) This measure barred the use of funds provided in the continuing resolution to initiate any project or activity that was not funded in the previous fiscal year.

STRUCTURE AND CONTENT OF APPROPRIATIONS MEASURES

All regular appropriations acts have three standard features: an enacting clause that designates the fiscal year for which the appropriations are made, account-by-account appropriations, and general provisions (exhibit 9-12).

The basic unit of appropriation is an account. Every unnumbered paragraph in an appropriations act is a single account, and all provisions enacted within the paragraph pertain only to that account unless the text gives them broader scope. The unnumbered accounts are the source of the governmentwide accounting system maintained by the Treasury. Laws governing the expenditure of funds (for example, that spending may not exceed appropriations and may be used only for the purposes of the appropriation) pertain to each account. Thus an account limits both the amount and purpose of expenditures.

Over the years, appropriations have been consolidated into a relatively small number of accounts. The budget now contains more than 1,000 accounts, but the 200 largest cover more than 90 percent of all federal expenditures. Many federal agencies have a single "salary and expenses" account for all their operating expenditures; some have additional accounts for special purposes such as procurement or construction. When Congress establishes a new program, the appropriation for it usually is folded into an existing account. Most appropriations provide a lump sum for all the activities or projects financed by the account, though the appropriations committees often specify in their reports how the money is to be allocated among various projects or activities. Sometimes the appropriations act itself specifies that a portion of the money in the account be used for designated purposes. The appropriation might specify that "not less than" a certain amount should be spent on a particular activity. When this or similar language appears in an appropriations act, the spending agency usually "fences off" the money by treating it as a subaccount.

In addition to provisions attached to particular accounts, each appropriations act has general provisions that apply to all accounts in the act. (An appropriations act that covers two or more departments may be subdivided into titles, each of which has its own general provisions.) The general provisions appear as numbered sections at the end of the title or act (exhibit 9-13). Most general provisions contain either limitations (restrictions on the use of appropriations) or legislation (changes in law); some earmark funds to particular uses. Most are reenacted year after year with little or no change. With some new ones added each year, there has been a steady rise in the number of general provisions; table 9-9 shows this increase at five-year intervals since fiscal 1964. In each such period, excluding 1994, there were more general provisions than in the previous period. The fiscal 1999 appropriations had more than six times the number of general provisions than did the fiscal 1964 appropriations. This steep increase reflects strained relations between Congress and executive agencies, the growing tendency of the appropriations committees to earmark funds and restrict their use, incremental behavior that impels these committees to retain old provisions while adding new ones, and the inclusion of more legislation in appropriations acts.

General provisions have become the most prominent and controversial features of some appropriations acts. Provisions have been inserted to restrict the use of federal money to finance abortions, to curb the enforcement of environmental protection laws, to bar certain military operations, and to induce changes in the speed limit on federally aided highways. The 147 general provisions in the fiscal 1999

▶ EXHIBIT 9-12
Structure of a Regular Appropriations Act

ENACTING CLAUSE

Making appropriations for the Department of Defense for the fiscal year ending September 30, 1998, and for other purposes.

Be it enacted by the Senate and House of Representatives of the United States of America in Congress assembled, That the following sums are appropriated, out of any money in the Treasury not otherwise appropriated, for the fiscal year ending September 30, 1998, for military function administered by the Department of Defense, and for other purposes, namely . . .

APPROPRIATIONS

CENTRAL INTELLIGENCE AGENCY RETIREMENT AND DISABILITY SYSTEM FUND

For payment to the Central Intelligence Agency Retirement and Disability System Fund, to maintain proper funding level for continuing the operation of the Central Intelligence Agency Retirement and Disability System; $196,900,000.

GENERAL PROVISIONS

Sec. 8020. None of the funds available to the Department of Defense may be used to demilitarize or dispose of M-1 Carbines, M-1 Garand rifles, M-14 rifles, .22 caliber rifles, .30 caliber rifles, or M-1911 pistols.

Source: *Department of Defense Appropriations Act for Fiscal Year 1998*, P.L. 105-56.

(a) An appropriations act has three main components: the enacting clause; appropriations to specified accounts; and general provisions.

(b) The enacting clause specifies the fiscal year for which appropriations are made. Unless otherwise stipulated, all funds provided in the act are available for obligation only in that fiscal year. All substantive provisions in an appropriations act expire at the end of the fiscal year unless the text gives them a longer period of effectiveness.

(c) Each unnumbered paragraph constitutes a single appropriations account. Most agencies have a single account providing for salaries and expenses; some have additional accounts for procurement or special activities. Provisions in an unnumbered paragraph pertain only to that account unless the text provides otherwise. Funds may be transferred between accounts only with the approval of Congress.

(d) The general provisions (which may limit the use of funds or contain new legislation) have numbered sections. These provisions apply to all accounts in the act. Appropriations that cover several departments, such as Commerce-Justice-State, are divided into several separate acts, each with its own general provisions.

▶ **EXHIBIT 9-13**
Types of General Provisions

LIMITATION

Sec. 513. No funds appropriated by this Act shall be available to pay for an abortion, or the administrative expenses in connection with any health plan under the Federal employees health benefit program which provides any benefits or coverage for abortions.

Sec. 514. The provisions of section 513 shall not apply where the life of the mother would be endangered if the fetus were carried to term, or the pregnancy is the result of an act of rape or incest.

LEGISLATION

Sec. 123. Notwithstanding any other provision of law, the Secretary of the Treasury shall establish the port of Kodiak, Alaska as a port of entry and United States Customs Service personnel in Anchorage, Alaska shall serve such port of entry. There are authorized to be appropriated such sums as necessary to cover the costs associated with the performance of customs functions using such United States Customs Service personnel.

GOVERNMENTWIDE

Sec. 610. No part of any appropriation for the current fiscal year contained in this or any other Act shall be paid to any person for the filling of any position for which he or she has been nominated after the Senate has voted not to approve the nomination of said person.

Source: *Treasury and General Government Appropriations Act for Fiscal Year 1998*, P.L. 105-61.

(a) General provisions (usually numbered sections) pertain to all accounts in the appropriations act. Some appropriations acts are divided into titles, which are designated as distinct appropriations acts. In these instances, the general provisions pertain only to the particular title in which they are found.

(b) The number of general provisions has increased greatly over the past twenty years. Most are limitations or legislation; many are reenacted year after year.

(c) Limitations typically begin with language similar to that shown here: "no funds appropriated." Some limitations pertain to broad policy manners, such as the use of appropriated funds to pay for abortions; some pertain to specific matters.

(d) Legislation often begins with the words "notwithstanding any other provision of law." The purpose of this phrase is to expressly override any existing provision of law that is contrary to the new measure.

(e) The annual Treasury–Postal Service Appropriations Act contains governmentwide provisions that pertain to all appropriations and all federal agencies. Note the words "in this or any other Act."

TABLE 9-9
General Provisions in Regular Appropriations Acts, Five-Fiscal-Year Intervals, 1964–99[a]

Bill	1964	1969	1974	1979	1984	1989	1994	1999
Agriculture	7	9	8	11	4	46	28	74
Defense	41	42	46	63	111	141	175	147
District of Columbia	14	17	18	24	31	46	42	70
Energy/Public Works	13	14	7	11	20	19	9	23
Foreign Operations/Aid	20	20	17	26	1	82	75	95
HUD/Independent Offices	7	11	6	8	15	15	18	77
Interior	5	11	10	18	33	41	25	115
Labor	10	19	20	23	31	47	24	54
Legislative Branch	3	5	3	31	21	42	29	45
Military Construction	12	12	10	13	22	31	24	27
State-Justice-Commerce	15	20	19	21	22	37	31	84
Transportation	[b]	10	15	18	22	53	41	72
Treasury-Postal Service	0	2	22	29	25	87	92	101
Total	147	192	201	296	371	687	613	984[c]

Source: *United States Statutes at Large*, selected sessions, 1963–98.

a. Each numbered section, except for those with a sense of the Congress (House or Senate) provision, is counted as a general provision; administrative provisions are included in the count. Sections with a capital letter following the designation are counted as a separate section.

b. There was no separate appropriation bill for Transportation in 1964.

c. Does not include sections from the emergency supplemental section of the Omnibus Appropriations Act for fiscal 1999.

defense appropriations act sprawl over forty-six pages; the actual appropriations take fewer than twenty pages.

Appropriations Accounts

Each appropriation account specifies the purposes for which the appropriation is made and the amount appropriated (exhibit 9-14). It may also contain one or more provisions limiting or earmarking funds or changing existing law. In contrast to the general provisions, limitations or legislation embedded in an account pertain only to the money spent out of that account unless the language gives them broader application.

An appropriation that does not specify the period for which the funds are available is a one-year appropriation. The funds may be obligated only during the fiscal year mentioned in the enacting clause; they lapse if not obligated by the end of that fiscal year. Congress sometimes makes multiyear appropriations that extend the period of availability for two or more years. The current practice in defense appropriations, for example, is for research and development funds to be available for two years, procurement funds for three years, and shipbuilding money for five years. Congress also makes no-year appropriations by specifying that the funds shall remain available until expended. No-year funds may be carried over to future years indefinitely, even if they have not been obligated. Exhibit 9-15 shows examples of appropriations with different periods of availability.

Appropriations acts contain a variety of accounts that serve special purposes. These include appropriations to liquidate contract authority, limit administrative expenses paid out of certain trust funds, transfer funds from one account to another, or finance the subsidy cost of direct or guaranteed loans.

▶ **EXHIBIT 9-14**
Structure of an Appropriations Account

COAST GUARD
Operating Expenses

For necessary expenses for the operation and maintenance of the Coast Guard, not otherwise provided for; purchase of not to exceed five passenger motor vehicles for replacement only; payments pursuant to section 156 of Public Law 97-377, as amended (42 U.S.C. 402 note), and section 229(b) of Social Security Act (42 U.S.C. 429(b)); and recreation and welfare; $2,700,000,000 of which $300,000,000 shall be available for defense-related activities; and of which $25,000,000 shall be derived from the Oil Spill Liability Trust Fund: Provided, That none of the funds appropriated in this or any other Act shall be available for pay or administrative expenses in connection with shipping commissioners in the United States: Provided further, That none of the funds provided in this Act shall be available for expenses incurred for yacht documentation under 46 U.S.C. 12109, except to the extent fees are collected from yacht owners and credited to this appropriation: Provided further, That the Commandant shall reduce both military and civilian employment levels for the purpose of complying with Executive Order No. 12839: Provided further, That up to $615,000 in user fees collected pursuant to section 1111 of Public Law 104-324 shall be credited to this appropriation as offsetting collections in fiscal year 1999: Provided further, That the Secretary may transfer funds to this account, from Federal Aviation Administration "Operations," not to exceed $71,705,000 in total for the fiscal year, fifteen days after written notification to the House and Senate Committees on Appropriations solely for the purpose of providing additional funds for drug interdiction activities: Provided further, That none of the funds in this Act shall be available for the Coast Guard to plan, finalize, or implement any regulation that would promulgate new maritime user fees not specifically authorized by law after the date of enactment of this Act.

Source: *Omnibus Consolidated and Emergency Supplemental Appropriations for Fiscal Year 1999*, P.L. 105-277.

(a) This unnumbered paragraph constitutes a single appropriations account; all provisions in the paragraph pertain only to this account unless the text indicates otherwise. Appropriation accounts generally are referenced by title—in this case, Coast Guard Operating Expenses.

(b) The Coast Guard received an appropriation of $2.7 billion for all its operating expenses. Notice, however, that a portion of this money is reserved for particular purposes and additional funds may be transferred to this account from other sources.

(c) Although the appropriations language provides little detail on how the funds are to be spent, the appropriations committees' reports and other documents specify many of the particular projects and activities on which the funds are to be spent.

(d) Most of the appropriations language is taken by a series of provisions that limit or dictate the use of funds. The first such provision is written broadly to restrict the use of "funds appropriated in this or any other Act"; the text of the second restriction is more common, it only limits use of "funds appropriated in this Act." Several of the provisions exhibited here pertain to user fees.

▶ **EXHIBIT 9-15**
Period during Which Funds Are Available

ONE-YEAR

NATIONAL CEMETERY SYSTEM

For necessary expenses for the maintenance and operation of the National Cemetery System, not otherwise provided for, including uniforms or allowances therefore; cemeterial expenses as authorized by law; purchase of three passenger motor vehicles for use in cemeterial operations; and hire of passenger motor vehicles, $84,183,000.

MULTIYEAR

MEDICAL AND PROSTHETIC RESEARCH

For necessary expenses in carrying out programs of medical and prosthetic research and development as authorized by 38 U.S.C. chapter 73, to remain available until September 30, 1999, $272,000,000, plus reimbursements.

NO-YEAR (INDEFINITE)

VETERANS INSURANCE AND INDEMNITIES

For military and naval insurance, national service life insurance, servicemen's indemnities, service-disabled veterans insurance, and veterans mortgage life insurance as authorized by 38 U.S.C. chapter 19; 70 Stat. 887; 72 Stat. 487, $51,360,000, to remain available until expended.

Source: *Departments of Veterans Affairs and Housing and Urban Development and Independent Agencies Appropriations Act for Fiscal Year 1998*, P.L. 105-65.

(a) Appropriations differ in the period for which the budget authority is available for obligation. The three excerpts displayed here are one-year, multiyear, and no-year appropriations. Other variants are appropriations that become available during only a portion of a fiscal year or that become available in advance of the fiscal year for which they were made.

(b) When an appropriations account does not specify a period of availability (as in the first example here),

the funds are available for only the fiscal year specified in the enacting clause of the appropriations act.

(c) The multiyear funds exhibited here are available for one fiscal year beyond the fiscal year for which the appropriation is made. Although these funds are available for two years, the entire amount is scored as budget authority in the year covered by the appropriations act.

(d) The phrase "to remain available until expended" provides a no-year appropriation that does not have to be obligated in a particular fiscal year. The availability of these funds carries over into subsequent fiscal years even if they have not been obligated.

LEGISLATION AND LIMITATIONS IN APPROPRIATIONS ACTS

The inclusion of legislative provisions and limitations in appropriations acts has been referred to several times in this chapter. Despite the rules barring legislation in appropriations acts, the House and Senate manage to insert legislation when a majority so desires. In some cases, entire laws have been enacted in appropriations measures, but the more common practice is to insert particular provisions. Congress legislates by ignoring or waiving the rules, inserting substantive law in continuing resolutions, and making policy in the guise of limitations. Although the appropriations committees are often characterized as interlopers who disregard jurisdictional boundaries and congressional rules, they frequently are force-fed legislation sought by others. They insert legislation in some cases at the behest of authorizing committee members and other times because congressional leaders see appropriations bills as their only or best opportunity to move stalled legislation.

Limitations are another matter. These provisions, which typically begin with the phrase, "none of the funds shall be used for," have become the stock in trade of members who want to change policy through the appropriations process. Hundreds of limitations are enacted in appropriations measures each year—some in the accounts, many in general provisions. Many limitations deal with relatively minor aspects of agency operations, such as the relocation of field offices, but some deal with major or controversial issues, such as the deployment of weapons and funding of abortions. Some are straightforward restrictions on the use of appropriations; others have the barely disguised purpose of altering or blocking the implementation of federal laws.

The thin line between limitations and legislation depends on parliamentary precedents and interpretations. If a provision sets conditions on the use of appropriations or requires a federal agency or official to make a determination or take some action, it is likely to be ruled legislation. If it is negative, unconditional, and entails no action, it is likely to be ruled a limitation. Appropriations committee members (and others) are adept at wording provisions negatively so they are held to be limitations, even when the obvious purpose is to change existing policy.

INTERPRETING APPROPRIATIONS MEASURES

In carrying out their responsibilities, agencies need to know the amounts they have to spend, as well as any conditions Congress imposes on the use of funds. The text of the appropriations act usually provides some guidance, but it rarely is sufficiently detailed to cover all the matters of interest to the appropriations committees. In spending money, agencies go beyond the text of relevant appropriations to also consider other legislation, budget justifications, and the reports on appropriations bills.

Substantive Law

The basic principle laid down in the previous chapter—that appropriations must be spent according to the requirements and restrictions set in authorizing legislation—makes it essential for spenders to consult substantive laws. These laws may prescribe certain activities and prohibit others, and they often specify reports spending agencies are to file or establish priorities and funding levels for projects and activities. Authorizing law typically covers many matters not dealt with in appropriations acts: how the agency is to be organized and operate, the duties of its officials, and the manner in which finances are to be managed.

In some instances, however, authorizing law and the annual appropriations act cover the same matters but differ on the procedures or policies to be followed. The authorization may earmark funds to certain projects, the appropriations to others. One law might require that money be spent on a particular activity; the other might bar use of funds for the very same activity. In sorting out conflicts between these laws, slight differences in wording may spawn big differences in legal interpretation. Interpreting the appropriation and authorization in ways that enable the agency to satisfy both dictates can deflect collisions between laws. When conflict is unavoidable, the basic rule is that the last enacted law prevails. But agencies understand that conflicts between authorizations and appropriations are not merely matters of statutory construction; they often reflect political conflict between different committees and members. Simply following the letter of the law may not enable the agency to stay in the good graces of both the authorizers and appropriators.

Budget Justifications

Agency budget justifications normally break down the amount requested by activities and items of expenditure. The appropriations subcommittees generally expect agencies to adhere to their budget justifications to the extent practicable. Of course, agencies must disregard the justifications when the appropriations committees instruct them to spend the money in a different way. In addition, agencies sometimes deviate from the justifications by going through the reprogramming procedures discussed in the next chapter or by unilaterally making minor adjustments that do not require them to notify Congress.

Appropriations Committee Reports

The long-standing practice of the appropriations committees has been to provide detailed guidance on how funds are to be spent in their reports rather than in the body of appropriations acts. This arrangement gives both the appropriations committees and spending agencies somewhat more flexibility than if the details were enacted into law (exhibit 9-16). The reports do not comment on every agency request or item of expenditure. Guidance is most likely when the committee disagrees with the president's request or the distribution of money among activities specified by an agency in its budget justification or when it wants to earmark funds, restrict their use, or dictate agency policies or operations. Since the 1970s, guidance and earmarks have become much more detailed and numerous, leading some to complain that Congress is micromanaging agencies and denying them the freedom to operate efficiently. Regardless of whether this charge is warranted, there is ample evidence that a generation of divided government and bickering over budget policies and priorities have abraded the relationship between the appropriations committees and spending agencies.

Agencies are expected to follow the guidance of all reports (House Appropriations, Senate Appropriations, and the joint statement of managers on the conference report), except when they conflict with one another. For example, if the House report earmarks a portion of the funds in an account to project A, the Senate report earmarks to project B, and the conference report to project C, the agency is expected to allocate the specified funds to each of the projects. The same rule applies to other types of guidance in appropriations reports.

In these reports, wording is crucial because it conveys the extent to which the committee allows latitude in carrying out instructions; report language is carefully selected and sometimes is negotiated with the affected agency. The reports frequently use words such as as-

EXHIBIT 9-16
Appropriations Committee Report: Guidance to Agencies

The OMH [Office of Minority Health] is urged to make community development and coordination grants to indigenous organizations with a history of supporting community development efforts in health promotion and disease prevention that would support the development of leadership coalitions to conduct needs assessments and planning processes for the purpose of integrating HIV, STD, TB, substance abuse prevention, treatment and care services. These funds should also be used to address the HIV epidemic in the territories such as in the Virgin Islands where, for example, the HIV/AIDS case rate is more than twice the national case rate of 24.1 per 100,000.

The conference agreement expects HHS to maintain the current level of support for Meharry Medical College to continue a cooperative agreement to support the development of an integrated health delivery system in a historically underserved community, and that the Office of Minority Health should provide no more than $1,000,000 of the total amount provided for the effort. The remainder shall be provided by other agencies of HHS. The conference agreement includes funds within the Office of Minority Health to continue a study on managed care and historically minority health professions schools.

The Secretary is encouraged to work with Greater Southeast Medical Center in Southeast Washington, DC to develop a telemedicine network designed to provide access to modern health information systems.

Source: *Conference Report on the Omnibus Consolidated and Emergency Supplemental Appropriations for Fiscal Year 1999*, H. Rept. 825, 105th Cong., 2d sess., 1998, p. 1289.

(a) The reports of the House and Senate appropriations committees, which are drafted by their subcommittees, provide detailed guidance to agencies on spending appropriated funds and carrying out activities. Although report language does not have statutory effect, agencies generally heed these directives. The guidance might be positive—specifying how the funds are to be spent—or negative—directing the affected agency not to undertake certain activities or expenditures.

(b) The reports comment on most items in the appropriations bills, but they concentrate on changes from the previous year's level, earmarks, restrictions on the use of funds, and disagreements with the agency or the president's budget. For virtually all appropriations bills, report language has become more detailed and pointed than it was one or two decades earlier.

(c) The language used here to convey the committee's views is varied. Words such as "is urged," "expects," "should," and "is encouraged" (which appear in this exhibit) indicate the committee's strong interest in having its dictates implemented. Other words, such as "directs" or "requires," may convey an even stronger message, while still others—"notes" or "assumes"—might soften the guidance. But regardless of wording, the appropriations committees expect agencies to follow their guidance.

(d) This exhibit is drawn from the joint explanatory statement of the conference report on fiscal 1999 appropriations. Additional guidance appears in the reports of the House and Senate appropriations committees. As a general rule, all guidance should be followed, except when there is a conflict, in which case the conference report is determinative.

sumes, notes, requests, expects, directs, and requires. These words are not synonymous—
each has its own nuance and intent. However,
even the most permissive words offer guidance
that agencies do not lightly disregard.

What gives the appropriations reports special force is not their legal status but the fact
that the next appropriations cycle is always less
than one year away. An agency that willfully
violates report language risks retribution the
next time it asks for money. It may find this
year's report language relocated to the next appropriations act, thereby giving it even less lee-
way than it had before. Or it may find the next
time that the appropriations committees'
guidance is more detailed and onerous or that
its appropriation has been cut. The appropriations committees also punish noncompliant
agencies by writing tough limitations into the
appropriations act, cutting the agency's priority programs, trimming the offending official's
staff, issuing more earmarks, and/or curtailing
its operating flexibility. In most cases, the
committees do not have to use these weapons
because agencies comply with the report language. When they find it difficult to do so,
their best course of action is to explain their
predicament to staff (or less frequently to
members) and seek an accommodation that
satisfies the committee's interest while enabling them to run their operations. An
agency that maintains ongoing contact with
subcommittee members and staff, and consults with them on problems in implementing
report language, will obtain more flexibility
than one that acts unilaterally.

CONCLUSION

For more than two centuries, making appropriations has been a source of congressional
power and a key factor in organizing the legislative calendar. The process has always re-

volved around the annual review of spending
requests and congressional decisions on the
amounts to be made available. In making
these decisions, the appropriations committees
have usually decided on what should be provided for the next year by looking back at what
was provided for the current year.

This tradition-bound process has evolved
incrementally, with a premium placed on both
procedural continuity and program stability.
As the political-budgeting world in which they
operate was transformed, the appropriations
committees held on to tradition—retaining
the same subcommittee structure and boundaries despite the vast expansion of government, allowing each subcommittee substantial
operating autonomy, and holding on to quaint
practices. This unresponsiveness contributed
to a shrinkage of their effective jurisdiction
with the advance of entitlements and the cre-
ation of the congressional budget process.
With little choice in the matter, the committees made modest concessions to the growth of
government (by consolidating accounts), new
congressional budget rules (by fitting their
spending decisions into predetermined totals),
spending limits (by paying greater attention to
outlays), and conflict with the president (by
producing omnibus spending measures).

But even when they produce an omnibus
measure, the appropriations committees uphold tradition by treating each of the regular
appropriations bills enacted in it as if it were
separate legislation. The 950-page omnibus
appropriations act for fiscal 1999 contains
eight regular appropriations acts, dozens of
"emergency supplemental" appropriations,
and a substantial amount of unrelated legislation. The omnibus act is virtually inaccessible
to outsiders; it has no table of contents or
other information to convey when one appropriations act or substantive law ends and another begins. Furthermore, each appropria-

tions act and substantive law has its own numbering arrangement so that the same section number appears numerous times in the omnibus measure (see box 5-4). This closed world has been penetrated, however, by outsiders who have an interest in what the appropriations committees are doing. Through the Internet and other modern information technologies, it is possible to quickly locate anything in an appropriations act or report.

Tradition leaves the appropriations committees in charge, but only over the discretionary accounts. The fact that a shrinking portion of total spending is in their domain is of less consequence to the appropriations committees than that they still effectively control large amounts of money.

Traditions erode when they are at variance with practice. In the case of the appropriations process, the progressive elaboration of budget rules and the escalation of budget conflict threatened its old ways. The former calls into question the logic of annual appropriations; the latter weakens the special conflict-abating procedures and norms of the appropriations committees. In the 1990s Congress enacted caps that limited discretionary spending for each of the next five years. Arguably, multiyear caps weaken the case for annual appropriations. Why fight over marginal amounts each year when the boundaries for appropriations have been set in advance? While this issue is discussed in the last chapter, it turns out that the annual character of appropriations has as much to do with norms and behavior as with legislative calendars and fiscal years. The appropriations committees have been acculturated through two centuries of congressional work to control spending one year at a time. Making annual appropriations is what these committees do—just about the only thing they do. If Congress were to switch to two-year appropriations, the leverage exercised by

these committees vis-à-vis spending agencies and other congressional participants would be weakened. But it is highly likely that a two-year cycle would open the door to much wider use of supplemental appropriations.

Biennial appropriations would call into question the relationship of authorizing and appropriations committees. Every discretionary program has the potential for duplication of effort in Congress and friction between the two sets of committees. Duplication and conflict tend to be low for programs that have permanent authorizations and high for those that are reauthorized annually. The increase in temporary authorizations has raised the odds that authorizers and appropriators will get in each other's way, even when they go about their own business. Yet there are enormous differences in the relationships between the two types of committees—ranging from defense programs, where the armed services committees and the defense appropriations subcommittees review the same budget submissions and decide many of the same spending issues each year, to various natural resources programs, which have continued for years without significant authorizing legislation.

Because of these differences, merging the authorizations and appropriations processes would have modest impact on some programs and profound impact on others. Some have argued that merging the two sets of committees would weaken congressional spending control while generating more conflict over appropriations. If the appropriations function were folded into authorizing committees, Congress's responsibility for the federal budget would be even more fragmented than it now is. Others counter that with section 302 allocations in place, effective control can be maintained even when many committees share jurisdiction.

Combining the two processes might make for a more efficient Congress but one less open to divergent perspectives. Congress benefits from authorizing committees that emphasize program needs and objectives and from appropriating committees that emphasize costs and financial constraints. Both perspectives need to be considered in making public policy; having separate committees gives each a platform for presenting its views. If the two processes were combined, appropriations actions would be hostage to conflict over substantive legislation, and the tendency of Congress to attach unrelated riders to appropriations measures might become more pronounced.

Although change comes slowly to the appropriations processes, it does come. By increments, the process has been made more open and transparent, more partisan and program-matic, and more closely linked to overall budget policies. Many of the procedures discussed here—the statements of administration policy, section 302(b) allocations, Senate initiative on appropriations bills, omnibus spending measures, OMB's seven-day estimates on appropriations acts, and summit negotiations between presidential aides and congressional leaders across a range of spending issues—were unknown two decades ago. Even as they uphold tradition, the appropriations committees have been molded and transformed by changes in national politics and congressional institutions. Twenty years hence additional reforms will have been introduced to modernize the appropriations process and adapt it to changing conditions.

10

Managing Federal Expenditures

Appropriations are supposed to be made by the time the fiscal year begins. But even when they are delayed, the start of a fiscal year compels agencies to shift to the next stage of budgeting, which involves managing federal expenditures.

The fiscal year starts on October 1, approximately eighteen months after federal agencies began preparing their budgets and eight months after the president submitted his budget to Congress. Key conditions affecting the budget are likely to change during these long intervals. The cost of goods and services may vary from earlier estimates, turnover within agency staff will be higher or lower than expected, and new problems and priorities will come to the fore. In spending appropriated funds, agencies must adhere to congressional intent while adjusting to changing conditions and emergency needs. They must be compliant and flexible—responsive to the will of Congress and responsible for getting the job done.

Implementing the budget is a balancing act that begins before the fiscal year starts and ends after the fiscal year is over. From beginning to end, agencies make thousands of operating decisions that affect spending. Many are routine and conform to original plans, but some adjust spending plans in light of new conditions. Implementing the budget receives much less attention than do presidential and congressional actions, but what an agency does with the money appropriated to it materially affects its performance. Agency budget staffs generally spend more time and effort on this phase of the process than on any other.

Decisions made and problems encountered while executing one year's budget strongly influence future budgets. Agencies often free up resources in their current budget for seed money to initiate activities that may become priorities in the next budget cycle. They may shift staff from old tasks to new ones or redirect operating resources (such as money for contracts or consultants) to new ones. Sometimes they make the adjustments internally, without notifying congressional committees or the Office of Management and Budget (OMB). Once in a while, they formally reprogram funds and adjust their accounts to reflect the changed allocation.

Managing expenditures is decentralized; within broad rules and guidelines, each spending agency handles its own finances. The federal government is too big and its activities too diverse to centralize financial operations in a single command post. Each agency receiving appropriations or other budget resources from Congress has primary responsibility for assuring the legality, propriety, and efficiency of its expenditures. Agencies usually make their own decisions on these matters, but they sometimes consult the General Accounting Office (GAO), which serves as the government's principal auditing and evaluation agency, or OMB, which shares responsibility with the Treasury Department for financial management. OMB's role in executing the budget is necessarily selective and limited. On any particular matter, it may intervene to guide the use of federal dollars, but it is much too small to oversee all transactions. Each agency has its own budget and accounting staffs; major subunits are also staffed with budget and finance specialists.

The next section of this chapter traces the normal sequence in which funds are spent as in-

tended by the appropriation, as well as variances from the normal pattern due to reprogramming, impoundment, and other actions. The second section examines financial management practices in federal agencies, including the relationship of budgeting and accounting, internal control, and changes spurred by the Chief Financial Officers Act of 1990 and the Government Performance and Results Act of 1993.

SPENDING BUDGET RESOURCES

Appropriated funds are not instantly available to agencies. The Antideficiency Act requires that appropriations be apportioned by periods within the fiscal year (typically by quarters) or among the projects to be undertaken. The purpose of apportionment is to deter agencies from spending at a rate that would exhaust their budget resources before the end of the fiscal year. In some instances, such as for national defense and threats to health and safety, funds may be apportioned at a rate that would necessitate supplemental appropriations.

The amount apportioned may not exceed the amount available for obligation. Only unobligated resources are subject to apportionment. Apportionment is managed by OMB, which reviews the requests agencies submit via the form shown in exhibit 10-1. This form has a complete listing of the types of unobligated budget resources in each fund or account. These resources may derive from current or permanent appropriations, transfers from other accounts, direct spending, unobligated balances carried forward from previous years, income earned from user charges, and other sources. OMB may withhold resources from apportionment but must report any such action to Congress via the impoundment procedures discussed later in this chapter.

Although apportionment is largely a technical procedure, it is the last point at which

EXHIBIT 10-1
Apportionment of Budgetary Resources

Description	Amount on Latest S.F. 132	Agency Request	Action by OMB
BUDGETARY RESOURCES			
1. Budget authority:			
A. Appropriations			
B. Borrowing authority			
C. Contract authority			
D. Net transfers, current year authority (+ or −)			
E. Other			
2. Unobligated balance:			
A. Brought forward October 1			
B. Net transfers prior year balance, actual (+ or −)			
C. Anticipated transfers prior year balance (+ or −)			
3. Spending authority from offsetting collections (Gross):			
A. Earned:			
1. Collected			
2. Receivable from Federal sources			
***			
4. Recoveries of prior year obligations:			
A. Actual			
B. Anticipated			
5. Temporarily not available pursuant to P.L. ———— (−)			
6. Permanently not available:			
A. Cancellations of expired and no-year accounts (−)			
B. Enacted rescissions of prior year balances (−)			
***			
7. TOTAL BUDGETARY RESOURCES			
APPLICATION OF BUDGETARY RESOURCES			
8. Apportioned:			
Category A:			
(1) First quarter			
(2) Second quarter			
(3) Third quarter			
(4) Fourth quarter			
***			
9. Withheld pending rescission			
10. Deferred			
11. Unapportioned balance of revolving fund			
12. TOTAL BUDGETARY RESOURCES			

Source: OMB Standard Form 132, September 1995.

(a) Standard Form 132 shows the amount requested for apportionment by the agency and OMB's decision. A single apportionment is made for each appropriation or fund account.

(b) The top part of this form (lines 1–7) itemizes all the resources available for apportionment; the bottom part (lines 8–12) shows apportionments by quarter or project and amounts withheld from apportionment. The total on line 12 must equal the total on line 7.

OMB formally controls agency spending. OMB sometimes uses apportionment to impose conditions on agency spending or to demand changes in agency practices.

Allotment

OMB makes a single apportionment for each appropriation account or fund; it does not formally subdivide the money among programs or organizational units, although it may advise them that particular funds are to be used for specified purposes. However, agencies need to notify program managers of the resources that will be available to them during the year. This information is provided through allotments, which distribute funds among bureaus, divisions, field offices, and other organizational subunits. Allotment procedures vary among agencies—they tend to be formal in large agencies, informal in small ones—and the total allotted may not exceed the OMB apportionment.

The allotment gives each operating unit its budget for the fiscal year. Within its allotment, a unit hires and pays staff, purchases supplies and equipment, and keeps track of its obligations. In most agencies, units do not have to obtain approval from headquarters before taking these actions, although special circumstances may intervene to restrict spending discretion. For example, an agency concerned that available resources will not suffice through the fiscal year might impose a hiring freeze or take back some of the money allotted to subunits at the start of the year. Normally, however, program managers can plan for the full year based on allotted resources.

Allotments, like much of the information agencies produce in the course of implementing their budgets, are not confidential, but neither are they public. Nowadays allotments are usually held in computerized data bases and distributed internally as printouts that are updated throughout the year to show the status of obligations and other spending actions. These internal budgets have more program and financial detail than is available in public budget documents. They show the money flows within departments, how funds are parceled among programs and activities, and provide insights into how the department is structured and operates.

Obligations

Once funds have been allocated, managers may obligate them. An obligation is an agency's binding commitment to another party concerning goods or services to be provided, amounts to be paid, and other material elements of the transaction. Internal actions, such as setting aside funds for particular purposes, are not bona fide obligations. Each obligation has to be supported by documents—such as purchase orders, signed contracts, letters of credit, or personnel records—attesting to the commitment.

Funds may be obligated only during the period that they are available. Beyond that period the funds lapse and authority to obligate expires. In addition, exhibit 10-2 shows that the obligation must be related to the purpose for which the appropriation was made. In recent times, some appropriations subcommittees have insisted that agencies within their jurisdiction spend funds according to the detailed justification schedules prepared for the appropriation hearings.

Agencies generally have accurate and timely information on the status of obligations. They know that overobligation violates the Antideficiency Act and that underobligation may cause them to lose resources. As the fiscal year winds down, agencies closely monitor obligations to ensure that virtually all remaining funds are used.

> **EXHIBIT 10-2**
> **Comptroller General Decision on Propriety of Expenditure**

The Principal Deputy General Counsel of the Central Intelligence Agency (CIA) requests our opinion on the propriety of using appropriated funds to purchase refrigerators for placement in the workplace. For the reasons stated below, should the CIA administratively determine that equipping the workplace with the refrigerators is reasonably related to the efficient performance of agency activities, we would not object to the CIA using appropriated funds to purchase refrigerators for the workplace. . . .

The issue here is whether the purchase of refrigerators may be considered a "necessary expense" of operating the facility. The general rule is that where an appropriation is not specifically available for a particular item, its purchase may be authorized as a "necessary expense" if there is a reasonable relationship between the object of the expenditure and the general purposes for which the funds were appropriated and the expenditure is not otherwise prohibited. B-210433, April 15, 1983. This rule of reason recognizes an agency's discretion in using its appropriation to fulfill its purpose.

We have addressed situations analogous to the one presented here. In 47 Comp. Gen. 657 (1968), we objected to the purchase of a coffee maker and related items because a purpose of the purchase was to enable the agency to provide coffee at meetings to its employees and others. We reached a different result where the agency determined that the purchase was necessary to compensate for a lack of available eating facilities. . . .

Accordingly, we would not object to the purchase of refrigerators should CIA administratively determine that equipping the headquarters facility with refrigerators is reasonably related to the efficient performance of agency activities, and not just for the personal convenience of individual employees.

Source: Comptroller General of the United States, *Central Intelligence Agency—Availability of Appropriations to Purchase Refrigerators for Placement in the Workplace*, B-276601, 158619, June 26, 1997.

(a) In most cases, spending agencies make their own decisions, based on accumulated precedents on the legality and propriety of expenditures.

(b) In the decision excerpted here, the issue was referred by the CIA to the comptroller general, who made an authoritative decision, which then may serve as precedent for other decisions.

(c) A key issue in this and many other rulings is whether the expenditure would benefit the government or only its employees. If only the latter benefit, the expenditure might be disallowed as not being a "necessary expense" that is reasonably related to the performance of agency activities. In this case, the comptroller general held that the purchase of refrigerators is a permissible public expense because it would enhance employee performance.

Guarding against overobligation depends not only on timely information, but also on prudent financial management. At the start of a fiscal year, many agencies compare the resources on hand with the amounts projected for salaries, supplies, and other operating expenses to determine whether they have enough to last through the year. Many make conservative assumptions, such as low turnover, and set aside money for unbudgeted contingencies. They often slow spending on contracts, equipment, and other discretionary items to ensure that they are not caught short before the year is over. As the fiscal year nears a close, many agencies find that they have been overly cautious and risk losing unspent funds. At this point, they typically accelerate spending on matters treated more conservatively earlier, leading them to obligate a large proportion of contract and procurement money during the last months of the fiscal year. Although the resulting year-end bulge in spending may appear to be wasteful, it is often the result of prudent financial management.

Outlays

Once the goods or services for which funds were obligated have been provided, the obligation is paid off and the amount is recorded as an outlay on agency accounts. Outlays are normally processed through administrative routines that are handled by disbursement offices, not by program managers. Payments are made pursuant to vouchers or invoices that indicate the account from which the funds are drawn, the payee, amount to be paid, and other relevant information. Before payment, the spending agency preaudits vouchers to determine that the amount is correct, the goods and services have been provided according to specification, and the account or fund from which the payment is to be made is available for that purpose. Nowadays most payments

are made in electronic form through disbursing offices operated by Treasury.

Agencies prepare monthly budget execution reports, detailing the volume of obligations and outlays during the latest month and cumulatively during the fiscal year. In addition to these reports, each agency maintains its own accounts, which are much more detailed than those recorded on a governmentwide basis.

Although outlays come too late in the expenditure process to be an effective instrument of financial control, they cannot be ignored in managing federal expenditures. The timing and rate of outlays are important to the Treasury for managing the government's cash and debt. Also, the difference between outlays and receipts determines the size of the budget surplus or deficit. As long as the federal budget is accounted for on a cash basis, outlays will exert a strong influence on budget actions.

Closing Accounts

The final step in the spending process is the closing of appropriations accounts. When an account is closed, all remaining balances are canceled and are no longer available for expenditure. Fixed accounts (those whose budget resources are available for obligation for a limited period) are closed according to a preset schedule. No-year funds that are available without a time limit remain open until all budget resources have been depleted or canceled.

The procedures for closing fixed accounts stretch over six or more fiscal years. The account is open during the period that funds are available for obligation—one year in the case of most appropriations. When this period ends, the account is in *expired* status for five years, during which no new obligations may be incurred but old ones are paid off as they become due. At the end of the five years, the account is *closed*, and any remaining balance is canceled.

Deviations from Spending Plans

The sequence of steps from apportionment through the closing of accounts sometimes occurs as provided for in annual appropriations. Often, however, these plans are altered during implementation of the budget, and resources are augmented, diminished, or shifted from one purpose to another. Some of these actions are taken by Congress, others by the spending agency. Some of the variances are intended to change policy; most are means of coping with needs and opportunities that arise during the year.

Supplemental Appropriations

A supplemental appropriation provides additional funding after the regular appropriation has been enacted. Supplemental funds may be provided for unanticipated needs or to cover a shortfall. As recently as the 1980s, agencies routinely received supplementals if they faced a shortage. Because the president's budget and regular appropriations are based on the current rather than the next year's federal pay scale, the practice was to finance annual pay increases in a supplemental. In the course of compiling this measure, the president typically requested, and Congress provided, additional money for other purposes as well. Congress also voted supplemental funds for emergencies and other unanticipated needs.

The discretionary spending caps crimped supplemental appropriations; these became less common in the 1990s than was previously the case. Agencies were expected to absorb pay increases and other unbudgeted expenses out of their regular appropriations.

Transfers and Reprogrammings

Nowadays agencies frequently finance unbudgeted needs by shifting funds within appropri-ations. These shifts are *transfers* when budget resources move from one account to another and *reprogrammings* when budget resources are switched from one activity to another within the same account.

Inasmuch as an appropriation is a legal limit on expenditure, funds may be transferred only pursuant to statutory authorization. Congress sometimes authorizes designated departments, such as the Defense Department, to transfer up to a certain amount or percentage of their appropriations among their accounts. An agency granted general transfer authority is usually required to notify relevant congressional committees when it moves funds from one account to another. In other instances Congress directs certain agencies to transfer a portion of their appropriation to other agencies. When funds are transferred, the receiving account (whose resources are augmented) must abide by any restrictions or conditions pertaining to the original appropriation. For example, if one-year money is transferred to an account that has no-year funds, the transferred money retains its one-year status.

Transfers are easy to monitor because some accounts lose resources and others gain. Transfer inflows and outflows are recorded in the program and financing schedules (see exhibit 5-4) published in the president's budget and in the apportionment schedule shown in exhibit 10-1. Reprogrammings, however, may be difficult to identify because appropriation accounts are not broken down by program. Reprogramming practices are affected by the definition of programs and by guidelines provided in appropriations bills or in the committee reports accompanying these bills. There are no governmentwide reprogramming rules (the rules vary considerably among the appropriations subcommittees), nor is there a comprehensive register of these actions. Some rules only require that the relevant subcommittees be given advance notice of reprogrammings; others require advance approval by the sub-committees (and in some cases by the cognizant authorizing committees as well). In still others, the reprogramming takes effect unless the relevant committees or subcommittees disapprove it during a waiting period. Exhibit 10-3 shows some appropriations subcommittees' reprogramming rules and practices.

Over the past two decades there has been a marked tightening of reprogramming rules. Matters that once were handled informally now have prescribed procedures and reporting requirements; matters that once required only notification now require advance approval. Reprogramming thresholds—the amount of money above which the reprogramming rules are triggered—have been set very low for some agencies. Box 10-1 highlights a reprogramming conflict between the Department of Veterans Affairs and the Senate VA-HUD Appropriations Subcommittee. The agency maintained that it did not violate reprogramming rules when it shifted funds without notifying Congress, but a GAO investigation concluded otherwise—that the shift in funds should have been reported to the subcommittee.

In a typical year, federal agencies report a total of fewer than one thousand reprogrammings. Most of these are concentrated in a few areas, such as defense and foreign assistance. Yet agencies are constantly moving funds from one use to another, juggling resources in response to pressures or opportunities encountered during the year. If all such adjustments were reported, the number of reprogrammings would add up to many thousands.

Why are there so few formal reprogrammings? Part of the answer lies in the broad scope of appropriations. At one time appropriations were extremely detailed; everything from authorized positions to supplies and travel were itemized. This type of appropria-

tion narrowed agency discretion and restricted their freedom in shifting funds. But as the size and scope of government grew, appropriations were progressively consolidated into broad accounts so that many agencies now receive a lump sum for all salaries and operating expenses. Although the appropriations committees earmark or direct the use of funds in their reports, agencies have considerable flexibility in using appropriations, and they exercise this discretion routinely without calling formal reprogramming procedures into play. But when the appropriations committees demand that a particular shift be classified as a reprogramming, agencies must behave accordingly. As a general rule, reprogramming is taking funds from a "program, project, or activity" (these usually are specified annually in appropriation committee reports) or from a "congressional interest" item—an expenditure mentioned in the text of the appropriations act or the appropriation committee reports.

Reprogramming operates in a murky area of executive-legislative relations. Many are undertaken under an arrangement that permits the appropriations committees to review and block the proposed shift of funds. This "committee veto" is exercised despite the 1983 Supreme Court ruling in *INS* v. *Chadha* that all legislative vetoes violate the Constitution. A legislative veto gives the House, the Senate, or both the power to disapprove a pending executive action. Arguably, if vetoes by the House or Senate are unconstitutional, then vetoes by congressional committees should be as well. Nevertheless, committee review of reprogramming and of many other types of executive action has become common during the years since the *Chadha* decision.

Committee vetoes flourish because they are part of a quid pro quo in which Congress gives agencies discretion in exchange for retaining authority to review and disapprove proposed ac-

▶ EXHIBIT 10-3
Reprogramming Law and Practice

LAW: DEFENSE APPROPRIATIONS ACT

No part of the funds in this Act shall be available to prepare or present a request to the Committees on Appropriations for reprogramming of funds, unless for higher priority items, based on the unforeseen military requirements, than those for which originally appropriated and in no case where the item for which reprogramming is requested has been denied by the Congress.

PRACTICE: HOUSE APPROPRIATIONS COMMITTEE REPORT

The Committee's perspective is one of ensuring that the funds made available in appropriations acts are in fact put to the use intended by the elected members of Congress, under the terms and conditions the Congress and the House and Senate Appropriations Committees place on the funding in question. . . . Regrettably, in recent years the Committee has observed a steady erosion of [Defense Department] compliance with these standards. . . .

In its fiscal year 2000 budget the Air Force acquisition community continues to blithely ignore specific Committee direction and law intended to ensure that funds appropriated for one purpose—for example, weapons procurement—are in fact used for that purpose and not for other efforts, such as research and development by:

1) Requesting hundreds of millions of dollars in various procurement programs, when in fact the intended use is to support operation and maintenance funding needs (in violation of DoD policy). . . .

Sources: *Department of Defense Appropriations Act for Fiscal Year 2000*, P.L. 106-79; and *Department of Defense Appropriations Bill for Fiscal Year 2000*, H. Rept. 244, 106th Cong., 1st sess., 1999, pp. 8–9.

(a) There are no governmentwide reprogramming rules; each set of appropriations subcommittees provides guidelines for the agencies in their jurisdiction. Sometimes (as in the first entry above), the guidelines are in the appropriations act, sometimes in the appropriations committee report. Pursuant to these directives, each agency has procedures for initiating reprogrammings and (when required) submitting them for congressional review.

(b) The rule exhibited here reflects a trend to more restrictive reprogramming procedures. Typical restrictions pertain to using programs to start or eliminate other programs or to finance an activity for which Congress denied an appropriations request.

(c) The report excerpted here sharply criticizes the Defense Department for violating reprogramming rules by starting new activities, using funds to continue programs terminated by Congress, and asking more than needed for one purpose in order to shift money to another purpose.

(d) Pursuant to these findings, the appropriations committees tightened the reprogramming rules for the Defense Department.

▼

BOX 10-1
Reprogramming Wars: Who Controls the Details of Federal Spending

For two centuries Congress and federal agencies have vied for control of the details of expenditure. Claiming the constitutionally prescribed power of the purse, Congress often insists that agencies spend money according to the fine print in appropriations acts and committee reports. But claiming that they need flexibility in carrying out authorized activities, agencies often deviate from the precise spending plan approved by Congress. Who wins this battle tells us a great deal about legislative-executive relations at different points in history.

The reprogramming rules prescribed by the VA-HUD Appropriations Subcommittees reflect congressional insistence that it control the details. The following report language was inserted in Senate Appropriations reports during the 1990s:

"The Committee continues to have a particular interest in being informed of reprogrammings which, although they may not change either the total amount available in an account or any of the purposes for which the appropriation is legally available, represent a significant departure from budget plans presented to the Committee in an agency's budget justifications. Consequently, the Committee directs the Departments of Veterans' Affairs and Housing and Urban Development, and the agencies funded through this bill, to notify the chairman of the Committee prior to each reprogramming of funds in excess of $250,000 between programs, activities, or elements unless an alternative amount for the agency or department in question is specified elsewhere in this report. The Committee desires to be notified of reprogramming actions which involve less than the above-mentioned amounts if such actions would have the effect of changing an agency's funding requirements in future years or if programs or projects specifically cited in the Committee's reports are affected."

This language is extraordinarily restrictive in a number of ways. First, it has a very low threshold—$250,000—for notifying the appropriations committee of reprogramming. Second, it defines reprogramming to include actions that do not change the purpose of appropriations. Third, it requires that the committee be informed of reprogramming below this amount that would change future funding requirements.

continued

tions (such as reprogramming). If Congress were barred from exercising this veto, it would probably withhold discretion from agencies and give them less flexibility in managing their budgets.

Impoundment

In addition to limiting the amounts that may be spent, appropriations establish the strong expectation that the funds Congress provides will be spent on planned activities. When an agency impounds—refuses to use all or part of an appropriation—it violates congressional intent. For example, if Congress were to appropriate $5 billion for education grants to states but the government spent only $4 billion, Congress's intent would go unfulfilled.

Most postwar presidents impounded some

▼
BOX 10-1
Continued

Despite these rules, the Department of Veterans Affairs (VA) shifted funds among line items without going through reprogramming procedures. A 1999 investigation by the General Accounting Office (GAO) found that during fiscal years 1993 through 1998, VA used $61 million of travel funds on other operating expenses, such as salaries and equipment. According to the GAO report, VA systematically overestimated travel costs in preparing its annual budget and then switched the excess funds to other object classes (see exhibit 5-6 for a list of object classes). GAO took the position that these reprogrammings should have been reported to the appropriations committees; VA argued that the reprogramming rules refer to shifts between "programs, activities, or elements," not to shifts between object classes. In a letter to the GAO disagreeing with its conclusions, VA wrote that it

"maintains an open dialogue with the Appropriations Committee staff. Over the years we have agreed that reprogramming requirements would apply to the major program activity components listed in the Program and Financing Schedule contained in the Appendix to the President's budget. . . . At no time was VA's interpretation of congressional expectations regarding reprogrammings challenged. . . . Redefining reprogramming requirements to apply to an object class level is inconsistent with the objectives of the Government Performance and Results Act and reinvention efforts, which encourage a focus on the performance not the categories of expenses."

Despite its view that the VA action constituted a reprogramming, GAO noted that the report language "does not have the force and effect of law and is not legally binding on an agency." If the same language were in the text of an appropriations act (as in exhibit 10-3), it would have a stronger legal basis. Why then do appropriations committees use report language rather than law? Possibly because they want to give affected agencies more flexibility. Why then do they criticize agencies for exercising their flexibility, as VA did? Possibly because they still want agencies to know that Congress controls the purse. Having it both ways generates friction between spending agencies and the committees, but it also establishes conditions under which they coexist, not always in peace, but with enough mutual accommodation that each can get on with its work until the next battle.

appropriated funds, but their actions were limited to particular projects. The volume of impoundments escalated during the Vietnam War, when Lyndon Johnson sought to dampen an overheated economy by withholding some expenditures. Impoundment became a full-scale political battleground in the early 1970s, when Richard Nixon refused to spend billions of dollars Congress had added to his budget. Nixon claimed an inherent power to impound, but many in Congress insisted that the president must spend appropriated money—even when doing so would mean higher total spending (or a bigger deficit) than he wanted. To resolve this conflict, the Impoundment Control Act of 1974 (enacted in the same measure as the Congressional Budget Act) prescribed rules and procedures for dealing with cases in which the president or an executive official withholds budget resources.

Due to its eroded relationship with Nixon, Congress defined impoundment in exceedingly broad terms as any "action or inaction" that delays or withholds funds. This language could be read to include routine financial operations, such as a delay in awarding a contract to check the vendor's reliability. In practice, however, impoundment is narrowly applied to actions whose purpose is to curtail spending; actions that only incidentally affect the amount spent are not treated as impoundments. The line between routine financial management and impoundment is not always clear, and disputes sometimes arise as to how particular actions should be handled. One area of controversy is known as *de facto impoundment*—a situation in which the federal agency does not directly slow the rate of spending but takes indirect action that has the same effect. Suppose, for example, that an agency drags its feet in hiring examiners to process disability claims. The effect will be to reduce the amount spent on these claims. Should this tactic be treated as an impoundment? Program advocates typically argue that it should, but OMB rarely reports it as an impoundment.

The 1974 act divides impoundment into two categories and prescribes distinct procedures for each. A *deferral* delays the use of funds; a *rescission* cancels budget authority. Every impoundment is either a deferral or a rescission; it cannot be both or something else.

When the president defers funds, he submits a message to Congress setting forth the amount, the program and account affected, the estimated fiscal and program impact, and the length of time the funds are to be deferred (exhibit 10-4). The president may not defer funds beyond the end of the fiscal year nor for a duration that would cause the budget authority to lapse or prevent the agency from spending the

money prudently. The original Impoundment Control Act permitted the president to defer funds for policy reasons—for example, because he opposes a particular program or wants to spend less than Congress appropriated. In exchange for giving the president this broad authority, Congress reserved for itself the power to disapprove any deferral by vote of the House or Senate. This arrangement was one of the legislative vetoes invalidated by the *Chadha* decision. In response to its loss of the legislative veto, Congress took away much of the president's deferral power. Under current rules, the president may defer spending only for the specific reasons permitted by the Antideficiency Act: to provide for contingencies or to achieve savings made possible through changes in requirements or efficiency in operations. The president may not use the deferral power to change budget or program policies. The comptroller general reviews each impoundment message and notifies Congress concerning the accuracy of the information, the legal status of the impoundment, and the probable impacts. If Congress does not enact a rescission bill within "45 days of continuous session," the president must release the funds. If not, the comptroller general may sue to compel their release.

The deferral rules demonstrate reciprocity in executive-legislative relations. When Congress retained the capacity to uphold its position by reviewing executive policies, it granted the president power to defer. But when Congress was denied that capacity, it curtailed presidential power. Both branches were weakened: the president had less control of federal finances; Congress had less ability to influence executive actions.

Rescission

The relationship between the president and Congress is different in rescissions, and so too

▶ EXHIBIT 10-4
Presidential Rescissions Message

Rescission Proposal No. R98-10

PROPOSED RESCISSION OF BUDGET AUTHORITY
Report Pursuant to Section 1012 of P.L. 93-344

Agency: Department of Agriculture	New budget authority $1,348,377,000 (P.L. 105-83)
Bureau: Forest Service	Other budgetary resources $270,000,000 Total budgetary resources $1,618,377,000
Appropriations title and symbol: National forest system 12X1106	Amount proposed for rescission $1,094,000
OMB identification code: 12-1106-0-1-302	*Legal authority (in addition to sec. 1012):* __x__ Antideficiency Act _____ Other
Grant program: _____ Yes __x__ No	*Type of budget authority:*
Type of account or fund: _____ Annual _____ Multi-year _____ __x__ No-Year *(expiration date)*	__x__ Appropriation _____ Contract authority _____ Other _____

Justification: The national forest system (NFS) provides for the delivery of goods and services associated with the principal NFS programs of land management planning, inventory, and monitoring; recreation use; law enforcement; general administration; and management of: wildlife and fisheries habitat; rangeland; forestland; soil, water, and air; minerals and geology; landownership; infrastructure. The proposed rescission is based on the affected program's FTE level and an estimate of its impact on the Department's civil rights resources, and is intended to offset supplemental appropriations for the Department's Civil Rights initiative. This action is taken pursuant to the Antideficiency Act (31 U.S.C. 1512).

Outlay Effect (in thousands of dollars)

1998 Outlay Estimate		Outlay Changes					
Without Rescission	With Rescission	FY 1998	FY 1999	FY 2000	FY 2001	FY 2002	FY 2003
1,400,000	1,399,070	−930	−164	. . .	. . .	. . .	. . .

Source: *Proposed Rescission of Budgetary Resources,* H. Doc. 215, 105th Cong., 2d sess., February 24, 1998.

(a) The president notifies Congress of every proposed rescission or deferral in a message that sets forth the reasons for the action and the estimated program and financial effects. The message exhibited here deals with rescissions; a similar one is used for deferrals. If the president fails to report an impoundment, the comptroller general may notify Congress. This notification has the same legal status as a presidential message.

(b) Every proposed rescission and deferral is assigned an alphanumeric identification. Rescissions are prefaced with the letter "R" and deferrals with the letter "D." The proposed rescission here, R98-10, was the tenth reported for fiscal 1998.

are the rules. The president may propose a rescission by submitting a message to Congress specifying the amount to be rescinded, the reasons, the accounts and programs involved, and the estimated budgetary and program impacts. After receiving the message, Congress has forty-five days of continuous session (usually a larger number of calendar days) during which it may consider a bill rescinding all, part, or none of the funds.

If Congress does not rescind the budget resources by the end of the forty-five days, the president must release the funds and make them available for obligation. The comptroller general, who reviews all proposed rescissions and deferrals, may bring suit to compel the release of the impounded funds, but this has been a rare occurrence.

The president's record on rescissions is a measure of his budgetary influence and of his standing with Congress. The high-water mark for president-initiated rescissions came in fiscal 1981 and 1982, when Ronald Reagan proposed more than $23 billion in cancellations shortly after he became president, and Congress rescinded more than 65 percent of his request. Table 10-1 indicates that Reagan's rescissions amounted to nearly two-thirds of the total rescinded pursuant to presidential request since the impoundment process was initiated in 1974. Over the years Congress has enacted only one-third of the rescissions proposed by the president. With fiscal 1981 and 1982 excluded, the rescission approval rate would drop below 20 percent.

Rescissions stir conflict between the president and Congress. Every rescission the White House requests is a demand that Congress cancel resources it previously appropriated. By implication, and sometimes by press release as well, proposed rescissions make the point that Congress erred when it appropriated the money. This is not a message that appeals to

legislators, especially when it comes from a president who has different budget priorities. In this contest, Congress has the advantage because the president must release the money if it refuses to pass a rescission bill. Over the past quarter of a century, presidents have been compelled to spend more than $50 billion of the $76 billion they wanted rescinded.

Table 10-1 also suggests that Congress has another advantage in these budget wars. It can rescind funds on its own initiative—without waiting for a presidential request—simply by passing a bill canceling previous appropriations. In fact, for every dollar Congress has rescinded pursuant to the president's impoundment request, it has rescinded four dollars by enacting legislation on its own initiative. At first glance, this behavior may seem puzzling. Why would Congress take the initiative in rescinding funds it had appropriated? Why, if it does not like rescissions requested by the president, has it been so active on its own? The puzzle evaporates when it is recognized that Congress initiates rescissions either to thwart the president or to make room in the budget for other expenditures. When Congress refuses to approve a president's rescission, he can portray it as a cabal of spendthrift politicians who think nothing of wasting taxpayer money. To buffer itself against this charge, Congress sometimes rescinds items other than those the president wanted. It may even rescind more than the president requested, taking care to cancel spending on his priorities. In 1992, for example, George Bush proposed almost $8 billion in rescissions, indicating that he would demand additional rescissions as the year progressed and the presidential election neared. Congress rescinded about $2 billion of the amount requested, but it then added another $22 billion of rescissions into the pot, taking money from his priorities rather than from areas he wanted cut. Bush

TABLE 10-1
Rescissions by Presidential and Congressional Initiative, 1974–98

Millions of dollars unless otherwise specified

President	Fiscal years	Presidential initiative			Congressional initiative	
		Amount proposed for rescission	Amount rescinded	Percent rescinded	Amount rescinded	Percent of total rescinded
Ford	1974–77	7,935	1,252	16	1,405	53
Carter	1977–81	4,608	2,116	46	3,526	62
Reagan	1981–89	43,437	15,657	36	33,400	68
Bush	1989–93	13,293	2,354	18	26,821	92
Clinton	1993–98	6,586	3,611	55	39,742	92
Total	1974–98	75,859	24,990	33	104,894	81

Source: U.S. General Accounting Office, *Impoundment Control Act: Use and Impact of Rescission Procedures*, GAO/T–OGC–99–56, July 30, 1999.

got the message and refrained from proposing additional rescissions.

Congress may also generate rescissions when the budget is tight and it wants to make room for additional spending. In some years Congress has rescinded funds to pay for supplemental spending without exceeding the discretionary caps; in others it has used rescissions as "earnest money" to show that even though it is spending more than the president wants, the additional amount has been offset by canceling old appropriations. Many congressionally initiated rescissions are of dormant or inactive funds, such as for weapons systems that have been delayed by technical problems or housing funds that have been reserved for future use.

Because they were devised during the Vietnam/Watergate era, when Congress was determined to rein in presidential power, the current rescission rules favor Congress. Some have suggested that the president's hand should be strengthened by forcing Congress to vote up or down on every requested rescission. This "expedited rescission authority" would

still give Congress the last word, but it would no longer be able to win by inaction. However, inasmuch as the prevailing arrangements let Congress win by doing nothing, it has been unwilling to change the rescission rules.

MANAGING AGENCY FINANCES

Implementing the budget not only entails spending the money; it also means using resources efficiently and having timely and accurate information on the financial status and performance of programs and accounts. Implementing the budget brings into play financial accounting and reporting, management and internal control systems, performance measurement, and audit and evaluation. OMB has defined financial management to include systems that collect, analyze, and report data for financial decisionmaking, that control and account for financial transactions and resources, and that generate financial information in support of agency missions. Financial management goes beyond budget formulation and execution; it also includes property and inventory control, managing grants and contracts, debt and cash management, personnel and payroll systems, and procurement practices. Only those elements of financial management closely linked to budgeting are discussed here.

Fragmentation in Financial Management

It would be misleading to speak of a single financial management system for the federal government. Instead, there are many systems and even more subsystems within them—some operating independently, some coupled together. During the 1990s, emphasis was placed on integrating financial management systems, but this proved to be a time-consuming and sometimes frustrating task. Table 10-2 sets forth the responsibilities of major federal entities in financial management. The picture that emerges is of many participants, both at the center of government and in federal agencies, each with its own niche and ways of going about its work. In sharp contrast to the many countries that entrust a broad range of financial responsibilities to the treasury or finance ministry, the United States splinters key functions among several entities. OMB has the lead role in compiling the budget and overseeing federal expenditures, the Treasury reports on the financial operations and condition of government, and the General Accounting Office reviews agency accounting systems and financial statements. Over the years these entities have cooperated through the Joint Financial Management Improvement Program (JFMIP), a small unit that disseminates information on developments in financial management.

Fragmentation is built into the structure of the federal government. GAO works mostly for Congress, though it also has an array of quasi-judicial and administrative responsibilities. OMB serves the president and uses its budget powers to advance his policies and objectives. The Treasury is responsible for collecting taxes and managing the government's vast portfolio of debt. Each has a distinctive perspective on the critical features of financial management. The budget is at the center of OMB's universe, with management ancillary to this core activity. GAO's world revolves around the review and evaluation of federal programs, and it views management as a tool for upholding legality and prudence in the use of public money. The Treasury handles cash flows and maintains governmentwide accounting systems, for which it needs consistent and reliable data.

Accounting and Budgeting

For decades, fragmentation resulted in weak coordination of budgeting and accounting, with each operating in its own sphere and having its own way of counting money. It was not supposed to be this way, for the Budget and Accounting Act of 1921 conceived of budgeting and accounting as interdependent processes. The budget would provide the basis for the accounting structure, and the accounting system would provide data for budget decisions. Over the years, however, budgeting and accounting drifted apart: the former was oriented toward obligations, the latter to cash and resources consumed. Budgeting was forward looking, a means of planning the programs and objectives of government. Accounting was backward looking, a means of recording transactions that had already occurred. The two were usually lodged in separate organizational units, and their data often were incompatible.

Moreover, accounting itself fragmented into numerous specialized systems. Beginning with budget and accounting legislation enacted in 1950 and 1956 and continuing into

TABLE 10-2
Major Financial Management Roles and Responsibilities, by Entity

Entity	Budget execution	Audit and evaluation	Financial management systems
Congress	Acts on supplementals, impoundments, and reprogrammings; sometimes monitors activities or expenditures	Imposes reporting requirements; conducts oversight; requests audits and evaluations from GAO and others	Establishes accounting structure; legislates policy on financial management systems and practices
Office of Management and Budget	Apportions budget resources; maintains full-time equivalent controls; monitors agency performance	Reviews agency spending and programs; focuses on high-risk areas; promotes performance measurement	Issues directives on management control, financial management systems, and other management practices; oversees CFO and GPRA implementation
Treasury	Manages cash and debt; matches spending against resources	None	Maintains governmentwide accounting system
Agencies	Spend resources and carry out activities; report to Congress, OMB, and others	Conduct internal audits and evaluations; respond to congressional and executive requests; compare planned and actual performance	Design and use financial management systems; maintain management controls; report on material weaknesses
Agency chief financial officer	Monitors financial execution of budget	Prepares financial statements, including data on performance	Promotes integration of accounting and budgeting systems
General Accounting Office	Reviews and reports on impoundments; settles certain claims	Reviews programs and operations; audits financial statements of government corporations	Certifies agency accounting systems; advises Congress on material weaknesses in internal control systems
Inspector General	None	Audits financial statements; investigates spending and other actions; evaluates programs	Recommends changes to improve systems and performance
Federal Accounting Standards Advisory Board	None	None	Formulates accounting standards and principles

the 1980s, agencies were encouraged to devise accounting systems that served their particular needs. Within large departments, individual bureaus and operating units were permitted to customize their accounting systems. This decentralized framework resulted in the federal government operating hundreds of separate systems that were unable to communicate with one another. It was not uncommon for the various systems to record transactions inconsistently and for the accounts maintained by bureaus to be incompatible with those maintained by their departments.

Within this fragmented arrangement, GAO took the lead in prescribing governmentwide accounting standards and in certifying agency compliance with the standards. But because the accounting standards were muddled and agencies had multiple systems, GAO found that many of the systems were not in compliance. Furthermore, GAO's standards were not the only ones—both OMB and the Treasury had their own practices and requirements. Having a plurality of standard-setting agencies left the federal government without generally accepted accounting standards.

Since the 1990s strong efforts have been made to integrate accounting and budgeting as part of a broad effort to improve financial management in the federal government. A key development has been the appointment of a chief financial officer (CFO) in all federal departments and major agencies. As prescribed by the Chief Financial Officers Act of 1990, the CFO is responsible for developing and maintaining an integrated accounting and financial management system, overseeing all financial operations relating to the agency's programs and activities, and monitoring the financial execution of the budget (box 10-2). The act does not expressly give the CFO a role in formulating agency budgets, but many have become involved. The law established the position of deputy director for management within OMB to serve as the CFO of the federal government, as well as the Office of Federal Financial Management.

Another important development in 1990 was the establishment of the Federal Accounting Standards Advisory Board (FASAB) by GAO, OMB, and the Treasury—the three agencies that claim lead authority over accounting standards. When FASAB recommends a standard, each of the three agencies promulgates it, thereby assuring conformity while allowing each agency to uphold its own role. During the 1990s FASAB issued a series of statements of financial accounting standards relating to the treatment of assets and liabilities, cost accounting concepts, accounting for inventory, property and equipment, and other matters. In 1996 FASAB issued a report that identified four principal objectives of federal finance reporting (box 10-3).

Standardization has enabled federal agencies to prepare annual financial statements and for the Treasury to develop a consolidated statement for the federal government. However, GAO has found many of these statements to have material weaknesses that impair their accuracy. Prodded by various legislative initiatives, such as the Government Management and Reform Act of 1994 (which requires the audit of agency financial statements and the preparation of a consolidated financial statement for the federal government) and the Federal Financial Management and Improvement Act of 1996 (which directs auditors to report on whether agency financial statements comply with federal standards), agencies can be expected to improve financial reporting.

As budgeting and accounting become more closely linked, federal authorities may face the question of whether accounting standards, which currently pertain only to financial statements, should be applied to the budget and re-

---

BOX 10-2
Provisions of the Chief Financial Officers Act of 1990

Organization
- Establishes a deputy director for management in OMB to be the chief financial officer responsible for financial management in the federal government, and the Office of Federal Financial Management, headed by the controller.
- Provides for the appointment of a chief financial officer in all federal departments and major agencies.
- Establishes a CFO council, headed by the OMB deputy director for management and including the agencies' chief financial officers. The council is an advisory body that coordinates the activities of agencies relating to modernization of financial systems, internal controls, financial data and information standards, and legislation affecting financial operations.

Functions of CFO
- Oversees all financial management activities relating to the agency's programs and operations.
- Develops and maintains an integrated accounting and financial management system that complies with accounting and internal control principles, standards, and requirements.
- Ensures that the agency's system provides complete, reliable, consistent, and timely information, including cost information and information that facilitates the systematic measurement of performance.
- Monitors the financial execution of the budget.

Reporting Elements
- Agency five-year plans setting forth the agency's financial management strategy, including planned accomplishments and target dates.
- A governmentwide five-year plan submitted by OMB describing steps to be taken in improving federal financial management.
- Annual reports by agencies analyzing the status of financial management and including required financial statements and a summary of reports on internal accounting and administrative control systems.
- Annual financial statements, supported by relevant financial and program performance data, audited by the agency inspector general (or an outside auditor).

Source: *Chief Financial Officers Act of 1990*, P.L. 101-576.

---

lated documents. The basic accounting rule is that financial information prepared for use by outside parties (such as bondholders or share owners) must comply with standards, but an entity may maintain internal records in any form it prefers. In business, the budget is an internal document that is not bound by accounting rules. In government, however, it is one of the principal means of communicating with citizens. At present, the federal budget does not

▼

BOX 10-3
Objectives of Federal Financial Reporting

Budget Integrity

Federal financial reporting should assist in fulfilling the government's duty to be publicly accountable for monies raised through taxes and other means, and for their expenditure in accordance with the appropriations laws that establish the government's budget for a particular fiscal year and related laws and regulations. Federal financial reporting should provide information that helps the reader to determine

- how budgetary resources have been obtained and used and whether their acquisition and use were in accordance with the legal authorization
- the status of budgetary resources and
- how information on the use of budgetary resources relates to information on the costs of program operations and whether information on the status of budgetary resources is consistent with other accounting information on assets and liabilities.

Operating Performance

Federal financial reporting should assist report users in evaluating the service efforts, costs, and accomplishments of the reporting entity, the manner in which these efforts and accomplishments have been financed, and the management of the entity's assets and liabilities. Federal financial reporting should provide information that helps the reader to determine the

- costs of providing specific activities and programs and the composition of and changes in these costs
- efforts and accomplishments associated with federal programs and the changes over time and in relation to costs and
- the efficiency and effectiveness of the government's management of its assets and liabilities.

Stewardship

Federal financial reporting should assist report users in assessing the impact on the nation of the government's operations and investments, and how, as a result, the government's and the nation's financial conditions have changed and may change in the future.

Systems and Controls

Federal financial reporting should assist users in understanding whether financial management systems, internal accounting, and administrative controls are adequate to ensure that

- transactions are executed in accordance with budgetary and financial laws and other requirements, consistent with the purposes authorized, and recorded in accordance with federal accounting standards
- assets are properly safeguarded to deter fraud, waste, and abuse and
- performance measurement information is adequately supported.

Source: Federal Accounting Standards Advisory Board, *Overview of Federal Accounting Concepts and Standards*, Report 1, December 31, 1996, pp. 8–9.

comply with accounting principles, but there will likely be greater correspondence in the future. An increasing number of state and local governments present their budget on the basis of generally accepted accounting principles, as do a number of national governments. The U.S. government has not yet moved in this direction, but under the impetus of recent financial management reforms, it may do so.

Traditionally, financial reporting has served such external requirements as assuring legality in expenditure. For this limited purpose, it sufficed to account for transactions in terms of obligations authorized or incurred, and cash received or paid out. Accounting for obligations is essential to ensure that funds are spent in accordance with applicable law and that the agencies adhere to Congress's intent in making appropriations. Accounting for cash is essential for the Treasury's management of the government's debt.

In addition to these external requirements, agencies need timely and accurate financial data to manage their own operations. In particular, they need information on the cost of the goods and services they are providing. In cost-based (or accrual) accounting, income is recorded when it is earned, not when it is received, and costs are recorded when goods and services are consumed, not when money is disbursed. Cost-based budgets are useful in measuring the resources used in carrying out activities, controlling expenses, and improving efficiency in operations. They also provide useful data for preparing performance-based budgets, which show the outputs resulting from government expenditures.

The Federal Balance Sheet

It is common practice for businesses to report their financial condition on a balance sheet, which lists assets, liabilities, and net worth. The balance sheet is constructed on the basis of generally accepted accounting principles, which provide rules for evaluating assets and liabilities, setting aside reserves for financial risks such as bad debts, and recognizing income and payments. Because of inadequate accounting practices and critical differences between it and business, the federal government did not prepare a balance sheet until the late 1990s. However, accounting improvements and pressure on the government to provide a true picture of its financial condition have induced OMB, GAO, and the Treasury to draft a balance sheet for the government.

OMB's exercise indicated that the government's liabilities exceeded its assets by $3.2 trillion in fiscal 1998. GAO's balance sheet reported that excess as $6 trillion, and the Treasury reported that it was $3.6 trillion. Various entries on one of these agency's balance sheet did not have corresponding entries on the other's. Thus while the three agencies each produced a balance sheet for the federal government, they did not treat entries consistently.

Care must be taken in interpreting the entries on a federal balance sheet. If a commercial entity had a negative net worth running into trillions of dollars, it would be insolvent. But the federal government has sovereign powers that do not appear on its balance sheet; foremost is the power to tax. If the present value of future revenue that would be generated by the tax laws now on the books were shown as an asset, the government might show a positive net worth. In other words, the balance sheet does a better job recognizing past liabilities than the value of assets.

Management Control

Federal financial management is guided by the doctrine of management control (sometimes referred to as internal control). Under this doctrine, program managers have primary responsibility for ensuring that resources are used properly and efficiently.

At one time (generally before the 1950s), federal agencies had to obtain external approval before spending funds. Nowadays each agency generally handles the transaction on its own, determining the amount of money available for a purpose and whether management rules (concerning personnel, travel, purchases, and other administrative actions) have been complied with. Each agency keeps its own books, preaudits its operations, and reports on its financial performance and condition. The Federal Financial Integrity Act of 1982 requires every agency to establish systems of internal control that are in accordance with standards prescribed by the comptroller general. The systems must provide "reasonable assurance" that obligations and costs are in compliance with applicable law, that funds, property, and other assets are safeguarded against waste, loss, or abuse, and that revenues and expenditures are properly recorded.

OMB and GAO share oversight responsibility for management control. OMB Circular A-123 requires agencies and their managers to "take systematic and proactive measures to (i) develop and implement appropriate, cost-effective management controls for results-oriented management; (ii) assess the adequacy of management controls in Federal programs and operations; (iii) identify needed improvements; (iv) take corresponding corrective action; and, (v) report annually on management controls." OMB guidelines emphasize that agencies should not set up separate management control processes. Instead, appropriate controls should be integrated into agency management systems. In addition to agency self-assessment, OMB occasionally singles out high-risk areas for close attention.

As required by law, GAO also reviews internal control systems and reports on material weaknesses. In assessing whether a deficiency constitutes a material weakness, GAO advises agencies to consider the magnitude and sensitivity of the resources involved, conflicts of interest, violations of statutory requirements, and adverse publicity that would harm an agency's credibility. GAO's annual report on management control typically finds considerable waste and mismanagement in federal agencies.

Performance-Based Management

Since the late 1970s Congress has enacted six laws affecting financial management (box 10-4). The earliest of these laws, the Inspector General Act and the Federal Managers' Financial Integrity Act, focused on wrongdoing and mismanagement by federal officials. The second pair of laws, beginning with the Chief Financial Officers Act, aimed to establish sturdy management systems. The last set has concentrated on spurring agencies to improve their performance and effectiveness.

A potentially important step in using the budget and related management processes to improve performance was taken in the Government Performance and Results Act of 1993. GPRA (or the Results Act, as it is sometimes called) prescribes a sequence of actions beginning with the development of performance measures, progressing to multiyear strategic plans, and concluding with agency and governmentwide plans linked to budget decisions (box 10-5). Once these instruments are in place, agencies are to report annually on performance and to periodically revise their strategic plans to reflect changes in objectives and priorities. GPRA also calls for the pilot testing of performance-based budgeting—an arrangement in which the money appropriated or spent is directly linked to the outputs or results the agency produces.

BOX 10-4
Laws Affecting Financial Management

Inspector General Act of 1978 (P.L. 95-452)
- Establishes independent inspector general offices in all federal departments and major agencies
- Conducts audits and investigations
- Recommends policies to promote economy, efficiency, and effectiveness
- Detects and prevents fraud and abuse
- Informs the agency head and Congress on problems and deficiencies

Federal Managers' Financial Integrity Act of 1982 (P.L. 97-255)
- Requires agencies to maintain internal accounting and administrative controls in compliance with standards prescribed by the comptroller general, to evaluate their management accountability and control systems, and to report yearly to Congress and the president on plans to correct material weaknesses

Chief Financial Officers Act of 1990 (P.L. 101-576)
- Requires twenty-four federal agencies to have a chief financial officer (CFO) responsible for overseeing all financial management activities relating to the agency's programs and operations and to prepare five-year plans, including milestones, for improving financial management.
- CFO council, headed by OMB deputy director for management, reviews and recommends improvements in financial management

Government Performance and Results Act of 1993 (P.L. 103-62)
- Mandates that agencies submit initial strategic plans, with updates every three years, and performance plans covering each program activity
- On the basis of these plans, OMB includes a performance plan for the federal government in the president's budget
- Beginning in 2000, agencies report each year on the previous year's performance

Government Management Reform Act of 1994 (P.L. 103-356)
- Requires the audit of agency financial statements and the preparation and audit of a consolidated financial statement for the federal government

Federal Financial Management Improvement Act of 1996 (P.L. 104-208)
- Directs auditors to report on whether agency financial statements comply with federal financial management systems' requirements, federal accounting standards, and the U.S. government's Standard General Ledger

▼

BOX 10-5

Major Features of the Government Performance and Results Act of 1993

Purpose

To improve program effectiveness and public accountability by focusing on results, service quality, and customer satisfaction; to help managers improve service delivery by planning for program objectives and providing them with information on program results and service quality; and to improve congressional decisionmaking by providing objective information on the relative effectiveness and efficiency of federal programs and expenditures.

Pilot Projects

Three sets of pilots: performance measures and reports (1994–96), managerial accountability and flexibility (1995–96), and performance budgeting (1998–99). (Some of the pilots were not conducted, and agencies moved directly to implementation.)

Strategic Plans

Agencies submit five-year strategic plans updated at least every three years. Plans are prepared in consultation with Congress and are to include a comprehensive mission statement, goals and objectives, how goals and objectives are to be achieved, relationship of annual performance goals to strategic objectives, external factors affecting achievement of goals, and program evaluation.

Performance Plans

Annual performance plans, consistent with the strategic plan, specify the performance to be achieved by each program activity, express goals in measurable form, describe processes and resources needed to meet performance goals, specify performance indicators, and provide a basis of comparing actual and planned performance.

Performance Reports

Annual program performance reports review whether goals for the previous year were achieved and if they were not, explaining why they were not met.

Performance Budgeting

Following pilot tests of performance budgeting, the OMB director issues a report (by March 31, 2001) assessing the feasibility and advisability of including a performance budget (which shows the varying levels of performance that would result from different budgeted amounts) in the president's budget.

Source: *Government Performance Results Act of 1993*, P.L. 103-62.

GPRA specifies six critical components for the strategic plans (see box 10-5). GPRA provides for agencies to consult with Congress during preparation of strategic plans and in subsequent updates or revisions. The first batch of plans was submitted in 1997; updates are required every three years, though some have suggested that the schedule be revised to synchronize planning with presidential terms. In 1997 the House majority leadership established special teams to oversee the implementation of this phase of GPRA. At the behest of various congressional committees, GAO has assessed the initial round of strategic plans and found that they do not sufficiently define a strategic path for agencies to take in setting goals and measuring performance. In GAO's view, the early strategic plans should be viewed as only the starting points in the broad transformation needed to implement performance-based management.

The next step in the GPRA process has been the submission of annual performance plans (that are consistent with each agency's strategic objectives) in tandem with its annual budget request to OMB. This guidance by OMB provides for each agency to revise its performance plan on the basis of financial and program decisions made in the president's budget. Agency plans must specify performance goals and indicators for the fiscal year, describe the operational processes and resources that will be needed to meet performance goals, and describe the means that will be used to verify measured results. OMB also requires that each program activity in an agency's program and financing schedules (described in exhibit 5-4) be covered by at least one performance goal or indicator. It also expresses the expectation that in time, the annual performance plan will become an integral part of agency budget requests and budget justification submitted to Congress, and that

agencies will restructure their appropriation accounts to provide a more systematic or functional presentation of budget and performance information. GPRA stipulates that on the basis of agency plans, OMB must include a governmentwide performance plan in the president's budget. In reviewing OMB's first governmentwide plan in the fiscal 1999 budget, GAO found that it did not always provide a clear and complete picture of performance. It urged that future plans go beyond the formal requirements of GPRA to more fully address the needs of Congress and other users.

The culmination of the GPRA process may be the introduction of performance-based budgets in which the level of resources is expressly linked to the level of outputs. This form of budgeting was tried in the 1950s and 1960s with little success, but in view of the overall emphasis on financial management reform, its prospects may be better this time. Much will depend on the inroads GPRA makes in implanting a culture of performance in federal agencies and in orienting congressional committees to outputs and results. It is too early to assess GPRA's impact, but one can already discern that it is following the path of previous reforms—a big investment by agencies at the outset, leading to the generation of vast amounts of paperwork that satisfy formal requirements but provide little evidence that the innovations have made a dent in behavior or decisions. The one big difference this time is that Congress is involved. Most of the appropriations subcommittees have prodded agencies to highlight information on objectives and performance in their budget justifications. Yet it is one thing for Congress to request information on performance and results and quite another for it to appropriate money on this basis and to give federal managers sufficient freedom and incentive to improve operations. When Congress earmarks money to projects or activities and writes detailed operating rules into legislation and committee reports, it undermines the performance ethic that GPRA promotes.

CONCLUSION

Managing expenditures involves a tug of war between the executive branch and Congress. Executives want flexibility; Congress wants control. During the nineteenth century and the early decades of the twentieth century, Congress generally dominated the relationship, as it leveraged its power of the purse to enact detailed appropriations that restricted executive discretion. The balance tilted in favor of the executive branch from the New Deal through the Great Society—a period in which laws accorded broad operating freedom to federal executives and appropriation accounts were broadened. But the tide turned again in the Vietnam/Watergate era, as Congress imposed numerous restrictions on executive action, enacted the first formal limits on presidential impoundments, and issued numerous directives in laws and committee reports. Congress was spurred by real or perceived abuses of executive power and by prolonged conflict between it and the president. As legislative controls and restrictions multiplied, Congress was accused of micromanaging the executive branch and of meddling in the details of administration.

During the 1990s there was a burst of initiatives to improve federal management. As well-intentioned as these initiatives may be, they do not address the basic relationship between federal managers and congressional paymasters. Congress wants more by way of performance, but it has not been willing to surrender any of the controls and habits that stand in the way of improved performance. It hogties managers and then bashes them for not producing. This arrangement gives Congress the best of both worlds: it gets the control it wants and passes the blame on to bureaucrats. It passes laws (such as GPRA), which instruct agencies to file voluminous reports, but then it goes about its old ways in parceling out money and legislating restrictions. Maybe the formula will work and managers will perform despite the restrictions on their operating discretion. Yet if they fall short of the mark, it will only confirm the legislative belief that even more restraints are needed.

The National Performance Review, the centerpiece of Vice President Al Gore's campaign to "reinvent government," produced anecdotal evidence that federal managers dutifully follow the rules and spend just about every dollar provided to them. They have little flexibility and take few risks. Even when they see opportunities to spend money more wisely, they have little discretion to do so. This probably is an overstated picture of federal management, but it has more than a kernel of truth: managers value compliance more than performance. Paradoxically, GPRA itself has become a vast compliance machine. Agencies produce strategic plans, not because they seek to transform themselves but because the GPRA calendar dictates that they do so. They generate performance measures because the law tells them to; whether the measures make a difference in their performance is another matter.

One of the great conceits of GPRA is that having more or different information changes behavior. But a reading of past reforms—performance budgeting in the 1950s, program budgeting and planning-programming-budgeting systems in the 1960s, zero-based budgeting in the 1970s—tells us that information by itself does not change anything. At the core, change is a matter of will and incentives—the drive to transform organizations and the inducement to do so. GPRA offers little of either, so it may end up as a legislated substitute for change.

11

The Self-Correcting
Budget Process

T his book demonstrated that federal budgeting operates with many rules, procedures, and constraints. It is not the case that anything goes in budgeting, that spenders and tax cutters get whatever they want regardless of the budget's condition, and that vote-seeking politicians have no means of rebuffing powerful demands. Budgeting is a regulated and balanced process, with checkpoints and controls at various stages of presidential and congressional action. But budgeting also is a political process that is highly sensitive to the preferences of voters and interest groups and to the strong inclination of elected leaders to satisfy constituents. Thus budgeting is a contest between rules that block demands and political tendencies that open it to demands. Sometimes in the course of this contest the budget is thrown out of kilter and large imbalances between revenues and outlays emerge. When this occurs, proposals are made for a constitutional amendment or legislative action to restore balance.

This concluding chapter considers proposals that would modify budget rules and procedures to produce more balanced outcomes. In reviewing proposed reforms, it becomes clear that budgeting is inherently a self-correcting process in which political pressure, either to avoid blame for unsatisfactory outcomes or to do the right thing, restores equilibrium. Self-correction involves not only changes in revenue and spending policy but also legislative and procedural changes, such as the

Budget Enforcement Act, to rebalance fiscal outcomes. The self-correction hypothesis leads one to be wary of fundamental changes in budgeting that would strip elected majorities of power to work their political will. Nevertheless, it must also be acknowledged that self-correction is flawed and costly and that modifications to various features of budgeting may improve outcomes or reduce political friction.

At times, budgeting seems to be anything but regulated and self-correcting. Such was the case throughout the 1980s and the early 1990s, when federal spending annually exceeded revenues by hundreds of billions of dollars. The deficit appeared to be so intractable that virtually all observers (this author included) saw little prospect that the budget could be brought back into balance. But it was, and when this book was completed, Washington politicians were fighting over surpluses that were projected to exceed $3 trillion during the first decade of the new millennium. The remarkable transition from deficits to surpluses was described in chapter 2; policy mistakes that spawned high deficits were followed by policy corrections that restored budgetary balance. This episode will not be the final shift in the budget's fortunes; one can reasonably expect deficits to reemerge in the not-too-distant future. In budgeting, self-correction works in both directions, liquidating both big deficits and big surpluses. Politicians act when the deficit is perceived to be too high and spend more or tax less when the surplus seems too large.

These adjustments are neither automatic nor painless. They do not follow a set course, and changes in policy or in economic conditions can slow or accelerate them. The path to self-correction is lined with tricky turns, and neither the timing of the adjustment nor the manner in which it is accomplished can be foretold. Consider the 1990s, a decade which began and ended with divided government.

Early in the decade, when the deficit approached $300 billion, budget pundits blamed divided government for the sorry outcome. Democrats and Republicans, the explanation ran, preferred to point the finger of blame at one another rather than make the hard choices to stanch the red ink. But at the decade's end, when surpluses emerged, experts credited divided government for the turnaround, explaining that it blocked both Republicans' attempts to trim taxes and Democrats' proposals to boost spending.

By all accounts, divisions between the two political parties have been a critical feature of recent American political history, but the political incentives that drive elected officials to abhor both oversized deficits and burgeoning surpluses ultimately prevail, regardless of the party lineup in Washington. Federal taxes were raised in 1990 with a Republican in the White House and the Democrats in control of Congress; they were raised again in 1993 when Democrats ran both political branches. Why were taxes raised? The answers differ slightly for the two presidents who signed the revenue increases into law. Congressional Democrats and budget aides pressured George Bush, who knew that taxes had to be raised to avoid sequestration. Clinton took the initiative in proposing tax increases; he perceived that, without action to reduce the deficit, chronic deficits would hobble his presidency. Though their motives differed, both presidents put the budget on a self-correcting course.

Self-correction does not mean that revenues and spending are stable in real or nominal terms or relative to the gross domestic product. These aggregates escalated steeply during the past sixty years; it is highly unlikely that they will ever recede to pre–New Deal or pre–World War II levels, or even to the levels experienced during the 1950s. The size of government reflects political judgments on the programs Americans want and are willing to pay for. Self-correction refers to the balance between revenue and spending, not to the absolute or relative size of government. The size of government is a political question decided by democratically elected leaders, not by preset limits on revenues or expenditures.

Some observers argue that the steep rise in revenue and spending is due to a built-in bias in democratic politics and that the size of government has expanded because the benefits of spending are concentrated among a relatively small number of recipients while the costs are dispersed among the taxpaying population. Beneficiaries therefore have a much stronger incentive to campaign for higher spending than taxpayers have to mobilize against higher taxes. But if budgeting is so markedly skewed in favor of higher spending, why is federal spending a significantly smaller share of the U.S. economy in 2000 than it was a decade earlier? And why is total government spending a much smaller share of GDP in the United States than in virtually all other developed countries? It is a mistake to assume there are no counterpressures against government spending and taxation. If there were not, politicians would easily disable or evade constitutional or statutory restrictions on their power to tax and spend.

In budgeting, rules are important because they make it easier or harder for politicians to take corrective action. Most of the lasting rules changes made in the congressional budget process since it was inaugurated in 1975 have encouraged self-correction. These include lengthening the time frame of budget resolutions, the reconciliation process, discretionary spending caps, pay-as-you-go (PAYGO) limits on revenue and direct spending legislation, and the use of baselines to score budget actions. But not all reforms have succeeded; the abortive Gramm-Rudman-Hollings Act pro-

vides ample evidence that politicians sometimes substitute bookkeeping tricks for genuine adjustment.

Self-correction can be painful, especially when it is necessitated by policy mistakes that have destabilized the budget. The turnaround from deficit to surplus took two decades and countless budget battles between the president and Congress, as well as within the legislative branch. Looking back at this protracted struggle leads one to wonder whether changes in the machinery of budgeting and in the behavior of participants might ease the process, block serious policy mistakes, reduce friction and pain, and accelerate correction. Correcting from deficit to surplus is a fractious process that leaves few combatants unbloodied. Political trust and capacity take a beating, as does budgeting itself. Why go through years of deficits and conflict that could be averted by preventing the emergence of big deficits in the first place? More to the point, why not implement stronger budget controls and thereby forestall the accumulation of trillions of dollars in public debt?

There are other signs of the toll the budget battles have taken. For most of the 1980s and 1990s, legislative debate and program policies were decided predominantly in terms of budgetary impact rather than substance. Budgetary friction disabled much of the authorizations process in Congress, leading it to cram major legislative actions into omnibus budget reconciliation and appropriations bills. In these decades, budgeting became a game of political brinksmanship, as key decisions were resolved in last-minute summit negotiations between the president and congressional leaders. Such negotiations undermined the normal committee process in Congress. Provisions have frequently been enacted in omnibus bills without prior legislative consideration. The finger pointing by the parties and the lies and gimmicks sometimes used to make budgetary peace have taken a heavy toll, such as the diminished public trust and confidence in national political institutions. The scars that decades of budgetary warfare have left tempt one to conclude that there must be a better way.

Short of imposing constitutional handcuffs, can the machinery of budgeting be calibrated to ease self-correction, make it more expeditious and fluid, and do less damage to presidential-congressional relations and to legislative order and budget routines? This chapter seeks answers by assessing existing budgetary institutions, the impact of impending demographic pressures on the budget, and several reform proposals.

THE ADEQUACY OF BUDGET CONTROLS

At its core, budgeting is a process for deciding how much should be raised and spent. In budgeting for revenues, there is widespread agreement that it is unwise to reconsider the tax code annually. Businesses and households make decisions in light of their tax situation; neither should be subject to the vagaries of revenue legislation. It is on the spending side of the ledger that the adequacy of budget control is often called into question.

Table 11-1 indicates that the budget effectively controls discretionary spending through a sequence of actions linking the totals to individual transactions. This chain of control is designed to ensure that the sum of the many millions of obligations or outlays made each year does not exceed approved discretionary totals. Although there are some exceptions, each step in this table is governed by the rule that it may not exceed the amount the previous step allows. For example, the amount apportioned for an account may not exceed the amount available for obligation from appropriations and other budgetary sources. The controls are not

quite as airtight as these examples imply, but the sequence keeps discretionary spending within or close to preset totals.

This is not the case for mandatory programs. Past legislative actions, rather than current budget decisions, almost entirely determine the amounts spent each year on entitlements. In mandatory programs, the chain of control is inverted—rather than the totals constraining individual programs, the amounts spent on programs determine the total. This inversion impedes, but does not prevent, self-correction in budgeting.

Simply because the budget does not constrain entitlements to the same degree as discretionary appropriations does not mean that spending is out of control. Current arrangements can be defended on two grounds. One is that in establishing entitlements the government accords priority to values other than budget control. The other is that two decades of experience with reconciliation procedures indicate that the government can regulate entitlements (although Social Security is exempt from this procedure). Spending control is not the sole objective of budget decisions; Congress and the president have other political concerns, which sometimes preempt control. Social Security assures workers that they will have a financial safety net in retirement, Medicare and Medicaid give elderly and low income Americans access to health care, and unemployment insurance restores a portion of discharged workers' lost income. The government finances food stamps and other assistance programs that enable low income families to maintain an acceptable standard of living. Through prescribed cost-of-living adjustments, the government protects recipients of various transfer programs against inflation. The common element in these programs is that their objectives are fulfilled by entitling beneficiaries to federal payments. Making

TABLE 11-1
Sequence of Discretionary Spending Control

Limitation or action	Control
Discretionary spending limits	Caps on total discretionary budget authority and outlays, set by the Budget Enforcement Act and adjusted periodically by Congress.
Budget resolution aggregates	Ceilings on total budget authority and outlays (covering both discretionary and direct spending). These aggregates may not assume more for discretionary spending than the limits allow.
Section 302(a) allocations	Total budget authority and outlays in the budget resolution are allocated to committees with spending jurisdiction. All discretionary spending is allocated to the appropriations committees.
Section 302(b) subdivisions	Each appropriation committee subdivides its allocation of budget authority and outlays among its thirteen subcommittees. The total allocated to these subcommittees may not exceed the amount allocated to the full committee.
Appropriations	The budget authority provided and outlays deriving from each appropriations bill are compared with the relevant subcommittees' 302(b) allocation. A point of order may be raised in the House or Senate against an appropriations bill that would cause the relevant 302(b) allocation to be exceeded.
Apportionment	Appropriations and other available budgetary resources are apportioned by OMB to each account, either by projects or by quarters of the fiscal year. The total apportioned may not exceed available resources.
Allotment	Each department or agency allots apportioned resources to its subunits. The total allotted may not exceed the amount apportioned.
Obligation	Obligations by agencies that commit the government to future payments. Agencies may not (with few exceptions) obligate in excess of available budget resources.
Outlay	Payment by the Treasury to liquidate obligations incurred by agencies.

these payments discretionary would bolster budget control but diminish the protections afforded Americans.

Americans widely share the values underlying most entitlements. Public opinion polls show overwhelming support for Social Security, Medicare, and other major entitlements. While Americans do not like "welfare" programs, they endorse the view that government should assist low-income people in meeting basic needs. Americans may not favor every entitlement program, but the more a program costs, the more support it is likely to have. Americans are concerned about the cost of

government but show little inclination to sacrifice income stability, health care, and other objectives on the altar of budget control.

For the government to have perfect fiscal control, each year's budget would be made anew, unencumbered by past commitments. Congress would annually decide how much to spend on pensions, medical assistance, food stamps, disability aid, unemployment insurance, and so on. The old days would be back; just about all spending would be discretionary.

However, a world of perfect budget control would not be a perfect world. Social insecurity would be widespread, with workers, employers, the aged, and others facing an uncertain and in many cases bleak future. Retired workers would have to go through the annual budget gyrations before knowing what the next year's Social Security payments or health services would be.

A strong case can be made that the country is better off because of the wide net cast by entitlements. Of course, not all such programs are equally meritorious, but their combined effect is to cushion households against the cyclical shocks of recession and temporary disability, and against the secular shocks of old age and infirmity. Entitlements ease anxieties about inflation, unemployment, illness, and disability. Entitlements dominate the budget because the biggest of these programs distribute benefits to a broad swath of Americans. In other words, the biggest programs do the most damage to budget control but the most good to society.

In principle, entitlements are incompatible with budget control; in practice, the two must be reconciled. The president and Congress must deal with annual budgets that include entitlements. They do so principally through reconciliation, which enables them to make marginal adjustments in entitlements while retaining the core benefits that affected programs provide. Congress occasionally makes big changes in entitlements through reconciliation, as it did in the 1996 overhaul of the welfare program, but the typical use of reconciliation is to prune a little here and there to meet the savings targets laid out in reconciliation instructions. After twenty years of cutting hundreds of billions of dollars from Medicare in this fashion, this program is pretty much the same as it was in 1980. Arguably, reconciliation has survived because it has not dismantled popular entitlements. It saves both money and programs by trimming expenditures at the margins and shifting some costs to beneficiaries and service providers.

Congress can continue to use reconciliation to whittle programs, but long-term projections of the imbalance between revenues and expenditures suggest that this ploy might not suffice when Medicare and Social Security spending surge in the future. But even if budget deficits return, it is highly unlikely that Congress will roll back entitlements to the point that they claim no greater a share of the budget than they did a decade or two ago. The entitlement state is here to stay, but lively debate and frequent budget action on the role and obligations of the government in transferring money to American households will continue.

THE FUTURE OF SELF-CORRECTION

The federal government faces two very different budget futures—a ten-year horizon of sustained surpluses, and then a period twenty to forty years out, during which the balances built up in Social Security will vanish, Medicare will have recurring financial crises, and Washington will have to make far-reaching changes in payments to the elderly or extract far more revenue from taxpayers. The two futures are joined in several ways. First, U.S. fiscal performance during the years of projected surplus will directly affect the ease with which the nation transitions to budgets beholden to aging baby boomers. It makes a big difference whether surpluses or deficits characterize the period immediately preceding the retirement surge. The former would cushion the inevitable future shocks to the budget; the latter would add to them. Second, decisions on shoring up the long-term viability of Social Security and Medicare will have to be taken during the next decade, before the baby boom generation affects the budget's bottom line. If political leaders delay action on the grounds that the budget is in good shape, they will have a much more difficult time making needed adjustments later on when the budget is in bad shape. The surplus years offer the best opportunity for dealing with the demographic time bomb.

Both the Office of Management and Budget (OMB) and the Congressional Budget Office (CBO) have drawn rosy scenarios for the first decade of the twenty-first century. They project that the annual budget surplus will rise from $100 billion in 1999 to about $400 billion ten years later. These surpluses are expected to add up to $3 trillion over the period—two-thirds in Social Security funds, the remainder in all other budget accounts. Recent budget history should warn us that such projections are likely to be wrong and that there is all the difference in the world between expecting a surplus and actually earning one. Yet the budget projections are based on prudent assumptions—more modest growth rates over the next decade than during the previous one and a slower rise in tax collections. But even reasonable forecasts can be derailed by force majeure in budgetary practice: war, economic downturn, or just political pressure to spend more or tax less.

The main flaw in the projections is that they assume prolonged constraint on discretionary spending; this will not happen. The self-correction hypothesis leads one to expect that changes in budgetary behavior will absorb much of the projected surplus. At this writing, there already are strong efforts to alter the course of budget policy. In 1999 the Republican-controlled Congress passed and Clinton vetoed a tax cut that would have depleted most of the projected non–Social Security surplus. But this was not the last tax-cutting effort driven by the surplus. The next year the president and Congress joined ranks to pass the first of what may be many tax cuts if the surplus persists. In 1999 Congress and the president also wrestled with the difficulties of accommodating spending pressures within the limit on discretionary appropriations. While pledging fidelity to the caps, they conspired to spend tens of billions above them.

In view of the bleak long-term budgetary prognosis, liquidation of the surplus is the wrong policy path. It would leave the country unprepared for the spending demands in the new century and take away the government's capacity to compensate for low household savings by running a surplus.

In 1999 Congress and the president muddled through to an arrangement that may inhibit self-correcting dissipation of the surplus. Both pledged that the Social Security surplus would not be used to finance other government programs. If this "lockbox" were enforced, the Social Security surplus would grow each year, as would the unified budget surplus. Of course, if the rest of the budget were to incur a deficit, the government would have to cover the shortfall with borrowed funds. In terms of future economic well-being, it makes little difference whether money is borrowed from Social Security or from other sources.

By the following year, the political commitment to protect Social Security surpluses was solidified by burgeoning surpluses in the rest of the budget. With more than $1 trillion in such surpluses projected over the next decade, politicians could spend more and tax less without touching Social Security. But a new political marker was brought into play—pay down the $3.5 trillion public debt by 2015. Once again Democrats and Republicans rushed to embrace the new budgetary religion, though each party took the position that there still would be ample money left over for spending initiatives or tax cuts. For the debt elimination goal to be achieved, the budget would have to produce rising surpluses over the next decade. The odds of this happening are relatively small, but if it does, self-correction will have been thwarted.

FIGURE 11-1

U.S. Population 65 Years and Older and Covered Workers per OASDI Beneficiary, Five-Year Intervals, 1960–2050[a]

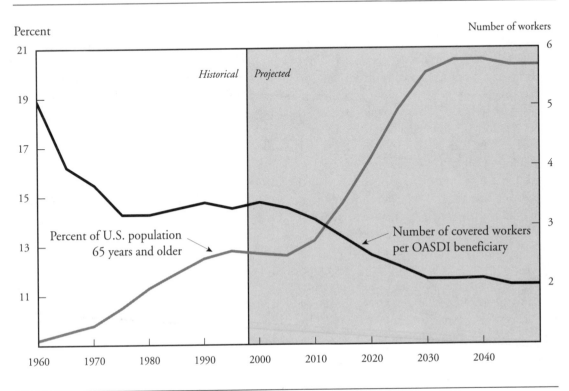

Sources: *2000 Annual Report of the Trustees of OASDI,* table II.F19, p. 122; and Census Bureau database, January 2000.

   a. The data here are based on intermediate assumptions.

Social Security and Medicare

Rising surpluses will not outlast the influx of baby boomers into the retirement stream. It is a sure bet that if current Medicare and Social Security policies continue without change, big deficits will emerge in the second decade of the new century. The budget predicament can be summed up in a few bits of data (shown in figures 11-1 and 11-2). First, the number of Americans age sixty-five and older is expected to double from 35 million (12.7 percent of the population in 2000) to 69 million (20 percent of the population) in 2030. Second, the number of active workers per Social Security recipient will drop from 3.4 in 2000 to 2.1 by 2030 and 1.3 by 2075. More money will flow out of the Social Security fund at a time when relatively less will be flowing in. Third, over the next thirty years, combined Social Security and Medicare outlays are projected to soar from $600 billion to more than $4 trillion, from less than 7 percent of GDP to over 10 percent. According to some estimates, these programs will account for 80 percent of federal spending by the middle of the new century.

Obviously, these trends are not sustainable. Normal self-correction will not suffice to deal with future Social Security and Medicare de-

FIGURE 11-2
Social Security Trust Fund, Medicare Hospital Insurance Trust Fund, and Combined Incurred Disbursements, 1970–2070ᵃ

Percent of GDP

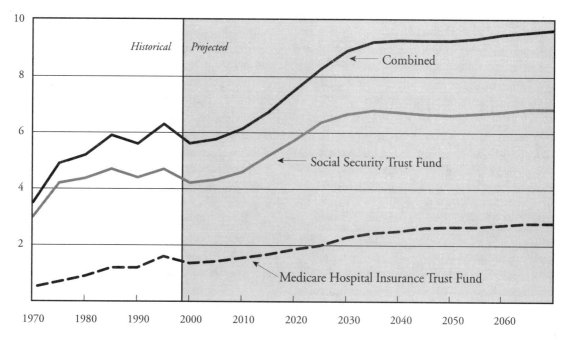

Source: *Budget of the United States, Historical Tables, Fiscal Year 2001,* table 1.2, table 13.1, and *2000 Annual Report of the Trustees of OASDI,* table III.C1, p. 189.
a. The data do not include the Medicare Supplemental Medical Insurance Trust Fund, which is mostly financed by current appropriations.

mands on the budget. But before yelling "crisis," it is appropriate to put the problem in perspective. First, Stein's Law (by economist Herbert Stein) predicts that trends that cannot persist will not. That is, there is no possibility of worst-case scenarios, or anything close to them, materializing. The federal budget will not be swallowed up by Social Security and Medicare. Long before it is, significant adjustments will be made in these programs. Second, as the population ages, the composition of spending will change; more public and private money will be spent on the elderly. In the same way that individuals change their consumption

patterns as they go through different life stages, so too does a government faced with a changing age structure. There is nothing amiss in spending a rising share of national income on the elderly when there are more elderly to spend it on. Third, because spending on the elderly cannot be permitted to crowd out other budgetary (and private) needs, significant changes will be made in Social Security and Medicare, though perhaps not as expeditiously or efficiently as some want. Social Security and Medicare will survive; both will be restructured long before they bankrupt the Treasury.

Although they are often lumped together,

Social Security and Medicare face different financial situations and are treated differently in the budget. Social Security is off-budget; Medicare is included in the budget. Social Security is changed infrequently and never in reconciliation bills; Medicare is adjusted frequently, usually through the reconciliation process. Adjustments to Social Security are made only to shore up its financial condition; Medicare changes have often been made to improve the overall budget condition.

Financial difficulties will come earlier to Medicare than to Social Security. Medicare's hospital insurance trust fund is expected to be depleted by 2023, while Social Security is projected to remain solvent until 2037 (figure 11-3). Future increases in Social Security payments will be due almost entirely to wage and price changes and increases in the number of recipients. In addition to being affected by these factors, Medicare spending is sensitive to the diffusion of medical technology, utilization rates for medical services, and inflation in the health sector. These variables are less predictable than those driving up Social Security expenditures.

Both Social Security and Medicare have attracted a slew of proposals to resolve their financial difficulties. For both programs, some advocate higher taxes, while others favor benefit cuts. Some promote privatization of all or a portion of these programs as a means of offloading the financial problems; others vigorously insist on public funding and operation. Some endorse an injection of general revenue; others fear that this remedy would shift much of the burden to taxpayers. The key issue is who should pay for keeping the programs solvent: active workers or beneficiaries? young or older Americans?

The political lineup in Washington will go a long way toward influencing the answers to these questions. Whole or partial privatization may advance if Republicans were to control both the White House and Congress but would be impeded if Democrats had control. Divided government might induce the two parties to craft a reform package that retains basic Social Security and Medicare benefits, trims future costs, and adds a layer of privatized pensions or medical insurance. On the other hand, continued economic growth may further delay action as additional revenue extends the solvency of these programs.

Fixing Social Security may be easier than ensuring the future fiscal soundness of Medicare. The actuarial shortfall in Social Security receipts over the next seventy-five years has been estimated at approximately 2 percent of covered payrolls; the gap is smaller early in this period, much greater in the latter part. This means that a two percentage point increase in the payroll tax (one percentage point each for employees and employers) would eliminate the entire gap. Any combination of policy changes (such as raising the retirement age, adjusting payment formulas, or increasing the penalty for taking Social Security before the retirement age) that adds up to two percentage points would put this program on a sound basis.

Medicare is a tougher call. One proposed remedy—raising the eligibility age—would add millions to the ranks of Americans lacking health insurance. Another proposal—enabling Americans to opt out of Medicare by acquiring their own insurance or by establishing medical savings accounts to pay health care expenses—would burden the program with poorer or sicker people. Despite the impending shortfall in Medicare finances, Congress faces enormous pressure to expand benefits.

Like Social Security, Medicare will continue intact, though with modifications that enable it to survive the financial storm. Premiums and other charges might be means-tested in the future, requiring wealthier participants to pay more than poorer ones. The program will be contoured to produce cost savings, and pay-

FIGURE 11-3
Projected Actuarial Balance of Social Security Trust Fund and Medicare Hospital Insurance Trust Fund, Five-Year Intervals, 2000–75ᵃ

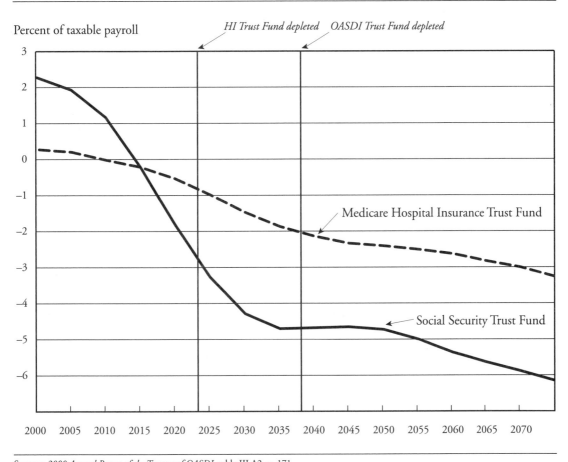

Sources: *2000 Annual Report of the Trustees of OASDI,* table III.A2, p. 171.
a. The data here are based on intermediate assumptions.

ments to providers will be trimmed from time to time. If the past is a guide, Medicare will continue to be a heavily legislated program, with numerous adjustments made every few years (or more frequently). Politicians will strive to avoid explicit rationing of health services, but they will devise forms of implicit rationing that dampen the use of various services.

The long-term viability of Social Security and Medicare will depend not only on policy adjustments, but also on the performance of the economy over the next twenty-five years and beyond. In fact, a robust economy will make these programs sustainable over an extended period; a weak economy will make it difficult for the government to meet these expenses even if it were to trim Social Security and Medicare benefits. The effect of the economy can be quite dramatic, as shown by earlier projections forecasting the depletion of Social Security and Medicare hospital insurance trust funds (see figure 11-3). In 1999 the trustees of these funds estimated that Social Security would be able to make payments until 2034, while Medicare would run out of money in 2015. Just one year later, the viability of Social Security was extended by three years, while eight years were added to the estimated life of Medicare. The revised projections for Social Security were due to the economy's strong performance and the Medicare revisions to both general economic conditions and a slowdown in inflation in the health care sector.

Even a seemingly small variation in economic conditions can make a substantial difference in the future affordability of Social Security and Medicare. For example, if the economy were to grow 2 percent a year during the first twenty-five years of the new millennium, GDP would grow (in 1999 dollars) from $9 trillion to approximately $15 trillion. But if growth were slightly higher, 2.3 percent a year, GDP would be about $16.5 trillion. This additional money would greatly ease the burden of financing Social Security and Medicare payments.

Although many factors go into determining economic performance, it is highly probable that the economy will be markedly larger in 2025 if the federal government runs a budget surplus by saving the money built up in the Social Security trust fund. These surpluses would provide a pool of money for investments and over time lead to a more productive work force and a bigger economy.

Looking thirty to fifty years ahead, one can envision successful self-correction in Social Security and Medicare. Government will spend much less on these programs than it would under current law but much more (as a share of GDP and of budget outlays) than it now does. To repeat what was said earlier: it is inevitable that when the elderly are a higher proportion of the population, government will spend correspondingly more on them. Any other outcome would be politically untenable.

IMPROVING SELF-CORRECTION

The tone of this chapter is upbeat. Budgeting is an adaptive process that reinvents itself in response to changes in financial and political conditions. But the adjustment process is fractious and painful. The concluding section examines four proposed budget reforms that might facilitate self-correction:

— amend the Constitution to require a balanced budget

— impose caps on entitlements

— convert budgeting from an annual to a biennial cycle

— convert the budget resolution from an internal congressional action into a shared legislative-executive responsibility

The first two deal with substantive policy, the last two with budget procedures.

Balanced Budget Amendment

During the high deficit era, repeated demands were made for a constitutional amendment requiring a balanced budget. In 1995 the House approved a balanced budget amendment by 300-132, but the Senate fell one vote short of the two-thirds that is needed for constitutional amendments (the text of that amendment is shown in exhibit 11-1). Now that the budget is balanced, demands for constitutional change have abated, but efforts to amend the Constitution will reemerge when deficits return. Yet, the best time to act on a balanced budget amendment may be when the budget has a surplus and dire measures are not needed rather than when deficits are rampant and balance appears to be unattainable.

Balanced budget amendments come in several forms. Some would merely require a planned balance at the time budget decisions were made; others would go further and require an actual balance. Most versions would waive the balance requirement during wartime

▶ EXHIBIT 11-1
Proposed Constitutional Amendment to Require a Balanced Budget

SECTION 1. Total outlays for any fiscal year shall not exceed total receipts for that fiscal year, unless three-fifths of the whole number of each House of Congress shall provide by law for a specific excess of outlays over receipts by a rollcall vote.

SECTION 2. The limit on the debt of the United States held by the public shall not be increased, unless three-fifths of the whole number of each House shall provide by law for such an increase by a rollcall vote.

SECTION 3. Prior to each fiscal year, the President shall transmit to the Congress a proposed budget for the United States Government for that fiscal year in which total outlays do not exceed total receipts.

SECTION 4. No bill to increase revenue shall become law unless approved by a majority of the whole number of each House by a rollcall vote.

SECTION 5. The Congress may waive the provisions of this article for any fiscal year in which a declaration of war is in effect.
The provisions of this article may be waived for any fiscal year in which the United States is engaged in military conflict which causes imminent and serious military threat to national security and is so declared by a joint resolution, adopted by a majority of the whole number of each House, which becomes law.

SECTION 6. The Congress shall enforce and implement this article by appropriate legislation, which may rely on estimates of outlays and receipts.

SECTION 7. Total receipts shall include all receipts of the United States Government except those derived from borrowing. Total outlays shall include all outlays of the United States Government except for those for repayment of debt principal.

SECTION 8. This article shall take effect beginning with fiscal year 2002 or with the second fiscal year beginning after its ratification, whichever is later.

Source: *Balanced Budget Amendment*, H.J. Res. 1, 104th Cong., 1st sess., 1995.

or by a supermajority (such as a three-fifths) vote in the House and Senate. Rather than consider textual differences, the discussion here focuses on two overriding questions: Do inadequacies in self-correction justify a constitutional restriction? What would be the likely impact of a balanced budget rule on budget procedures and outcomes?

The case for amending the Constitution rests on the conviction that all deficits are irresponsible, regardless of their size or cause, and that statutory remedies do not work. A constitutional rule would not distinguish between big deficits and small ones, nor between deficits that result from cyclical weakness in the economy and those embedded in a structural imbalance between revenues and outlays.

Throughout American history, the prevailing sentiment has been that deficits are injurious to the well-being of the country. The main concern has been that, by spending beyond its income, the government burdens future generations, which have no voice in making the decision and do not directly benefit from it. At times the argument is couched in moral terms, as if it were utterly wrong for government to finance operations with borrowed funds. This moral stance has been relaxed during wartime, when supporting military forces has been deemed to be of a higher order than making ends meet. And it has been overtaken by events during recession, when the drop-off in revenues has compelled government to borrow.

In my view, reformers should be wary of imposing constitutional restrictions on democratic majorities. Statutory remedies have enormous advantages, as the successful implementation of budget enforcement rules in the 1990s indicates. Statutory rules can more readily distinguish between big deficits and small ones, those stemming from cyclical disturbances and those caused by structural problems, those that are temporary and those that persist, and between those based on willful miscalculation and those due to circumstances that the president and Congress could not foresee when they made the budget. Statutory requirements can be fine-tuned as experience accumulates and as politicians learn what works and what does not.

One such adjustment—the shift from the Gramm-Rudman-Hollings Act (GRH) of the 1980s to the Budget Enforcement Act of 1990 (BEA)—speaks to the value of experimenting with statutory controls. GRH was not effective, but Congress was able to supersede it with new legislation. GRH prescribed a balanced budget but never met its target; BEA does not require a balanced budget, but it spurred liquidation of the deficit. GRH barred politicians from tinkering with the deficit targets, so they lied instead. BEA permits the president to adjust the targets, with the result that budget projections have become more honest.

Even if a balanced budget amendment were inscribed in the Constitution, its implementation would depend on legislation that defines the scope of the budget, establishes accounting rules for receipts, outlays, and other transactions, and specifies what is to be done in case of unplanned deficits. Implementing legislation would have to take account of faulty estimates, changing economic conditions, emergencies, and other occurrences not foreseen when the budget was approved. It would have to prescribe rules for determining which entities are federal and included in the budget and which are not. And it would have to deal with the budgetary treatment of capital investments, loans, asset sales, and several other types of transactions.

In many years, the economy has the final say as to whether the budget is balanced. The odds are overwhelming that in periods of moderate to severe economic weakness, the Constitution would have to retreat in the face of economic realities. In fact, most versions of the balanced budget rule permit Congress to waive the requirement in time of emergency. But waiver would not be automatic; it would have to be supported by a congressional majority (or supermajority), leaving open the possibility that a waiver would not be approved and that balance would not be achieved. If a balanced budget amendment may be suspended for economic necessity, it will also be overridden for political expedience.

Perhaps the most troubling aspect of a constitutional amendment is that it might induce governmental paralysis. The rule could open the door to situations in which Congress lacks both a majority to pass a balanced budget and a supermajority to permit deficit spending. A balanced budget amendment infringes on the fundamental democratic principle that elected officials should make policy. In my view, if the political process spawns unwanted deficits, correction should be sought through statutory remedies.

Entitlement Caps

As discussed earlier, entitlements impede self-correction. One idea for remedying this deficiency is to impose a cap on mandatory spending similar to those levied on discretionary programs. The cap could be applied to total entitlement spending, the total minus certain exclusions (such as Social Security), or to specific programs. It could operate through automatic cuts triggered by excess spending or by legislative action pursuant to notice that the cap has been exceeded.

Presumably the law establishing such caps would dictate how they would be enforced. The law might provide for across-the-board cuts in payments to recipients (or, in health programs, to providers), or according to some other formula. The formula might require that all of the excess spending be offset in a single year or that remedying the problem be spread over several years. It might allow for excess entitlement spending to be paid by tax increases, and it

might distinguish between budgets that have surpluses or deficits. These are only a few of the options for operationalizing an entitlement cap.

Although the government has little experience with entitlement caps, they have been used in other countries and can be made to work here. The relevant question, however, is whether they make good policy. An automatic cap probably would have hidden, unwanted side effects, such as denying health services to some people or curtailing financial assistance to needy families. Spending in excess of the cap would most likely occur during a recession, when personal incomes were depressed and federal income security spending rose. This is the most inapt time to cut income support or other payments to households.

Automatic caps give priority to spending control over other objectives served by entitlements. The best way to balance competing objectives would be to let Congress decide what to do when spending exceeds a preset limit. In 1993 Bill Clinton issued an executive order providing for the president to recommend a course of action when entitlement spending exceeds budgeted levels. Congress would have to act, but it would not be bound by the president's recommendation, nor would it be required to roll back entitlement spending to the budgeted level.

If Congress decides that spending should exceed the caps, its action should not be seen as a breakdown of budgetary discipline but as an affirmation of other public objectives. The important thing is that competing objectives have a fair chance of prevailing, not that the process be rigged for or against a particular outcome.

Biennial Budgeting and Appropriations

Lengthening the budget process to a biennial cycle has been a recurring goal of reformers. Such a cycle would set a two-year minimum for authorizing legislation and provide for the president to submit a full budget every other year. Congress would switch to a biennial schedule for the budget resolution and regular appropriations bills. However, the president and Congress would have the option of making supplemental budget decisions in the off year. Inasmuch as the appropriations process is the main sticking point in biennial proposals, it is the focus of the present discussion.

Advocates in both the executive and legislative branches have advanced a barrage of arguments in favor of a two-year process. Most address the internal operations of Congress or federal agencies and seek to ease congestion of legislative calendars and agency budget schedules. The 1993 National Performance Review (NPR) proposed biennial budgeting as a means of liberating the process from the details of expenditure and orienting it to larger policy issues. Freed from the tight deadlines of an annual cycle, NPR reasoned, agencies would have more time for strategic planning and program review.

Legislative supporters of a biennial budget complain about the amount of time the thirteen annual appropriations bills take, the crowding-out effect on other legislative business, and the conflicts generated by the need to settle the same matters every year. They blame the appropriations process for the decline in authorizing activity, and they view appropriations as a grinding process that is often completed behind schedule long after the fiscal year has started. To critics, the appropriations committees hold on to the annual process because it enables them to earmark money to favored projects.

Congressional reformers envision a two-year schedule in which substantive legislation would be considered the first year and spending bills the second. They believe this arrangement would encourage more active congressional oversight of government agencies and performance.

In terms of budget control, the argument for a biennial budget rests on expected changes in the focus of appropriations. A one-year appropriations process inevitably concentrates on year-to-year changes in spending items at the expense of considering the long-term direction of federal programs. A lengthier cycle might be less incremental and more change-oriented, less locked onto inputs and details and more focused on outputs and results, less interested in micromanaging agencies and more concerned about strategy and priorities.

Are these expectations realistic? Not if past reforms, such as the planning-programming-budgeting system (PPBS) introduced in the 1960s and the zero-based budgeting tried in the 1970s, are a guide. Both reforms sought to break budgeting away from incremental routines and to frame financial decisions more strategically. Neither succeeded, and their failure was most pronounced in the appropriations arena. Reformers counter with the argument that past budget innovations would have retained annual appropriations; the current one would do away with them. Moreover, they insist that the results would be more favorable this time because changes would be made in congressional operations, not just in executive branch budget formulation, and because the biennial process would be reinforced by other innovations moving forward under the aegis of the Government Performance and Results Act.

If the federal government were to shift to biennial appropriations, the United States would be the first major democracy to take this step, though not the first to establish a multiyear budget cycle. A number of countries have adopted a medium-term expenditure framework, a device that allows them to make annual budget policy within a multiyear context. Governments in some countries have given agencies discretion to carry over unused operational money from one year to the next, and a few even allow agencies to prespend a small portion of the next year's appropriation. Some have developed multiyear budgets that specify the operating resources agencies will receive for each of the next several years and the programs they will carry out during that period. Significantly, however, interyear flexibility and multiyear arrangements have not preempted annual appropriations. The lesson from other countries is that it is feasible to reduce the work burden of annual appropriations and to lengthen the policy horizon while continuing to make appropriations every year.

In fact, Congress has moved substantially away from annual spending control. For one thing, discretionary appropriations control only one-third of federal spending. For another, a sizable portion of these appropriations are made on a no-year basis, and the funds remain available for obligation indefinitely. Moreover, when it sets discretionary caps, Congress makes multiyear spending decisions.

It seems odd that for many programs the only choice available is the short leash of annual appropriations or the freedom of permanent entitlements. Biennial appropriations would provide an additional option that would be sensible for many programs, such as capital expenditures and military procurement, that have long planning cycles.

Despite the strong arguments for lengthening the budget process, one should be wary of changing a critical process that has operated on an annual basis since the start of American democracy without considering the broader implications for the political system. Shifting to a biennial cycle would ripple beyond the appropriations process to the operation of Congress and its relations with executive institutions. Congress would still have the power of the purse, but it would hold the strings more loosely. How loosely would depend on the extent to which two-year appropriations bring

about the behavioral changes its advocates expect. The behavioral response would provide answers to a number of questions. Will a biennial cycle enhance or impair the government's capacity for self-correction when changes in political or economic conditions warrant adjustments in budget policy? Will agencies regard the second year of a biennial appropriation as a floor from which to campaign for supplemental funds? Will the president and Congress make such substantial use of supplemental appropriations in the off year that the process would be biennial in name only? What changes have to be made in congressional operations and committee work to assure vigilant oversight of federal programs and agencies? The biennial appropriations issue should be considered in tandem with related matters, including adjustments in fiscal policy, the rules under which supplemental funds may be provided, and relations between Congress and the president.

Presidential Role in the Congressional Budget Resolution

As discussed in chapter 6, the budget resolution process established in 1974 was conceived as a means by which Congress would stake out its own position on the budget and would no longer be dependent on the president's recommendations. For this reason, the budget resolution was devised as an internal congressional procedure without any involvement by the president. Over the years, however, both the resolution and Congress's budget relations with the president have changed. During the 1990s there were frequent budget summit negotiations between the president and Congress. These typically took place near the end of the session, after Congress unilaterally passed its own budget resolution but before it completed work on appropriations.

The president and Congress are interdependent on budget matters. The president cannot get his budget adopted without legislative action, and Congress cannot get its budget resolution implemented without the president's concurrence. If they have become interdependent, does it not make sense for the president and Congress to seek agreement early in the process? Why wait until the last minute when positions have hardened and shutdown is imminent? Why should Congress unilaterally formulate a budget resolution when it cannot unilaterally enact the legislation needed to implement the resolution?

In considering these questions, it is necessary to take account of how switching from a concurrent to a joint resolution (that would require the president's signature to become law) might affect the willingness and capacity of warring politicians to make budgetary peace. Conflict is ubiquitous in budgeting because it is a process in which some pay and others benefit. But precisely because conflict is unavoidable, it is essential that the process be engineered so as to encourage opposing sides to seek accommodation.

One of the virtues of the existing congressional budget process is that it is tailored to each year's circumstances. Congress takes up reconciliation bills in some years but not in others. In some it adopts status quo budgets; in others it reaches for major policy changes. In some years the president and Congress go to the summit on budget disputes; in others they work out disagreements through routine work on legislation and appropriations. The elasticity of the process has enabled the two branches to formally negotiate when the prospect of agreement is favorable and to go their separate ways when the gap between them is so wide that agreement is beyond reach.

It is true that by the end of the process, when the final appropriations bills are negotiated, there has to be some meeting of the minds. But resolving appropriations disputes is usually a more placid matter than resolving budgetary differences. The former typically deals with discrete activities and spending items, the latter with budget totals and program priorities. Appropriations fragment budget conflict into bite-size decisions that can be resolved one at a time; the budget resolution aggregates them into comprehensive statements of national policy. Until the second half of the 1990s, Congress normally made appropriations decisions in a bipartisan manner, in contrast with its budget resolutions, which generated partisan wrangling and party-line votes. In view of this voting pattern, giving the president a formal role may make it more difficult for the two sides to bridge their differences. Each would be emboldened to uphold its position by emphasizing the differences between it and the other political branch.

Some have suggested that injecting the president into the budget resolution would spur the two branches to reach agreement early in the session and not wait until the last moment, when federal agencies are about to run out of money. In budgeting, however, real deadlines encourage compromise, but contrived deadlines merely postpone the day of reckoning. Congress and the president know that if they fail to agree on the resolution, they still have until much later in the session to work out their differences. Moreover, even if they do agree on a budget framework in the spring, they may still fight later in the year when appropriations and other implementing measures are considered.

The budget resolution must be a process for all political seasons, when big policy shifts are in the air and when only incremental adjustments are made, when the two branches lock horns on the budget and when they see things the same way. The best way to ensure that the budget resolution works under all conditions is to keep it flexible. Arming the president with a pen might leave him with nothing to sign or veto.

Federal Budget–Related
Internet Sites

OFFICE OF MANAGEMENT AND BUDGET
Internet address: www.whitehouse.gov/OMB
Agencies' communications to Congress
Appropriations reports within seven days of enactment
Circulars, bulletins, press releases, and testimony
Executive budget and supporting documents
Financial management policies
Midsession Review
PAYGO reports and estimates of PAYGO balances
Governmentwide performance plan
Management reform/GPRA
Sequester Update Report
Statements of administration policy (SAPs)

CONGRESSIONAL BUDGET OFFICE
Internet address: www.cbo.gov
Analysis of budgetary topics and the president's budget
Cost estimates, studies and reports, and testimony
Economic and Budget Outlook
Economic and budget projections
Current status of discretionary appropriations
Emergency spending under the Budget Enforcement Act
Monthly budget review
Options for changing and spending revenue
Projected federal tax revenues and the effect of changes in tax law
Unauthorized appropriations and expiring authorizations

LIBRARY OF CONGRESS

Internet address: thomas.loc.gov
Congressional bill summary since 1973
Congressional bill text since 1989
Congressional directory and committee
    membership
Congressional Record since 1989
Committee reports since 1995
House committees' hearings transcripts
Roll call votes since 1990
Public laws since 1973

GOVERNMENT ACCOUNTING OFFICE

Internet address: www.gao.gov
Comptroller General decisions and opinions
Performance and accountability
Policy and guidance material
Reports on federal agencies' rules
Testimony

HOUSE APPROPRIATIONS COMMITTEE

Internet address: www.house.gov/
    appropriations
302(b) allocations
Committee and subcommittee membership
Committee letters to the administration
News releases
Program terminations since fiscal 1996
Schedule of markups and hearings
Status and summary of current
    appropriations bills

HOUSE BUDGET COMMITTEE

Internet address: www.house.gov/budget
Budget resolution
Committee membership
Hearings transcripts
Issue papers
Press releases
Schedule

GOVERNMENT PRINTING OFFICE

Internet address: www.access.gpo.gov
Committee prints since 1997
Committee hearings since 1997
Congressional bills since 1993
Congressional Record since 1994
Congressional reports since 1995
Economic Report of the President since 1995
Executive budget since 1995
Public laws since 1995
United States Code

TREASURY DEPARTMENT

Internet address: www.treas.gov
Annual report
Daily and monthly Treasury statements
Press releases and speeches
Treasury Bulletin

SENATE APPROPRIATIONS COMMITTEE

Internet address: www.senate.gov/
    ~appropriations
302(b) allocations
Committee and subcommittee membership
Hearings, markup, and conference schedule
Press releases
Status and summary of current
    appropriations bills

SENATE BUDGET COMMITTEE

Internet address: www.senate.gov/~budget
Analysis of president's budget
Budget Bulletin
Chairman's mark
Economic Bulletin
Hearings transcripts
Press releases
Schedule

Glossary

ACCRUAL BASIS—the basis of accounting that records revenues when they are earned and expenditures when costs are incurred, regardless of the period in which money is received or payments made.

ACCRUED EXPENDITURES—charges that reflect liabilities incurred for services received, goods or other property received, or amounts becoming owed under programs for which no current service or performance is required. Expenditures accrue regardless of when cash payments are made.

ADVANCE APPROPRIATIONS—budget authority provided in an appropriations act to become available in a fiscal year beyond the one for which the act is enacted. The amount is included in the budget totals for the fiscal year in which the amount will become available for obligation. *Also see* Forward funding.

ADVANCE FUNDING—budget authority that may be obligated or spent during the current fis-cal year from the next year's appropriation. When obligated in advance, budget authority is increased for the current fiscal year and decreased for the next fiscal year.

ALLOCATION—in executive budgeting, allocations are budget authorities or other resources transferred to another account to carry out the purposes of the parent account. For use in congressional budgeting, *see* Committee allocation.

ALLOTMENT—a distribution by an agency to officials or administrative units authorizing them to incur obligations within a specified amount and period. The total amount allotted by an agency cannot exceed the amount apportioned by the Office of Management and Budget.

ALLOWANCE LETTER—a letter sent to each agency by the Office of Management and Budget after the president's budget has been submitted to Congress. The letter advises the agency of budget decisions and multiyear planning estimates, employment ceilings, and other significant policy and administrative matters.

ALLOWANCES—amounts included in the budget to cover possible additional expenditures for statutory pay increases, contingencies, and other requirements.

ANNUAL AUTHORIZATION—an authorization of appropriations for a single fiscal year, usually for a definite amount of money. Ongoing programs with annual authorizations are supposed to be reauthorized each year. If they are not reauthorized, Congress often enables them to continue by appropriating money for them.

APPORTIONMENT—a distribution made by the Office of Management and Budget of amounts available for obligation. Apportionments divide these amounts by periods (usually quarters) or projects. The apportionment limits the amount that may be obligated. When an account is apportioned, some resources may be reserved pursuant to the Antideficiency Act or may be proposed for rescission pursuant to the Impoundment Control Act.

APPROPRIATED ENTITLEMENT—an entitlement whose budget authority is provided in annual appropriations acts instead of in substantive law. These entitlements are classified as direct spending by the Budget Enforcement Act.

APPROPRIATION—a provision of law providing budget authority that enables an agency to incur obligations and to make payments out of the Treasury for specified purposes. Appropriations are the most common means of providing budget authority. Annual appropriations are provided in appropriations acts; most permanent appropriations are enacted in substantive law.

APPROPRIATION LIMITATION—a provision in an appropriations act that limits the amount that may be obligated or spent for specified

purposes. The limitation may be applied to direct loan obligations, guaranteed loan commitments, administrative expenses financed out of trust funds, or other purposes.

APPROPRIATIONS ACT—a law making annual appropriations. The law may be a regular, supplemental, or continuing appropriation.

AUTHORIZATION ACT—a law that establishes or continues one or more federal programs or agencies, establishes the terms and conditions under which they operate, sets other policy requirements or restrictions, authorizes the enactment of appropriations, and specifies how apportioned funds are to be used.

BACKDOOR SPENDING—*see* Direct Spending and Spending Authority.

BALANCED BUDGET—a budget in which receipts equal or exceed outlays.

BALANCES OF BUDGET AUTHORITY—budget authority provided in previous years that has not been spent. Obligated balances are amounts that have not been liquidated; unobligated balances are amounts that remain available for obligation.

BASELINE—a projection of revenues, expenditures, and other budget amounts under assumed economic conditions and participation rates, and assuming no change in current policy. The baseline is usually projected annually by the Congressional Budget Office for each of the next ten (or less) years. It is used in preparing the congressional budget resolution, scoring the budgetary impact of legislation under pay-as-you-go rules, and estimating the budgetary impact of provisions in reconciliation bills.

BIENNIAL BUDGET—a budget for a period of two years. The federal government has an annual budget, but proposals have been made that it adopt a biennial budget.

BORROWING AUTHORITY—a type of spending authority that permits a federal agency to incur obligations and to make payments for specified purposes out of funds borrowed from the Treasury or the public. Except for trust funds and certain other entities, borrowing authority is effective only to the extent provided in appropriations acts.

BUDGET AMENDMENT—a revision to a pending budget request submitted by the president before Congress has completed action on the original request.

BUDGET RESOURCES—the amounts available (regardless of source) for obligation in a fund or account. These resources include new budget authority, recoveries or restoration of budget authority provided in previous years, transfers from other accounts, fees and other collections deposited in the account, and unobligated balances.

BUDGET AUTHORITY—authority provided by law to enter into obligations that normally result in outlays. The main forms of budget authority are appropriations, borrowing authority, and contract authority. Budget authority also includes the subsidy cost of direct and guaranteed loans but not the unsubsidized portion. Budget authority may be classified by the period of availability (one year, multiyear, or no year), by the timing of congressional action (current or permanent), or by the specificity of the amount available (definite or indefinite).

BUDGET ENFORCEMENT ACT OF 1990—an act of Congress that established limits on discretionary spending and pay-as-you-go rules for revenue and direct spending.

BUDGET RESOLUTION—a concurrent resolution passed by both houses of Congress that presents the congressional budget for each of the succeeding ten (or less) fiscal years. The budget resolution sets forth budget totals and functional allocations and may include reconciliation instructions to designated House or Senate committees. *Also see* Reconciliation instruction.

BUDGET SURPLUS OR DEFICIT—the arithmetic difference between budget receipts and outlays. The deficit is the excess of outlays over receipts; the surplus is the excess of receipts over outlays.

BUDGETARY RESERVES—funds withheld from apportionment by the Office of Management and Budget, as authorized by the Antideficiency Act. Unless expressly authorized by other laws, such reserves may be set aside only because of savings due to changes in requirements or efficiency of operations. Reserves are reported to Congress, as required by the Impoundment Control Act.

BUSINESS-TYPE STATEMENTS—financial statements (published in the budget) for government corporations, certain revolving funds, and government-sponsored enterprises. These statements differ from budget schedules in that they principally focus on assets and liabilities rather than on budgetary resources.

CAPITAL BUDGET—a budget that segregates capital investments from operating expenditures. Investment in capital assets is excluded from calculation of the surplus or deficit, but the operating budget is charged for depreciation and/or debt service. The federal government does not have a capital budget, but investment expenditures are shown in supplementary budget schedules.

CASH BASIS—the accounting method in which revenues are recorded when received and expenditures are recorded when paid, without regard to the accounting period in which the revenues were earned or the costs incurred.

CHIEF FINANCIAL OFFICER—an official appointed pursuant to the Chief Financial Officers Act of 1990 to oversee financial management activities relating to the programs and operations of an agency, develop and maintain an integrated accounting and financial management system, and monitor the financial execution of the agency's budget.

CLOSED ACCOUNT—an account whose balance is canceled and is no longer available for obligation or expenditure. An account (such as a one-year appropriation) that is available for obligation for a limited period is closed five years after obligations may no longer be drawn against it. *Also see* Expired account.

COMMITTEE ALLOCATION—the distribution, pursuant to section 302 of the Congressional Budget Act, of new budget authority, entitlement authority, and outlays to House and Senate committees. The allocation, which may not exceed the relevant amounts in the budget resolution, usually is made in the joint explanatory statement that accompanies the conference report on the budget resolution.

COMPARATIVE STATEMENT OF NEW BUDGET AUTHORITY—a table, in the report of the House or Senate appropriations committee on an appropriations bill, which compares the amount recommended for each account with the amount appropriated for the previous fiscal year and the amount requested by the president.

CONCURRENT RESOLUTION ON THE BUDGET—*see* Budget Resolution.

CONSTANT DOLLARS—the dollar value of goods and services, adjusted for changes in prices. Constant dollar series are used to compute the inflation-adjusted level of budget receipts and outlays.

CONTINGENT LIABILITY—a conditional obligation that may become an actual liability if certain events occur or fail to occur. Contingent liabilities include loan guarantees, bank deposit insurance, and price guarantees.

CONTINUING RESOLUTION (CONTINUING APPROPRIATION)—a joint resolution that provides budget authority for programs or agencies whose regular appropriation was not enacted by the start of the fiscal year. A continuing resolution is usually a temporary measure that expires at a specified date or is superseded by enactment of the regular appropriations act. Some continuing resolutions, however, are in effect for the entire fiscal year and serve as the means of enacting regular appropriations.

CONTRACT AUTHORITY—legislation that permits obligations to be incurred in advance of appropriations. With certain exceptions, contract authority is effective only to the extent provided in appropriations acts. When contract authority is provided, Congress appropriates funds to pay off obligations incurred pursuant to it.

COST-BASED BUDGET—a budget whose expenditures are based on the goods and services consumed rather than on the amounts obligated or outlayed.

COST ESTIMATE—an estimate prepared by the Congressional Budget Office of the outlays that would ensue from reported legislation over a five-year period. The cost estimate, which is required by the Congressional Budget Act, is usually published in the report accompanying the legislation.

CREDIT PROGRAM ACCOUNT—the budget account into which an appropriation is made to cover the subsidy cost and/or administrative expenses of a direct or guaranteed loan. The appropriated funds are then disbursed to a financing account.

CREDIT SUBSIDY COST—the estimated cost, over the duration of a direct or guaranteed loan and calculated on the basis of the net present value, of the projected cash flows of the loan or guarantee, excluding administrative expenses. For direct loans, the subsidy cost is the net present value of the following cash flows: disbursements, payments of interest and principal, recoveries, fees, and other payments. For loan guarantees, the subsidy cost is the net present value of government payments for defaults, interest subsidies, and other payments less the estimated payments to the government for fees, other charges, and recoveries.

CURRENT DOLLARS—the dollar value of a good or service in terms of prices paid at the time the good or service is sold. *Also see* Constant dollars.

CURRENT LEVEL—classification used by the House Budget Committee in making section 302 allocations to committees. It refers to new budget authority and outlays resulting from existing law, in contrast to discretionary action—the new budget authority and outlays resulting from new legislation.

CURRENT SERVICE ESTIMATE—estimates in the president's budget of the levels of budget authority and outlays that would be required in the next and subsequent fiscal years to continue existing services. These estimates reflect the projected cost of continuing federal programs if there are no policy changes. *Also see* Baseline.

DEFERRAL—an action or inaction that temporarily withholds, delays, or precludes the obligation or expenditure of budget authority. Deferrals may be made only for the purposes authorized by the Antideficiency Act (or another law), not for policy reasons.

DEFICIENCY APPORTIONMENT—an apportionment (by the Office of Management and Budget) of available budgetary resources in an amount that may compel the enactment of supplemental budget authority. Such apportionments may be made only under the conditions allowed by the Antideficiency Act.

DIRECT LOAN—a disbursement of funds (not in exchange for goods or services) that is contracted to be repaid. An appropriation is made to cover the subsidy cost and administrative expenses of each direct loan program.

DIRECT SPENDING—budget authority and ensuing outlays provided in laws other than appropriations acts, including annually appropriated entitlements. Direct spending is distinguished by the Budget Enforcement Act from discretionary spending and is subject to pay-as-you-go rules.

DISCRETIONARY SPENDING—budget authority, other than appropriated entitlements, and ensuing outlays provided in annual appropriations acts. The Budget Enforcement Act limits discretionary budget authority and outlays.

DISCRETIONARY SPENDING LIMITS—ceilings set by the Budget Enforcement Act on budget authority and outlays for discretionary programs. Appropriations causing budget authority or outlays to exceed the limit may compel a sequestration.

EARMARKING—earmarked revenues are dedicated by law to a specific purpose or program. The revenues include trust funds, special funds, and offsetting collections credited to appropriations accounts. Earmarked expenditures are dedicated by an appropriations act or the accompanying committee report to a particular project or activity.

EMERGENCY SPENDING—an appropriation that the president and Congress have designated as an emergency. Under BEA, an emergency appropriation causes an increase in the relevant discretionary spending limits to accommodate the additional spending.

ENTITLEMENT AUTHORITY—a provision of law that obligates the federal government to make payments to eligible recipients. Entitlement authority may be funded in either an annual or permanent appropriation.

EXPIRED ACCOUNT—an appropriation or fund account whose balances are no longer available for incurring new obligations because the time available for incurring such obligations has expired. Outlays may be made from expired accounts to liquidate previously made obligations. *Also see* Closed Account.

FEDERAL DEBT—the total amount of Treasury debt and agency debt, consisting of debt held by the public and debt held by trust or special funds.

FEDERAL FUNDS—all monies collected and spent by the federal government, other than those designated as trust funds. Federal funds include general, special, public enterprise, and intergovernmental funds.

FINANCIAL STATEMENTS—statements reporting on the financial condition of agencies or other federal entities, including statements of financial condition, results of operations, cash flows, and a reconciliation to the budget.

FINANCING ACCOUNT—an account established pursuant to the Federal Credit Reform Act of 1990 that receives disbursements from a credit program account and handles all other cash flows to or from the government resulting from direct or guaranteed loans. Financing accounts are not included in the budget totals.

FISCAL POLICY—federal policies concerning revenues, spending, and the deficit intended to promote the nation's macroeconomic goals with respect to employment, output, prices, and the balance of payments.

FISCAL YEAR—the accounting period for the budget. The fiscal year for the federal government begins on October 1 and ends the next September 30. The fiscal year is designated by the calendar year in which it ends; for example, fiscal year 2000 began October 1, 1999, and ended September 30, 2000.

FIXED ACCOUNT—an account whose funds are available for a definite period, in contrast to accounts that have no-year funds. Unobligated balances in fixed accounts expire (are no longer available for obligation) at the end of the period for which they are available.

FORWARD FUNDING—budget authority that becomes available for obligation during one fiscal year and continues to be available through the next fiscal year. The budget authority is counted in the fiscal year for which the appropriation is made.

FULL FUNDING—the provision of budget authority to finance the full estimated cost of a project or activity, such as ship construction, that will be completed in subsequent years. Full funding also refers to the appropriation of the full amount authorized in authorizing legislation.

FUNCTION OR FUNCTIONAL CLASSIFICATION—a classification of budgetary resources in terms of the principal purposes they serve. A function may be divided into two or more subfunctions. The last three digits of an account's identification code represent the subfunction into which the account has been classified.

GOVERNMENT-SPONSORED ENTERPRISE—an enterprise established by the federal government but privately owned and operated. These enterprises are excluded from the budget totals because they are private entities. However, financial information concerning them is included in the budget.

GRAMM-RUDMAN-HOLLINGS PROCESS—the process established by the Balanced Budget and Emergency Deficit Control Act of 1985 (commonly known as the Gramm-Rudman-Hollings Act), which included fixed deficit targets and the sequestration of budgetary resources if the projected deficit was greater than the target. The Budget Enforcement Act of 1990 superseded these procedures.

GROSS DOMESTIC PRODUCT (GDP)—the market value of all final goods and services produced within the borders of a country in a given period. GDP can be expressed in current or constant dollars.

IDENTIFICATION CODE—the eleven-digit code assigned to each appropriation or fund account that identifies the agency, account, timing of the transmittal to Congress, type of fund, and account's functional classification.

IMPOUNDMENT—an action or inaction by a government officer or employee that precludes or delays the obligation or expenditure of budget authority. *Also see* Deferral, Rescission.

INTERNAL CONTROL—the systems and practices of an agency to safeguard its assets, ensure the accuracy and reliability of accounts, and foster compliance with prescribed financial management policies. Sometimes referred to as management control.

JUSTIFICATION MATERIAL—the documents and schedules submitted by an agency to the appropriations committees in support of its budget request. The material typically explains changes between the current appropriation and the amounts requested for the next fiscal year.

LINE-ITEM VETO—the power of the president to veto part of a bill passed by Congress. The Line Item Veto Act of 1996 authorized the president to cancel parts of legislation containing discretionary budget authority, new direct spending, or limited tax benefits. This act was ruled unconstitutional by the Supreme Court in 1998. At present, therefore, the president must veto or sign the entire measure.

LIQUIDATING ACCOUNT—an account (established pursuant to the Federal Credit Reform Act) to handle all cash flows resulting from direct or guaranteed loans made before fiscal 1992.

LIQUIDATING APPROPRIATION—an appropriation to pay obligations incurred pursuant to substantive legislation, usually contract authority. A liquidating appropriation is not recorded as budget authority.

LOAN GUARANTEE—a commitment by the federal government to pay part or all of the loan principal or interest to the lender in the event of default by the borrower. The subsidy cost of new loan guarantees is included in the computation of budget authority and outlays.

MANAGEMENT FUND—an account authorized by law to receive budgetary resources from two or more appropriations to carry out a common purpose or activity not involving a continuing cycle of operations.

MEANS OF FINANCING—certain financial flows to the federal government that are not included in budget receipts or outlays. These include funds borrowed from the public, seigniorage, and credit-financing accounts.

MIDSESSION REVIEW OF THE BUDGET—an updated summary of the president's budget containing revised estimates of revenues, budget authority, and outlays, as well as other information. The midsession review is supposed to be issued by July 15.

MONTHLY TREASURY STATEMENT—a summary statement issued each month by the Treasury presenting data on receipts, outlays, and the surplus or deficit for the latest completed month and for the fiscal year to date, with comparisons to the same period in the previous year.

MULTIYEAR APPROPRIATION—budget authority provided in an appropriations act for a period in excess of one fiscal year. Multiyear appropriations may cover periods that do not coincide with the start or end of a fiscal year.

MULTIYEAR AUTHORIZATION—an authorization of appropriations for a period in excess of one fiscal year. Programs with multiyear authorizations must be reauthorized periodically.

NATIONAL INCOME AND PRODUCT ACCOUNTS—quarterly and annual accounts providing data on aggregate economic activity. Federal revenues and outlays in these accounts differ in some details from those reported in the budget.

NO-YEAR APPROPRIATION—budget authority provided in an appropriations act that remains available for obligation for an indefinite period. These funds do not lapse if they are not obligated by the end of the fiscal year.

OBJECT CLASSIFICATION—a classification identifying expenditures by the goods or services purchased (such as personnel, supplies, and equipment). An object classification schedule is included in the budget for each appropriation account.

OBLIGATED BALANCE—the amount of obligations incurred for which payment has not yet been made. This balance usually is carried forward until the obligations are paid.

OBLIGATION—binding agreement (such as a contract awarded, service received, or similar transaction) that will require payment.

OFF-BUDGET—budget authority, outlays, or receipts of federal entities that are excluded by law from the budget. These entities currently include the Social Security trust funds and the Postal Service.

OFFSETTING COLLECTIONS—receipts from the public that result from business-type activities and collections from other government accounts. These collections are not counted as receipts but are netted against budget authority and outlays.

ONE-YEAR APPROPRIATION—budget authority provided in an appropriations act that is available for obligation only during a single fiscal year, usually the fiscal year specified in the enacting clause of the appropriations act.

OUTLAYS—payments made (usually through the issuance of checks, disbursement of cash, or electronic transfer) to liquidate obligations. Outlays during a fiscal year may be for payment of obligations incurred in previous years or in the same year.

PAYGO (pay-as-you-go)—the procedure established by the Budget Enforcement Act to ensure that direct spending and revenue legislation does not cause an increase in the deficit or reduce the surplus. PAYGO requires that an increase in the deficit or reduction in the surplus due to new legislation be offset by other legislation or sequestration.

PERFORMANCE BUDGETING—a form of budgeting that relates resources provided in the budget to measurable results.

PERFORMANCE PLANS—annual plans, prescribed by the Government Performance and Results Act of 1993, to inform Congress and the public of each agency's major programs and activities, the measures used to gauge performance, the strategies and resources required to achieve goals, and the procedures used to verify performance information.

PERMANENT APPROPRIATION—budget authority that becomes available without any current action by Congress. Budget authority is deemed to be permanent if it derives from legislation enacted in previous sessions of Congress.

PROGRAM ACCOUNT—*See* Credit Program Account.

PROGRAM AND FINANCING SCHEDULE—a schedule published in the president's budget that presents data on each account. The schedule consists of several sections that provide data on obligations (by program), gross budgetary resources, new budget authority, outlays, and offsets.

PROGRAM, PROJECT, OR ACTIVITY (PPA)—an element within a budget account. For annually appropriated accounts, PPAs are defined by appropriations acts or accompanying reports. For accounts not funded by annual appropriations, PPAs are defined by the program listing in program and financing schedules.

PUBLIC DEBT—funds borrowed by the Treasury from the public or from a fund or account. The public debt, which is subject to a statutory limit, does not include agency debt (funds borrowed by other federal agencies).

PUBLIC ENTERPRISE FUND—a revolving account for business-type activities that is financed by offsetting collections credited to the account.

REAPPROPRIATION—congressional action that continues the availability of all or part of the unobligated portion of budget authority that has expired or would otherwise expire. Reappropriations are counted as new budget authority in the fiscal year for which the availability is extended.

RECEIPTS (or BUDGET RECEIPTS)—collections from the public, including tax receipts and social insurance premiums. Budget receipts do not include various offsetting collections, which are accounted for as negative outlays.

RECONCILIATION BILL—a bill containing changes in law recommended by House or Senate committees pursuant to reconciliation instructions in a budget resolution.

RECONCILIATION INSTRUCTION—a provision in a budget resolution directing one or more House or Senate committees to recommend legislation changing existing law to bring spending, revenues, or the debt limit into conformity with the budget resolution. The instructions specify the committees to which they are directed, the dollar changes to be achieved, and usually a deadline by which the legislation is to be reported.

RECONCILIATION PROCESS—procedures established in the Congressional Budget Act by which Congress changes existing laws to conform revenues and spending to the levels set in a budget resolution.

REPROGRAMMING—the shift of funds from one purpose to another within the same appropriations account. Reprogramming often entails formal notification and the opportunity for congressional committees to disapprove the shift.

RESCISSION—the cancellation of budget authority previously provided by Congress. The Impoundment Control Act prescribes procedures for presidential notification and congressional action on rescission proposals.

RESCISSION BILL—a bill reported pursuant to a president's rescission message that cancels budget authority previously provided by Congress.

RESERVES—*See* Budgetary Reserves.

REVOLVING FUND—an account or fund in which the income derived from its operations is available to finance the fund's continuing operations without fiscal year limitations.

SCOREKEEPING—procedures for tracking and reporting on the status of congressional budget actions affecting receipts, budget authority, outlays, the surplus or deficit, and the public debt.

SCORING—procedures and rules for measuring the budget impact of legislation for purposes of the Budget Enforcement Act. The Office of Management and Budget is responsible for scoring enacted legislation to determine whether a sequester is required.

SECTION 302—*See* Committee Allocation.

SEQUESTER—the cancellation of budgetary resources pursuant to the Budget Enforcement Act, in response to a violation of the discretionary spending limits or the pay-as-you-go rules.

SPECIAL FUND—funds earmarked by law for special purposes. There sometimes is little practical difference between a special fund and a trust fund, but special funds are classified as federal funds.

SPENDING AUTHORITY—the term designated by the Congressional Budget Act for borrowing authority, contract authority, entitlement authority, and authority to forgo offsetting collections (the borrowing authority for which is not provided in advance by appropriations acts). *Also see* Direct Spending.

SPENDOUT RATE—the rate at which new budget authority provided by Congress is spent by federal agencies, hence the rate at which outlays occur. Sometimes referred to as the outlay rate.

STATUTORY DEBT LIMIT—the maximum amount, established by law, of public debt that may be outstanding. The limit covers virtually all debt issued by the federal government, including borrowing from trust funds, but excludes some debt incurred by agencies.

STRATEGIC PLANS—multiyear plans required by the Government Performance and Results Act, containing a mission statement, general goals and objectives, strategies for achieving the goals, the relationship between the strategic goals and annual performance goals, key external factors, and program evaluations.

SUBSIDY COST—*See* Credit Subsidy Cost.

SUPPLEMENTAL APPROPRIATION—an act appropriating funds in addition to those provided in an annual or continuing appropriations act.

TAX EXPENDITURE—revenue losses attributable to provisions of federal law that allow a special exclusion or deduction from income, or that provide a special credit, preferential tax rate, or deferral of tax liability.

Tax expenditures entail no payment from the government. Rather, the Treasury forgoes some of the revenue it would otherwise have collected, and affected taxpayers pay lower taxes than they otherwise would have had to pay.

TRANSFER—the shift of budgetary resources from one appropriations account or fund to another—in contrast to reprogramming, which shifts resources within the same account. Funds may be transferred only as authorized by law.

TRANSFER PAYMENTS—payments the government makes to individuals for which no current or future goods or services are provided in return. These payments include Social Security, unemployment insurance, veterans' benefits, and various welfare payments.

TRUST FUNDS—accounts designated by law as trust funds for receipts and expenditures earmarked for specified purposes.

UNDISTRIBUTED OFFSETTING RECEIPTS—receipts that are recorded as offsets against total spending rather than against particular accounts or functions. These include income from the sale of major assets and from offshore oil leases.

UNIFIED BUDGET—a comprehensive budget that includes all receipts and outlays from federal funds and trust funds. Off-budget entities (the Postal Service and Social Security) are excluded from the unified budget, but data relating to them are presented in the budget.

UNOBLIGATED BALANCE—the portion of budget authority that has not been obligated. Unobligated balances are carried forward until the period for which they are available ends.

USER FEES—fees charged to users for goods or services provided by the government. In levying or authorizing these fees, Congress determines whether the revenue should revert to the Treasury or should be available to the agency providing the goods or services.

VIEWS AND ESTIMATES—a report issued each year within six weeks after submission of the president's budget by each House or Senate committee with jurisdiction over federal programs. Each views and estimates report contains committees' comments or recommendations on budgetary matters in their jurisdictions.

WORKING FUND ACCOUNTS—funds established to receive advance payments from other agencies or accounts. Consolidated working funds do not finance the work directly; they reimburse the appropriation or fund account that finances the work performed.

Index

Accounting: agency systems, 256–58; application to budget, 258–61; budget authority, 37, 38; cost-based, 261; deficit and surplus, 37, 44; functional allocations, 114; fund types, 40; government-owned and -sponsored enterprises, 39, 41–42; guaranteed and direct loans, 42–44; on-budget totals, 44–46; outlays, 36, 37–38; relationship to budgeting, 256; revenues, 36–37; rules and conventions, 36–37, 258

Accounts, appropriations, 189, 191, 192, 229, 232, 246

AFDC. *See* Aid to Families with Dependent Children

Agencies, federal: adjustments to budget, 242, 247, 248; allotments of funds within, 244; apportionments to, 242–44; appropriations, 186–87; authorizing legislation, 164, 235–36; budget and accounting staff, 242; budget authority, 37; budget requests, 30–31, 78, 81, 84, 89, 265; budget responsibilities, 81, 82t; chief financial officers, 258, 259, 257t; congressional hearings on budget requests, 90, 191, 204; financial management responsibilities, 257t; implementation of budget, 34, 241–42, 255; impoundments, 250; internal budgets, 98, 244; interpretations of appropriations bills, 235–38; justification material, 86, 98, 191, 204, 209, 236; numbers of employees, 86; obligations, 244–46; OMB oversight, 87, 262; president's role in budgets, 84–85; relations with appropriations committees, 189, 191, 204, 236, 237, 251; repro-gramming, 236, 247–51; spending requests to Congress before budget process, 13–14; strategic plans, 82, 262, 264, 265, 282; transfers of funds, 247. *See also* Budget, president's; Financial management

Agriculture: appropriations bills, 95; price supports, 69

Aid to Families with Dependent Children (AFDC), 19t, 69

Allocations, 32, 34, 53, 131; of budget authority, 109, 114, 131; functional, 109, 114, 119; section *302*(a), 53, 114, 131; section *302*(b), 53, 114, 131, 204–08, 215, 219

Antideficiency Act, 15, 242

Apportionment, 242–44

Appropriations, 8–9; accounts, 189, 191, 192, 229, 232, 246; advance, 37, 63, 66, 68t; annual, 52, 187, 239, 284; apportionment, 242–44; and authorizations, 165, 171, 175; availability periods, 232; continuing, 187, 188, 223, 227; direct spending, 50, 52, 184; discretionary spending, 50–52, 53; emergency spending, 62, 63, 64–65, 68t, 95, 188; evolution of process, 189–93, 238–39; incrementalism, 209–11, 282; limits on executive branch, 186; line-item veto, 95–97; made before budget process, 10, 189–90; offsets, 62–63, 69; permanent, 187; and president's budget, 209; process, 202–03, 208–11; proposals for biennial, 187, 239, 281–83; regular, 187; reprogramming, 236,

quirement, 14; media coverage, 90; narrow range of options, 3, 78–79; performance-based, 262, 264, 265; as policy tool, 3–4, 17, 74, 79–80; as political statement, 89–90, 98; preparation, 30–31, 55, 78, 81–86, 89–90; program and financing schedule, 98; relationship to appropriations, 209; revenues, 139; revisions, 90; two-track process, 85–86; unrealistically high numbers, 92–94

Budget, unified 39–40, 44, 45, 47, 110

Budget and Accounting Act of *1921*, 14, 15, 22, 74–75, 87, 89, 191, 256

Budget authority: allocation to committees, 109; in appropriations bills, 186; new, 37, 110, 114; permanent, 37; relationship to outlays, 38, 49t

Budget Committees. *See* House Budget Committee; Senate Budget Committee

Budget Enforcement Act of *1990* (BEA), 15, 181; adjustable deficit targets, 24, 49; effects, 280; enforcement mechanisms, 22–24, 49–50, 52, 134, 184. *See also* Pay-as-you-go rules; Spending caps, discretionary

Budget process: allocation and redistribution of resources, 4; annual cycle, 30–34, 284; biennial process proposed, 187, 239, 281–83; change-oriented and status quo years, 6–7, 106, 108, 117, 125; conflict in, 1, 2–4, 107, 109, 269–70, 284; direct and discretionary spending, 49–54; economic assumptions, 54, 55–56, 72, 92; enforcement of rules, 54–56; evolution, 8, 9, 269; fragmentation in Congress, 106–08; incrementalism, 5, 84, 209–11, 282; legislative dominance, 9–14; managing public perceptions of spending increases, 58–60, 69; milestones, 15; multiyear cycle in other countries, 282–83; negotiations between president and Congress, 55–56, 80–81, 90, 91, 92, 93–94, 193, 206–08; participants, 2–3; political factors, 1, 2, 5, 53–56, 267, 269–70; presidential dominance, 14–18, 79–80, 107; president's roles, 14, 17, 18–19, 75, 81, 82t, 84–85, 86, 90, 108–09; reform proposals, 138, 239–40, 266, 278–84; requirement for resolution, 4–5, 20; self-correction, 267–70, 273, 278; timetable, 30, 31t, 81. *See also* Appropriations; Authorizations; Congressional budget resolution; Scoring; Scorekeeping

Budget reconciliation: bills, 117, 125, 127–29; bills vetoed, 199; changes to entitlements, 272; establishment of process, 134; in future, 129; instructions, 108, 109–10, 125–27; omnibus bills, 32, 127, 128; process, 53, 125–29; scope, 125; spending cuts, 184; timing, 137–38; unrelated provisions in bills, 128

Budget Reconciliation Act of *1987*, 141t

Bureau of the Budget: establishment, 14, 74–75, 87. *See also* Office of Management and Budget

Bush, George H. W.: approach to budgets, 75–76, 85, 93, 104; budget documents, 98; domestic spending cuts, 211; 1990 budget summit, 24–25, 76; relations with Congress, 91, 211, 268; rescissions, 254–55; tax increase, 24–25, 29–30, 75, 151–52, 157; vetoes, 96

Bush administration: budgets, 22–25, 98, 211; capital gains tax rates, 147

Byrd, Robert, 65

Byrd rule, 128

Carr, Bob, 178

Carter, Jimmy, 91, 255t

CBA. *See* Congressional Budget and Impoundment Control Act of *1974*

CBO. *See* Congressional Budget Office

Chief Financial Officers Act of *1990*, 258, 259, 262, 263

Civil War, 13, 93

Clinton, Bill: balanced budget, 26–30; balanced budget deal (*1997*), 63, 75, 79, 94, 151, 180; budget documents, 98; budget policies, 25–26, 85; budget tactics, 90, 91–92, 93–94, 104; children's health insurance, 29, 56; compared with other presidents, 75–77; deficit reduction as priority, 6, 24–26, 91–92, 268; discretionary spending increases, 26, 63, 67; election (*1996*), 201; election campaign (*1992*), 6, 24, 75; emergency spending, 62, 64–65, 95; entitlement spending, 281; fiscal *1994* budget, 3–4, 6–7, 25–26, 58, 75, 80, 91–92, 108; fiscal *1995* budget, 6–7, 78; fiscal *1996* budget battle, 26, 75, 77, 79, 80–81, 128, 199–201; fiscal *1998* budget, 26–30, 79; fiscal *1999* budget, 26, 79, 94–95; fiscal *2000* budget, 31t, 63; fiscal *2001* budget, 38–39, 63, 66, 67; government shutdowns and, 77, 80–81, 200–01; health care reform, 6, 7, 26, 55, 77; Medicare, 58, 59–60, 69, 128; opposition to tax cuts, 69–70; proposed use of surplus, 95, 110; rescissions, 255t; relations with Congress, 79, 80, 91, 93–94, 96; Social Security, 110; statements of administration policy, 219; State of the Union Address (*1998*), 110; tax increases, 25, 29, 140, 151, 152, 157, 268; transportation acts signed, 179, 180; use of CBO numbers, 55; vetoes, 79, 95, 96, 128, 140, 199, 200, 201, 223, 273

Cold War: end of, 28, 84

Congress: appropriations power, 186; balanced budget deal (*1997*), 63, 75, 79, 94, 151, 180; budget responsibilities, 1, 8, 9; decentralized budget process, 106–08; divided government, 3, 20, 80, 94, 268; dominance of budget process, 9–14; legislative power, 164; legislative vetoes, 248, 252; number of laws passed, 3, 174; presidential influence on budget process, 75, 90, 92, 107; reforms of *1970*s, 142–43,

Obligations, 37, 244–46; accounting for, 261; delayed, 66, 68t

OBRA-*90. See* Omnibus Budget Reconciliation Act

Office of Management and Budget (OMB): accounting practices, 258; apportionment, 242–44; appropriations hearings, 203; balance sheets, 261; baseline projections, 57, 59–60; budget implementation, 34, 242; budget preparation, 31, 55, 81, 82t, 85, 89–90; in Bush administration, 75; Circular A-*10*, 89; Circular A-*11*, 89; Circular A-*123*, 262; deficit estimates, 26, 27; deputy director for management, 258, 259; disagreements with CBO, 55–56, 87; economic assumptions, 55–56, 63, 70; financial management definition, 255; financial management role, 256, 257t; history, 87; Indian tribe trust funds and, 40; monitoring of appropriations, 204, 221; oversight of agencies, 87, 262; performance-based management, 265; political role, 55, 87, 88; relations with Congress, 87, 88, 90; report on appropriations bill, 223; responsibilities, 86–87, 88; scoring of legislation, 50, 60, 71–72, 147; staff, 87, 88; statements of administration policy, 219–21; surplus estimates, 273; user charges guidelines, 160. *See also* Bureau of the Budget

Offsets, 62–63, 68t, 69

Offsetting collections, 161

Omnibus appropriations acts: emergency spending in, 62, 64–65, 95, 188; fiscal *1996*, 198t, 201; fiscal *1999*, 60, 62, 64–65, 95, 188, 238–39; use of, 188

Omnibus Budget Reconciliation Act of *1990* (OBRA-*90*), 24–25, 76, 141t

O'Neill, June, 118–19, 120, 121

Outlays, 37–38, 246. *See also* Spending

Panetta, Leon, 7, 78

Patent and Trademark Office, 160

Pay-as-you-go (PAYGO) rules: for direct spending, 24, 28–29, 49, 50, 52, 69, 134; effects on deficits, 69; enforcement, 146–47; establishment, 25; impact on congressional behavior, 147–48, 152; not applied to existing laws, 184; for revenues, 24, 49, 50, 69–70, 134, 146–48; in time of surplus, 153–54

Pension Benefit Guaranty Corporation, 42

Performance-based management, 262–66

Planning-programming-budgeting system (PPBS), 82, 84, 282

Political action committees, 140

Political factors in budget process, 1, 2, 5, 53–56, 267, 269–70

Postal Service, 41, 44

Presidents: action on appropriations bills, 223; authoriz-

ing legislation initiated by, 174; budget conflicts with Congress, 1, 18–22, 26, 79, 80–81, 107, 227, 269–70; budget responsibilities, 1, 8, 9–10, 74–75; divided government, 3, 20, 80, 94, 268; dominance of budget process, 14–18, 79–80, 107; impoundments, 192, 250–52; individual styles, 75–77, 91–92; negotiations with Congress, 55–56, 80–81, 90, 91, 92, 93–94, 193, 206–08; proposed role in congressional budget resolution, 283–84; rescissions, 252–55; roles in budget process, 14, 17, 18–19, 75, 81, 82t, 84–85, 86, 90, 108–09; statements of administration policy, 219–21; use of media, 91; veto power, 94–97. *See also* Budget, president's; *and individual presidents*

President's Commission on Budget Concepts, 15, 39, 161

Reagan, Ronald: approach to budgets, 76–77, 85, 92, 104; budget deficits, 21–22; comparison to Clinton, 76–77; defense spending, 38; domestic spending cuts, 66, 92, 174, 211; economic program, 21–22, 72; fiscal *1982* budget, 3–4, 76, 108; relations with Congress, 79, 81, 91, 92, 96, 211; rescissions, 254, 255t; tax cuts, 21, 150; tax increases, 76, 144, 145, 151; use of media, 91

Reconciliation. *See* Budget reconciliation

Reid, Harry, 166

Reinventing government campaign. *See* National Performance Review

Reprogramming, 236, 247–51

Republicans: attempts to influence CBO, 118–19, 120–21; balanced budget agreement with Clinton (*1997*), 75, 79, 94; battles with Clinton, 59–60, 79, 80–81, 94–95, 96, 128; blamed for government shutdowns, 80, 200–01; budget policy differences, 121; control of Congress after *1994* elections, 26, 80, 193, 199, 213; divided government, 20, 268; efforts to cut spending, 211, 212–23t; emergency spending, 62, 63, 64–65, 95; tax cuts proposed, 94–95, 273

Rescissions, 252–55

Results Act. *See* Government Performance and Results Act

Revenue legislation: "Christmas treeing," 146, 147, 148; committees responsible, 32t, 33, 108; conference committees, 146, 147; congressional initiatives, 139–40; estimated revenues, 56; frequency, 143; House, 10, 140–43; line-item veto, 95–97; lobbying, 140; politics of, 139–40, 143; scoring, 146–48; Senate, 140–42, 144–46, 147; tax expenditures, 148–50

Revenues: accounting rules and conventions, 36–37; from asset sales, 60; baseline projections, 56, 127, 146; business-type, 37, 160; in congressional budget